ALSO BY CRAIG FEHRMAN

Author in Chief

THE BEST
PRESIDENTIAL
WRITING

FROM 1789
TO THE PRESENT

Edited by

CRAIG FEHRMAN

AVID READER PRESS
New York London Toronto Sydney New Delhi

AVID READER PRESS
An Imprint of Simon & Schuster, Inc.
1230 Avenue of the Americas
New York, NY 10020

First Avid Reader Press hardcover edition October 2020

AVID READER PRESS and colophon are trademarks of Simon & Schuster, Inc.

For information about special discounts for bulk purchases,
please contact Simon & Schuster Special Sales at 1-866-506-1949
or business@simonandschuster.com.

The Simon & Schuster Speakers Bureau can bring authors to
your live event. For more information or to book an event,
contact the Simon & Schuster Speakers Bureau at 1-866-248-3049
or visit our website at www.simonspeakers.com.

Interior design by Kyle Kabel

Manufactured in the United States of America

1   3   5   7   9   10   8   6   4   2

Library of Congress Cataloging-in-Publication Data has been applied for.

ISBN 978-1-4767-8853-1
ISBN 978-1-4767-8858-6 (ebook)

Contents

CALVIN COOLIDGE

HERBERT HOOVER

FRANKLIN D. ROOSEVELT

HARRY S. TRUMAN

DWIGHT EISENHOWER

JOHN F. KENNEDY

Introduction

In 1906, a young soldier named Douglas MacArthur received some thrilling news: he'd been chosen to serve as an assistant to the president, Theodore Roosevelt. The job turned out to be rather boring, with MacArthur mostly helping at White House dinners and enduring the hectoring of self-important congressmen. Still, the setting—and the boss—made up for it. MacArthur marveled at Roosevelt's intelligence, his energy, his certainty. A few times, in quiet moments, they talked about foreign policy, but one day MacArthur raised a domestic concern. What, the soldier asked, explained Roosevelt's political success? To Roosevelt, the answer was simple: the people loved him, he said, because he "put into words what is in their hearts and minds but not their mouths."

This skill—of identifying and focusing on the right problems, of describing their significance and arguing for the right solutions, of writing and writing well—has always been essential to the presidency. In essays and addresses, Roosevelt coined phrases that still mark his era more than a century later: the "strenuous life," the "square deal," the muckrakers of the press and their opposite, "the man in the arena." Most presidents have tried to do this, though not always with Roosevelt's success. The presidency is a position won through words, defined through words, and carried out through words. America's chief executives have talked and written their way into the White House; once there, they've explained not just their policies but their own role as president, often expanding that role's powers along the way; after they depart, they usually reflect on the experience, defending their choices and sharing what it felt like to lead.

This anthology, for the first time, collects the best and most important examples of each of these kinds of writing: campaign, presidential, and postpresidential. It contains the story of America, told by the presidents themselves.

That story, like most stories from history, is one of continuity and change. Certain themes emerge, with even the most famous speeches finding new meanings or fresh connections—so that George Washington's Farewell Address leads to Ulysses S. Grant's defense of the Fifteenth Amendment, which leads to Lyndon B. Johnson's call to pass a Voting Rights Act that would make this amendment actually mean something, which leads to Barack Obama's address, fifty years on, that shows how the amendment has been weakened once again.

One theme that spans this anthology is how presidents campaign. During the eighteenth century, and for long stretches of the nineteenth, candidates did not go out and stump. In keeping quiet they followed Washington's example, proving their fitness for the office by proving their lack of interest in it. This changed, of course, but slowly, with candidates getting involved through campaign biographies and pub-lished letters, then front-porch speeches and bestselling books. Technol-ogy was changing, too, with new forms supplementing (if never quite replacing) old ones: from newspapers to widely affordable books, from the telegraph and the locomotive to newsreels and radio, television and Twitter.* Each form encouraged its own style of writing, but they all seemed to benefit from the same basic material: a charming backstory, a big idea, a clever bit of symbolism linking the two. Seeing candidates sell their ideas, and seeing them sell themselves, reveals much about America and its desires.

Another theme is how presidents govern. The Constitution—itself a piece of writing—provides few details about the presidency and its powers. It has fallen to the presidents themselves to describe their job and then to

---

* One thing that hasn't changed is ghostwriting. While some pieces in this anthology came from a speechwriter (or several speechwriters), they were published or declaimed under the name of the president, usually after that president offered detailed guidance and careful review. The history of ghostwriting in America is as old as the history of America itself. Just take John Adams's word for it: "If I could persuade my friend Rush," he once wrote, "or perhaps my friend Jefferson, to write such a thing for me, I know not why I might not transcribe it as Washington did so often. Borrowed eloquence, if it contains as good stuff, is as good as own eloquence."

do it. They have pursued both steps aggressively through writing—through the "bully pulpit," to use another of Roosevelt's phrases.

One can see this expansion of executive power in the State of the Union address, which has grown from a written progress report to a detailed and executive-driven platform, delivered in prime time with a "STATE OF THE UNION" chyron flashing underneath. (While that name didn't stick until the twentieth century, this anthology calls all annual addresses "State of the Unions"; for more on such modernizing, see the Note on Texts, Sources, and Permissions on page 461.) One can see this expansion in impromptu remarks, in prepared statements, in inaugural addresses or addresses that mourn a tragedy or dedicate a place. Every speech or statement is an opportunity to demonstrate and enact executive power. "There have been periods of our history," Woodrow Wilson once wrote, "when presidential messages were utterly without practical significance, perfunctory documents which few persons except the editors of newspapers took the trouble to read." This changed because of presidential writing, and presidential writing changed because of this.

One can also see this expansion in the content of presidential writing—in the evolution of foreign policy, to choose another prominent theme. While the Constitution does dwell on the role of commander in chief, that role has shifted as America has shifted, from a provincial nation with no standing army to a postatomic superpower. America's foreign policy has shifted as well, moving from the isolationism of Washington's Farewell Address to the durability of the Monroe Doctrine and then the violent revisions of the twentieth century: World War I, World War II, the Cold War. These shifts occurred on the battlefield, but they occurred in the bully pulpit, too.

Another theme is how presidents view history. America's politicians have long specialized in using history to justify their decisions or to push new policies. (Grant invoked Washington in his statement on the Fifteenth Amendment because Grant wanted to tie it to, in his phrase, the "Father of his country.") Presidents have analyzed the writing of their predecessors, theorizing about what makes an effective address. They have tried to write history themselves, privately in diaries and unpublished manuscripts and publicly in presidential memoirs. Here especially one can feel the human side of the presidency, though it exists in each kind of writing. In this anthology, presidents open up about a key battle in the Revolutionary War, about the assassination of other presidents, about the bombing of Pearl Harbor. Taken together, these excerpts show how autobiography has changed across the centuries—and just as much how the self has changed, the *auto* in autobiography.

The self remains an alluring concept for most presidents. It is how they see the world, and it is how they see history. In his own presidential memoirs, Harry S. Truman wrote about his lifelong love of history—a favorite high school teacher, a beloved set of books, a standing appointment at his local library. But Truman also wrote about how history worked, to his mind, at least: "It takes men to make history or there would be no history. History does not make the man."

Another way to say this is that it takes presidents to write history—to end a war "with malice toward none," to begin a war on "a date which will live in infamy," to urge another leader to "tear down this wall."

And yet history does make the man. There are forces and contexts that no president can escape—something proven by the fact that so many leaders have tried and failed to escape them.

One example is America's current partisan moment and the limits it puts on a president's ability to persuade. While most presidents have attempted to address the entire nation—to channel Roosevelt, to "put into words what is in their hearts and minds but not their mouths"—their modern speeches have sometimes backfired. The president may be the only official elected by the entire nation, but when a president of one party takes a stand, it compels the other party to take the opposite stand. This reality has altered the goals of presidential writing—from persuading America to persuading half of it, from shifting public opinion to organizing a party's agenda, setting its biggest issues, and defining its greatest enemies.

Still, even recent presidents have kept trying to describe and shape America's values, to put into words what the nation is and what it should be. It is this lasting impulse that most unifies these presidential texts. What is America? Who is America for? What will America become? For more than two centuries, different presidents have offered different answers. Sometimes, these answers have been paradoxical or even dishonorable, including Thomas Jefferson's views on Black Americans and Andrew Jackson's on Native Americans—"those children of the forest," in another bully pulpit phrase.

But this, the good and the bad, is the story of America, told by the presidents themselves. Their words live in two senses, as this anthology makes clear. A president's words represent an account of America, of history rendered in language. But they also represent action and power—their words are history, the thing itself.

From His Notes for an Early Biographer

"They then from every little rising tree, stump, stone, and bush kept up a constant galling fire"

George Washington was a general and a president, but he was not a writer—not in his own mind, at least. After the Revolutionary War, David Humphreys, one of Washington's aides-de-camp, urged him to write an autobiography. "I am conscious of a defective education," Washington replied, "and want of capacity to fit me for such an undertaking." Humphreys turned to a biography of Washington instead, convincing his subject to answer some key questions. Washington wrote eleven pages in the third person, the closest he ever came to telling his own story. This passage describes part of the French and Indian War: Washington's defeat at Fort Necessity in 1754, and his early bristling at the British treatment of American troops.

About 9 o'clock on the 3rd of July, the enemy advanced with shouts and dismal Indian yells to our entrenchments, but was opposed by so warm, spirited, and constant a fire, that to force the works in that way was abandoned by them. They then from every little rising tree, stump, stone, and bush kept up a constant galling fire upon us, which was returned in the best manner we could till late in the afternoon, when there fell the most tremendous rain that can be conceived—filled our trenches with water, wet not only the ammunition in the cartouche boxes and firelocks but that which was in a small temporary stockade in the middle of the entrenchment called Fort Necessity, erected for the sole purpose of its security and that of the few stores we had, and left us nothing but a few (for all were not provided with them) bayonets for defense.

In this situation, with no prospect of bettering it, terms of capitulation were offered to us by the enemy which with some alterations that were insisted upon were the more readily acceded to, as we had no salt provisions, and but indifferently supplied with fresh foods, which, from the heat of the weather, would not keep, and because a full third of our numbers, officers as well as privates were, by this time, killed or wounded. The next morning, we marched out with the honors of war, but were plundered, contrary to the articles of capitulation, of great part of our baggage by the savages. Our sick and wounded were left with a detachment under the care and command of the worthy Doctor Craik (for he was not only surgeon to the regiment but a lieutenant therein) with such necessities as we could collect, and the remains of the regiment and the detachment of regulars took up their line for the interior country. . . .

In this manner the winter was employed, when advice was received of the force destined for this service under the orders of General Braddock and the arrival of Sir Jonathan St. Clair, the quartermaster general, with some new arrangement of rank by which no officer who did not immediately derive his commission from the king could command one who did. This was too degrading for George Washington to submit to; accordingly, he resigned his military employment, determining to serve the next campaign as a volunteer.

First Inaugural Address

(1789)

"I was summoned by my country"

As America's first president, Washington set many lasting precedents, including the delivery of an inaugural address after taking the oath of office. Another precedent was the use of ghostwriters. For Washington's first inaugural, which he gave on April 30, 1789, David Humphreys tried and failed to write a draft; most of the final prose seems to have come from James Madison. While Humphreys stuffed his version with specific proposals, Washington and Madison chose a broader, thematic approach, a speech that aligned with Washington's most lasting precedent of all: that the president should be a humble figure, an executive who deferred to the legislature on domestic issues, who was reluctantly called to serve.

Among the vicissitudes incident to life, no event could have filled me with greater anxieties than that of which the notification was transmitted by your order, and received on the fourteenth day of the present month. On the one hand, I was summoned by my country, whose voice I can never hear but with veneration and love, from a retreat which I had chosen with the fondest predilection and, in my flattering hopes, with an immutable decision as the asylum of my declining years; a retreat which was rendered every day more necessary as well as more dear to me by the addition of habit to inclination, and of frequent interruptions in my health to the gradual waste committed on it by time. On the other hand, the magnitude and difficulty of the trust to which the voice of my country called me, being sufficient to awaken in the wisest and most experienced of her citizens a distrustful scrutiny into his qualifications, could not but overwhelm with despondence one who, inheriting inferior endowments from nature and unpracticed in the duties of civil administration, ought to be peculiarly conscious of his own deficiencies. In this conflict of emotions, all I dare aver is that it has been my faithful study to collect my duty from a just appreciation of every circumstance by which it might be affected. All I dare hope is that if in executing this task I have been too much swayed by a grateful remembrance of former instances, or by an affectionate sensibility to this transcendent proof of the confidence of my fellow-citizens, and have thence too little consulted my incapacity as well as disinclination for the weighty and untried cares before me, my error will be palliated by the motives which misled me, and its consequences be judged by my country with some share of the partiality in which they originated.

Such being the impressions under which I have, in obedience to the public summons, repaired to the present station, it would be peculiarly improper to omit in this first official act my fervent supplications to that Almighty Being who rules over the universe, who presides in the councils of nations, and whose providential aids can supply every human defect, that his benediction may consecrate to the liberties and happiness of the people of the United States a government instituted by themselves for these essential purposes, and may enable every instrument employed in its administration to execute with success the functions allotted to his charge. In tendering this homage to the Great Author of every public and private good, I assure myself that it expresses your sentiments not less than my own; nor those of my fellow-citizens at large, less than either. No people can be bound to acknowledge and adore the invisible hand which conducts the affairs of men more than the people of the United States. Every step by which they have advanced to the character of an independent nation seems to have been distinguished by some token of providential agency. And in the important revolution just accomplished in the system of their united government, the tranquil deliberations and voluntary consent of so many distinct communities, from which the event has resulted, cannot be compared with the means by which most governments have been established without some return of pious gratitude along with a humble anticipation of the future blessings which the past seem to presage. These reflections, arising out of the present crisis, have forced themselves too strongly on my mind to be suppressed. You will join with me I trust in thinking that there are none under the influence of which the proceedings of a new and free government can more auspiciously commence.

By the article establishing the executive department, it is made the duty of the president "to recommend to your consideration such measures as he shall judge necessary and expedient." The circumstances under which I now meet you will acquit me from entering into that subject further than to refer to the great constitutional charter under which you are assembled, and which, in defining your powers, designates the objects to which your attention is to be given. It will be more consistent with those circumstances, and far more congenial with the feelings which actuate me, to substitute in place of a recommendation of particular measures the tribute that is due to the talents, the rectitude, and the patriotism which adorn the characters selected to devise and adopt them. In these honorable qualifications, I behold the surest pledges that as on one side, no local prejudices or attachments, no separate views, nor party animosities will misdirect the comprehensive and equal eye which ought to watch over this great assemblage of communities and interests; so, on another, that the foundations of our national policy will be laid in the pure and immutable principles of private morality and the pre-eminence of free government, be exemplified by all the attributes which can win the affections of its citizens, and command the respect of the world.

I dwell on this prospect with every satisfaction which an ardent love for my country can inspire since there is no truth more thoroughly established than that there exists in the economy and course of nature an indissoluble union between virtue and happiness, between duty and advantage, between the genuine maxims of an honest and magnanimous policy and the solid rewards of public prosperity and felicity; since we ought to be no less persuaded that the propitious smiles of heaven can never be expected on a nation that disregards the eternal rules of order and right, which Heaven itself has ordained; and since the preservation of the sacred fire of liberty and the destiny of the republican model of government are justly considered as deeply, perhaps as finally staked on the experiment entrusted to the hands of the American people.

Besides the ordinary objects submitted to your care, it will remain with your judgment to decide how far an exercise of the occasional power delegated by the Fifth Article of the Constitution is rendered expedient at the present juncture by the nature of objections which have been urged against the system, or by the degree of inquietude which has given birth to them.

Instead of undertaking particular recommendations on this subject, in which I could be guided by no lights derived from official opportunities, I shall again give way to my entire confidence in your discernment and pursuit of the public good. For I assure myself that while you carefully avoid every alteration which might endanger the benefits of a united and effective government, or which ought to await the future lessons of experience, a reverence for the characteristic rights of freemen and a regard for the public harmony will sufficiently influence your deliberations on the question how far the former can be more impregnably fortified, or the latter be safely and advantageously promoted.

To the preceding observations I have one to add, which will be most properly addressed to the House of Representatives. It concerns myself and will therefore be as brief as possible. When I was first honored with a call into the service of my country, then on the eve of an arduous struggle for its liberties, the light in which I contemplated my duty required that I should renounce every pecuniary compensation. From this resolution I have in no instance departed. And being still under the impressions which produced it, I must decline as inapplicable to myself any share in the personal emoluments which may be indispensably included in a permanent provision for the executive department, and must accordingly pray that the pecuniary estimates for the station in which I am placed may, during my continuance in it, be limited to such actual expenditures as the public good may be thought to require.

Having thus imparted to you my sentiments, as they have been awakened by the occasion which brings us together, I shall take my present leave, but not without resorting once more to the benign Parent of the human race, in humble supplication that since He has been pleased to favor the American people with opportunities for deliberating in perfect tranquility and dispositions for deciding with unparalleled unanimity on a form of government, for the security of their union and the advancement of their happiness, so His divine blessing may be equally conspicuous in the enlarged views, the temperate consultations, and the wise measures on which the success of this government must depend.

GEORGE WASHINGTON

Farewell Address

(1796)

"The baneful effects of the spirit of party"

Washington considered retiring after one term, and in 1792 he had Madison draft a statement announcing his departure. Madison and a few others convinced Washington to seek a second term, but the president returned to the statement in 1796. This time, he asked Alexander Hamilton for help with a longer version. Washington still shaped the ideas, the structure, even the tone—"a plain style," he told Hamilton. The final text ran in virtually every American newspaper, allowing Washington to make the case for national unity and to outline the looming threats to that unity: geographical schisms, international meddling, and especially "the common and continual mischiefs of the spirit of party."

The period for a new election of a citizen to administer the executive government of the United States being not far distant, and the time actually arrived when your thoughts must be employed in designating the person who is to be clothed with that important trust, it appears to me proper, especially as it may conduce to a more distinct expression of the public voice, that I should now apprise you of the resolution I have formed, to decline being considered among the number of those out of whom a choice is to be made.

I beg you, at the same time, to do me the justice to be assured that this resolution has not been taken without a strict regard to all the considerations appertaining to the relation which binds a dutiful citizen to his

7

country; and that in withdrawing the tender of service which silence in my situation might imply I am influenced by no diminution of zeal for your future interest, no deficiency of grateful respect for your past kindness, but am supported by a full conviction that the step is compatible with both.

The acceptance of and continuance hitherto in the office to which your suffrages have twice called me have been a uniform sacrifice of inclination to the opinion of duty, and to a deference for what appeared to be your desire. I constantly hoped that it would have been much earlier in my power, consistently with motives, which I was not at liberty to disregard, to return to that retirement from which I had been reluctantly drawn. The strength of my inclination to do this, previous to the last election, had even led to the preparation of an address to declare it to you, but mature reflection on the then perplexed and critical posture of our affairs with foreign nations, and the unanimous advice of persons entitled to my confidence, impelled me to abandon the idea.

I rejoice that the state of your concerns, external as well as internal, no longer renders the pursuit of inclination incompatible with the sentiment of duty or propriety, and am persuaded, whatever partiality may be retained for my services, that in the present circumstances of our country you will not disapprove my determination to retire.

The impressions with which I first undertook the arduous trust were explained on the proper occasion. In the discharge of this trust, I will only say that I have with good intentions contributed towards the organization and administration of the government, the best exertions of which a very fallible judgment was capable. Not unconscious, in the outset, of the inferiority of my qualifications, experience in my own eyes, perhaps still more in the eyes of others, has strengthened the motives to diffidence of myself, and every day the increasing weight of years admonishes me more and more that the shade of retirement is as necessary to me as it will be welcome. Satisfied that if any circumstances have given peculiar value to my services, they were temporary, I have the consolation to believe that while choice and prudence invite me to quit the political scene, patriotism does not forbid it.

In looking forward to the moment which is intended to terminate the career of my public life, my feelings do not permit me to suspend the deep acknowledgment of that debt of gratitude which I owe to my beloved country for the many honors it has conferred upon me; still more for the steadfast confidence with which it has supported me, and for the opportunities I have thence enjoyed of manifesting my inviolable attachment by services faithful and persevering, though in usefulness unequal to my zeal. If benefits have resulted to our country from these services, let it always be remembered to your praise, and as an instructive example in our annals, that under circumstances in which the passions, agitated in every direction, were liable to mislead; amidst appearances sometimes dubious, vicissitudes of fortune often discouraging; in situations in which not infrequently want of success has countenanced the spirit of criticism, the constancy of your support was the essential prop of the efforts and a guarantee of the plans by which they were effected.

Profoundly penetrated with this idea, I shall carry it with me to my grave as a strong incitement to unceasing vows that heaven may continue to you the choicest tokens of its beneficence; that your union and brotherly affection may be perpetual; that the free Constitution, which is the work of your hands, may be sacredly maintained; that its administration in every department may be stamped with wisdom and virtue; that, in fine, the happiness of the people of these states, under the auspices of liberty, may be made complete by so careful a preservation and so prudent a use of this blessing as will acquire to them the glory of recommending it to the applause, the affection, and adoption of every nation which is yet a stranger to it.

Here, perhaps, I ought to stop. But a solicitude for your welfare, which cannot end but with my life, and the apprehension of danger, natural to that solicitude, urge me on an occasion like the present to offer to your solemn contemplation and to recommend to your frequent review some sentiments which are the result of much reflection of no inconsiderable observation, and which appear to me all important to the permanency of your felicity as a people. These will be offered to you with the more freedom, so you can only see in them the disinterested warnings of a parting friend who can possibly have no personal motive to bias his counsel. Nor can I forget, as an encouragement to it, your indulgent reception of my sentiments on a former and not dissimilar occasion.

Interwoven as is the love of liberty with every ligament of your hearts, no recommendation of mine is necessary to fortify or confirm the attachment.

The unity of government, which constitutes you one people, is also now dear to you. It is justly so, for it is a main pillar in the edifice of your real independence, the support of your tranquility at home, your peace abroad, of your safety, of your prosperity, of that very liberty which you so highly prize. But as it is easy to foresee that from different causes and from different quarters much pains will be taken, many artifices employed, to weaken in your minds the conviction of this truth, as this is the point in your political fortress against which the batteries of internal and external enemies will be most constantly and actively (though often covertly and insidiously) directed, it is of infinite moment that you should properly estimate the immense value of your national union to your collective and individual happiness; that you should cherish a cordial, habitual, and unmovable attachment to it, accustoming yourselves to think and speak of it as of the palladium of your political safety and prosperity, watching for its preservation with jealous anxiety, discountenancing whatever may suggest even a suspicion that it can in any event be abandoned, and indignantly frowning upon the first dawning of every attempt to alienate any portion of our country from the rest or to enfeeble the sacred ties which now link together the various parts.

For this you have every inducement of sympathy and interest. Citizens by birth or choice of a common country, that country has a right to concentrate your affections. The name of American, which belongs to you in your national capacity, must always exalt the just pride of patriotism, more than any appellation derived from local discriminations. With slight shades of difference, you have the same religion, manners, habits, and political principles. You have in a common cause fought and triumphed together; the independence and liberty you possess are the work of joint councils and joint efforts, of common dangers, sufferings, and successes.

But these considerations, however powerfully they address themselves to your sensibility, are greatly outweighed by those which apply more immediately to your interest. Here every portion of our country finds the most commanding motives for carefully guarding and preserving the union of the whole.

The north, in an unrestrained intercourse with the south, protected by the equal laws of a common government, finds in the productions of the latter great additional resources of maritime and commercial enterprise and precious materials of manufacturing industry. The south in the same intercourse, benefitting by the agency of the north, sees its agriculture grow and its commerce expand. Turning partly into its own channels the seamen of the north, it finds its particular navigation invigorated, and while it contributes, in different ways, to nourish and increase the general mass of the national navigation, it looks forward to the protection of a maritime strength, to which itself is unequally adapted. The east, in a like intercourse with the west, already finds, and in the progressive improvement of interior communications by land and water will more and more find, a valuable vent for the commodities which it brings from abroad, or manufactures at home. The west derives from the east supplies requisite to its growth and comfort, and what is perhaps of still greater consequence, it must of necessity owe the secure enjoyment of indispensable outlets for its own productions to the weight, influence, and the future maritime strength of the Atlantic side of the union, directed by an indissoluble community of interest as one nation. Any other tenure by which the west can hold this essential advantage, whether derived from its own separate strength or from an apostate and unnatural connection with any foreign power, must be intrinsically precarious.

While then every part of our country thus feels an immediate and particular interest in union, all the parts combined cannot fail to find in the united mass of means and efforts greater strength, greater resource, proportionally greater security from external danger, a less frequent interruption of their peace by foreign nations; and, what is of inestimable value, they must derive from union an exemption from those broils and wars between themselves which so frequently afflict neighboring countries, not tied together by the same government, which their own rivalships alone would be sufficient to produce, but which opposite foreign alliances, attachments and intrigues would stimulate and embitter. Hence likewise they will avoid the necessity of those overgrown military establishments which under any form of government are inauspicious to liberty and which are to be regarded as particularly hostile to republican liberty; in this sense it is that your union ought to be considered as a main prop of your liberty, and that the love of the one ought to endear to you the preservation of the other.

These considerations speak a persuasive language to every reflecting and virtuous mind and exhibit the continuance of the union as a primary object of patriotic desire. Is there a doubt, whether a common government can embrace so large a sphere? Let experience solve it. To listen to mere speculation in such a case were criminal. We are authorized to hope that a proper organization of the whole, with the auxiliary agency of governments for the respective subdivisions, will afford a happy issue to the experiment. It is well worth a fair and full experiment. With such powerful and obvious motives to union, affecting all parts of our country, while experience shall not have demonstrated its impracticability, there will always be reason to distrust the patriotism of those who in any quarter may endeavor to weaken its bands.

In contemplating the causes which may disturb our union, it occurs as matter of serious concern that any ground should have been furnished for characterizing parties by geographical discriminations—northern and southern, Atlantic and western—whence designing men may endeavor to excite a belief that there is a real difference of local interests and views.

One of the expedients of party to acquire influence, within particular districts, is to misrepresent the opinions and aims of other districts. You cannot shield yourselves too much against the jealousies and heartburnings which spring from these misrepresentations; they tend to render alien to each other those who ought to be bound together by fraternal affection. The inhabitants of our western country have lately had a useful lesson on this head: they have seen, in the negotiation by the executive and in the unanimous ratification by the Senate of the treaty with Spain, and in the universal satisfaction at that event throughout the United States, a decisive proof how unfounded were the suspicions propagated among them of a policy in the general government and in the Atlantic states unfriendly to their interests in regard to the Mississippi; they have been witnesses to the formation of two treaties, that with Great Britain and that with Spain, which secure to them everything they could desire in respect to our foreign relations towards confirming their prosperity. Will it not be their wisdom to rely for the preservation of these advantages on the union by which they were procured? Will they not henceforth be deaf to those advisers, if such there are, who would sever them from their brethren and connect them with aliens?

To the efficacy and permanency of your union, a government for the whole is indispensable. No alliances, however strict, between the parts can be an adequate substitute; they must inevitably experience the infractions and interruptions which all alliances in all times have experienced. Sensible of this momentous truth, you have improved upon your first essay, by the adoption of a constitution of government better calculated than your former for an intimate union and for the efficacious management of your common concerns. This government, the offspring of our own choice, uninfluenced and unawed, adopted upon full investigation and mature deliberation, completely free in its principles, in the distribution of its powers, uniting security with energy, and containing within itself a provision for its own amendment, has a just claim to your confidence and your support. Respect for its authority, compliance with its laws, acquiescence in its measures, are duties enjoined by the fundamental maxims of true liberty. The basis of our political systems is the right of the people to make and to alter their constitutions of government. But the Constitution which at any time exists, till changed by an explicit and authentic act of the whole people, is sacredly obligatory upon all. The very idea of the power and the right of the people to establish government presupposes the duty of every individual to obey the established government.

All obstructions to the execution of the laws, all combinations and associations under whatever plausible character with the real design to direct, control, counteract, or awe the regular deliberation and action of the constituted authorities, are destructive of this fundamental principle and of fatal tendency. They serve to organize faction, to give it an artificial and extraordinary force, to put in the place of the delegated will of the nation, the will of a party, often a small but artful and enterprising minority of the community, and, according to the alternate triumphs of different parties, to make the public administration the mirror of the ill-concerted and incongruous projects of faction, rather than the organ of consistent and wholesome plans digested by common councils and modified by mutual interests.

However combinations or associations of the above description may now and then answer popular ends, they are likely in the course of time and things to become potent engines by which cunning, ambitious, and unprincipled men will be enabled to subvert the power of the people and to usurp for themselves the reins of government, destroying afterwards the very engines which have lifted them to unjust dominion.

Towards the preservation of your government and the permanency of your present happy state, it is requisite not only that you steadily discountenance irregular oppositions to its acknowledged authority, but also that you resist with care the spirit of innovation upon its principles, however specious the pretexts. One method of assault may be to effect in the forms of the Constitution alterations which will impair the energy of the system and thus to undermine what cannot be directly overthrown. In all the changes to which you may be invited, remember that time and habit are at least as necessary to fix the true character of governments as of other human institutions; that experience is the surest standard by which to test the real tendency of the existing constitution of a country; that facility in changes upon the credit of mere hypothesis and opinion exposes to perpetual change, from the endless variety of hypothesis and opinion; and remember especially that for the efficient management of your common interests, in a country so extensive as ours, a government of as much vigor as is consistent with the perfect security of liberty is indispensable. Liberty itself will find in such a government, with powers properly distributed and adjusted, its surest guardian. It is, indeed, little else than a name where the government is too feeble to withstand the enterprises of faction, to confine each member of the society within the limits prescribed by the laws, and to maintain all in the secure and tranquil enjoyment of the rights of person and property.

I have already intimated to you the danger of parties in the state, with particular reference to the founding of them on geographical discriminations. Let me now take a more comprehensive view and warn you in the most solemn manner against the baneful effects of the spirit of party, generally.

This spirit, unfortunately, is inseparable from our nature, having its root in the strongest passions of the human mind. It exists under different shapes in all governments, more or less stifled, controlled, or repressed, but in those of the popular form it is seen in its greatest rankness and is truly their worst enemy.

The alternate domination of one faction over another, sharpened by the spirit of revenge, natural to party dissension, which in different ages and countries has perpetrated the most horrid enormities, is itself a frightful despotism. But this leads at length to a more formal and permanent despotism. The disorders and miseries which result gradually incline the minds of men to seek security and repose in the absolute power of an individual, and sooner or later the chief of some prevailing faction more able or more fortunate than his competitors turns this disposition to the purposes of his own elevation, on the ruins of public liberty.

Without looking forward to the extremity of this kind (which nevertheless ought not to be entirely out of sight), the common and continual mischiefs of the spirit of party are sufficient to make it the interest and duty of a wise people to discourage and restrain it.

It serves always to distract the public councils and enfeeble the public administration. It agitates the community with ill-founded jealousies and false alarms, kindles the animosity of one part against another, foments occasionally riot and insurrection. It opens the door to foreign influence and corruption, which find a facilitated access to the government itself through the channels of party passions. Thus the policy and the will of one country are subjected to the policy and will of another.

There is an opinion that parties in free countries are useful checks upon the administration of the government and serve to keep alive the spirit of liberty. This within certain limits is probably true, and in governments of a monarchical cast patriotism may look with indulgence if not with favor upon the spirit of party. But in those of the popular character, in governments purely elective, it is a spirit not to be encouraged. From their natural tendency, it is certain there will always be enough of that spirit for every salutary purpose. And there being constant danger of excess, the effort ought to be by force of public opinion to mitigate and assuage it.

A fire not to be quenched, it demands a uniform vigilance to prevent its bursting into a flame, lest, instead of warming, it should consume.

It is important, likewise, that the habits of thinking in a free country should inspire caution in those entrusted with its administration to confine themselves within their respective constitutional spheres, avoiding in the exercise of the powers of one department to encroach upon another. The spirit of encroachment tends to consolidate the powers of all the departments in one and thus to create, whatever the form of government, a real despotism. A just estimate of that love of power, and proneness to abuse it which predominates in the human heart, is sufficient to satisfy us of the truth of this position. The necessity of reciprocal checks in the exercise of political power, by dividing and distributing it into different depositories and constituting each the guardian of the public weal against invasions by the others, has been evinced by experiments ancient and modern, some of them in our country and under our own eyes. To preserve them must be as necessary as to institute them. If, in the opinion of the people, the distribution or modification of the constitutional powers be in any particular wrong, let it be corrected by an amendment in the way which the Constitution designates. But let there be no change by usurpation, for though this in one instance may be the instrument of good, it is the customary weapon by which free governments are destroyed. The precedent must always greatly overbalance in permanent evil any partial or transient benefit which the use can at any time yield.

Of all the dispositions and habits which lead to political prosperity, religion and morality are indispensable supports. In vain would that man claim the tribute of patriotism who should labor to subvert these great pillars of human happiness, these firmest props of the duties of men and citizens. The mere politician, equally with the pious man, ought to respect and to cherish them. A volume could not trace all their connections with private and public felicity. Let it simply be asked where is the security for property, for reputation, for life, if the sense of religious obligation desert the oaths which are the instruments of investigation in courts of justice? And let us with caution indulge the supposition that morality can be maintained without religion. Whatever may be conceded to the influence of refined education on minds of peculiar structure, reason and experience both forbid us to expect that national morality can prevail in exclusion of religious principle.

It is substantially true that virtue or morality is a necessary spring of popular government. The rule indeed extends with more or less force to every species of free government. Who that is a sincere friend to it can look with indifference upon attempts to shake the foundation of the fabric?

Promote, then, as an object of primary importance, institutions for the general diffusion of knowledge. In proportion as the structure of a government gives force to public opinion, it is essential that public opinion should be enlightened.

As a very important source of strength and security, cherish public credit. One method of preserving it is to use it as sparingly as possible, avoiding occasions of expense by cultivating peace but remembering also that timely disbursements to prepare for danger frequently prevent much greater disbursements to repel it; avoiding likewise the accumulation of debt, not only by shunning occasions of expense but by vigorous exertions in time of peace to discharge the debts which unavoidable wars may have occasioned, not ungenerously throwing upon posterity the burden which we ourselves ought to bear. The execution of these maxims belongs to your representatives, but it is necessary that public opinion should cooperate. To facilitate to them the performance of their duty, it is essential that you should practically bear in mind that towards the payment of debts there must be revenue, that to have revenue there must be taxes, that no taxes can be devised which are not more or less inconvenient and unpleasant, that the intrinsic embarrassment inseparable from the selection of the proper objects (which is always a choice of difficulties) ought to be a decisive motive for a candid construction of the conduct of the government in making it and for a spirit of acquiescence in the measures for obtaining revenue which the public exigencies may at any time dictate.

Observe good faith and justice towards all nations, cultivate peace and harmony with all; religion and morality enjoin this conduct and can it be that good policy does not equally enjoin it? It will be worthy of a free, enlightened, and at no distant period a great nation to give to mankind the magnanimous and too novel example of a people always guided by an exalted justice and benevolence. Who can doubt that in the course of time and things the fruits of such a plan would richly repay any temporary advantages which might be lost by a steady adherence to it? Can it be that Providence has not connected the permanent felicity of a nation with its virtue? The experiment at least is recommended by every sentiment which ennobles human nature. Alas! Is it rendered impossible by its vices?

In the execution of such a plan, nothing is more essential than that permanent, inveterate antipathies against particular nations, and passionate attachments for others, should be excluded; and that, in place of them, just and amicable feelings towards all should be cultivated. The nation which indulges towards another a habitual hatred or a habitual fondness is in some degree a slave. It is a slave to its animosity or to its affection, either of which is sufficient to lead it astray from its duty and its interest. Antipathy in one nation against another disposes each more readily to offer insult and injury, to lay hold of slight causes of umbrage, and to be haughty and intractable when accidental or trifling occasions of dispute occur. Hence frequent collisions, obstinate, envenomed and bloody contests. The nation, prompted by ill will and resentment, sometimes impels to war the government, contrary to the best calculations of policy. The government sometimes participates in the national propensity and adopts through passion what reason would reject; at other times, it makes the animosity of the nation subservient to projects of hostility instigated by pride, ambition, and other sinister and pernicious motives. The peace often, sometimes perhaps the liberty, of nations has been the victim.

So, likewise, a passionate attachment of one nation for another produces a variety of evils. Sympathy for the favorite nation, facilitating the illusion of an imaginary common interest in cases where no real common interest exists and infusing into one the enmities of the other, betrays the former into a participation in the quarrels and wars of the latter, without adequate inducement or justification. It leads also to concessions to the favorite nation of privileges denied to others, which is apt doubly to injure the nation making the concessions, by unnecessarily parting with what ought to have been retained and by exciting jealousy, ill will, and a disposition to retaliate in the parties from whom equal privileges are withheld; and it gives to ambitious, corrupted, or deluded citizens (who devote themselves to the favorite nation) facility to betray or sacrifice the interests of their own country without odium, sometimes even with popularity, gilding with the appearances of a virtuous sense of obligation a commendable deference for public opinion or a laudable zeal for public good, the base or foolish compliances of ambition, corruption, or infatuation.

As avenues to foreign influence in innumerable ways, such attachments are particularly alarming to the truly enlightened and independent patriot. How many opportunities do they afford to tamper with domestic factions, to practice the acts of seduction, to mislead public opinion, to influence or awe the public councils! Such an attachment of a small or weak towards a great and powerful nation dooms the former to be the satellite of the latter.

Against the insidious wiles of foreign influence (I conjure you to believe me, fellow-citizens), the jealousy of a free people ought to be constantly awake since history and experience prove that foreign influence is one of the most baneful foes of republican government. But that jealousy to be useful must be impartial, else it becomes the instrument of the very influence to be avoided instead of a defense against it. Excessive partiality for one foreign nation, and excessive dislike for another, cause those whom they actuate to see danger only on one side and serve to veil and even second the arts of influence of the other. Real patriots, who may resist the intrigues of the favorite, are liable to become suspected and odious, while its tools and dupes usurp the applause and confidence of the people, to surrender their interests.

The great rule of conduct for us, in regard to foreign nations, is in extending our commercial relations, to have with them as little political connection as possible. So far as we have already formed engagements, let them be fulfilled with perfect good faith. Here let us stop.

Europe has a set of primary interests, which to us have none or a very remote relation. Hence she must be engaged in frequent controversies, the causes of which are essentially foreign to our concerns. Hence, therefore, it must be unwise in us to implicate ourselves, by artificial ties, in the ordinary vicissitudes of her politics or the ordinary combinations and collisions of her friendships or enmities.

Our detached and distant situation invites and enables us to pursue a different course. If we remain one people under an efficient government, the period is not far off when we may defy material injury from external annoyance, when we may take such an attitude as will cause the neutrality we may at any time resolve upon to be scrupulously respected, when belligerent nations under the impossibility of making acquisitions upon us will not lightly hazard the giving us provocation, when we may choose peace or war as our interest, guided by justice, shall counsel.

Why forego the advantages of so peculiar a situation? Why quit our own to stand upon foreign ground? Why, by interweaving our destiny with that of any part of Europe, entangle our peace and prosperity in the toils of European ambition, rivalship, interest, humor, or caprice?

It is our true policy to steer clear of permanent alliances with any portion of the foreign world; so far, I mean, as we are now at liberty to do it, for let me not be understood as capable of patronizing infidelity to existing engagements. I hold the maxim no less applicable to public than to private affairs that honesty is always the best policy. I repeat it, therefore: let those engagements be observed in their genuine sense. But in my opinion it is unnecessary and would be unwise to extend them.

Taking care always to keep ourselves by suitable establishments on a respectable defensive posture, we may safely trust to temporary alliances for extraordinary emergencies.

Harmony, liberal intercourse with all nations, are recommended by policy, humanity, and interest. But even our commercial policy should hold an equal and impartial hand, neither seeking nor granting exclusive favors or preferences; consulting the natural course of things; diffusing and diversifying by gentle means the streams of commerce, but forcing nothing; establishing with powers so disposed in order to give trade a stable course, to define the rights of our merchants, and to enable the government to support them, conventional rules of intercourse, the best that present circumstances and mutual opinion will permit, but temporary, and liable to be from time to time abandoned or varied as experience and circumstances shall dictate; constantly keeping in view that it is folly in one nation to look for disinterested favors from another, that it must pay with a portion of its independence for whatever it may accept under that character, that by such acceptance it may place itself in the condition of having given equivalents for nominal favors and yet of being reproached with ingratitude for not giving more. There can be no greater error than to expect or calculate upon real favors from nation to nation. It is an illusion which experience must cure, which a just pride ought to discard.

In offering to you, my countrymen, these counsels of an old and affectionate friend, I dare not hope they will make the strong and lasting impression I could wish, that they will control the usual current of the passions or prevent our nation from running the course which has hitherto marked the destiny of nations; but if I may even flatter myself that they may be productive of some partial benefit, some occasional good, that they may now and then recur to moderate the fury of party spirit, to warn against the mischiefs of foreign intrigue, to guard against the impostures of pretended patriotism, this hope will be a full recompense for the solicitude for your welfare by which they have been dictated.

How far in the discharge of my official duties I have been guided by the principles which have been delineated, the public records and other evidences of my conduct must witness to you and to the world. To myself, the assurance of my own conscience is that I have at least believed myself to be guided by them.

In relation to the still subsisting war in Europe, my Proclamation of the 22nd of April, 1793, is the index to my plan. Sanctioned by your approving voice and by that of your representatives in both houses of Congress, the spirit of that measure has continually governed me, uninfluenced by any attempts to deter or divert me from it.

After deliberate examination with the aid of the best lights I could obtain, I was well satisfied that our country, under all the circumstances of the case, had a right to take and was bound in duty and interest to take a neutral position. Having taken it, I determined, as far as should depend upon me, to maintain it with moderation, perseverance, and firmness.

The considerations which respect the right to hold this conduct it is not necessary on this occasion to detail. I will only observe that according to my understanding of the matter that right, so far from being denied by any of the belligerent powers, has been virtually admitted by all.

The duty of holding a neutral conduct may be inferred, without anything more, from the obligation which justice and humanity impose on every nation in cases in which it is free to act, to maintain inviolate the relations of peace and amity towards other nations.

The inducements of interest for observing that conduct will best be referred to your own reflections and experience. With me, a predominant motive has been to endeavor to gain time to our country to settle and mature its yet recent institutions and to progress without interruption to that degree of strength and consistency which is necessary to give it, humanly speaking, the command of its own fortunes.

Though in reviewing the incidents of my administration, I am unconscious of intentional error, I am nevertheless too sensible of my defects not to think it probable that I may have committed many errors. Whatever they may be, I fervently beseech the Almighty to avert or mitigate the evils to which they may tend. I shall also carry with me the hope that my country will never cease to view them with indulgence, and that after forty-five years of my life dedicated to its service with an upright zeal, the faults of incompetent abilities will be consigned to oblivion, as myself must soon be to the mansions of rest.

Relying on its kindness in this as in other things, and actuated by that fervent love towards it which is so natural to a man who views in it the native soil of himself and his progenitors for several generations, I anticipate with pleasing expectation that retreat in which I promise myself to realize, without alloy, the sweet enjoyment of partaking in the midst of my fellow-citizens the benign influence of good laws under a free government—the ever favorite object of my heart, and the happy reward, as I trust, of our mutual cares, labors, and dangers.

JOHN ADAMS

From His Autobiography

"My children may be assured that no illegitimate brother or sister exists"

Washington's authorial reluctance meant that John Adams was the first president to attempt his memoirs, a process he began a few months after leaving the White House in 1801. Writing an autobiography in this period was much different than in later eras: more formal, less personal, and almost always intended to be published after the subject's death. While Adams tried to follow these rules, his blunt and impulsive nature often overwhelmed them. Again and again in his unfinished manuscript, Adams would nod to some convention—go light on the youthful anecdotes, say—only to get carried away in the writing of a charming story or bitter political memory. In this excerpt, on his childhood and study at Harvard, one can see Adams's honesty, emotion, and moral certainty.

My father married Susanna Boylston in October 1734, and on the 19th of October, 1735, I was born. As my parents were both fond of reading, and my father had destined his firstborn long before his birth to a public education, I was very early taught to read at home and at a school of Mrs. Belcher, the mother of Deacon Moses Belcher who lived in the next house on the opposite side of the road. I shall not consume much paper in relating the anecdotes of my youth. I was sent to the public school close by the stone church, then kept by Mr. Joseph Cleverly, who died this year 1802 at the age of ninety. Mr. Cleverly was through his whole life the most indolent man I ever knew, though a tolerable scholar and a gentleman.

21

His inattention to his scholars was such as gave me a disgust to schools, to books, and to study, and I spent my time as idle children do in making and sailing boats and ships upon the ponds and brooks, in making and flying kites, in driving hoops, playing marbles, playing Quoits, wrestling, swimming, skating, and above all in shooting, to which diversion I was addicted to a degree of ardor which I know not that I ever felt for any other business, study, or amusement.

My enthusiasm for sports and inattention to books alarmed my father, and he frequently entered into conversation with me upon the subject. I told him I did not love books and wished he would lay aside the thoughts of sending me to college.

"What would you do, child?"

"Be a farmer."

"A farmer? Well I will show you what it is to be a farmer. You shall go with me to Penny Ferry tomorrow morning and help me get thatch."

"I shall be very glad to go, sir."

Accordingly next morning he took me with him, and with great good humor kept me all day with him at work. At night at home he said, "Well, John, are you satisfied with being a farmer?"

Though the labor had been very hard and very muddy I answered, "I like it very well, sir."

"Ay, but I don't like it so well, so you shall go to school today."

I went but was not so happy as among the creek thatch. My schoolmaster neglected to put me into arithmetic longer than I thought was right, and I resented it. I procured me Cocker's [*Decimal Arithmetic*], I believe, and applied myself to it at home alone and went through the whole course, overtook and passed by all the scholars at school without any master at all. I dared not ask my father's assistance because he would have disliked my inattention to my Latin. In this idle way, I passed on till fourteen and upwards, when I said to my father very seriously I wished he would take me from school and let me go to work upon the farm.

"You know," said my father, "I have set my heart upon your education at college and why will you not comply with my desire."

"Sir, I don't like my schoolmaster. He is so negligent and so cross that I never can learn anything under him. If you will be so good as to persuade Mr. Marsh to take me, I will apply myself to my studies as closely as my nature will admit and go to college as soon as I can be prepared." Next morning the first I heard was, "John, I have persuaded Mr. Marsh to take you, and you must go to school there today."

This Mr. Marsh was a son of our former minister of that name who kept a private boarding school but two doors from my father's. To this school I went where I was kindly treated, and I began to study in earnest. My father soon observed the relaxation of my zeal for my fowling piece and my daily increasing attention to my books. In a little more than a year, Mr. Marsh pronounced me fitted for college. On the day appointed at Cambridge for the examination of candidates for admission, I mounted my horse and called upon Mr. Marsh, who was to go with me.

The weather was dull and threatened rain. Mr. Marsh said he was unwell and afraid to go out. I must therefore go alone. Thunder struck at this unforeseen disappointment, and terrified at the thought of introducing myself to such great men as the president and fellows of a college, I at first resolved to return home. But foreseeing the grief of my father and apprehending he would not only be offended with me but my master, too, whom I sincerely loved, I aroused myself and collected resolution enough to proceed. Although Mr. Marsh had assured me that he had seen one of the tutors the last week and had said to him all that was proper for him to say if he should go to Cambridge; that he was not afraid to trust me to an examination and was confident I should acquit myself well and be honorably admitted, yet I had not the same confidence in myself and suffered a very melancholy journey.

Arrived at Cambridge, I presented myself according to my directions and underwent the usual examination by the president, Mr. Holyoke, and the tutors, Flint, Hancock, Mayhew, and Marsh. Mr. Mayhew, into whose class we were to be admitted, presented me a passage of English to translate into Latin. It was long and casting my eye over it I found several words the Latin for which did not occur to my memory. Thinking that I must translate it without a dictionary, I was in a great fright and expected to be turned by, an event that I dreaded above all things. Mr. Mayhew went into his study and bid me follow him.

"There, child," said he, "is a dictionary, and there a grammar, and there paper, pen, and ink, and you may take your own time."

This was joyful news to me, and I then thought my admission safe. The Latin was soon made, and I was declared admitted and a theme given me to write on in the vacation. I was as light when I came home as I had been heavy when I went. My master was well pleased and my parents very happy. I spent the vacation not very profitably, chiefly in reading magazines and a British *Apollo*. I went to college at the end of it and took the chamber assigned me and my place in the class under Mr. Mayhew. I found some better scholars than myself, particularly Lock, Hemmenway, and Tisdale. The last left college before the end of the first year, and what became of him I know not. Hemmenway still lives a great divine, and Lock has been president of Harvard College, a station for which no man was better qualified. With these I ever lived in friendship, without jealousy or envy. I soon became intimate with them and began to feel a desire to equal them in science and literature. In the sciences, especially mathematics, I soon surpassed them, mainly because, intending to go into the pulpit, they thought divinity and the classics of more importance to them. In literature I never overtook them.

Here it may be proper to recollect something which makes an article of great importance in the life of every man. I was of an amorous disposition and very early from ten or eleven years of age was very fond of the society of females. I had my favorites among the young women and spent many of my evenings in their company, and this disposition, although controlled for seven years after my entrance into college, returned and engaged me too much till I was married.

I shall draw no characters nor give any enumeration of my youthful flames. It would be considered as no compliment to the dead or the living. This I will say: they were all modest and virtuous girls and always maintained this character through life. No virgin or matron ever had cause to blush at the sight of me, or to regret her acquaintance with me. No father, brother, son, or friend ever had cause of grief or resentment for any intercourse between me and any daughter, sister, mother, or any other relation of the female sex. My children may be assured that no illegitimate brother or sister exists or ever existed.

These reflections, to me consolatory beyond all expression, I am able to make with truth and sincerity, and I presume I am indebted for this blessing to my education. My parents held every species of libertinage in such contempt and horror and held up constantly to view such pictures of disgrace, of baseness, and of ruin, that my natural temperament was always overawed by my principles and sense of decorum. This blessing has been rendered the more precious to me as I have seen enough of the effects of a different practice. Corroding reflections through life are the never-failing consequence of illicit amours, in old countries as well as in new countries. The happiness of life depends more upon innocence in this respect than upon all the philosophy of Epicurus, or of Zeno without it. I could write romances or histories as wonderful as romances of what

I have known or heard in France, Holland, and England, and all would serve to confirm what I learned in my youth in America: that happiness is lost forever if innocence is lost, at least until a repentance is undergone so severe as to be an overbalance to all the gratifications of licentiousness. Repentance itself cannot restore the happiness of innocence, at least in this life.

JOHN ADAMS

From "A Dissertation on the Canon and the Feudal Law"

(1765)

"Liberty must at all hazards be supported. We have a right to it, derived from our Maker"

Adams also published thousands of pages during his lifetime: fiery newspaper essays, dense books of political theory, and pamphlets that were debated before, during, and after the Revolutionary War. One such pamphlet, "A Dissertation on the Canon and the Feudal Law," first appeared serially in 1765, and in it Adams summarized the character of his fellow Americans. In this excerpt, he celebrates the colonies' passion for self-education and a free press—two qualities that would ensure their ability to function as an independent nation.

A native of America who cannot read and write is as rare an appearance as a Jacobite or a Roman Catholic—i.e., as rare as a comet or an earthquake. It has been observed that we are all of us lawyers, divines, politicians, and philosophers. And I have good authorities to say that all candid foreigners who have passed through this country and conversed freely with all sorts of people here will allow that they have never seen so much knowledge and civility among the common people in any part of the world. It is true, there has been among us a party for some years, consisting chiefly not of the descendants of the first settlers of this country

26

but of high churchmen and high statesmen imported since, who affect to censure this provision for the education of our youth as a needless expense and an imposition upon the rich in favor of the poor and as an institution productive of idleness and vain speculation among the people whose time and attention it is said ought to be devoted to labor and not to public affairs or to examination into the conduct of their superiors. And certain officers of the crown, and certain other missionaries of ignorance, foppery, servility, and slavery, have been most inclined to countenance and increase the same party. Be it remembered, however, that liberty must at all hazards be supported. We have a right to it, derived from our Maker.

But if we had not, our fathers have earned and bought it for us at the expense of their ease, their estates, their pleasure, and their blood. And liberty cannot be preserved without a general knowledge among the people, who have a right, from the frame of their nature, to knowledge, as their great Creator who does nothing in vain has given them understandings and a desire to know—but besides this they have a right, an indisputable, unalienable, indefeasible divine right to that most dreaded and envied kind of knowledge, I mean of the characters and conduct of their rulers. Rulers are no more than attorneys, agents, and trustees for the people, and if the cause, the interest, and trust is insidiously betrayed or wantonly trifled away the people have a right to revoke the authority that they themselves have deputed and to constitute abler and better agents, attorneys, and trustees.

And the preservation of the means of knowledge, among the lowest ranks, is of more importance to the public than all the property of all the rich men in the country. It is even of more consequence to the rich themselves, and to their posterity. The only question is whether it is a public emolument, and if it is, the rich ought undoubtedly to contribute in the same proportion, as to all other public burdens, i.e. in proportion to their wealth which is secured by public expenses.

But none of the means of information are more sacred or have been cherished with more tenderness and care by the settlers of America than the press. Care has been taken that the art of printing should be encouraged and that it should be easy and cheap and safe for any person to communicate his thoughts to the public. And you, Messieurs Printers, whatever the tyrants of the earth may say of your paper, have done important service to your country, by your readiness and freedom in publishing the speculations of the curious. The stale, impudent insinuations of slander and sedition with which the gormandizers of power have endeavored to discredit your paper are so much the more to your honor; for the jaws of power are always opened to devour, and her arm is always stretched out if possible to destroy, the freedom of thinking, speaking, and writing. And if the public interest, liberty, and happiness have been in danger from the ambition or avarice of any great man or number of great men—whatever may be their politeness, address, learning, ingenuity, and in other respects integrity and humanity—you have done yourselves honor and your country service by publishing and pointing out that avarice and ambition.

THOMAS JEFFERSON

From His Autobiography, Including His Draft of the Declaration of Independence

"When in the course of human events"

Like Adams, Thomas Jefferson started but never completed his memoirs. Jefferson did better at sticking to his era's autobiographical conventions, focusing on his public actions instead of his private feelings. The one exception came in Jefferson's rich, behind-the-scenes stories of authorship: how he wrote "A Summary View of the Rights of British America," the pamphlet that made his name in 1774; how he published Notes on the State of Virginia, *the book that contained some of his most controversial opinions; and how he drafted the Declaration of Independence in 1776. This excerpt includes Jefferson's Declaration draft and his account of how that draft came to be, an account that, in its contradictory blend of assertion and self-deprecation, is fully Jeffersonian.*

It appearing in the course of these debates that the colonies of New York, New Jersey, Pennsylvania, Delaware, Maryland, and South Carolina were not yet matured for falling from the parent stem, but that they were fast advancing to that state, it was thought most prudent to wait a while for them and to postpone the final decision to July 1. But that this might occasion as little delay as possible, a committee was appointed to prepare a declaration of independence. The committee [members] were John Adams, Dr. Franklin, Roger Sherman, Robert R. Livingston, and myself. Committees were also appointed at the same time to prepare a plan of confederation for the colonies and to state the terms proper to be proposed for foreign alliance.

The committee for drawing the Declaration of Independence desired me to do it. It was accordingly done, and being approved by them, I reported it to the house on Friday the 28th of June, when it was read and ordered to lie on the table. On Monday the 1st of July, the house resolved itself into a committee of the whole and resumed the consideration of the original motion made by the delegates of Virginia, which being again debated through the day was carried in the affirmative by the votes of New Hampshire, Connecticut, Massachusetts, Rhode Island, New Jersey, Maryland, Virginia, North Carolina, and Georgia. South Carolina and Pennsylvania voted against it. Delaware having but two members present, they were divided; the delegates for New York declared they were for it themselves and were assured their constituents were for it, but that their instructions having been drawn near a twelvemonth before, when reconciliation was still the general object, they were enjoined by them to do nothing which should impede that object. They therefore thought themselves not justifiable in voting on either side and asked leave to withdraw from the question, which was given them.

The committee rose and reported their resolution to the house. Mr. Edward Rutledge of South Carolina then requested the determination might be put off to the next day, as he believed his colleagues, though they disapproved of the resolution, would then join in it for the sake of unanimity. The ultimate question, whether the house would agree to the resolution of the committee, was accordingly postponed to the next day, when it was again moved and South Carolina concurred in voting for it. In the meantime, a third member had come post from the Delaware counties and turned the vote of that colony in favor of the resolution. Members of a different sentiment attending that morning from Pennsylvania also, their vote was changed, so that the whole twelve colonies who were authorized to vote at all gave their voices for it; and within a few days the convention of New York approved of it and thus supplied the void occasioned by the withdrawing of their delegates from the vote.

Congress proceeded the same day to consider the Declaration of Independence, which had been reported and laid on the table the Friday preceding and on Monday referred to a committee of the whole. The pusillanimous idea that we had friends in England worth keeping terms with still haunted the minds of many. For this reason those passages which conveyed censures on the people of England were struck out, lest they should give them offense. The clause, too, reprobating the enslaving the inhabitants of Africa, was struck out in complaisance to South Carolina and Georgia, who had never attempted to restrain the importation of slaves and who on the contrary still wished to continue it. Our northern brethren also, I believe, felt a little tender under those censures; for though their people have very few slaves themselves yet they had been pretty considerable carriers of them to others.

The debates having taken up the greater parts of the 2nd, 3rd, and 4th days of July were in the evening of the last closed. The declaration was reported by the committee, agreed to by the house, and signed by every member present except Mr. [John] Dickinson. As the sentiments of men are known not only by what they receive, but what they reject also, I will state the form of the declaration as originally reported. The parts struck out by Congress shall be distinguished by a black line drawn under them, and those inserted by them shall be placed in [italics] . . .

A Declaration by the Representatives of the United States of America, in General Congress Assembled

When in the course of human events it becomes necessary for one people to dissolve the political bands which have connected them with another, and to assume among the powers of the earth the separate and equal station to which the laws of nature and of nature's God entitle them, a decent respect to the opinions of mankind requires that they should declare the causes which impel them to the separation.

We hold these truths to be self-evident: that all men are created equal; that they are endowed by their creator with inherent and *certain* inalienable rights; that among these are life, liberty, and the pursuit of happiness; that to secure these rights, governments are instituted among men, deriving their just powers from the consent of the governed; that whenever any form of government becomes destructive of these ends, it is the right of the people to alter or abolish it and to institute new government, laying its foundation on such principles and organizing its powers in such form, as to them shall seem most likely to effect their safety and happiness. Prudence indeed will dictate that governments long established should not be changed for light and transient causes; and accordingly all experience has shown that mankind are more disposed to suffer while evils are sufferable than to right themselves by abolishing the forms to which they are accustomed. But when a long train of abuses and usurpations <u>begun at a distinguished period and</u> pursuing invariably the same object evinces a design to reduce them under absolute despotism, it is their right, it is their duty to throw off such government and to provide new guards for their future security. Such has been the patient sufferance of these colonies, and such is now the necessity which constrains them to <u>expunge</u> *alter* their former systems of government. The history of the present king of Great Britain is a history of <u>unremitting</u> *repeated* injuries and usurpations, <u>among which appears no solitary fact to contradict the uniform tenor of the rest but all have</u> *all having* in direct object the establishment of an absolute tyranny over these states. To prove this let facts be submitted to a candid world <u>for the truth of which we pledge a faith yet unsullied by falsehood.</u>

He has refused his assent to laws the most wholesome and necessary for the public good.

He has forbidden his governors to pass laws of immediate and pressing importance, unless suspended in their operation, till his assent should be obtained; and when so suspended, he has utterly neglected to attend to them.

He has refused to pass other laws for the accommodation of large districts of people, unless those people would relinquish the right of representation in the legislature, a right inestimable to them and formidable to tyrants only.

He has called together legislative bodies at places unusual, uncomfortable, and distant from the depository of their public records, for the sole purpose of fatiguing them into compliance with his measures.

He has dissolved representative houses repeatedly <u>and continually</u> for opposing with manly firmness his invasions on the rights of the people.

He has refused for a long time after such dissolutions to cause others to be elected, whereby the legislative powers, incapable of annihilation, have returned to the people at large for their exercise, the state remaining in the meantime exposed to all the dangers of invasion from without and convulsions within.

He has endeavored to prevent the population of these states, for that purpose obstructing the laws for naturalization of foreigners, refusing to pass others to encourage their migrations hither, and raising the conditions of new appropriations of lands.

He has <u>suffered</u> *obstructed* the administration of justice <u>totally to cease in some of these states</u> *by* refusing his assent to laws for establishing judiciary powers.

He has made <u>our</u> judges dependent on his will alone for the tenure of their offices and the amount and payment of their salaries.

He has erected a multitude of new offices <u>by a self-assumed power</u> and sent hither swarms of new officers to harass our people and eat out their substance.

He has kept among us in times of peace standing armies <u>and ships of war</u> without the consent of our legislatures.

He has affected to render the military independent of and superior to the civil power.

He has combined with others to subject us to a jurisdiction foreign to our constitutions and unacknowledged by our laws, giving his assent to their acts of pretended legislation for quartering large bodies of armed troops among us; for protecting them by a mock trial from punishment for any murders which they should commit on the inhabitants of these states; for cutting off our trade with all parts of the world; for imposing taxes on us without our consent; for depriving us *in many cases* of the benefits of trial by jury; for transporting us beyond seas to be tried for pretended offences; for abolishing the free system of English laws in a neighboring province, establishing therein an arbitrary government and enlarging its boundaries so as to render it at once an example and fit instrument for introducing the same absolute rule into these <u>states</u> *colonies*; for taking away our charters, abolishing our most valuable laws, and altering fundamentally the forms of our governments; for suspending our own legislatures and declaring themselves invested with power to legislate for us in all cases whatsoever.

He has abdicated government here, <u>withdrawing his governors and declaring us out of his allegiance and protection</u> *by declaring us out of his protection and waging war against us.*

He has plundered our seas, ravaged our coasts, burned our towns, and destroyed the lives of our people.

He is at this time transporting large armies of foreign mercenaries to complete the works of death, desolation, and tyranny already begun with circumstances of cruelty and perfidy *scarcely paralleled in the most barbarous ages and totally* unworthy the head of a civilized nation.

He has constrained our fellow citizens taken captive on the high seas to bear arms against their country, to become the executioners of their friends and brethren, or to fall themselves by their hands.

He has *excited domestic insurrections amongst us and has* endeavored to bring on the inhabitants of our frontiers the merciless Indian savages, whose known rule of warfare is an undistinguished destruction of all ages, sexes, and conditions of existence.

He has incited treasonable insurrections of our fellow-citizens, with the allurements of forfeiture and confiscation of our property.

He has waged cruel war against human nature itself, violating its most sacred rights of life and liberty in the persons of a distant people who never offended him, captivating and carrying them into slavery in another hemisphere or to incur miserable death in their transportation thither. This piratical warfare, the opprobrium of infidel powers, is the warfare of the Christian king of Great Britain. Determined to keep open a market where men should be bought and sold, he has prostituted his negative for suppressing every legislative attempt to prohibit or to restrain this execrable commerce. And that this assemblage of horrors might want no fact of distinguished die, he is now exciting those very people to rise in arms among us and to purchase that liberty of which he has deprived them by murdering the people on whom he also obtruded them, thus paying off former crimes committed against the liberties of one people, with crimes which he urges them to commit against the lives of another.

In every stage of these oppressions we have petitioned for redress in the most humble terms: our repeated petitions have been answered only by repeated injuries. A prince whose character is thus marked by every act which may define a tyrant is unfit to be the ruler of a *free* people who mean to be free. Future ages will scarcely believe that the hardiness of one man adventured, within the short compass of twelve years only, to lay a foundation so broad and so undisguised for tyranny over a people fostered and fixed in principles of freedom.

Nor have we been wanting in attentions to our British brethren. We have warned them from time to time of attempts by their legislature to extend a *an unwarrantable* jurisdiction over these our states *us*. We have reminded them of the circumstances of our emigration and settlement here, no one of which could warrant so strange a pretension that these were effected at the expense of our own blood and treasure, unassisted by the wealth or the strength of Great Britain; that in constituting indeed our several forms of government we had adopted one common king, thereby laying a foundation for perpetual league and amity with them; but that submission to their parliament was no part of our constitution, nor ever in idea, if history may be credited and, we *have* appealed to their native justice and magnanimity as well as to *and we have conjured them by* the ties of our common kindred to disavow these usurpations which were likely to *would inevitably* interrupt our connection and correspondence. They too have been deaf to the voice of justice and of consanguinity, and when occasions have been given them by the regular course of their laws of removing from their councils the disturbers of our harmony, they have, by their free election, re-established them in power. At this very time too they are permitting their chief magistrate to send over not only soldiers of our common blood, but Scotch and foreign mercenaries to invade and destroy us. These facts have given the last stab to agonizing affection, and manly spirit bids us to renounce forever these unfeeling brethren. We must endeavor to forget our former love for them and to hold them as we hold the rest of mankind, enemies in war, in peace friends. We might have been a free and a great people together, but a communication of grandeur and of freedom it seems is below their dignity. Be it so, since they will have it. The road to happiness and to glory is open to us too. We will tread it apart from them, and *We must therefore* acquiesce in the necessity which denounces our eternal separation *and hold them as we hold the rest of mankind, enemies in war, in peace friends*!

We therefore, the representatives of the United States of America in general Congress assembled, *appealing to the Supreme Judge of the world for the rectitude of our intentions,* do in the name and by the authority of the good people of these states reject and renounce all allegiance and subjection to the kings of Great Britain and all the good people of these colonies, others who may hereafter claim by, through, or under them; we utterly dissolve all political connection which may heretofore have subsisted between us and the people or parliament of Great Britain; and finally we do assert and declare these colonies to be free and independent states, *colonies solemnly publish and declare that these united colonies are and of right ought to be free and independent states; that they are absolved from all allegiance to the British crown; and that all political connection between them and the state of Great Britain is and ought to be totally dissolved,* and that as free and independent states, they have full power to levy war, conclude peace, contract alliances, establish commerce, and to do all other acts and things which independent states may of right do. And for the support of this declaration, *with a firm reliance on the protection of Divine Providence,* we mutually pledge to each other our lives, our fortunes, and our sacred honor.

THOMAS JEFFERSON

From *Notes on the State of Virginia*

"To justify a general conclusion requires many observations"

As its title suggests, **Notes on the State of Virginia** *surveyed Jefferson's home state: its laws, its commerce, its resources, and so forth. But Jefferson used this structure to disguise a more ambitious book—a book that, from its first edition in 1785, introduced and defended America on an international stage. "I had always made it a practice," Jefferson explained in his autobiography, "of obtaining any information of our country." In the* Notes, *he used that information to rebut America's critics, most notably the Count de Buffon, a French intellectual whose theory of degeneracy held that the New World and its inferior climate produced "degenerated" animals and, perhaps, "degenerated" people and nations. Jefferson answered de Buffon with statistical tables and reports on America's robust fauna, but he also answered him with wide-ranging arguments and a scientific, step-by-step style. In the* Notes, *Jefferson was always ready for a playful tangent, and in this passage he engages the question of whether America's intellectuals were themselves degenerated.*

I am induced to suspect there has been more eloquence than sound reasoning displayed in support of [de Buffon's] theory, that it is one of those cases where the judgment has been seduced by a glowing pen; and while I render every tribute of honor and esteem to the celebrated zoologist, who has added and is still adding so many precious things to the treasures of science, I must doubt whether in this instance he has not cherished error also, by lending her for a moment his vivid imagination and bewitching language.

So far the Count de Buffon has carried this new theory of the tendency of nature to belittle her productions on this side the Atlantic. Its application to the race of whites, transplanted from Europe, remained for the Abbé Raynal: "On doit etre etonné (he says) que l'Amerique n'ait pas encore produit un bon poëte, un habile mathematicien, un homme de genie dans un seul art, ou une seule science." *America has not yet produced one good poet.* When we shall have existed as a people as long as the Greeks did before they produced a Homer, the Romans a Virgil, the French a Racine and Voltaire, the English a Shakespeare and Milton, should this reproach be still true, we will inquire from what unfriendly causes it has proceeded, that the other countries of Europe and quarters of the earth shall not have inscribed any name in the roll of poets.

But neither has America produced *one able mathematician, one man of genius in a single art or a single science.* In war we have produced a Washington, whose memory will be adored while liberty shall have votaries, whose name will triumph over time and will in future ages assume its just station among the most celebrated worthies of the world, when that wretched philosophy shall be forgotten which would have arranged him among the degeneracies of nature. In physics we have produced a Franklin, than whom no one of the present age has made more important discoveries, nor has enriched philosophy with more or more ingenious solutions of the phenomena of nature. We have supposed [David] Rittenhouse second to no astronomer living, that in genius he must be the first, because he is self-taught. As an artist he has exhibited as great a proof of mechanical genius as the world has ever produced. He has not indeed made a world, but he has by imitation approached nearer its Maker than any man who has lived from the creation to this day.*

As in philosophy and war, so in government, in oratory, in painting, in the plastic art, we might show that America, though but a child of yesterday, has already given hopeful proofs of genius, as well of the nobler kinds which arouse the best feelings of man, which call him into action, which substantiate his freedom and conduct him to happiness, as of the

---

* There are various ways of keeping truth out of sight. Mr. Rittenhouse's model of the planetary system has the plagiary appellation of an Orrery; and the quadrant invented by Godfrey, an American also, and with the aid of which the European nations traverse the globe, is called Hadley's Quadrant.

subordinate, which serve to amuse him only. We therefore suppose that this reproach is as unjust as it is unkind and that, of the geniuses which adorn the present age, America contributes its full share. For comparing it with those countries where genius is most cultivated, where are the most excellent models for art and scaffoldings for the attainment of science, as France and England, for instance, we calculate thus: the United States contain three millions of inhabitants; France twenty millions; and the British islands ten. We produce a Washington, a Franklin, a Rittenhouse. France then should have half a dozen in each of these lines, and Great Britain half that number, equally eminent.

It may be true that France has; we are but just becoming acquainted with her, and our acquaintance so far gives us high ideas of the genius of her inhabitants. It would be injuring too many of them to name particularly a Voltaire, a Buffon, the constellation of Encyclopedists, the Abbé Raynal himself, etc., etc. We therefore have reason to believe she can produce her full quota of genius. The present war having so long cut off all communication with Great Britain, we are not able to make a fair estimate of the state of science in that country. The spirit in which she wages war is the only sample before our eyes, and that does not seem the legitimate offspring either of science or of civilization. The sun of her glory is fast descending to the horizon. Her philosophy has crossed the Channel, her freedom the Atlantic, and herself seems passing to that awful dissolution whose issue is not given human foresight to scan.

Despite Jefferson's many tangents, he always wrote with America and its international reputation in mind. While describing Virginia's scenery, for instance, Jefferson attempted some literary prose of his own. Perhaps he had Raynal's dismissal of American letters in mind; either way, Jefferson used his description to show readers that America's resources could measure up to any other nation's. The description would become one of the Notes' *most famous passages.*

The passage of the Potomac through the Blue Ridge [Mountains] is perhaps one of the most stupendous scenes in nature. You stand on a very high point of land. On your right comes up the Shenandoah, having ranged along the foot of the mountain a hundred miles to seek a vent. On your left approaches the Potomac, in quest of a passage also. In the moment of their junction, they rush together against the mountain, rend it asunder, and pass off to the sea. The first glance of this scene hurries our senses into the opinion that this earth has been created in time, that the mountains were formed first, that the rivers began to flow afterwards, that in this place particularly they have been dammed up by the Blue Ridge of mountains and have formed an ocean which filled the whole valley, that continuing to rise they have at length broken over at this spot and have torn the mountain down from its summit to its base. The piles of rock on each hand, but particularly on the Shenandoah, the evident marks of their disrupture and avulsion from their beds by the most powerful agents of nature, corroborate the impression.

But the distant finishing which nature has given to the picture is of a very different character. It is a true contrast to the foreground. It is as placid and delightful as that is wild and tremendous. For the mountain being cloven asunder, she presents to your eye, through the cleft, a small catch of smooth blue horizon, at an infinite distance in the plain country, inviting you, as it were, from the riot and tumult roaring around, to pass through the breach and participate of the calm below. Here the eye ultimately composes itself; and that way too the road happens actually to lead. You cross the Potomac above the junction, pass along its side through the base of the mountain for three miles, its terrible precipices hanging in fragments over you, and within about twenty miles reach Frederick Town and the fine country round that. This scene is worth a voyage across the Atlantic.

During his chapter on Virginia's laws, Jefferson paused to discuss two of his pet issues, religion and education. In truth, it was an even broader discussion: about democracy and good government, about how to strengthen them both by making education a public concern while keeping religion a private one. But it was Jefferson's secular asides—"it does me no injury for my neighbor to say there are twenty gods, or no god"—that would haunt him. His enemies would attack him with these lines from the Notes *for the rest of his career, particularly during his runs for president.*

The first stage of this education being the schools of the hundreds, wherein the great mass of the people will receive their instruction, the principal foundations of future order will be laid here. Instead therefore of putting the Bible and Testament into the hands of the children, at an age when their judgments are not sufficiently matured for religious inquiries, their memories may here be stored with the most useful facts from Greek, Roman, European, and American history. . . . History by apprising them of the past will enable them to judge of the future; it will avail them of the experience of other times and other nations; it will qualify them as judges of the actions and designs of men; it will enable them to know ambition under every disguise it may assume and, knowing it, to defeat its views. In every government on earth is some trace of human weakness, some germ of corruption and degeneracy, which cunning will discover and wickedness insensibly open, cultivate, and improve. Every government degenerates when trusted to the rulers of the people alone. The people themselves therefore are its only safe depositories. And to render even them safe their minds must be improved to a certain degree. . . .

By [Virginia's] own act of assembly of 1705, c. 30, if a person brought up in the Christian religion denies the being of a God, or the Trinity, or asserts there are more gods than one, or denies the Christian religion to be true, or the scriptures to be of divine authority, he is punishable. . . . This is a summary view of that religious slavery under which a people have been willing to remain, who have lavished their lives and fortunes for the establishment of their civil freedom. The error seems not sufficiently eradicated, that the operations of the mind, as well as the acts of the body, are subject to the coercion of the laws. But our rulers can have authority over such natural rights only as we have submitted to them. The rights of conscience we never submitted, we could not submit. We are answerable for them to our God. The legitimate powers of government extend to such acts only as are injurious to others. But it does me no injury for my neighbor to say there are twenty gods, or no god. It neither picks my pocket nor breaks my leg. . . .

Reason and free inquiry are the only effectual agents against error. Give a loose to them, they will support the true religion by bringing every false one to their tribunal, to the test of their investigation. They are the natural enemies of error, and of error only. Had not the Roman government permitted free inquiry, Christianity could never have been introduced. Had not free inquiry been indulged, at the era of the Reformation, the corruptions of Christianity could not have been purged away. If it be restrained now, the present corruptions will be protected and new ones encouraged. Was the government to prescribe to us our medicine and diet, our bodies would be in such keeping as our souls are now. Thus in France the emetic was once forbidden as a medicine, and the potato as an article of food.

Government is just as infallible too when it fixes systems in physics. Galileo was sent to the Inquisition for affirming that the earth was a sphere; the government had declared it to be as flat as a trencher, and Galileo was obliged to abjure his error. This error, however, at length prevailed, the earth became a globe, and Descartes declared it was whirled round its axis by a vortex. The government in which he lived was wise enough to see that this was no question of civil jurisdiction, or we should all have been involved by authority in vortices. In fact, the vortices have been exploded, and the Newtonian principle of gravitation is now more firmly established, on the basis of reason, than it would be were the government to step in and to make it an article of necessary faith. Reason and experiment have been indulged, and error has fled before them. It is error alone which needs the support of government. Truth can stand by itself.

Another of the Notes' *most famous passages has a far uglier legacy. While Jefferson was willing to criticize slavery abstractly—as in the passage Congress deleted from his Declaration draft, a passage Jefferson carefully preserved in his autobiography—he remained a slave owner. Indeed, Jefferson never stopped believing that Blacks were inferior to whites. In another of the* Notes' *tangents, and in a troubling, pseudoscientific tone, he detailed his reasons for this belief. These reasons would be widely discussed and reprinted during the nineteenth century, with pro-slavery politicians using Jefferson's fame to justify their brutal treatment of Black Americans.*

The first difference which strikes us is that of color. Whether the black of the negro resides in the reticular membrane between the skin and scarf-skin or in the scarf-skin itself, whether it proceeds from the color of the blood, the color of the bile, or from that of some other secretion, the difference is fixed in nature and is as real as if its seat and cause were better known to us. And is this difference of no importance? Is it not the foundation of a greater or less share of beauty in the two races? Are not the fine mixtures of red and white, the expressions of every passion by greater or less suffusions of color in the one, preferable to that eternal monotony which reigns in the countenances, that immoveable veil of black which covers all the emotions of the other race? Add to these flowing hair, a more elegant symmetry of form, their own judgment in favor of the whites, declared by their preference of them as uniformly as is the preference of the orangutan for the black women over those of his own species. The circumstance of superior beauty is thought worthy attention in the propagation of our horses, dogs, and other domestic animals; why not in that of man?

Besides those of color, figure, and hair, there are other physical distinctions proving a difference of race. They have less hair on the face and body. They secrete less by the kidneys and more by the glands of the skin, which gives them a very strong and disagreeable odor. This greater degree of transpiration renders them more tolerant of heat and less so of cold than the whites. Perhaps too a difference of structure in the pulmonary apparatus, which a late ingenious experimentalist has discovered to be the principal regulator of animal heat, may have disabled them from extricating in the act of inspiration so much of that fluid from the outer air, or obliged them in expiration to part with more of it. They seem to require less sleep. A black after hard labor through the day will be induced by the slightest amusements to sit up till midnight or later, though knowing he must be out with the first dawn of the morning.

They are at least as brave and more adventuresome. But this may perhaps proceed from a want of forethought, which prevents their seeing a danger till it be present. When present, they do not go through it with more coolness or steadiness than the whites. They are more ardent after their female, but love seems with them to be more an eager desire than a tender delicate mixture of sentiment and sensation. Their griefs are transient. Those numberless afflictions, which render it doubtful whether heaven has given life to us in mercy or in wrath, are less felt and sooner forgotten with them. In general, their existence appears to participate more of sensation than reflection. To this must be ascribed their disposition to sleep when abstracted from their diversions and unemployed in labor. An animal whose body is at rest, and who does not reflect, must be disposed to sleep of course.

Comparing them by their faculties of memory, reason, and imagination, it appears to me, that in memory they are equal to the whites; in reason much inferior, as I think one could scarcely be found capable of tracing and comprehending the investigations of Euclid; and that in imagination they are dull, tasteless, and anomalous. It would be unfair to follow them to Africa for this investigation. We will consider them here, on the same stage with the whites, and where the facts are not apocryphal on which a judgment is to be formed. It will be right to make great allowances for the difference of condition, of education, of conversation, of the sphere in which they move. Many millions of them have been brought to and born in America. Most of them indeed have been confined to tillage, to their own homes and their own society, yet many have been so situated that they might have availed themselves of the conversation of their masters; many have been brought up to the handicraft arts, and from that circumstance have always been associated with the whites. Some have been liberally educated, and all have lived in countries where the arts and sciences are cultivated to a considerable degree and have had before their eyes samples of the best works from abroad. The Indians, with no advantages of this kind, will often carve figures on their pipes not destitute of design and merit. They will crayon out an animal, a plant, or a country, so as to prove the existence of a germ in their minds which only wants cultivation. They astonish you with strokes of the most sublime oratory; such as prove their reason and sentiment strong, their imagination glowing and elevated. But never yet could I find that a black had uttered a thought above the level of plain narration. . . .

The opinion, that they are inferior in the faculties of reason and imagination, must be hazarded with great dissidence. To justify a general conclusion requires many observations, even where the subject may be submitted to the anatomical knife, to optical glasses, to analysis by fire or by solvents. How much more then where it is a faculty, not a substance, we are examining, where it eludes the research of all the senses, where the conditions of its existence are various and variously combined, where the effects of those which are present or absent bid defiance to calculation; let me add, too, as a circumstance of great tenderness, where our conclusion would degrade a whole race of men from the rank in the scale of beings which their Creator may perhaps have given them. To our reproach it must be said that though for a century and a half we have had under our eyes the races of black and of red men, they have never yet been viewed by us as subjects of natural history. I advance it therefore as a suspicion only that the blacks, whether originally a distinct race, or made distinct by time and circumstances, are inferior to the whites in the endowments both of body and mind.

THOMAS JEFFERSON

First Inaugural Address

(1801)

"We are all Republicans; we are all Federalists"

When Jefferson delivered his first inaugural address, on March 4, 1801, he delivered it to a divided nation. Despite Washington's warnings about "the spirit of party," the elections of 1796 and 1800 had turned highly partisan, with Adams and the Federalists facing off against Jefferson and the Democratic-Republicans. (One of the most heated issues, driven by excerpts from the Notes, *was Jefferson's religion.) Now, in his inaugural, Jefferson crafted a call for Americans to come together, to remember what they had in common and what they had already achieved. It's a call many presidents have echoed since, though few have done so with Jefferson's elegance.*

Called upon to undertake the duties of the first executive office of our country, I avail myself of the presence of that portion of my fellow citizens which is here assembled to express my grateful thanks for the favor with which they have been pleased to look towards me, to declare a sincere consciousness that the task is above my talents and that I approach it with those anxious and awful presentiments which the greatness of the charge and the weakness of my powers so justly inspire. A rising nation, spread over a wide and fruitful land, traversing all the seas with the rich productions of their industry, engaged in commerce with nations who feel power and forget right, advancing rapidly to destinies beyond the reach of mortal eye: when I contemplate these transcendent objects and see the honor, the happiness, and the hopes of this beloved country committed to the issue and the auspices of this day, I shrink from the contemplation and humble myself before the magnitude of the undertaking. Utterly indeed should I despair did not the presence of many whom I here see remind me that, in the other high authorities provided by our Constitution, I shall find resources of wisdom, of virtue, and of zeal on which to rely under all difficulties. To you, then, gentlemen, who are charged with the sovereign functions of legislation, and to those associated with you, I look with encouragement for that guidance and support which may enable us to steer with safety the vessel in which we are all embarked amidst the conflicting elements of a troubled world.

During the contest of opinion through which we have passed, the animation of discussions and of exertions has sometimes worn an aspect which might impose on strangers unused to think freely and to speak and to write what they think; but this being now decided by the voice of the nation, announced according to the rules of the Constitution, all will of course arrange themselves under the will of the law, and unite in common efforts for the common good. All too will bear in mind this sacred principle, that though the will of the majority is in all cases to prevail, that will to be rightful must be reasonable; that the minority possess their equal rights, which equal laws must protect, and to violate would be oppression.

Let us then, fellow citizens, unite with one heart and one mind, let us restore to social intercourse that harmony and affection without which liberty and even life itself are but dreary things. And let us reflect that having banished from our land that religious intolerance under which mankind so long bled and suffered, we have yet gained little if we countenance a political intolerance as despotic, as wicked and capable of as bitter and bloody persecutions. During the throes and convulsions of the ancient world, during the agonizing spasms of infuriated man, seeking through blood and slaughter his long lost liberty, it was not wonderful that the agitation of the billows should reach even this distant and peaceful shore, that this should be more felt and feared by some and less by others and should divide opinions as to measures of safety, but every difference of opinion is not a difference of principle. We have called by different names brethren of the same principle. We are all Republicans; we are all Federalists.

If there be any among us who would wish to dissolve this union, or to change its republican form, let them stand undisturbed as monuments of the safety with which error of opinion may be tolerated where reason is left free to combat it. I know indeed that some honest men fear that a republican government cannot be strong, that this government is not strong enough. But would the honest patriot, in the full tide of successful experiment, abandon a government which has so far kept us free and firm, on the theoretic and visionary fear that this government, the world's best hope, may by possibility want energy to preserve itself? I trust not. I believe this, on the contrary, the strongest government on earth. I believe it the only one where every man, at the call of the law, would fly to the standard of the law, and would meet invasions of the public order as his own personal concern. Sometimes it is said that man cannot be trusted with the government of himself. Can he then be trusted with the government of others? Or have we found angels, in the form of kings, to govern him? Let history answer this question.

Let us then with courage and confidence pursue our own Federal and Republican principles, our attachment to union and representative government. Kindly separated by nature and a wide ocean from the exterminating havoc of one quarter of the globe; too high minded to endure the degradations of the others; possessing a chosen country with room enough for our descendants to the thousandth and thousandth generation; entertaining a due sense of our equal right to the use of our own faculties, to the acquisitions of our own industry, to honor and confidence from our fellow citizens resulting not from birth but from our actions and their sense of them; enlightened by a benign religion, professed indeed and practiced in various forms yet all of them inculcating honesty, truth, temperance, gratitude, and the love of man, acknowledging and adoring an overruling Providence, which by all its dispensations proves that it delights in the happiness of man here and his greater happiness hereafter; with all these blessings, what more is necessary to make us a happy and a prosperous people? Still one thing more, fellow citizens, a wise and frugal government, which shall restrain men from injuring one another, shall leave them otherwise free to regulate their own pursuits of industry and improvement, and shall not take from the mouth of labor the bread it has earned. This is the sum of good government, and this is necessary to close the circle of our felicities.

About to enter, fellow citizens, on the exercise of duties which comprehend everything dear and valuable to you, it is proper you should understand what I deem the essential principles of our government and consequently those which ought to shape its administration. I will compress them within the narrowest compass they will bear, stating the general principle but not all its limitations: equal and exact justice to all men, of whatever state or persuasion, religious or political; peace, commerce, and honest friendship with all nations, entangling alliances with none; the support of the state governments in all their rights as the most competent administrations for our domestic concerns and the surest bulwarks against anti-republican tendencies; the preservation of the general government in its whole constitutional vigor as the sheet anchor of our peace at home and safety abroad; a jealous care of the right of election by the people, a mild and safe corrective of abuses which are lopped by the sword of revolution where peaceable remedies are unprovided; absolute acquiescence in the decisions of the majority, the vital principle of republics, from which is no appeal but to force, the vital principle and immediate parent of the despotism; a well-disciplined militia, our best reliance in peace and for the first moments of war, till regulars may relieve them; the supremacy of the civil over the military authority; economy in the public expense, that labor may be lightly burthened; the honest payment of our debts and sacred preservation of the public faith; encouragement of agriculture and of commerce as its handmaid; the diffusion of information and arraignment of all abuses at the bar of the public reason; freedom of religion, freedom of the press, and freedom of person, under the protection of the habeas corpus, and trial by juries impartially selected.

These principles form the bright constellation which has gone before us and guided our steps through an age of revolution and reformation. The wisdom of our sages and blood of our heroes have been devoted to their attainment; they should be the creed of our political faith, the text of civic instruction, the touchstone by which to try the services of those we trust, and should we wander from them in moments of error or of alarm, let us hasten to retrace our steps and to regain the road which alone leads to peace, liberty, and safety.

I repair then, fellow citizens, to the post you have assigned me. With experience enough in subordinate offices to have seen the difficulties of this, the greatest of all, I have learned to expect that it will rarely fall to the lot of imperfect man to retire from this station with the reputation and the favor which bring him into it. Without pretensions to that high confidence you reposed in our first and greatest revolutionary character, whose pre-eminent services had entitled him to the first place in his country's love and destined for him the fairest page in the volume of faithful history, I ask so much confidence only as may give firmness and effect to the legal administration of your affairs. I shall often go wrong through defect of judgment. When right, I shall often be thought wrong by those whose positions will not command a view of the whole ground. I ask your indulgence for my own errors, which will never be intentional, and your support against the errors of others, who may condemn what they would not if seen in all its parts. The approbation implied by your suffrage is a great consolation to me for the past, and my future solicitude will be to retain the good opinion of those who have bestowed it in advance, to conciliate that of others by doing them all the good in my power, and to be instrumental to the happiness and freedom of all.

Relying then on the patronage of your good will, I advance with obedience to the work, ready to retire from it whenever you become sensible how much better choices it is in your power to make. And may that Infinite Power, which rules the destinies of the universe, lead our councils to what is best, and give them a favorable issue for your peace and prosperity.

THOMAS JEFFERSON

From His State of the Union

(1801)

"The states themselves have principal care of our persons, our property, and our reputation"

Jefferson's initial State of the Union is significant for two reasons. First, Jefferson demonstrated the powers—or at least the pose—of a humble, Washington-style presidency: focused on international matters but otherwise deferential to Congress and, even more, to the states. Second, Jefferson delivered his address not orally, as Washington and Adams had done, but as a written document that a clerk read to Congress. It was another way to downplay the chief executive, and Jefferson's approach would remain the norm until Woodrow Wilson's presidency.

It is a circumstance of sincere gratification to me that, on meeting the great council of our nation, I am able to announce to them on grounds of reasonable certainty that the wars and troubles which have for so many years afflicted our sister nations have at length come to an end, and that the communications of peace and commerce are once more opening among them. While we devoutly return thanks to the beneficent Being who has been pleased to breathe into them the spirit of conciliation and forgiveness, we are bound with peculiar gratitude to be thankful to Him that our own peace has been preserved through so perilous a season, and ourselves permitted quietly to cultivate the earth and to practice and improve those arts which tend to increase our comforts. The assurances, indeed, of friendly disposition received from all the powers with whom we have principle relations had inspired a confidence that our peace with them would not have been disturbed. But a cessation of irregularities which had affected the commerce of neutral nations and of the irritations and injuries produced by them cannot but add to this confidence, and strengthens at the same time the hope that wrongs committed on unoffending friends under a pressure of circumstances will now be reviewed with candor, and will be considered as founding just claims of retribution for the past and new assurance for the future.

Among our Indian neighbors also a spirit of peace and friendship generally prevails, and I am happy to inform you that the continued efforts to introduce among them the implements and the practice of husbandry and the household arts have not been without success; that they are becoming more and more sensible of the superiority of this dependence for clothing and subsistence over the precarious resources of hunting and fishing, and already we are able to announce that instead of that constant diminution of their numbers produced by their wars and their wants, some of them begin to experience an increase of population.

To this state of general peace with which we have been blessed, one only exception exists. Tripoli, the least considerable of the Barbary States, had come forward with demands unfounded either in right or in compact and had permitted itself to denounce war on our failure to comply before a given day.

The style of the demand admitted but one answer. I sent a small squadron of frigates into the Mediterranean, with assurances to that power of our sincere desire to remain in peace but with orders to protect our commerce against the threatened attack. The measure was seasonable and salutary. The Bey [of Tripoli] had already declared war. His cruisers were out. Two had arrived at Gibraltar. Our commerce in the Mediterranean was blockaded and that of the Atlantic in peril. The arrival of our squadron dispelled the danger. One of the Tripolitan cruisers having fallen in with and engaged the small schooner *Enterprise*, commanded by Lieutenant Sterett, which had gone as a tender to our larger vessels, was captured after a heavy slaughter of her men, without the loss of a single one on our part. The bravery exhibited by our citizens on that element will, I trust, be a testimony to the world that it is not the want of that virtue which makes us seek their peace, but a conscientious desire to direct the energies of our nation to the multiplication of the human race and not to its destruction.

Unauthorized by the Constitution, without the sanction of Congress to go beyond the line of defense, the vessel, being disabled from committing further hostilities, was liberated with its crew.

The legislature will doubtless consider whether, by authorizing measures of offense also, they will place our force on an equal footing with that of its adversaries. I communicate all material information on this subject that in the exercise of this important function, confided by the Constitution to the legislature exclusively, their judgment may form itself on a knowledge and consideration of every circumstances of weight.

I wish I could say that our situation with all the other Barbary States was entirely satisfactory. Discovering that some delays had taken place in the performance of certain articles stipulated by us, I thought it my duty, by immediate measures for fulfilling them, to vindicate to ourselves the right of considering the effect of departure from stipulation on their side. From the papers which will be laid before you, you will be enabled to judge whether our treaties are regarded by them as fixing at all the measure of their demands or as guarding from the exercise of force our vessels within their power, and to consider how far it will be safe and expedient to leave our affairs with them in their present posture.

I lay before you the result of the census lately taken of our inhabitants, to a conformity with which we are now to reduce the ensuing ration of representation and taxation. You will perceive that the increase of numbers during the last ten years, proceeding in geometric ratio, promises a duplication in little more than twenty-two years. We contemplate this rapid growth and the prospect it holds up to us, not with a view to the injuries it may enable us to do others in some future day, but to the settlement of the extensive country still remaining vacant within our limits, to the multiplication of men susceptible of happiness, educated in the love of order, habituated to self-government, and valuing its blessings above all price.

Other circumstances, combined with the increase of numbers, have produced an augmentation of revenue arising from consumption in a ratio far beyond that of population alone; and though the changes in foreign relations now taking place so desirably for the whole world may for a season affect this branch of revenue, yet weighing all probabilities of expense as well as of income, there is reasonable ground of confidence that we may now safely dispense with all the internal taxes comprehending excise, stamps, auctions, licenses, carriages, and refined sugars, to which the postage on newspapers may be added to facilitate the progress of information; and that the remaining sources of revenue will be sufficient to provide for the support of government, to pay the interest of the public debts, and to discharge the principals within shorter periods than the laws or the general expectation had contemplated. War, indeed, and untoward events may change this prospect of things and call for expenses which the imposts could not meet, but sound principles will not justify our taxing the industry of our fellow citizens to accumulate treasure for wars to happen we know not when, and which might not, perhaps, happen but from the temptations offered by that treasure.

These views, however, of reducing our burdens are formed on the expectation that a sensible and at the same time a salutary reduction may take place in our habitual expenditures. For this purpose, those of the civil government, the Army, and Navy will need revisal.

When we consider that this government is charged with the external and mutual relations only of these states—that the states themselves have principal care of our persons, our property, and our reputation, constituting the great field of human concerns—we may well doubt whether our organization is not too complicated, too expensive, whether offices and officers have not been multiplied unnecessarily and sometimes injuriously to the service they were meant to promote.

I will cause to be laid before you an essay toward a statement of those who, under public employment of various kinds, draw money from the Treasury or from our citizens. Time has not permitted a perfect enumeration, the ramifications of office being too multiplied and remote to be completely traced in a first trial. Among those who are dependent on executive discretion I have begun the reduction of what was deemed unnecessary. The expenses of diplomatic agency have been considerably diminished. The inspectors of internal revenue who were found to obstruct the accountability of the institution have been discontinued. Several agencies created by executive authorities, on salaries fixed by that also, have been suppressed and should suggest the expediency of regulating that power by law, so as to subject its exercises to legislative inspection and sanction.

Other reformations of the same kind will be pursued with that caution which is requisite in removing useless things, not to injure what is retained. But the great mass of public offices is established by law, and therefore by law alone can be abolished. Should the legislature think it expedient to pass this roll in review and try all its parts by the test of public utility, they may be assured of every aid and light which executive information can yield.

From His Notes on the Constitutional Convention

"Pinckney was for a vigorous executive"

James Madison kept a diary during the Constitutional Convention of 1787, preserving the fullest account of the delegates and their debates over what precisely the American government should be. One debate revolved around the American presidency. Did the nation need one president or a board of presidents? How many years should a president serve? Was "president" even the right name? This entry from Madison's diary covers the first of many days the delegates spent answering those questions. But it also reveals something about Madison as a writer—because he spent the rest of his life quietly revising and amplifying this "diary," creating a historical document that was also personal and political.

Friday, June 1, 1787

William Houston from Georgia took his seat.

The committee of the whole proceeded to Resolution 7: "that a national executive be instituted, to be chosen by the national legislature for the term of _____ years, etc., to be ineligible thereafter, to possess the executive powers of Congress, etc."

[Charles] Pinckney was for a vigorous executive, but was afraid the executive powers of the existing Congress might extend to peace and war, etc., which would render the executive a monarchy of the worst kind, to wit an elective one.

[James] Wilson moved that the executive consist of a single person. Mr. Pinckney seconded the motion, so as to read "that a national executive to consist of a single person be instituted."

A considerable pause ensuing, and the chairman asking if he should put the question, Dr. Franklin observed that it was a point of great importance and wished that the gentlemen would deliver their sentiments on it before the question was put.

[John] Rutledge animadverted on the shyness of gentlemen on this and other subjects. He said it looked as if they supposed themselves precluded by having frankly disclosed their opinions from afterwards changing them, which he did not take to be at all the case. He said he was for vesting the executive power in a single person, though he was not for giving him the power of war and peace. A single man would feel the greatest responsibility and administer the public affairs best.

[Roger] Sherman said he considered the executive magistracy as nothing more than an institution for carrying the will of the legislature into effect; that the person or persons ought to be appointed by and accountable to the legislature only, which was the depositary of the supreme will of the society. As they were the best judges of the business which ought to be done by the executive department and consequently of the number necessary from time to time for doing it, he wished the number might not be fixed but that the legislature should be at liberty to appoint one or more as experience might dictate.

Mr. Wilson preferred a single magistrate, as giving most energy, dispatch, and responsibility to the office. He did not consider the prerogatives of the British monarch as a proper guide in defining the executive powers. Some of these prerogatives were of legislative nature, among others that of war and peace, etc. The only powers he conceived strictly executive were those of executing the laws and appointing officers, not appertaining to and appointed by the legislature.

[Elbridge] Gerry favored the policy of annexing a council to the executive in order to give weight and inspire confidence.

[Edmund] Randolph strenuously opposed a unity in the executive magistracy. He regarded it as the fetus of monarchy. We had, he said, no motive to be governed by the British government as our prototype. He did not mean, however, to throw censure on that excellent fabric. If we were in a situation to copy it, he did not know that he should be opposed to it, but the fixed genius of the people of America required a different form of government. He could not see why the great requisites for the executive department, vigor, dispatch, and responsibility, could not be found in three men, as well as in one man. The executive ought to be independent. It ought therefore in order to support its independence to consist of more than one.

Mr. Wilson said that unity in the executive instead of being the fetus of monarchy would be the best safeguard against tyranny. He repeated that he was not governed by the British model, which was inapplicable to the situation of this country, the extent of which was so great, and the manners so republican, that nothing but a great confederated republic would do for it.

Mr. Wilson's motion for a single magistrate was postponed by common consent, the committee seeming unprepared for any decision on it, and the first part of the clause agreed to, viz., "that a national executive be instituted."

[James] Madison thought it would be proper, before a choice should be made between a unity and a plurality in the executive, to fix the extent of the executive authority, that as certain powers were in their nature executive and must be given to that department, whether administered by one or more persons, a definition of their extent would assist the judgment in determining how far they might be safely entrusted to a single officer. He accordingly moved that so much of the clause before the committee as related to the powers of the executive should be struck out and that after the words "that a national executive ought to be instituted" there be inserted the words following, viz., "with power to carry into effect the national laws, to appoint to offices in cases not otherwise provided for, and to execute such other powers 'not legislative nor judiciary in their nature,' as may from time to time be delegated by the national legislature." The words "not legislative nor judiciary in their nature" were added to the proposed amendment in consequence of a suggestion by General [Charles Cotesworth] Pinckney that improper powers might otherwise be delegated.

Mr. Wilson seconded this motion.

Mr. Pinckney moved to amend the amendment by striking out the last member of it, viz., "and to execute such other powers not legislative nor judiciary in their nature as may from time to time be delegated." He said they were unnecessary, the object of them being included in the "power to carry into effect the national laws."

Mr. Randolph seconded the motion.

Mr. Madison did not know that the words were absolutely necessary, or even the preceding words, "to appoint to offices," etc., the whole being perhaps included in the first member of the proposition. He did not, however, see any inconveniency in retaining them, and cases might happen in which they might serve to prevent doubts and misconstructions.

In consequence of the motion of Mr. Pinckney, the question on Mr. Madison's motion was divided, and the words objected to by Mr. Pinckney struck out by the votes of Connecticut, New York, New Jersey, Pennsylvania, Delaware, North Carolina, and Georgia, against; Massachusetts, Virginia, and South Carolina, the preceding part of the motion being first agreed to; Connecticut, divided; all the other states in the affirmative.

The next clause in Resolution 7, relating to the mode of appointing and the duration of the executive being under consideration, Mr. Wilson said he was almost unwilling to declare the mode which he wished to take place, being apprehensive that it might appear chimerical. He would say, however, at least that in theory he was for an election by the people. Experience, particularly in New York and Massachusetts, showed that an election of the first magistrate by the people at large was both a convenient and successful mode. The objects of choice in such cases must be persons whose merits have general notoriety.

Mr. Sherman was for the appointment by the legislature and for making him absolutely dependent on that body, as it was the will of that which was to be executed. An independence of the executive on the supreme legislature was in his opinion the very essence of tyranny if there was any such thing.

Mr. Wilson moved that the blank for the term of duration should be filled with three years, observing at the same time that he preferred this short period on the supposition that a re-eligibility would be provided for.

Mr. Pinckney moved for seven years.

Mr. Sherman was for three years and against the doctrine of rotation as throwing out of office the men best qualified to execute its duties.

[George] Mason was for seven years at least and for prohibiting a re-eligibility as the best expedient both for preventing the effect of a false complaisance on the side of the legislature towards unfit characters and a temptation on the side of the executive to intrigue with the legislature for a re-appointment.

[Gunning] Bedford was strongly opposed to so long a term as seven years. He begged the committee to consider what the situation of the country would be in case the first magistrate should be saddled on it for such a period and it should be found on trial that he did not possess the qualifications ascribed to him or should lose them after his appointment. An impeachment, he said, would be no cure for this evil, as an impeachment would reach misfeasance only, not incapacity. He was for a triennial election and for an ineligibility after a period of nine years.

On the question for seven years, Massachusetts, divided; Connecticut, no; New York, ay; New Jersey, ay; Pennsylvania, ay; Delaware, ay; Virginia, ay; North Carolina, no; South Carolina, no; Georgia, no. There being five ays, four noes, one divided, a question was asked whether a majority had voted in the affirmative? The president decided that it was an affirmative vote.

The mode of appointing the executive was the next question.

Mr. Wilson renewed his declarations in favor of an appointment by the people. He wished to derive not only both branches of the legislature from the people, without the intervention of the state legislatures but the executive also, in order to make them as independent as possible of each other, as well as of the states.

Col. Mason favored the idea, but thought it impracticable. He wished, however, that Mr. Wilson might have time to digest it into his own form. The clause "to be chosen by the national legislature" was accordingly postponed.

Mr. Rutledge suggested an election of the executive by the second branch only of the national legislature.

The committee then rose and the house adjourned.

JAMES MADISON

From an Essay on Benjamin Franklin

"I never passed half an hour in his company without hearing some observation or anecdote worth remembering"

Madison's diary of the Constitutional Convention was only one of his ongoing literary projects, most of which would not be published until after his death. Madison wrote a short and stilted autobiography and worked on a series of essays—one on banking, another on Washington, and a third on Benjamin Franklin, which is excerpted here. Madison captures Franklin's intelligence, wit, and larger-than-life stature among America's early politicians and presidents.

I did not become acquainted with Dr. Franklin till after his return from France and election to the chief magistracy of Pennsylvania. During the session of the Grand Convention, of which he was a member, and as long after as he lived, I had opportunities of enjoying much of his conversation, which was always a feast to me. I never passed half an hour in his company without hearing some observation or anecdote worth remembering.

Among those which I have often repeated, and can therefore be sure that my memory accurately retains, are the following.

Previous to the Convention, and while the states were seeking by their respective regulations to enlarge as much as possible their share of the general commerce, the doctor alluding to their jealousies and competitions remarked that it would be best for all of them to let the trade be free, in which case it would level itself and leave to each its proper share.

These contests, he said, put him in mind of what had once passed between a little boy and little girl eating milk and bread out of the same bowl. "Brother," cried the little girl, "eat on your own side, you get more than your share." . . .

While the last members were signing [the Constitution], Doctor Franklin, looking towards the president's chair, at the back of which a rising sun happened to be painted, observed to a few members near him that painters had found it difficult to distinguish in their art a rising from a setting sun. "I have," said he, "often and often in the course of the session, and the vicissitudes of my hopes and fears as to its issue, looked at that behind the president without being able to tell whether it was rising or setting. But now at length I have the happiness to know that it is a rising and not a setting sun."

In a conversation with him one day while he was confined to his bed, the subject of religion with its various doctrines and modes happening to turn up, the doctor remarked that he should be glad to see an experiment made of a religion that admitted of no pardon for transgressions, the hope of impunity being the great encouragement to them. In illustration of this tendency, he said that when he was a young man he was much subject to fits of indigestion brought on by indulgence at the table. On complaining of it to a friend, he recommended as a remedy a few drops of oil of wormwood whenever that happened, and that he should carry a little vial of it about him. On trial he found the remedy to answer, and then, said he, "having my absolution in my pocket, I went on sinning more freely than ever."

On entering his chamber in his extreme age, when he had been much exhausted by pain and was particularly sensible of his weakness, "Mr. Madison," said he, "these machines of ours, however admirably formed, will not last always. Mine I find is just worn out."

"It must have been an uncommonly good one," I observed, "to last so long."

From *The Federalist Papers*

"Ambition must be made to counteract ambition"

Once the Constitutional Convention had drafted its new document, the states had to decide whether to ratify it. The Federalist Papers were the attempt of Madison, Hamilton, and John Jay to persuade New York to do precisely that. Writing under a shared pseudonym, a common practice in eighteenth-century political writing, they published newspaper essays that evaluated the Constitution's biggest questions. Two of the most significant Federalist Papers are No. 10, which ran on November 22, 1787, and No. 51, which ran on February 6, 1788. Madison clearly wrote the first and almost certainly wrote the second, and together they examine the nature of political conflict and the best approaches, legislative and executive, for handling it.

The Federalist No. 10

Among the numerous advantages promised by a well-constructed union, none deserves to be more accurately developed than its tendency to break and control the violence of faction. The friend of popular governments never finds himself so much alarmed for their character and fate as when he contemplates their propensity to this dangerous vice. He will not fail therefore to set a due value on any plan which, without violating the principles to which he is attached, provides a proper cure for it. The instability, injustice, and confusion introduced into the public councils have in truth been the mortal diseases under which popular governments have everywhere perished, as they continue to be the favorite and fruitful topics from which the adversaries to liberty derive their most specious declamations. The valuable improvements made by the American constitutions on the popular models, both ancient and modern, cannot certainly be too much admired, but it would be an unwarrantable partiality to contend that they have as effectually obviated the danger on this side as was wished and expected. Complaints are everywhere heard from our most considerate and virtuous citizens, equally the friends of public and private faith and of public and personal liberty, that our governments are too unstable; that the public good is disregarded in the conflicts of rival parties; and that measures are too often decided not according to the rules of justice and the rights of the minor party, but by the superior force of an interested and over-bearing majority. However anxiously we may wish that these complaints had no foundation, the evidence of known facts will not permit us to deny that they are in some degree true. It will be found, indeed, on a candid review of our situation, that some of the distresses under which we labor have been erroneously charged on the operation of our governments, but it will be found at the same time that other causes will not alone account for many of our heaviest misfortunes, and particularly for that prevailing and increasing distrust of public engagements and alarm for private rights, which are echoed from one end of the continent to the other. These must be chiefly, if not wholly, effects of the unsteadiness and injustice, with which a factious spirit has tainted our public administration.

By a faction I understand a number of citizens, whether amounting to a majority or minority of the whole, who are united and actuated by some common impulse of passion or of interest adverse to the rights of other citizens or to the permanent and aggregate interests of the community.

There are two methods of curing the mischiefs of faction: The one by removing its causes; the other by controlling its effects.

There are again two methods of removing the causes of faction: The one by destroying the liberty which is essential to its existence; the other by giving to every citizen the same opinions, the same passions, and the same interests.

It could never be more truly said than of the first remedy, that it is worse than the disease. Liberty is to faction what air is to fire, an aliment without which it instantly expires. But it could not be a less folly to abolish liberty, which is essential to political life, because it nourishes faction, than it would be to wish the annihilation of air, which is essential to animal life because it imparts to fire its destructive agency.

The second expedient is as impracticable, as the first would be unwise. As long as the reason of man continues fallible, and he is at liberty to exercise it, different opinions will be formed. As long as the connection subsists between his reason and his self-love, his opinions and his passions will have a reciprocal influence on each other, and the former will be objects to which the latter will attach themselves. The diversity in the faculties of men from which the rights of property originate is not less an insuperable obstacle to a uniformity of interests. The protection of these faculties is the first object of government. From the protection of different and unequal faculties of acquiring property, the possession of different degrees and kinds of property immediately results, and from the influence of these on the sentiments and views of the respective proprietors ensues a division of the society into different interests and parties.

The latent causes of faction are thus sown in the nature of man, and we see them everywhere brought into different degrees of activity, according to the different circumstances of civil society. A zeal for different opinions concerning religion, concerning government, and many other points, as well of speculation as of practice, an attachment to different leaders ambitiously contending for pre-eminence and power, or to persons of other descriptions whose fortunes have been interesting to the human passions, have in turn divided mankind into parties, inflamed them with mutual animosity, and rendered them much more disposed to vex and oppress each other than to co-operate for their common good. So strong is this propensity of mankind to fall into mutual animosities that where no substantial occasion presents itself, the most frivolous and fanciful distinctions have been sufficient to kindle their unfriendly passions and excite their most violent conflicts. But the most common and durable source of factions has been the various and unequal distribution of property. Those who hold and those who are without property have ever formed distinct interests in society. Those who are creditors and those who are debtors fall under a like discrimination. A landed interest, a manufacturing interest, a mercantile interest, a moneyed interest, with many lesser interests, grow up of necessity in civilized nations and divide them into different classes, actuated by different sentiments and views. The regulation of these various and interfering interests forms the principal task of modern legislation and involves the spirit of party and faction in the necessary and ordinary operations of government.

No man is allowed to be a judge in his own cause because his interest would certainly bias his judgment and, not improbably, corrupt his integrity. With equal, nay with greater reason, a body of men are unfit to be both judges and parties at the same time; yet, what are many of the most important acts of legislation, but so many judicial determinations not indeed concerning the rights of single persons but concerning the rights of large bodies of citizens, and what are the different classes of legislators but advocates and parties to the causes which they determine? Is a law proposed concerning private debts? It is a question to which the creditors are parties on one side and the debtors on the other. Justice ought to hold the balance between them. Yet the parties are and must be themselves the judges, and the most numerous party, or in other words the most powerful faction, must be expected to prevail. Shall domestic manufactures be encouraged and in what degree by restrictions on foreign manufactures? are questions which would be differently decided by the landed and the manufacturing classes, and probably by neither with a sole regard to justice and the public good. The apportionment of taxes on the various descriptions of property is an act which seems to require the most exact impartiality, yet there is perhaps no legislative act in which greater opportunity and temptation are given to a predominant party to trample on the rules of justice. Every shilling with which they over-burden the inferior number is a shilling saved to their own pockets.

It is in vain to say that enlightened statesmen will be able to adjust these clashing interests and render them all subservient to the public good. Enlightened statesmen will not always be at the helm; nor, in many cases, can such an adjustment be made at all without taking into view indirect and remote considerations, which will rarely prevail over the immediate interest which one party may find in disregarding the rights of another, or the good of the whole.

The inference to which we are brought is that the causes of faction cannot be removed, and that relief is only to be sought in the means of controlling its effects.

If a faction consists of less than a majority, relief is supplied by the republican principle, which enables the majority to defeat its sinister views by regular vote; it may clog the administration, it may convulse the society, but it will be unable to execute and mask its violence under the forms of the constitution. When a majority is included in a faction, the form of popular government on the other hand enables it to sacrifice to its ruling passion or interest, both the public good and the rights of other citizens. To secure the public good and private rights against the danger of such a faction, and at the same time to preserve the spirit and the form of popular government, is then the great object to which our enquiries are directed.

Let me add that it is the great desideratum by which alone this form of government can be rescued from the opprobrium under which it has so long labored and be recommended to the esteem and adoption of mankind.

By what means is this object attainable? Evidently by one of two only. Either the existence of the same passion or interest in a majority at the same time must be prevented, or the majority, having such co-existent passion or interest, must be rendered by their number and local situation unable to concert and carry into effect schemes of oppression. If the impulse and the opportunity be suffered to coincide, we well know that neither moral nor religious motives can be relied on as an adequate control. They are not found to be such on the injustice and violence of individuals and lose their efficacy in proportion to the number combined together; that is, in proportion as their efficacy becomes needful.

From this view of the subject, it may be concluded that a pure democracy, by which I mean a society consisting of a small number of citizens who assemble and administer the government in person, can admit of no cure for the mischiefs of faction. A common passion or interest will, in almost every case, be felt by a majority of the whole; a communication and concert results from the form of government itself, and there is nothing to check the inducements to sacrifice the weaker party or an obnoxious individual. Hence it is that such democracies have ever been spectacles of turbulence and contention, have ever been found incompatible with personal security or the rights of property, and have in general been as short in their lives as they have been violent in their deaths. Theoretic politicians, who have patronized this species of government, have erroneously supposed that by reducing mankind to a perfect equality in their political rights they would, at the same time, be perfectly equalized and assimilated in their possessions, their opinions, and their passions.

A republic, by which I mean a government in which the scheme of representation takes place, opens a different prospect and promises the cure for which we are seeking. Let us examine the points in which it varies from pure democracy, and we shall comprehend both the nature of the cure and the efficacy which it must derive from the union.

The two great points of difference between a democracy and a republic are: first, the delegation of the government—in the latter, to a small number of citizens elected by the rest; secondly, the greater number of citizens and greater sphere of country over which the latter may be extended.

The effect of the first difference is, on the one hand, to refine and enlarge the public views by passing them through the medium of a chosen body of citizens whose wisdom may best discern the true interest of their country and whose patriotism and love of justice will be least likely to sacrifice it to temporary or partial considerations. Under such a regulation, it may well happen that the public voice pronounced by the representatives of the people will be more consonant to the public good than if pronounced by the people themselves convened for the purpose. On the other hand, the effect may be inverted. Men of factious tempers, of local prejudices, or of sinister designs may by intrigue, by corruption, or by other means first obtain the suffrages and then betray the interests of the people. The question resulting is, whether small or extensive republics are most favorable to the election of proper guardians of the public weal, and it is clearly decided in favor of the latter by two obvious considerations.

In the first place it is to be remarked that, however small the republic may be, the representatives must be raised to a certain number in order to guard against the cabals of a few; and that, however large it may be, they must be limited to a certain number in order to guard against the confusion of a multitude. Hence the number of representatives in the two cases not being in proportion to that of the constituents and being proportionally greatest in the small republic, it follows that if the proportion of fit characters be not less in the large than in the small republic, the former will present a greater option and consequently a greater probability of a fit choice.

In the next place, as each representative will be chosen by a greater number of citizens in the large than in the small republic, it will be more difficult for unworthy candidates to practice with success the vicious arts by which elections are too often carried, and the suffrages of the people being more free will be more likely to center on men who possess the most attractive merit and the most diffusive and established characters.

It must be confessed that in this, as in most other cases, there is a mean, on both sides of which inconveniencies will be found to lie. By enlarging too much the number of electors, you render the representative too little acquainted with all their local circumstances and lesser interests; as by reducing it too much, you render him unduly attached to these, and too little fit to comprehend and pursue great and national objects. The federal Constitution forms a happy combination in this respect; the great and aggregate interests being referred to the national, the local and particular to the state legislatures.

The other point of difference is the greater number of citizens and extent of territory which may be brought within the compass of republican than of democratic government, and it is this circumstance principally which renders factious combinations less to be dreaded in the former than in the latter. The smaller the society, the fewer probably will be the distinct parties and interests composing it; the fewer the distinct parties and interests, the more frequently will a majority be found of the same party; and the smaller the number of individuals composing a majority, and the smaller the compass within which they are placed, the more easily will they concert and execute their plans of oppression. Extend the sphere and you take in a greater variety of parties and interests; you make it less probable that a majority of the whole will have a common motive to invade the rights of other citizens, or if such a common motive exists, it will be more difficult for all who feel it to discover their own strength, and to act in unison with each other. Besides other impediments, it may be remarked that where there is a consciousness of unjust or dishonorable purposes, communication is always checked by distrust in proportion to the number whose concurrence is necessary.

Hence it clearly appears that the same advantage which a republic has over a democracy, in controlling the effects of faction, is enjoyed by a large over a small republic—is enjoyed by the union over the states composing it. Does this advantage consist in the substitution of representatives, whose enlightened views and virtuous sentiments render them superior to local prejudices and to schemes of injustice? It will not be denied that the representation of the union will be most likely to possess these requisite endowments. Does it consist in the greater security afforded by a greater variety of parties, against the event of any one party being able to outnumber and oppress the rest? In an equal degree does the increased variety of parties, comprised within the union, increase this security. Does it, in fine, consist in the greater obstacles opposed to the concert and accomplishment of the secret wishes of an unjust and interested majority? Here, again, the extent of the union gives it the most palpable advantage.

The influence of factious leaders may kindle a flame within their particular states, but will be unable to spread a general conflagration through the other states; a religious sect may degenerate into a political faction in a part of the confederacy, but the variety of sects dispersed over the entire face of it must secure the national councils against any danger from that source; a rage for paper money, for an abolition of debts, for an equal division of property, or for any other improper or wicked project will be less apt to pervade the whole body of the union than a particular member of it, in the same proportion as such a malady is more likely to taint a particular county or district than an entire state.

In the extent and proper structure of the union, therefore, we behold a republican remedy for the diseases most incident to republican government—and according to the degree of pleasure and pride we feel in being republicans, ought to be our zeal in cherishing the spirit and supporting the character of federalists.

The Federalist No. 51

To what expedient, then, shall we finally resort for maintaining in practice the necessary partition of power among the several departments, as laid down in the Constitution? The only answer that can be given is that as all these exterior provisions are found to be inadequate, the defect must be supplied by so contriving the interior structure of the government as that its several constituent parts may, by their mutual relations, be the means of keeping each other in their proper places. Without presuming to undertake a full development of this important idea, I will hazard a few general observations, which may perhaps place it in a clearer light and enable us to form a more correct judgment of the principles and structure of the government planned by the convention.

In order to lay a due foundation for that separate and distinct exercise of the different powers of government, which to a certain extent is admitted on all hands to be essential to the preservation of liberty, it is evident that each department should have a will of its own and consequently should be so constituted that the members of each should have as little agency as possible in the appointment of the members of the others. Were this principle rigorously adhered to, it would require that all the appointments for the supreme executive, legislative, and judiciary magistracies should be drawn from the same fountain of authority, the people, through channels having no communication whatever with one another. Perhaps such a plan of constructing the several departments would be less difficult in practice than it may in contemplation appear. Some difficulties, however, and some additional expense, would attend the execution of it. Some deviations therefore from the principle must be admitted. In the constitution of the judiciary department in particular, it might be inexpedient to insist rigorously on the principle; first, because peculiar qualifications being essential in the members, the primary consideration ought to be to select that mode of choice, which best secures these qualifications; secondly, because the permanent tenure by which the appointments are held in that department, must soon destroy all sense of dependence on the authority conferring them.

It is equally evident that the members of each department should be as little dependent as possible on those of the others for the emoluments annexed to their offices. Were the executive magistrate or the judges not independent of the legislature in this particular, their independence in every other would be merely nominal.

But the great security against a gradual concentration of the several powers in the same department consists in giving to those who administer each department the necessary constitutional means and personal motives to resist encroachments of the others. The provision for defense must in this, as in all other cases, be made commensurate to the danger of attack. Ambition must be made to counteract ambition. The interest of the man must be connected with the constitutional rights of the place. It may be a reflection on human nature that such devices should be necessary to control the abuses of government. But what is government itself but the greatest of all reflections on human nature? If men were angels, no government would be necessary. If angels were to govern men, neither external nor internal controls on government would be necessary. In framing a government which is to be administered by men over men, the great difficulty lies in this: you must first enable the government to control the governed, and in the next place oblige it to control itself. A dependence on the people is no doubt the primary control on the government, but experience has taught mankind the necessity of auxiliary precautions.

This policy of supplying by opposite and rival interests the defect of better motives might be traced through the whole system of human affairs, private as well as public. We see it particularly displayed in all the subordinate distributions of power, where the constant aim is to divide and arrange the several offices in such a manner as that each may be a check on the other; that the private interest of every individual may be a sentinel over the public rights. These inventions of prudence cannot be less requisite in the distribution of the supreme powers of the state.

But it is not possible to give to each department an equal power of self-defense. In republican government, the legislative authority necessarily predominates. The remedy for this inconveniency is to divide the legislature into different branches, and to render them by different modes of election, and different principles of action, as little connected with each other as the nature of their common functions and their common dependence on the society will admit. It may even be necessary to guard against dangerous encroachments by still further precautions. As the weight of the legislative authority requires that it should be thus divided, the weakness of the executive may require, on the other hand, that it should be fortified. An absolute negative on the legislature appears at first view to be the natural defense with which the executive magistrate should be armed. But perhaps it would be neither altogether safe nor alone sufficient. On ordinary occasions, it might not be exerted with the requisite firmness; and on extraordinary occasions, it might be perfidiously abused. May not this defect of an absolute negative be supplied by some qualified connection between this weaker department and the weaker branch of the stronger department, by which the latter may be led to support the constitutional rights of the former without being too much detached from the rights of its own department?

If the principles on which these observations are founded be just, as I persuade myself they are, and they be applied as a criterion to the several state constitutions and to the federal constitution, it will be found that if the latter does not perfectly correspond with them, the former are infinitely less able to bear such a test.

There are moreover two considerations particularly applicable to the federal system of America, which place that system in a very interesting point of view.

First: in a single republic, all the power surrendered by the people is submitted to the administration of a single government, and usurpations are guarded against by a division of the government into distinct and separate departments. In the compound republic of America, the power surrendered by the people is first divided between two distinct governments and then the portion allotted to each subdivided among distinct and separate departments. Hence a double security arises to the rights of the people. The different governments will control each other at the same time that each will be controlled by itself.

Second: it is of great importance in a republic not only to guard the society against the oppression of its rulers, but to guard one part of the society against the injustice of the other part. Different interests necessarily exist in different classes of citizens. If a majority be united by a common interest, the rights of the minority will be insecure. There are but two methods of providing against this evil: the one by creating a will in the community independent of the majority, that is, of the society itself; the other by comprehending in the society so many separate descriptions of citizens as will render an unjust combination of a majority of the whole very improbable, if not impracticable. The first method prevails in all governments possessing a hereditary or self-appointed authority. This at best is but a precarious security because a power independent of the society may as well espouse the unjust views of the major as the rightful interests of the minor party, and may possibly be turned against both parties. The second method will be exemplified in the federal republic of the United States. While all authority in it will be derived from and dependent on the society, the society itself will be broken into so many parts, interests, and classes of citizens that the rights of individuals or of the minority will be in little danger from interested combinations of the majority. In a free government, the security for civil rights must be the same as for religious rights. It consists in the one case in the multiplicity of interests and, in the other, in the multiplicity of sects. The degree of security in both cases will depend on the number of interests and sects, and this may be presumed to depend on the extent of country and number of people comprehended under the same government.

This view of the subject must particularly recommend a proper federal system to all the sincere and considerate friends of republican government since it shows that in exact proportion as the territory of the union may be formed into more circumscribed confederacies or states, oppressive combinations of a majority will be facilitated; the best security under the republican form for the rights of every class of citizens will be diminished; and consequently, the stability and independence of some member of the government, the only other security, must be proportionally increased. Justice is the end of government. It is the end of civil society. It ever has been and ever will be pursued until it be obtained, or until liberty be lost in the pursuit. In a society under the forms of which the stronger faction can readily unite and oppress the weaker, anarchy may as truly be said to reign as in a state of nature where the weaker individual is not secured against the violence of the stronger; and as in the latter state even the stronger individuals are prompted by the uncertainty of their condition to submit to a government which may protect the weak as well as themselves, so in the former state will the more powerful factions or parties be gradually induced by a like motive to wish for a government which will protect all parties, the weaker as well as the more powerful. It can be little doubted that if the state of Rhode Island was separated from the confederacy and left to itself, the insecurity of rights under the popular form of government within such narrow limits would be displayed by such reiterated oppressions of factious majorities that some power altogether independent of the people would soon be called for by the voice of the very factions whose misrule had proved the necessity of it.

In the extended republic of the United States, and among the great variety of interests, parties, and sects which it embraces, a coalition of a majority of the whole society could seldom take place on any other principles than those of justice and the general good, and there being thus less danger to a minor from the will of the major party, there must be less pretext also to provide for the security of the former by introducing into the government a will not dependent on the latter, or in other words, a will independent of the society itself. It is no less certain than it is important, notwithstanding the contrary opinions which have been entertained, that the larger the society, provided it lie within a practicable sphere, the more duly capable it will be of self government. And happily for the republican cause, the practicable sphere may be carried to a very great extent by a judicious modification and mixture of the federal principle.

From His Autobiography

"Shot down by a musket ball which passed through his breast"

During Washington's Christmas crossing of the Delaware River—and during the famous victory that followed—James Monroe was an eighteen-year-old lieutenant. Many years later, Monroe wrote about that battle and other important moments from his career as a soldier, diplomat, and president. His autobiography resembles Jefferson's and especially Madison's, sticking to the third person and emphasizing Monroe's public life. Still, he briefly considered publishing his book during his lifetime, and at times he provided a personal glimpse at key moments in American history—especially in this excerpt on the night he crossed the Delaware.

General Washington . . . perceived that the British commander, by the disposition which he had made of his troops, had estimated his success beyond their merit, that he considered the country as essentially conquered. The opportunity for profiting of that error, of depressing the British power and elevating the hopes and spirits of his country, was favorable, and he resolved to take advantage of it. The force at Trenton was small, but believed by the British commander to be superior to any that he could bring to bear on it. His other troops in Jersey were dispersed through the towns in a line from the Delaware to the Hudson, at Princeton, New Brunswick, Elizabethtown, and Newark.

The first attack was to be made on Trenton, on the result of which everything would depend. This was arranged in a general council, on great consideration and with consummate judgment. The command of the vanguard, consisting of fifty men, was given to Captain William Washington of the Third Virginia Regiment, an officer whose good conduct had already been noticed. This appointment having been communicated to the other officers by Colonel Weedon, Lieutenant Monroe promptly offered his services to act as a subaltern under him, which was promptly accepted. On the 25th of December, 1776, they passed the Delaware in front of the army, in the dusk of the evening, at Coryell's Ferry, ten miles above Trenton, and hastened to a point about one and one-half miles from it, at which the road by which they descended intersected that which led from Trenton to Princeton, for the purpose, in obedience to orders, of cutting off all communication between them and from the country to Trenton.

The night was tempestuous, as was the succeeding day, and made more severe by a heavy fall of snow. Captain Washington executed his orders faithfully. He soon took possession of the point to which he was ordered, and holding it through the night, intercepted and made prisoners of many who were passing in directions to and from Trenton. At the dawn of the day, our army approached, with the commander-in-chief at its head. Captain Washington then moved forward with the vanguard in front, attacked the enemy's picket, shot down the commanding officer, and drove it before him. A general alarm then took place among the troops in town. The drums were beat to arms, and two cannon were placed in the main street to bear on the head of our column as it entered. Captain Washington rushed forward, attacked, and put the troops around the cannon to flight, and took possession of them. Moving on afterwards, he received a severe wound and was taken from the field.

The command then devolved on Lieutenant Monroe, who advanced in like manner at the head of the corps and was shot down by a musket ball which passed through his breast and shoulder. He also was carried from the field. Our troops, then entering the town in several columns and attacking the enemy as they formed, soon overcame and made prisoners of them. Lieutenant Monroe was taken to the same room to which Captain Washington had been carried, and their wounds were dressed by Dr. Cochran, the Surgeon General of the army, and Dr. Riker, who had quartered with them in the country and accompanied them in the vanguard in the attack on the picket and advance in the city.

In the great events of which I have spoken, Mr. Monroe, being a mere youth, counted for nothing in comparison with those distinguished citizens who had the direction of public affairs. In adverting to the epoch of his commencement, I have thought it proper, and have taken delight in noticing in appropriate terms, the high character of that epoch and of those into whose hands its destiny fell. Taken together, they formed a school of practical instruction for many successful purposes, of which it is believed that history has furnished no equal example. It was a school of instruction in the knowledge of mankind, in the science of government, and what is of still great importance, for inculcating on the youthful mind those sound moral and political principles on which the success of our system depends.

From His State of the Union

(1823)

"We should consider any attempt on their part to extend their system to any portion of this hemisphere as dangerous to our peace and safety"

By the time Monroe became president, four decades after the Delaware crossing, America's influence in the world had changed dramatically. Monroe used his 1823 State of the Union to clarify that influence. In the Old World, Britain, Spain, and France were jockeying; in the New World, Mexico, Argentina, and others were winning their independence. In his written text, Monroe repeated the idea that America should stay out of the Eastern Hemisphere—what Washington in his Farewell Address had called the folly of "interweaving our destiny with that of any part of Europe." But Monroe added a second point: going forward, Europe needed to stay out of the Western Hemisphere. These ideas would shape America's foreign policy for decades to come as the Monroe Doctrine.

The citizens of the United States cherish sentiments the most friendly in favor of the liberty and happiness of their fellow men on that side of the Atlantic. In the wars of the European powers in matters relating to themselves we have never taken any part, nor does it comport with our policy so to do.

It is only when our rights are invaded or seriously menaced that we resent injuries or make preparation for our defense. With the movements in this hemisphere we are of necessity more immediately connected, and by causes which must be obvious to all enlightened and impartial observers.

The political system of the allied powers is essentially different in this respect from that of America. This difference proceeds from that which exists in their respective governments; and to the defense of our own, which has been achieved by the loss of so much blood and treasure and matured by the wisdom of their most enlightened citizens and under which we have enjoyed unexampled felicity, this whole nation is devoted.

We owe it, therefore, to candor and to the amicable relations existing between the United States and those powers to declare that we should consider any attempt on their part to extend their system to any portion of this hemisphere as dangerous to our peace and safety. With the existing colonies or dependencies of any European power we have not interfered and shall not interfere, but with the governments who have declared their independence and maintained it, and whose independence we have on great consideration and on just principles acknowledged, we could not view any interposition for the purpose of oppressing them or controlling in any other manner their destiny by any European power in any other light than as the manifestation of an unfriendly disposition toward the United States.

In the war between those new governments and Spain we declared our neutrality at the time of their recognition, and to this we have adhered and shall continue to adhere, provided no change shall occur which, in the judgment of the competent authorities of this government, shall make a corresponding change on the part of the United States indispensable to their security.

The late events in Spain and Portugal show that Europe is still unsettled. Of this important fact no stronger proof can be adduced than that the allied powers should have thought it proper, on any principle satisfactory to themselves, to have interposed by force in the internal concerns of Spain. To what extent such interposition may be carried, on the same principle, is a question in which all independent powers whose governments differ from theirs are interested, even those most remote and surely none more so than the United States.

Our policy in regard to Europe, which was adopted at an early stage of the wars which have so long agitated that quarter of the globe, nevertheless remains the same, which is not to interfere in the internal concerns of any of its powers; to consider the government de facto as the legitimate government for us; to cultivate friendly relations with it; and to preserve those relations by a frank, firm, and manly policy, meeting in all instances the just claims of every power, submitting to injuries from none.

But in regard to those continents, circumstances are eminently and conspicuously different. It is impossible that the allied powers should extend their political system to any portion of either continent without endangering our peace and happiness; nor can anyone believe that our southern brethren, if left to themselves, would adopt it of their own accord. It is equally impossible, therefore, that we should behold such interposition in any form with indifference. If we look to the comparative strength and resources of Spain and those new governments, and their distance from each other, it must be obvious that she can never subdue them. It is still the true policy of the United States to leave the parties to themselves, in the hope that other powers will pursue the same course.

If we compare the present condition of our union with its actual state at the close of our Revolution, the history of the world furnishes no example of a progress in improvement in all the important circumstances which constitute the happiness of a nation which bears any resemblance to it. At the first epoch our population did not exceed 3,000,000. By the last Census it amounted to about 10,000,000, and, what is more extraordinary, it is almost altogether native, for the immigration from other countries has been inconsiderable. At the first epoch half the territory within our acknowledged limits was uninhabited and a wilderness. Since then new territory has been acquired of vast extent, comprising within it many rivers, particularly the Mississippi, the navigation of which to the ocean was of the highest importance to the original states. Over this territory our population has expanded in every direction, and new states have been established almost equal in number to those which formed the first bond of our union. This expansion of our population and accession of new states to our union have had the happiest effect on all its highest interests.

That it has eminently augmented our resources and added to our strength and respectability as a power is admitted by all, but it is not in these important circumstances only that this happy effect is felt. It is manifest that by enlarging the basis of our system and increasing the number of states the system itself has been greatly strengthened in both its branches. Consolidation and disunion have thereby been rendered equally impracticable.

Each government, confiding in its own strength, has less to apprehend from the other, and in consequence each, enjoying a greater freedom of action, is rendered more efficient for all the purposes for which it was instituted.

It is unnecessary to treat here of the vast improvement made in the system itself by the adoption of this Constitution and of its happy effect in elevating the character and in protecting the rights of the nation as well as individuals. To what, then, do we owe these blessings? It is known to all that we derive them from the excellence of our institutions. Ought we not, then, to adopt every measure which may be necessary to perpetuate them?

JOHN QUINCY ADAMS

From His Diary, along with Three of His Poems

"My ambition would have been by some great work of literature to have done honor to my age"

John Quincy Adams was an important politician and diplomat. (As secretary of state, he wrote more of the Monroe Doctrine speech than did its namesake.) But Adams's heart belonged to books. "Americans have in Europe a sad reputation on the article of literature," he wrote as a young man. "I shall purpose to render a service to my country by devoting to {literature} the remainder of my life." While politics ended up taking most of his time, Adams still wrote books, including Letters on Silesia, *a travel narrative;* Dermot MacMorrogh, *an epic poem; and even a biography of his presidential father, though Adams never did complete that one. He also produced essays and translations and an intense, career-spanning diary. One of that diary's themes, as in the following entries, is Adams's love of books, and it is his diary more than any other piece of writing that stands as his true contribution to America's literary reputation.*

December 25, 1820

No attendance at the office. I gave the day to relaxation, and, with a view to make an experiment upon the taste of the younger part of our present family, after breakfast I read aloud Pope's "Messiah," a poem

79

suited to the day and of which my own admiration was great at an earlier age than that of my son Charles, the youngest person now in my family. Not one of them, excepting George, appeared to take the slightest interest in it; nor is there one of them who has any relish for literature. Charles has a great fondness for books and a meditative mind, but neither disposition nor aptitude for public speaking or correct reading. Charles must teach himself all that he learns. He will learn nothing from others.

Literature has been the charm of my life, and, could I have carved out my own fortunes, to literature would my whole life have been devoted. I have been a lawyer for bread, and a statesman at the call of my country. In the practice of the law I never should have attained the highest eminence, for the want of natural and spontaneous eloquence. The operations of my mind are slow, my imagination sluggish, and my powers of extemporaneous speaking very inefficient. But I have much capacity for, and love of, labor, habits on the whole of industry and temperance, and a strong and almost innate passion for literary pursuits. The business and sometimes the dissipations of my life have in a great measure withdrawn me from it. The summit of my ambition would have been by some great work of literature to have done honor to my age and country, and to have lived in the gratitude of future ages.

This consummation of happiness has been denied me. The portion of life allotted to me is that of my mortal existence, but even in this failure of my highest objects, literature has been to me a source of continual enjoyment and a powerful preservative from vice. It would have been a great comfort to me if all or either of my children inherited this propensity. George is not entirely without it. The others have it not, and I have found every effort to stimulate them to it, hitherto, fruitless. Pope says, "'tis education forms the common mind," and so it is; but the common mind will be always groveling in common objects. The uncommon mind must form itself.

September 24, 1829

In the evening I read several of Madame du Deffand's letters. It belongs probably to the effect of age upon the taste and judgment that these letters are more interesting to me than any novel. They are records of realities. In youth it was directly the reverse; fairy tales, the Arabian Nights, fictitious adventures of every kind delighted me. And the more there was in them of invention, the more pleasing they were. My imagination pictured them all as realities, and I dreamed of enchantments as if there was a world in which they existed. At ten years of age I read Shakespeare's *Tempest*, *As You Like It*, *Merry Wives of Windsor*, *Much Ado about Nothing*, and *King Lear*. The humors of Falstaff scarcely affected me at all. Bardolph and Pistol and Nym were personages quite unintelligible to me, and the lesson of Sir Hugh Evans to the boy William was too serious an affair. But the incantations of Prospero, the loves of Ferdinand and Miranda, the more than ethereal brightness of Ariel, and the worse than beastly grossness of Caliban made for me a world of revels and lapped me in Elysium.

With these books, in a closet of my mother's bedchamber, there was also a small edition, in two volumes, of Milton's *Paradise Lost*, which, I believe, I attempted ten times to read and never could get through half a book. I might as well have attempted to read Homer before I had learned the Greek alphabet. I was mortified, even to the shedding of solitary tears, that I could not even conceive what it was that my father and mother admired so much in that book, and yet I was ashamed to ask them an explanation. I smoked tobacco and read Milton at the same time, and from the same motive—to find out what was the recondite charm in them which gave my father so much pleasure. After making myself four or five times sick with smoking, I mastered that accomplishment and acquired a habit which, thirty years afterwards, I had much more difficulty in breaking off. But I did not master Milton. I was nearly thirty when I first read the *Paradise Lost* with delight and astonishment. But of late years I have lost the relish for fiction. I see nothing with sympathy but men, women, and children of flesh and blood. Madame du Deffand's suppers afford me savory food, and I was charmed this evening with her picture of the Lucan family sending a piano to her apartments, the father making his daughters play and sing an hour or two, Lady Stormont joining in the concert, the piano and the children being then sent home and leaving a party to sup. The visit of Dr. Franklin and Silas Deane with Mr. Le Roi is also very amusing, and her remark that all the company were in favor of the Americans excepting herself and Mr. De Guignes, who were for the Court, is more interesting to me than ten volumes of *Waverleys*. Can philosophy tell me why this is so?

October 17, 1833

I am copying the stanzas on the astrology of the zodiac for a revised edition of *Dermot MacMorrogh*. I received a letter from [the printer Melvin] Lord, with one to him from Mr. Pierpont, who objects to the term "bard" as applied to Cicero. Now that word was, of all others, the one which I could not possibly consent to strike out, and Mr. Pierpont's letter was otherwise not very encouraging to the publication of the proem. I showed it to my wife, who objected to two of the stanzas—precisely those which Lord thought the best of the whole. I immediately determined not to publish the proem now. I merely altered one stanza, supplied that which was in the first and second edition left in blank, and wrote to Lord to direct the contractor at Cincinnati to print from the second edition with these two alterations. I feel easier after this determination.

Scarcely any man in this country who has ever figured in public life has ever ventured into the field of general literature—none successfully. I have attempted it in the *Letters {on} Silesia*; in the *Lectures upon Rhetoric and Oratory*; in occasional fugitive pieces in verse, original and translated; and finally in this poem of *Dermot MacMorrogh*, which is original and at once a work of history, imagination, and poetry. It has come to a third edition, and will now be forgotten, as will be my other writings in prose and verse. Like the rest of American poetry, it resembles the juice of American grapes—it has not, in ripening, the property of acquiring alcohol enough to keep it in preservation. I have pushed my experiment on the public temper far enough.

Adams's most popular poem was probably "The Wants of Man," a meditation on what makes a meaningful life. While Adams included stanzas on political power, he also included ones on literary talent. Ralph Waldo Emerson, who as a young man had traveled to the Adamses' Massachusetts home to meet an aging John Adams, liked his son's poem enough to reprint it in his famed Parnassus *anthology, next to entries by Shakespeare and Milton.*

The Wants of Man

"Man wants but little here below,
Nor wants that little long."
    —{Oliver} Goldsmith's Hermit

I.

"Man wants but little here below,
Nor wants that little long."
'Tis not with me exactly so,
But 'tis so in the song.

My wants are many, and if told
Would muster many a score;
And were each wish a mint of gold,
I still should long for more.

II.

What first I want is daily bread,
And canvas backs and wine;
And all the realms of nature spread
Before me when I dine.
Four courses scarcely can provide
My appetite to quell,
With four choice cooks from France, beside,
To dress my dinner well.

III.

What next I want, at heavy cost,
Is elegant attire—
Black sable furs, for winter's frost,
And silks for summer's fire,
And Cashmere shawls, and Brussels lace
My bosom's front to deck,
And diamond rings my hands to grace,
And rubies for my neck.

IV.

And then I want a mansion fair,
A dwelling house, in style,
Four stories high, for wholesome air—
A massive marble pile;
With halls for banquets and balls,
All furnished rich and fine;
With stabled studs in fifty stalls,
And cellars for my wine.

V.

I want a garden and a park,
My dwelling to surround—
A thousand acres (bless the mark),
With walls encompassed round—
Where flocks may range and herds may low,
And kids and lambkins play,
And flowers and fruits commingled grow,
All Eden to display.

VI.

I want, when summer's foliage falls,
And autumn strips the trees,
A house within the city's walls,
For comfort and for ease.
But here, as space is somewhat scant,
And acres somewhat rare,
My house in town I only want
To occupy—a square.

VII.

I want a steward, butler, cooks;
A coachman, footman, grooms,
A library of well-bound books,
And picture-garnished rooms;
Corregios, Magdalen, and Night,
The matron of the chair;
Guido's fleet coursers in their flight,
And Claudes at least a pair.

VIII.

I want a cabinet profuse
Of medals, coins, and gems;
A printing press, for private use,
Of fifty thousand EMS;

And plants, and minerals, and shells;
Worms, insects, fishes, birds;
And every beast on earth that dwells,
In solitude or herds.

IX.

I want a board of burnished plate,
Of silver and of gold;
Tureens of twenty pounds in weight,
With sculpture's richest mold;
Plateaus, with chandeliers and lamps,
Plates, dishes—all the same;
And porcelain vases, with the stamps
Of Sevres, Angouleme.

X.

And maples, of fair glossy stain,
Must form my chamber doors,
And carpets of the Wilton grain
Must cover all my floors;
My walls, with tapestry bedecked,
Must never be outdone;
And damask curtains must protect
Their colors from the sun.

XI.

And mirrors of the largest pane
From Venice must be brought;
And sandalwood, and bamboo cane,
For chairs and tables bought;
On all the mantelpieces, clocks
Of thrice-gilt bronze must stand,
And screens of ebony and box
Invite the stranger's hand.

XII.

I want (who does not want?) a wife,
Affectionate and fair,
To solace all the woes of life,
And all its joys to share;
Of temper sweet, of yielding will,
Of firm, yet placid mind,
With all my faults to love me still,
With sentiment refined.

XIII.

And as Time's car incessant runs,
And Fortune fills my store,
I want of daughters and of sons
From eight to half a score.
I want (alas! can mortal dare
Such bliss on earth to crave?)
That all the girls be chaste and fair—
The boys all wise and brave.

XIV.

And when my bosom's darling sings,
With melody divine,
A pedal harp of many strings
Must with her voice combine.
A piano, exquisitely wrought,
Must open stand, apart;
That all my daughters may be taught
To win the stranger's heart.

XV.

My wife and daughters will desire
Refreshment from perfumes,
Cosmetics for the skin require,
And artificial blooms.

The civet fragrance shall dispense,
And treasured sweets return;
Cologne revive the flagging sense,
And smoking amber burn.

XVI.

And when at night my weary head
Begins to droop and dose,
A southern chamber holds my bed,
For nature's soft repose;
With blankets, counterpanes, and sheet,
Mattress and bed of down,
And comfortables for my feet,
And pillows for my crown.

XVII.

I want a warm and faithful friend,
To cheer the adverse hour,
Who ne'er to flatter will descend,
Nor bend the knee to power;
A friend to chide me when I'm wrong,
My inmost soul to see;
And that my friendship prove as strong
For him, as his for me.

XVIII.

I want a kind and tender heart,
For others wants to feel;
A soul secure from Fortune's dart,
And bosom armed with steel;
To bear divine chastisement's rod,
And mingling in my plan,
Submission to the will of God,
With charity to man.

XIX.

I want a keen, observing eye,
An ever-listening ear,
The truth through all disguise to spy,
And wisdom's voice to hear;
A tongue, to speak at virtue's need,
In Heaven's sublimest strain;
And lips, the cause of man to plead,
And never plead in vain.

XX.

I want uninterrupted health,
Throughout my long career,
And streams of never-failing wealth,
To scatter far and near;
The destitute to clothe and feed,
Free bounty to bestow;
Supply the helpless orphan's need,
And soothe the widow's woe.

XXI.

I want the genius to conceive,
The talents to unfold,
Designs, the vicious to retrieve,
The virtuous to uphold;
Inventive power, combining skill,
A persevering soul,
Of human hearts to mold the will,
And reach from pole to pole.

XXII.

I want the seals of power and place,
The ensigns of command,
Charged by the people's unbought grace,
To rule my native land.

Nor crown, nor scepter would I ask
But from my country's will,
By day, by night, to ply the task
Her cup of bliss to fill.

XXIII.

I want the voice of honest praise
To follow me behind,
And to be thought in future days
The friend of human kind;
That after ages, as they rise,
Exulting may proclaim,
In choral union to the skies,
Their blessings on my name.

XXIV.

These are the wants of mortal man;
I cannot want them long,
For life itself is but a span,
And earthly bliss a song.
My last great want, absorbing all,
Is, when beneath the sod,
And summoned to my final call,
The mercy of my God.

XXV.

And oh! while circles in my veins
Of life the purple stream,
And yet a fragment small remains
Of nature's transient dream,
My soul, in humble hope unscarred,
Forget not thou to pray,
That this thy want may be prepared
To meet the Judgment Day.

After Adams lost the White House to Andrew Jackson, in 1828, he returned to his family's home. Before long, his Massachusetts neighbors were urging him to run for the House of Representatives. While Adams mulled their request, he wrote this sonnet. It considers poetry's perennial topic of seizing the day, but from a political perspective that few other poets have ever felt.

To the Sun-Dial

Under the Window of the Hall of the House of Representatives of the
United States

Thou silent herald of Time's silent flight!
    Say, could'st thou speak, what warning voice were thine?
    Shade, who canst only show how others shine!
Dark, sullen witness of resplendent light
In day's broad glare, and when the moontide bright
    Of laughing fortune sheds the ray divine,
    Thy ready favors cheer us—but decline
The clouds of morning and the gloom of night.
Yet are thy counsels faithful, just, and wise;
    They bid us seize the moments as they pass—
Snatch the retrieveless sunbeam as it flies,
    Nor lose one sand of life's revolving glass—
Aspiring still, with energy sublime,
By virtuous deeds to give eternity to Time.

Adams's strongest poems tended to be religious or didactic: hymns, versifications of Scripture, and other forms that chimed with his cool and ordered mind.

My Shepherd is the Lord on High

My Shepherd is the Lord on high;
    His hand supplies me still;
In pastures green he makes me lie,
    Beside the rippling rill;
He cheers my soul, relieves my woes,
    His glory to display;
The paths of righteousness he shows,
    And leads me in his way.

Though walking through death's dismal shade,
    No evil will I fear;
Thy rod, thy staff shall lend me aid,
    For thou art ever near:
For me a table thou dost spread
    In presence of my foes;
With oil thou dost anoint my head;
    By thee my cup o'erflows.

Thy goodness and thy mercy sure
    Shall bless me all my days;
And I, with lips sincere and pure,
    Will celebrate thy praise.

Yes, in the temple of the Lord
    Forever I will dwell;
To after time thy name record,
    And of thy glory tell.

From *The Life of Andrew Jackson*

"To escape was impossible"

The election of 1824 featured a popular slogan: "John Quincy Adams / Who can write / Andrew Jackson / Who can fight." Yet it was Andrew Jackson— the former general and frontier rogue—who had a powerful book buoying his campaign. By this point, presidential elections were drawing more voters and becoming more personality driven. Still, candidates did not actively campaign for the same reason that ex-presidents did not actively publish their memoirs; both actions undercut the Washington ideal of the politician as humble servant. Jackson and his allies devised a workaround: a campaign biography written not by the candidate but by a supporter, even as Jackson stealthily sat for interviews and reviewed chapters, maintaining as much editorial control as most modern political authors. Jackson's campaign biography became a huge success, recounting his life but also spinning his life, especially in these opening pages that position the youthful Jackson as strong and patriotic, as someone who can fight.

Andrew Jackson was born on the 15th day of March, 1767. His father, Andrew, the youngest son of his family, emigrated to America from Ireland during the year 1765, bringing with him two sons, Hugh and Robert, both very young. Landing at Charleston, in South Carolina, he shortly afterwards purchased a tract of land in what was then called the Waxsaw settlement, about forty-five miles above Camden, at which place the subject of this history was born.

Shortly after his birth, his father died, leaving three sons to be provided for by their mother. She appears to have been an exemplary woman and to have executed the arduous duties which had devolved on her with great faithfulness and with much success. To the lessons she inculcated on the youthful minds of her sons was, no doubt, owing in a great measure that fixed opposition to British tyranny and oppression, which afterwards so much distinguished them. Often would she spend the winter's evenings in recounting to them the sufferings of their grandfather at the siege of Carrickfergus and the oppression exercised by the nobility of Ireland over the laboring poor, impressing it upon them as a first duty to expend their lives, if it should become necessary, in defending and supporting the natural rights of man.

Inheriting but a small patrimony from their father, it was impossible that all the sons could receive an expensive education. The two eldest were therefore only taught the rudiments of their mother tongue at a common country school. But Andrew, being intended by his mother for the ministry, was sent to a flourishing academy at the Waxsaw meeting house, superintended by Mr. Humphries. Here he was placed on the study of the dead languages and continued until the Revolutionary War, extending its ravages into that section of South Carolina where he then was, rendered it necessary that everyone should betake himself to the American standard, seek protection with the enemy, or flee his country. It was not an alternative that admitted of tedious deliberation. The natural ardor of his temper, deriving encouragement from the recommendations of his mother, whose feelings were not less alive on the occasion than his own, and excited by those sentiments in favor of liberty with which, by her conversation, his mind had been early endued, quickly determined him in the course to be pursued, and at the tender age of fourteen, accompanied by his brother Robert, he hastened to the American camp and engaged actively in the service of his country. His oldest brother, who had previously joined the army, had lost his life at the Battle of Stono [Ferry], from the excessive heat of the weather and the fatigues of the day.

Both Andrew and Robert, were, at this period, pretty well acquainted with the manual exercise and had some idea of the different evolutions of the field, having been indulged by their mother in attending the drill and general musters of the neighborhood.

The Americans, being unequal as well from the inferiority of their numbers as their discipline to engage the British army in battle, had retired before it into the interior of North Carolina; but when they learned that Lord Cornwallis had crossed the Yadkin, they returned in small detachments to their native state. On their arrival, they found Lord Rawdon in possession of Camden, and the whole country around in a state of desolation. The British commander being advised of the return of the settlers of Waxsaw, Major Coffin was immediately dispatched thither with a corps of light dragoons, a company of infantry, and a considerable number of Tories for their capture and destruction. Hearing of their approach, the settlers without delay appointed the Waxsaw meeting house as a place of rendezvous, that they might the better collect their scattered strength and concert some system of operations.

About forty of them had accordingly assembled at this point when the enemy approached, keeping the Tories, who were dressed in the common garb of the country, in front, whereby this little band of patriots was completely deceived, having taken them for Captain Nisbet's company, in expectation of which they had been waiting. Eleven of them were taken prisoners; the rest with difficulty fled, scattering and betaking themselves to the woods for concealment. Of those who thus escaped, though closely pursued, were Andrew Jackson and his brother who, entering a secret bend in a creek that was close at hand, obtained a momentary respite from danger and avoided, for the night, the pursuit of the enemy.

The next day, however, having gone to a neighboring house, for the purpose of procuring something to eat, they were broken in upon and made prisoners by Coffin's dragoons and a party of Tories who accompanied them. Those young men, with a view to security, had placed their horses in the wood, on the margin of a small creek, and posted on the road which led by the house a sentinel, that they might have information of any approach and in time to be able to elude it. But the Tories, who were well acquainted with the country and the passes through the forest, had unfortunately passed the creek at the very point where the horses and baggage of our young soldiers were deposited and taken possession of them. Having done this, they approached cautiously the house and were almost at the door before they were discovered.

To escape was impossible, and both were made prisoners. Being placed under guard, Andrew was ordered in a very imperious tone by a British officer to clean his boots, which had become muddied in crossing the creek. This order he positively and peremptorily refused to obey, alleging that he looked for such treatment as a prisoner of war had a right to expect. Incensed at his refusal, the officer aimed a blow at his head with a drawn sword, which would, very probably, have terminated his existence had he not parried its effects by throwing up his left hand, on which he received a severe wound, the mark of which he bears to this hour. His brother, at the same time, for a similar offense received a deep cut on the head, which subsequently occasioned his death.

They were both now taken to jail where, separated and confined, they were treated with marked severity until a few days after the battle before Camden, when, in consequence of a partial exchange, effected by the intercessions and exertions of their mother and Captain Walker of the militia, they were both released from confinement. Captain Walker had in a charge on the rear of the British army succeeded in making thirteen prisoners, whom he gave in exchange for seven Americans, of which number were these two young men. Robert, during his confinement in prison, had suffered greatly; the wound on his head all this time, having never been dressed, was followed by an inflammation of the brain, which, in a few days after his liberation, brought him to the grave.

To add to the afflictions of Andrew, his mother, worn down by grief and her incessant exertions to provide clothing and other comforts for the suffering prisoners who had been taken from her neighborhood, expired in a few weeks after her son, near the lines of the enemy, in the vicinity of Charleston. Andrew, the last and only surviving child, confined to a bed of sickness occasioned by the sufferings he had been compelled to undergo while a prisoner and by getting wet on his return from captivity, was thus left in the wide world, without a human being with whom he could claim a near relationship.

ANDREW JACKSON

From His State of the Union
(1830)

"The executive feels it has a right to expect the cooperation of Congress"

Once he defeated Adams, in 1828, Jackson declared himself a new kind of president. "The recent demonstration of public sentiment," he said in his inaugural address, "inscribes on the list of executive duties, in characters too legible to be overlooked, the task of reform." While previous presidents had typically deferred to the legislature, Jackson called for specific policies and wielded political power. One example came in the spring of 1830, when Jackson pushed through the Indian Removal Act, a cruel bill that would ultimately lead to the Trail of Tears. Later that year, in this excerpt from his written State of the Union, the president celebrated his legislation and reminded the various states that he expected their support in enforcing it.

The consequences of a speedy removal will be important to the United States, to individual states, and to the Indians themselves. The pecuniary advantages which it promises to the government are the least of its recommendations. It puts an end to all possible danger of collision between the authorities of the general and state governments on account of the Indians. It will place a dense and civilized population in large tracts of country now occupied by a few savage hunters. By opening the whole territory between Tennessee on the north and Louisiana on the south to the settlement of the whites it will incalculably strengthen the southwestern frontier and render the adjacent states strong enough to repel future invasions without remote aid. It will relieve the whole state of Mississippi and the western part of Alabama of Indian occupancy, and enable those states to advance rapidly in population, wealth, and power. It will separate the Indians from immediate contact with settlements of whites; free them from the power of the states; enable them to pursue happiness in their own way and under their own rude institutions; will retard the progress of decay, which is lessening their numbers, and perhaps cause them gradually, under the protection of the government and through the influence of good counsels, to cast off their savage habits and become an interesting, civilized, and Christian community. These consequences, some of them so certain and the rest so probable, make the complete execution of the plan sanctioned by Congress at their last session an object of much solicitude.

Toward the aborigines of the country no one can indulge a more friendly feeling than myself, or would go further in attempting to reclaim them from their wandering habits and make them a happy, prosperous people. I have endeavored to impress upon them my own solemn convictions of the duties and powers of the general government in relation to the state authorities. For the justice of the laws passed by the states within the scope of their reserved powers they are not responsible to this government. As individuals we may entertain and express our opinions of their acts, but as a government we have as little right to control them as we have to prescribe laws for other nations.

With a full understanding of the subject, the Choctaw and the Chickasaw tribes have with great unanimity determined to avail themselves of the liberal offers presented by the act of Congress and have agreed to remove beyond the Mississippi River. Treaties have been made with them, which in due season will be submitted for consideration. In negotiating these treaties they were made to understand their true condition, and they have preferred maintaining their independence in the western forests to submitting to the laws of the states in which they now reside. These treaties, being probably the last which will ever be made with them, are characterized by great liberality on the part of the government. They give the Indians a liberal sum in consideration of their removal, and comfortable subsistence on their arrival at their new homes. If it be their real interest to maintain a separate existence, they will there be at liberty to do so without the inconveniences and vexations to which they would unavoidably have been subject in Alabama and Mississippi.

Humanity has often wept over the fate of the aborigines of this country, and philanthropy has been long busily employed in devising means to avert it, but its progress has never for a moment been arrested, and one by one have many powerful tribes disappeared from the earth. To follow to the tomb the last of his race and to tread on the graves of extinct nations excite melancholy reflections. But true philanthropy reconciles the mind to these vicissitudes as it does to the extinction of one generation to make room for another. In the monuments and fortifications of an unknown people, spread over the extensive regions of the west, we behold the memorials of a once powerful race, which was exterminated or has disappeared to make room for the existing savage tribes. Nor is there anything in this which, upon a comprehensive view of the general interests of the human race, is to be regretted. Philanthropy could not wish to see this continent restored to the condition in which it was found by our forefathers. What good man would prefer a country covered with forests and ranged by a few thousand savages to our extensive republic, studded with cities, towns, and prosperous farms, embellished with all the improvements which art can devise or industry execute, occupied by more than twelve million happy people, and filled with all the blessings of liberty, civilization, and religion?

The present policy of the government is but a continuation of the same progressive change by a milder process. The tribes which occupied the countries now constituting the eastern states were annihilated or have melted away to make room for the whites. The waves of population and civilization are rolling to the westward, and we now propose to acquire the countries occupied by the red men of the south and west by a fair exchange and, at the expense of the United States, to send them to a land where their existence may be prolonged and perhaps made perpetual.

Doubtless it will be painful to leave the graves of their fathers; but what do they more than our ancestors did or than our children are now doing? To better their condition in an unknown land our forefathers left all that was dear in earthly objects. Our children by thousands yearly leave the land of their birth to seek new homes in distant regions. Does humanity weep at these painful separations from everything, animate and inanimate, with which the young heart has become entwined? Far from it. It is rather a source of joy that our country affords scope where our young population may range unconstrained in body or in mind, developing the power and faculties of man in their highest perfection.

These remove hundreds and almost thousands of miles at their own expense, purchase the lands they occupy, and support themselves at their new homes from the moment of their arrival. Can it be cruel in this government when, by events which it cannot control, the Indian is made discontented in his ancient home to purchase his lands, to give him a new and extensive territory, to pay the expense of his removal, and support him a year in his new abode? How many thousands of our own people would gladly embrace the opportunity of removing to the west on such conditions! If the offers made to the Indians were extended to them, they would be hailed with gratitude and joy.

And is it supposed that the wandering savage has a stronger attachment to his home than the settled, civilized Christian? Is it more afflicting to him to leave the graves of his fathers than it is to our brothers and children? Rightly considered, the policy of the general government toward the red man is not only liberal but generous. He is unwilling to submit to the laws of the states and mingle with their population. To save him from this alternative, or perhaps utter annihilation, the general government kindly offers him a new home, and proposes to pay the whole expense of his removal and settlement.

In the consummation of a policy originating at an early period, and steadily pursued by every administration within the present century—so just to the states and so generous to the Indians—the executive feels it has a right to expect the cooperation of Congress and of all good and disinterested men. The states, moreover, have a right to demand it. It was substantially a part of the compact which made them members of our confederacy. . . . May we not hope, therefore, that all good citizens, and none more zealously than those who think the Indians oppressed by subjection to the laws of the states, will unite in attempting to open the eyes of those children of the forest to their true condition and by a speedy removal to relieve them from all the evils, real or imaginary, present or prospective, with which they may be supposed to be threatened.

MARTIN VAN BUREN

From *Inquiry into the Origin and Course of Political Parties*

"Few had better opportunities for knowing
the state of feeling which prevailed at the
presidential mansion, while this matter
was in progress, than myself"

*Martin Van Buren wrote extensively after leaving the White House. He worked
on a thousand-plus-page autobiography and another book, a synthesis of historical and political analysis, though he planned for both titles to appear after
his death. The second one,* Inquiry into the Origin and Course of Political
Parties, *evaluates many key moments from American history and is still cited by
political scientists today. This excerpt focuses on a moment Van Buren experienced
himself: Jackson's contentious decision to veto a banking bill in 1832, a decision
based in part on his belief that the executive had as much claim to interpret the
Constitution as did the legislature or judiciary. The veto showed, once again,
how committed Jackson was to expanding executive power.*

Few had better opportunities for knowing the state of feeling which
prevailed at the presidential mansion, while this matter was in progress,
than myself. I arrived at New York from my brief mission to England after
the bank bill had passed both houses and on the day it was sent to President Jackson for his approval and left the next morning for Washington.
Arriving there at midnight, I proceeded at once to the White House, in

pursuance of an invitation he had sent to New York in anticipation of my coming.

I found the general in bed, supported by pillows, in miserable health but awake and awaiting and expecting me. Before suffering me to take a seat, and while still holding my hand, he with characteristic eagerness when in the execution of weighty concerns spoke to me of the bank—of the bill that had been sent for his approval, and of the satisfaction he derived from my arrival at so critical a moment—and I have not forgotten the gratification which beamed from his countenance when I expressed a hope that he would veto it and when I declared my opinion that it was in that way only he could discharge the great duty he owed to the country and to himself. Not that he was ignorant of my views upon the subject, for in all our conversations in respect to it before I left the country—and they had been frequent and anxious—my voice had been decided as well against the then existing [bank], as against any other national bank. Neither that he was himself in doubt as to the course that he ought to pursue, for he entertained none. But the satisfaction he evinced, and which he expressed in the most gratifying terms, arose solely from the relief he derived from finding himself so cordially sustained in a step he had determined to take but in respect to which he had been severely harassed by the stand taken by the leading members of his cabinet and by the remonstrances of many timid and not a few false friends, and had as yet been encouraged only by the few about him in comparatively subordinate positions who were alike faithful to principle and to himself.

The veto message was prepared and sent in while I remained at Washington. The manuscript was at all times open to my inspection, although I had but little direct agency in its construction. Had it been otherwise, the few words which subsequently made that part in which they appear so conspicuous could not have escaped my notice.

The paragraph in the message which sets forth the constitutional principles which President Jackson intended to avow contains the following declarations: first, that if the opinion of the Supreme Court covered the whole ground of the act under consideration, still it ought not to control the coordinate authorities of the government; second, that the Congress, the executive, and the court must each for itself be guided by its own opinions of the Constitution; third, that it is as much the duty of the House of Representatives, of the Senate, and of the president to decide upon any bill or resolution that may be presented to them for passage or approval, as it is for the supreme judges when brought before them for judicial decision; fourth, that the opinion of the judges has no more authority over Congress than the opinion of Congress has over the judges, and that on that point the president is independent of both; fifth, that the authority of the Supreme Court should not therefore be permitted to control the Congress or the executive when acting in their legislative capacities, but to have only such influence as the force of their reasoning may deserve. In none of these avowals is the principle of irresponsibility in respect to the opinion of the Supreme Court, by fair construction much less by necessary implication, carried farther than to include the president when discharging his official duties as the depository of the executive power of the Government in approving or disapproving of a Bill or Resolution sent to him by Congress for his executive action. That in all this he was perfectly right, it will be seen even [Daniel] Webster, latitudinarian as he was, did not venture to controvert.

But in the midst of these declarations are found these unguarded words: "Each public officer who takes an oath to support the Constitution swears that he will support it as he understands it and not as it is understood by others." Either this declaration was applied by the president only to all such officers as those of whom he had been speaking before and of whom alone he spoke afterwards, all in the same paragraph—to that class of officers who, singly as was his own case, or in conjunction with others as was the case with some, constituted the three great departments of the government while acting in their respective official capacities, as it was beyond all doubt intended to be applied—or he must be supposed to have held that the inferior judges of the federal courts had a right to say to the superior court, "We do not understand the Constitution as you have expounded it, and we will therefore not submit to your decision"; the same as to the judges of the state courts of every grade, and as to the officers of the custom-house and innumerable other officers of his own appointment, empowering the latter on the same ground to refuse to conform to the instructions sent to them, etc., etc. A construction, one would think, too preposterous for credulity itself to swallow.

The plain and well-understood substance of what he said was that in giving or withholding his assent to the bill for the re-charter of the bank it was his right and duty to decide the question of its constitutionality for himself, uninfluenced by any opinion or judgment which the Supreme Court had pronounced upon that point farther than his judgment was satisfied by the reason which it had given for its decision. This covered the whole ground. It explained fully his views of the Constitution in respect to what he was doing. All beyond was both uncalled for and unnecessary. To this view of the president's power and duty under the Constitution, Mr. Webster assented in the fullest manner. . . .

If the supporters of the bank had been willing to judge the president by the claim of power under the Constitution which he intended to advance in his veto message, there would have been a perfect accord of opinion between him and their great leader in the debate upon that document, and one disturbing element would have been withdrawn from the severe agitation to which the public mind was exposed. But this course neither suited the interest of the bank, nor would it have comported with the excited feelings of the implacable enemies of the president. Matters had worked to their liking. By forcing the bill through the two houses at the eve of the struggle for the president's reelection, and thus compelling him either to sign or to encounter the responsibility of defeating it, they felt that they had involved the great opponent of the bank—the only man whose power with the people they really dreaded—in toils from which his escape would be impossible. They were engaged in framing an issue with President Jackson and the Democratic Party, looking at that time only to the defeat of his reelection. . . .

Webster denounced him as a ruthless tyrant who was violating the Constitution and uprooting the foundations of society. Look at some of his fierce denunciations:

> . . . Social disorder, entire uncertainty in regard to individual rights and individual duties, the cessation of legal authority, confusion, the dissolution of free government—all these are inevitable consequences of the principles adopted by the [veto] message. . . . No president, and no public man, ever before advanced such doctrines in the face of the nation. There never was before a moment in which any president would have been tolerated in asserting such claim to despotic power. . . .

I cannot allow this great constitutional question, respecting the relation which the three great departments of the federal government—executive, legislative, and judicial—were by the Constitution designed to occupy toward each other, to pass without further notice. One more vitally important has not arisen nor can ever arise out of our complex and peculiar form of government. . . .

The Constitution requires from the president, and from him only, that he should, in addition to the oath of office, before he enter upon its duties, swear "that he will, to the best of his ability, preserve, protect, and defend the Constitution of the United States." . . . It seems very absurd to suppose that it was intended to oblige the president of the United States—the officer clothed with the whole executive power of the government; the only officer, except the vice-president, who is chosen by the whole people of the United States; the champion, designated by the Constitution itself to "preserve, protect, and defend" it in the performance of the executive duties committed to his charge, duties affecting what Hamilton happily describes as "the general liberty of the people," to distinguish it from affairs of *meum* and *tuum*—to keep his eye upon the Supreme Court calendar, and to gather from its decisions in respect to the private rights of parties litigant the measure of his constitutional powers, and to stop or go on in the execution of the important national offices assigned to his department as its judgments may be deemed to authorize or forbid his further proceeding.

JAMES POLK

From His Diary

"The people of the United States have no idea of the extent to which the president's time . . . is occupied by the voracious and often unprincipled persons"

Most presidents who followed Jackson did not share his broad views of executive power—something one can see in James Polk's White House diary. From 1845 to 1849, Polk wrote detailed entries about the Mexican-American War and the arguments over slavery spreading to new states. (He also wrote detailed entries about Washington intrigue: "This whole excitement in the Senate has grown out of the aspirations of senators and their friends for the presidency.") Yet many of Polk's entries, including the following ones, emphasize something more mundane: the crushing demands of the patronage system. Another Jacksonian innovation, this system let winning politicians—and the political bosses who supported them— fill tens of thousands of government jobs with their partisan allies. Polk grew to hate the "herd of loafers" patronage lured to his office every day.

August 26, 1846

Twelve months ago this day, a very important conversation took place in [the] cabinet between myself and Mr. [James] Buchanan on the Oregon question. This conversation was of so important a character that I deemed it proper on the same evening to reduce the substance of it to writing for the purpose of retaining it more distinctly in my memory. This

I did on separate sheets. It was this circumstance which first suggested to me the idea, if not the necessity, of keeping a journal or diary of events and transactions which might occur during my presidency. I resolved to do so and accordingly procured a blank book for that purpose on the next day, in which I have every day since noted whatever occurred that I deemed of interest. Sometimes I have found myself so much engaged with my public duties as to be able to make only a very condensed and imperfect statement of events and incidents which occurred, and to omit others altogether which I would have been pleased to have noted.

January 7, 1847

Many persons, members of Congress and others, called today, all of them or nearly all on what they may regard as the patriotic, but which I consider the contemptible, business of seeking office for themselves or their friends. The passion for office and the number of unworthy persons who seek to live on the public is increasing beyond former example, and I now predict that no president of the United States of either party will ever again be reelected. The reason is that the patronage of the government will destroy the popularity of any president, however well he may administer the government. The office seekers have become so numerous that they hold the balance of power between the two great parties of the country. In every appointment which the president makes he disappoints half a dozen applicants and their friends, who, actuated by selfish and sordid motives, will prefer any other candidate in the next election, while the person appointed attributes the appointment to his own superior merit and does not even feel obliged by it. . . .

Another great difficulty in making appointments which the president encounters is that he cannot tell upon what recommendations to rely. Members of Congress and men of high station in the country sign papers of recommendation, either from interested personal motives or without meaning what they say, and thus the president is often imposed on and induced to make bad appointments. When he does so the whole responsibility falls on himself, while those who have signed papers of recommendation and misled him take special care never to avow the agency they have had in the matter, or to assume any part of the responsibility.

I have had some remarkable instances of this during my administration. One or two of them I think worthy to be recorded as illustrations of many others. In the recess of Congress shortly after the commencement of my administration, I made an appointment upon the letter of recommendation of a senator. I sent the nomination to the Senate at the last session and it was rejected, and, as I learned, at the instance of the same senator who had made the recommendation.

A few days afterwards, the senator called to recommend another person for the same office. I said to him, "Well, you rejected the man I nominated."

"Oh yes," he replied, "he was without character and wholly unqualified."

I then asked him if he knew upon whose recommendation I had appointed him, to which he replied that he did not. I then handed to him his own letter and told him that was the recommendation upon which I had appointed him.

He appeared confused and replied, "Well, we are obliged to recommend our constituents when they apply to us."

The senator was Mr. Atchison of Missouri, and the person appointed and rejected was Mr. Hedges as surveyor of the port of St. Louis. Other like cases have occurred.

February 8, 1848

Though this was cabinet day I could not well avoid seeing members of Congress who called. All who did call were upon the important business of seeking office for their constituents or the throng of persons who flock to Washington to get office instead of going to work and making a living by honest industry. I am obliged to be civil and patient with members of Congress and others when they call on this business. Much of my time is taken up in this way, and I am sometimes exceedingly worried by it. They apply to me not only for offices that exist but for those which are expected to be created. If a bill is introduced into Congress proposing to create an office, it brings upon me a crowd of applicants with masses of papers recommending them. It is in vain that I repeat a dozen times in a day that no such offices exist by law. I am compelled to have my time taken up in listening to their importunities.

A strong illustration of this is afforded at this session of Congress. Bills are before Congress to create a number of assistant pursers in the Navy, to increase the military force, to increase the number of clerks, and to institute diplomatic relations with Rome and some of the South American states. The consequence is that a great crowd of persons have rushed to Washington, have enlisted members of Congress in their behalf; and whenever my doors are opened I am besieged by them and can do no business unless I lock my doors and refuse admittance to any.

A large proportion of those who thus trouble me are unworthy and unfit for the places they seek, and many of them are mere loafers who are too lazy to work and wish to be supported by the public. If an officer is taken ill, application is made for his office if he should die. A case of this kind (one out of many which have occurred since I have been president) has occurred within a few days. The marshal of this district is reported to be confined to his house by sickness, and I have had half a dozen applications for his place, if he should die. Four members of Congress waited on me this morning in behalf of one of these applicants. I am often disgusted with such scenes.

April 6, 1848

My office was crowded up to the hour of twelve o'clock with visitors, and I was greatly annoyed by the importunities of office seekers. It is most disgusting to be compelled to spend hour after hour almost every day in hearing the applications for office made by loafers who congregate in Washington, and by members of Congress in their behalf, and yet I am compelled to submit to it or offend or insult the applicants and their friends. The people of the United States have no idea of the extent to which the president's time, which ought to be devoted to more important matters, is occupied by the voracious and often unprincipled persons who seek office. If a kind Providence permits me length of days and health, I will, after I retire from the presidential office, write the secret and hitherto unknown history of the workings of the government in this respect.

April 10, 1848

In the midst of the annoyances of the herd of lazy, worthless people who come to Washington for office instead of going to work and by some honest calling making a livelihood, I am sometimes amused at their applications. A case of this kind occurred on Saturday last. One of these office seekers placed his papers of recommendation in the hands of Judge Mason to present to me. No particular office was specified in the papers, and the Judge reported to me that he enquired of him what office he wanted, to which he answered that he thought he would be a good hand at making treaties, and that as he understood there were some to be made soon he would like to be a minister abroad.

This is about as reasonable as many other applications which are made to me.

From His Autobiography

"In spite of myself, I burst out crying"

When Millard Fillmore was in his seventies, the Buffalo Historical Society asked him to write his autobiography. He agreed as long as it would stay sealed until after his death. Fillmore declined to write about his political career or his private experiences as president. But his account of growing up in upstate New York remains revealing. This excerpt offers a glimpse into the harsh world of indentured servitude. It also shows Fillmore's intense passion for self-education, a passion that placed him in the tradition of John Adams's description of American readers and John Quincy Adams's study of John Milton, even if Fillmore had to pursue that passion with far fewer resources than the Adamses had.

In the fall of 1814, a neighbor had been drafted into the military service for three months, and he offered me what I regarded as a very liberal sum to take his place as a substitute. I was foolish enough to desire to accept the offer, but at the same time a man by the name of Benjamin Hungerford, formerly a near neighbor but then living in Sparta, Livingston County, New York, where he had established the business of carding and cloth-dressing, came to my father and proposed to take me on trial for three months; then, if we were both suited, I was to become an apprentice to the business. My father persuaded me to abandon the idea of becoming a soldier, and to go home with Mr. Hungerford to learn a trade. He had come with an old team to purchase dye-woods and other materials for his business—his load was very heavy and the roads very bad—consequently I had to go on foot most of the way, something like a hundred miles, but I endured this very well.

Up to this time I had never spent two days away from home, and my habits and tastes were somewhat peculiar. For instance, I was very fond of bread-and-milk and usually ate it three times a day, regardless of what others ate. And here I will say, I think that this early habit, and the thorough training afforded by outdoor exercise on a farm, gave me a constitution and digestive powers which have enabled me to preserve my health under all the vicissitudes of a varied life, and to my uniform good health and temperate habits I am chiefly indebted, under Providence, for any success I have attained. But I found, when I got to Sparta, that milk was a luxury in which I could but seldom indulge. On the contrary, I was compelled to eat boiled salt pork, which I detested, with occasionally pudding and milk and buckwheat cakes, or starve. This was very hard, but I did not complain.

I was, however, more disappointed at the work I was required to do. I had become anxious to learn the trade and supposed I should be put at once into the shop, instead of which I was set to chopping wood for a coal pit. I probably manifested some disappointment, but I was reconciled to the work by being told that charcoal was indispensable for cloth dressing, that I might be so situated that I could not purchase, and that therefore it was necessary to know how to make and burn a coal pit.

I was the youngest apprentice and soon found that I had to chop most of the wood, having very little opportunity to work in the shop, and as it seemed to me that I was made to enslave myself without any corresponding benefit, I became exceedingly sore under this servitude. One day when I had been chopping in the woods, I came into the shop just before dark, tired and dissatisfied, and Mr. Hungerford told me to take my ax and go up on the hill and cut some wood for the shop. I took up my ax and said (perhaps not very respectfully) that I did not come there to learn to chop and immediately left without waiting for a reply. I went on to the hill, mounted a log, and commenced chopping. Mr. Hungerford soon followed me up and, coming near, asked me if I thought I was abused because I had to chop wood. I told him I did, that I came there for no such purpose and could learn to chop at home, and that I was not disposed to submit to it.

He said that I must obey his orders.

I said, "Yes, if they are right; otherwise I will not, and I have submitted to this injustice long enough."

He said, "I will chastise you for your disobedience," and stepped towards me as I stood upon the log with my ax in my hand.

I was burning with indignation and felt keenly the injustice and insult and said to him, "You will not chastise me"; and, raising my ax, said, "If you approach me I will split you down."

He looked at me for a minute, and I looked at him, when he turned and walked off. I am very glad that he did so, for I was in a frenzy of anger and know not what I might have done. I had dwelt in silence and solitude upon what I deemed his injustice until I had become morbidly sensitive, and his spark of insolent tyranny kindled the whole into a flame. I do not justify my threat, and sincerely regret it, but the truth must be told.

The next day he asked me if I wished to go home. I told him I was ready to go or would stay the three months for which I came, if I could be employed in the shop. He said I might be, and so I remained until the time was up, when I shouldered my knapsack, containing bread and dried venison, and returned to my father's on foot and alone. Mr. Hungerford came after me next year, but I refused to go with him.

I think that this injustice, which was no more than other apprentices have suffered and will suffer, had a marked effect upon my character. It made me feel for the weak and unprotected and hate the insolent tyrant in every station of life. Some acts of tyranny during the late rebellion have made my blood boil with indignation; but perhaps I was wrong since the country at large seems to have borne them with more than Christian patience and humility.

One other incident that occurred during these three months of servitude may be mentioned. The only holiday which I was allowed was the first day of January, 1815, when I went with the other employees of the shop to the house of a Mr. Duncan, where the day was to be celebrated. There I witnessed for the first time the rude sports in which people engage in a new country, such as wrestling, jumping, hopping, firing at turkeys and raffling for them, and drinking whisky. I was a spectator of the scene, taking no part except that I raffled once for the turkey that was perched up in one corner of the room and won it. No persuasion could induce me to raffle again, and that was the beginning and end of my gambling, if it might be called such, as I have never since gambled to the value of a cent.

In 1815, I commenced my apprenticeship with Zaccheus Cheney and Alvan Kellogg, who carried on the business of carding and cloth-dressing at Newhope, near my father's residence. I was not indentured, but the verbal bargain was that I was to serve during the season of wool-carding and cloth-dressing—which usually lasted from about the first of June to the middle of December—until I arrived at the age of twenty, for which

I was to be taught the trade and receive fifty-five dollars for each year, except the last, when the amount was to be increased. This was thought to be sufficient for my clothing and spending money, and all the rest of my time and earnings belonged to my father, who had a large family and a sickly wife to support.

I was well pleased with my situation, and all things went on smoothly and satisfactorily. The apparent impossibility of anything better or higher suppressed hope and enforced contentment. I went to school some, during the winters of 1816 and 1817, and worked on the farm during the spring. I had thus far had no access to books beyond the schoolbooks which I had, as my father's library consisted only of a Bible, hymn-book, and almanac, and sometimes a little weekly paper from Auburn; but in 1817 or 1818 a small circulating library was established in the town, and I managed to get a share, which cost me two dollars.

Then, for the first time, I began to read miscellaneous works. Still, I had very little leisure to indulge in this luxury. I read without method or object; nevertheless, I read enough to see the need of a better knowledge of the definition of words. I therefore bought a small dictionary and determined to seek out the meaning of every word occurring in my reading which I did not understand. While attending the carding machines, I used to place the dictionary on the desk—by which I passed every two minutes in feeding the machines and removing the rolls—and in this way I could have a moment in which to look at a word and read its definition and could then fix it in my memory. This I found quite successful.

The winter that I was eighteen years of age, I was employed to teach a country school in the town of Scott, at the head of Skaneateles Lake. This was at that time a very rough and uncultivated place where the boys, the winter before, had driven out the teacher and broken up the school. It was not long before I saw that the question who was master had got to be decided. One of the boys set my authority at defiance—evidently with the intention of bringing on a fight. I ordered him up for chastisement. Immediately, the larger boys sprang to their feet, and one attempted to seize the wooden poker, but I was too quick for him and, raising it, I stamped my foot and told them to sit down—and they obeyed. . . .

I returned to my apprenticeship in June and improved every leisure moment in studying and reading. My attempt to teach had made me conscious of my deficiency. I therefore decided to attend school, if possible the next winter. But the best school was in a different part of the town from that in which my father lived, and I had no means to pay my board. Nevertheless, I was determined to go to school, and I effected an arrangement with a farmer by which he was to board me and when the school closed I was to work for him, chopping two days for every week's board, which I did. I then, for the first time in my life, heard a sentence parsed, and had an opportunity to study geography with a map. I pursued much of my study with, and perhaps was unconsciously stimulated by the companionship of, a young lady whom I afterward married.

About this time my father sold his farm and removed to Montville, Cayuga County, where Judge Walter Wood resided. He was a gentleman somewhat advanced in years and reputed to be very wealthy. He had farms and tenants scattered over several counties on the Old Military Tract. The titles were often the subject of litigation, and his professional business was mostly limited to actions of ejectment. He had a good library and was a man of remarkable energy and of methodical business habits, and from his example and training I derived essential benefit, especially from his scrupulous punctuality. He was in religious sentiments a Quaker, using the Quakers' plain language, dressing in their style, and punctually attending the "meeting" twice a week, and his office the other days of the week from sunrise till nine o'clock in the evening.

Some persons, without my knowledge, had suggested to my father that it was possible for me to be something more than a carder of wool and dresser of cloth, and he was induced to apply to Judge Wood to know if he would receive me into his office on trial for a little time, before I went back to my apprenticeship, and he consented. I knew nothing of this until, at the dinner table, my mother informed me of it; and the news was so sudden and unexpected that, in spite of myself, I burst out crying and had to leave the table, much mortified at my weakness.

Suffice it to say, I went immediately into Judge Wood's office, and he handed me the first volume of Blackstone's *Commentaries*, and said, "Thee will please to turn thy attention to this."

From the Ottawa Debate with Stephen Douglas

(1858)

"There is no reason in the world why the negro is not entitled to all the natural rights enumerated in the Declaration of Independence"

When Abraham Lincoln challenged Stephen Douglas for his Senate seat, in 1858, he did so as a long shot. To increase his odds, Lincoln challenged Douglas to a series of debates. They argued about slavery and whether it should spread to America's new territories and states, and although Lincoln lost the race, he knew these issues would continue to dominate national politics. In 1860 Lincoln and Douglas faced off again, this time for the White House, and Lincoln worked obsessively to produce a book that gathered the texts of their old debates—not a Jackson-style campaign biography, in other words, but a new kind of political book made up of the candidates' own words. Lincoln's book became an enormous bestseller, presenting exchanges like this one, from Lincoln's response to Douglas at their first debate, directly to readers and voters.

Now, gentlemen, I hate to waste my time on such things, but in regard to that general abolition tilt that Judge Douglas makes—when he says that I was engaged at that time in selling out and abolitionizing the old Whig Party—I hope you will permit me to read a part of a printed speech that I made then at Peoria, which will show altogether a different view of the position I took in that contest of 1854:

> . . . It is wrong—wrong in its direct effect, letting slavery into Kansas and Nebraska, and wrong in its prospective principle, allowing it to spread to every other part of the wide world where men can be found inclined to take it. This declared indifference, but as I must think, covert real zeal for the spread of slavery, I cannot but hate. I hate it because of the monstrous injustice of slavery itself. I hate it because it deprives our republican example of its just influence in the world—enables the enemies of free institutions, with plausibility, to taunt us as hypocrites; causes the real friends of freedom to doubt our sincerity; and especially because it forces so many really good men amongst ourselves into an open war with the very fundamental principles of civil liberty, criticizing the Declaration of Independence. . . .

Now, gentlemen, I don't want to read at any greater length, but this is the true complexion of all I have ever said in regard to the institution of slavery and the black race. This is the whole of it, and anything that argues me into his idea of perfect social and political equality with the negro, is but a specious and fantastic arrangement of words, by which a man can prove a horse chestnut to be a chestnut horse.

I will say here, while upon this subject, that I have no purpose directly or indirectly to interfere with the institution of slavery in the states where it exists. I believe I have no lawful right to do so, and I have no inclination to do so. I have no purpose to introduce political and social equality between the white and the black races. There is a physical difference between the two, which in my judgment will probably forever forbid their living together upon the footing of perfect equality, and inasmuch as it becomes a necessity that there must be a difference, I, as well as Judge Douglas, am in favor of the race to which I belong, having the superior position. I have never said anything to the contrary, but I hold that notwithstanding all this, there is no reason in the world why the negro is not entitled to all the natural rights enumerated in the Declaration of Independence: the right to life, liberty, and the pursuit of happiness. I hold that he is as much entitled to these as the white man. I agree with Judge Douglas he is not my equal in many respects—certainly not in color, perhaps not in moral or intellectual endowment. But in the right to eat the bread, without leave of anybody else, which his own hand earns, he is my equal, and the equal of Judge Douglas, and the equal of every living man. . . .

I will dwell a little longer upon one or two of these minor topics upon which the Judge has spoken. He has read from my speech in Springfield, in which I say that "a house divided against itself cannot stand." Does the Judge say it can stand? I don't know whether he does or not. The Judge does not seem to be attending to me just now, but I would like to know if it is his opinion that a house divided against itself can stand. If he does then there is a question of veracity, not between him and me but between the Judge and an authority of a somewhat higher character.

Now, my friends, I ask your attention to this matter for the purpose of saying something seriously. I know that the Judge may readily enough agree with me that the maxim which was put forth by the Savior is true, but he may allege that I misapply it; and the Judge has a right to urge that, in my application, I do misapply it, and then I have a right to show that I do not misapply it. When he undertakes to say that because I think this nation, so far as the question of slavery is concerned, will all become one thing or all the other, I am in favor of bringing about a dead uniformity in the various states, in all their institutions, he argues erroneously. The great variety of the local institutions in the states, springing from differences in the soil, differences in the face of the country, and in the climate, are bonds of union. They do not make "a house divided against itself," but they make a house united. If they produce in one section of the country what is called for by the wants of another section, and this other section can supply the wants of the first, they are not matters of discord but bonds of union, true bonds of union.

But can this question of slavery be considered as among these varieties in the institutions of the country? I leave it to you to say whether, in the history of our government, this institution of slavery has not always failed to be a bond of union, and, on the contrary, been an apple of discord and an element of division in the house. I ask you to consider whether, so long as the moral constitution of men's minds shall continue to be the same, after this generation and assemblage shall sink into the grave, and another race shall arise, with the same moral and intellectual development we have—whether, if that institution is standing in the same irritating position in which it now is, it will not continue an element of division? If so, then I have a right to say that in regard to this question, the union is a house divided against itself, and when the Judge reminds me that I have often said to him that the institution of slavery has existed for eighty years in some states, and yet it does not exist in some others, I agree to the fact, and I account for it by looking at the position in which our fathers originally placed it—restricting it from the new territories where it had not gone and legislating to cut off its source by the abrogation of the slave trade, thus putting the seal of legislation against its spread.

The public mind did rest in the belief that it was in the course of ultimate extinction. But lately, I think—and in this I charge nothing on the Judge's motives—lately, I think, that he and those acting with him have placed that institution on a new basis, which looks to the perpetuity and nationalization of slavery. And while it is placed upon this new basis, I say, and I have said, that I believe we shall not have peace upon the question until the opponents of slavery arrest the further spread of it and place it where the public mind shall rest in the belief that it is in the course of ultimate extinction; or, on the other hand, that its advocates will push it forward until it shall become alike lawful in all the states, old as well as new, North as well as South.

Now, I believe if we could arrest the spread, and place it where Washington and Jefferson and Madison placed it, it would be in the course of ultimate extinction, and the public mind would, as for eighty years past, believe that it was in the course of ultimate extinction. The crisis would be past and the institution might be let alone for a hundred years, if it should live so long in the states where it exists, yet it would be going out of existence in the way best for both the black and the white races. . . .

Now my friends, I have but one branch of the subject, in the little time I have left, to which to call your attention, and as I shall come to a close at the end of that branch, it is probable that I shall not occupy quite all the time allotted to me. Although on these questions I would like to talk twice as long as I have, I could not enter upon another head and discuss it properly without running over my time. I ask the attention of the people here assembled and elsewhere, to the course that Judge Douglas is pursuing every day as bearing upon this question of making slavery national. Not going back to the records but taking the speeches he makes, the speeches he made yesterday and day before and makes constantly all over the country—I ask your attention to them.

In the first place, what is necessary to make the institution national? Not war. There is no danger that the people of Kentucky will shoulder their muskets and with a young nigger stuck on every bayonet march into Illinois and force them upon us. There is no danger of our going over there and making war upon them. Then what is necessary for the nationalization of slavery? It is simply the next Dred Scott decision. It is merely for the Supreme Court to decide that no state under the Constitution can exclude it, just as they have already decided that under the Constitution neither Congress nor the territorial legislature can do it. When that is decided and acquiesced in, the whole thing is done.

This being true, and this being the way as I think that slavery is to be made national, let us consider what Judge Douglas is doing every day to that end. In the first place, let us see what influence he is exerting on public sentiment. In this and like communities, public sentiment is everything. With public sentiment, nothing can fail; without it nothing can succeed. Consequently, he who molds public sentiment goes deeper than he who enacts statutes or pronounces decisions. He makes statutes and decisions possible or impossible to be executed.

This must be borne in mind, as also the additional fact that Judge Douglas is a man of vast influence, so great that it is enough for many men to profess to believe anything when they once find out that Judge Douglas professes to believe it. Consider also the attitude he occupies at the head of a large party—a party which he claims has a majority of all the voters in the country. This man sticks to a decision which forbids the people of a territory from excluding slavery, and he does so not because he says it is right in itself—he does not give any opinion on that—but because it has been decided by the court, and being decided by the court, he is, and you are, bound to take it in your political action as law—not that he judges at all of its merits, but because a decision of the court is to him a "Thus saith the Lord." He places it on that ground alone, and you will bear in mind that thus committing himself unreservedly to this decision, commits him to the next one just as firmly as to this. He did not commit himself on account of the merit or demerit of the decision, but it is a "Thus saith the Lord." The next decision, as much as this, will be a "Thus saith the Lord."

There is nothing that can divert or turn him away from this decision. It is nothing that I point out to him that his great prototype, General Jackson, did not believe in the binding force of decisions. It is nothing to him that Jefferson did not so believe. I have said that I have often heard him approve of Jackson's course in disregarding the decision of the Supreme Court pronouncing a National Bank constitutional. . . . But I cannot shake Judge Douglas' teeth loose from the Dred Scott decision. Like some obstinate animal (I mean no disrespect) that will hang on when he has once got his teeth fixed, you may cut off a leg, or you may tear away an arm, still he will not relax his hold. And so I may point out to the Judge, and say that he is bespattered all over, from the beginning of his political life to the present time with attacks upon judicial decisions—I may cut off limb after limb of his public record, and strive to wrench him from a single dictum of the court—yet I cannot divert him from it. He hangs to the last to the Dred Scott decision. These things show there is a purpose strong as death and eternity for which he adheres to this decision, and for which he will adhere to all other decisions of the same court.

ABRAHAM LINCOLN

From His Lecture on Discoveries and Inventions

"To emancipate the mind . . . is the great task which printing came into the world to perform"

Why was Lincoln the first president to publish a campaign book—especially at a time when most other candidates were still presenting themselves as humble, stump-averse servants? The answer can be found in a lecture he gave a few times after losing his Senate race to Douglas. In the lecture, Lincoln surveyed the history of human invention—and wondered why the rate of discovery seemed to be speeding up. It's a wonderful glimpse of Lincoln's curiosity and humor, but on one topic he adopted a more forceful tone: the invention of the printing press. Lincoln would not have used the metaphor of "emancipation" lightly, and it shows how deeply he believed in the power of printed texts, a belief that led him to create his bestselling campaign book.

In the world's history, certain inventions and discoveries occurred of peculiar value on account of their great efficiency in facilitating all other inventions and discoveries. Of these were the arts of writing and of printing, the discovery of America, and the introduction of patent laws. The date of the first, as already stated, is unknown, but it certainly was as much as fifteen hundred years before the Christian era; the second—printing—came in 1436, or nearly three thousand years after the first. The others followed more rapidly—the discovery of America in 1492, and the first patent laws in 1624.

Though not apposite to my present purpose, it is but justice to the fruitfulness of that period to mention two other important events—the Lutheran Reformation in 1517 and, still earlier, the invention of negroes, or of the present mode of using them, in 1434.

But to return to the consideration of printing, it is plain that it is but the other half—and in real utility, the better half—of writing, and that both together are but the assistants of speech in the communication of thoughts between man and man. When man was possessed of speech alone, the chances of invention, discovery, and improvement were very limited; but by the introduction of each of these, they were greatly multiplied. When writing was invented, any important observation likely to lead to a discovery had at least a chance of being written down and, consequently, a better chance of never being forgotten; and of being seen, and reflected upon, by a much greater number of persons; and thereby the chances of a valuable hint being caught, proportionally augmented. By this means the observation of a single individual might lead to an important invention years and even centuries after he was dead. In one word, by means of writing, the seeds of invention were more permanently preserved, and more widely sown.

And yet for the three thousand years during which printing remained undiscovered after writing was in use, it was only a small portion of the people who could write or read writing, and consequently the field of invention, though much extended, still continued very limited. At length printing came. It gave ten thousand copies of any written matter quite as cheaply as ten were given before; and consequently a thousand minds were brought into the field where there was but one before.

This was a great gain, and history shows a great change corresponding to it, in point of time. I will venture to consider it the true termination of that period called "the dark ages." Discoveries, inventions, and improvements followed rapidly and have been increasing their rapidity ever since. The effects could not come all at once. It required time to bring them out, and they are still coming. The capacity to read could not be multiplied as fast as the means of reading. Spelling books just began to go into the hands of the children; but the teachers were not very numerous, or very competent, so that it is safe to infer they did not advance so speedily as they do now-a-days. It is very probable—almost certain—that the great mass of men, at that time, were utterly unconscious; that their conditions, or their minds were capable of improvement. They not only looked upon the educated few as superior beings; but they supposed themselves to be naturally incapable of rising to equality. To emancipate the mind from this false and underestimate of itself is the great task which printing came into the world to perform. It is difficult for us, now and here, to conceive how strong this slavery of the mind was, and how long it did, of necessity, take to break its shackles and to get a habit of freedom of thought established.

It is, in this connection, a curious fact that a new country is most favorable—almost necessary—to the emancipation of thought, and the consequent advancement of civilization and the arts. The human family originated as is thought somewhere in Asia, and have worked their way principally westward. Just now, in civilization and the arts, the people of Asia are entirely behind those of Europe; those of the east of Europe behind those of the west of it; while we, here in America, think we discover and invent and improve faster than any of them. They may think this is arrogance, but they cannot deny that Russia has called on us to show her how to build steamboats and railroads, while in the older parts of Asia, they scarcely know that such things as steamboats and railroads exist. In anciently inhabited countries, the dust of ages—a real downright old-fogeyism—seems to settle upon and smother the intellects and energies of man. It is in this view that I have mentioned the discovery of America as an event greatly favoring and facilitating useful discoveries and inventions.

An Autobiographical Sketch

(1859)

"There is not much of it, for the reason,
I suppose, that there is not much of me"

While Lincoln disliked campaign biographies—he didn't trust other writers to present his life and his beliefs—he submitted to the practice when he ran for president. Lincoln even wrote a charming autobiographical sketch that journalists could crib from, though he added a cover letter reminding them of the era's humble expectations: "Of course it must not appear to have been written by myself."

My Dear Sir:

Herewith is a little sketch, as you requested. There is not much of it, for the reason, I suppose, that there is not much of me.

If anything be made out of it, I wish it to be modest, and not to go beyond the materials. If it were thought necessary to incorporate anything from any of my speeches, I suppose there would be no objection. Of course it must not appear to have been written by myself.

Yours very truly,
A. Lincoln

I was born February 12, 1809, in Hardin County, Kentucky. My parents were both born in Virginia, of undistinguished families—second families, perhaps I should say. My mother, who died in my tenth year, was of a family of the name of Hanks, some of whom now reside in Adams and others in Macon counties, Illinois. My paternal grandfather, Abraham Lincoln, emigrated from Rockingham County, Virginia, to Kentucky, about 1781 or 1782, where, a year or two later, he was killed by Indians, not in battle but by stealth when he was laboring to open a farm in the forest. His ancestors, who were Quakers, went to Virginia from Berks County, Pennsylvania. An effort to identify them with the New England family of the same name ended in nothing more definite than a similarity of Christian names in both families, such as Enoch, Levi, Mordecai, Solomon, Abraham, and the like.

My father, at the death of his father, was but six years of age, and he grew up literally without education. He removed from Kentucky to what is now Spencer County, Indiana, in my eighth year. We reached our new home about the time the state came into the Union. It was a wild region, with many bears and other wild animals still in the woods. There I grew up. There were some schools, so called, but no qualification was ever required of a teacher beyond "readin', writin', and cipherin'" to the rule of three. If a straggler supposed to understand Latin, happened to sojourn in the neighborhood, he was looked upon as a wizard. There was absolutely nothing to excite ambition for education. Of course when I came of age I did not know much. Still, somehow, I could read, write, and cipher to the rule of three; but that was all. I have not been to school since. The little advance I now have upon this store of education, I have picked up from time to time under the pressure of necessity.

I was raised to farm work, which I continued till I was twenty-two. At twenty-one I came to Illinois, and passed the first year in Macon County. Then I got to New Salem, at that time in Sangamon, now in Menard County, where I remained a year as a sort of clerk in a store. Then came the Black Hawk War, and I was elected a captain of volunteers—a success which gave me more pleasure than any I have had since. I went the campaign, was elated, ran for the legislature the same year (1832) and was beaten—the only time I ever have been beaten by the people. The next and three succeeding biennial elections, I was elected to the legislature. I was not a candidate afterwards. During this legislative period I had studied law, and removed to Springfield to practice it. In 1846, I was once elected to the lower house of Congress. Was not a candidate for reelection. From 1849 to 1854, both inclusive, practiced law more assiduously than ever before. Always a Whig in politics, and generally on the Whig electoral tickets, making active canvasses. I was losing interest in politics when the repeal of the Missouri Compromise aroused me again. What I have done since then is pretty well known.

If any personal description of me is thought desirable, it may be said I am in height six feet, four inches, nearly; lean in flesh, weighing, on an average, one hundred and eighty pounds; dark complexion, with coarse black hair, and grey eyes—no other marks or brands recollected.

Remarks at Independence Hall

(1861)

"If this country cannot be saved without giving up that principle, I was about to say I would rather be assassinated on this spot than to surrender it"

One of Lincoln's most reliable rhetorical strategies was appealing to America's history. In almost all of his major speeches—and even in his minor ones, like this one he extemporized at Philadelphia's Independence Hall, on his way to Washington to be sworn in as president—Lincoln used the past to frame or promote his present-day beliefs. It's a tendency that remains strong in American political rhetoric to this day.

I am filled with deep emotion at finding myself standing here in the place where were collected together the wisdom, the patriotism, the devotion to principle from which sprang the institutions under which we live. You have kindly suggested to me that in my hands is the task of restoring peace to our distracted country. I can say in return, sir, that all the political sentiments I entertain have been drawn, so far as I have been able to draw them, from the sentiments which originated and were given to the world from this hall in which we stand. I have never had a feeling, politically, that did not spring from the sentiments embodied in the Declaration of Independence.

I have often pondered over the dangers which were incurred by the men who assembled here and adopted that Declaration of Independence. I have pondered over the toils that were endured by the officers and soldiers of the army who achieved that Independence. I have often inquired of myself what great principle or idea it was that kept this confederacy so long together. It was not the mere matter of the separation of the colonies from the motherland, but something in that Declaration giving liberty not alone to the people of this country, but hope to the world for all future time. It was that which gave promise that in due time the weights should be lifted from the shoulders of all men, and that all should have an equal chance. This is the sentiment embodied in that Declaration of Independence.

Now, my friends, can this country be saved upon that basis? If it can, I will consider myself one of the happiest men in the world if I can help to save it. If it can't be saved upon that principle, it will be truly awful. But, if this country cannot be saved without giving up that principle, I was about to say I would rather be assassinated on this spot than to surrender it.

Now, in my view of the present aspect of affairs, there is no need of bloodshed and war. There is no necessity for it. I am not in favor of such a course, and I may say in advance, there will be no blood shed unless it be forced upon the government. The government will not use force unless force is used against it.

My friends, this is a wholly unprepared speech. I did not expect to be called upon to say a word when I came here—I supposed I was merely to do something towards raising a flag. I may, therefore, have said something indiscreet, but I have said nothing but what I am willing to live by and, in the pleasure of Almighty God, die by.

First Inaugural Address

(1861)

"The better angels of our nature"

On March 4, 1861, Lincoln delivered his first inaugural address. While seven states had already seceded from the Union, Lincoln tried to strike a cautious tone—or at least a more cautious one than his earlier drafts had managed. Lincoln revised the inaugural address carefully, piling up his reasons, legal and practical, for keeping the country together. They were not enough. In little more than a month, the first shots were fired at Fort Sumter.

In compliance with a custom as old as the government itself, I appear before you to address you briefly and to take, in your presence, the oath prescribed by the Constitution of the United States, to be taken by the president "before he enters on the execution of his office."

I do not consider it necessary, at present, for me to discuss those matters of administration about which there is no special anxiety or excitement.

Apprehension seems to exist among the people of the Southern states that by the accession of a Republican administration their property, and their peace and personal security, are to be endangered. There has never been any reasonable cause for such apprehension. Indeed, the most ample evidence to the contrary has all the while existed and been open to their inspection. It is found in nearly all the published speeches of him who now addresses you. I do but quote from one of those speeches when I declare that "I have no purpose, directly or indirectly, to interfere with the institution of slavery in the states where it exists. I believe I have no lawful right to do so, and I have no inclination to do so."

Those who nominated and elected me did so with full knowledge that I had made this and many similar declarations and had never recanted them. And more than this, they placed in the platform for my acceptance, and as a law to themselves, and to me, the clear and emphatic resolution which I now read:

Resolved: that the maintenance inviolate of the rights of the states, and especially the right of each state to order and control its own domestic institutions according to its own judgment exclusively, is essential to that balance of power on which the perfection and endurance of our political fabric depend; and we denounce the lawless invasion by armed force of the soil of any state or territory, no matter under what pretext, as among the gravest of crimes.

I now reiterate these sentiments, and in doing so, I only press upon the public attention the most conclusive evidence of which the case is susceptible, that the property, peace, and security of no section are to be in any wise endangered by the now incoming administration. I add, too, that all the protection which, consistently with the Constitution and the laws, can be given will be cheerfully given to all the states when lawfully demanded, for whatever cause—as cheerfully to one section as to another.

There is much controversy about the delivering up of fugitives from service or labor. The clause I now read is as plainly written in the Constitution as any other of its provisions:

No person held to service or labor in one state, under the laws thereof, escaping into another, shall, in consequence of any law or regulation therein, be discharged from such service or labor, but shall be delivered up on claim of the party to whom such service or labor may be due.

It is scarcely questioned that this provision was intended by those who made it for the reclaiming of what we call fugitive slaves, and the intention of the lawgiver is the law. All members of Congress swear their support to the whole Constitution—to this provision as much as to any other. To the proposition, then, that slaves whose cases come within the terms of this clause "shall be delivered up," their oaths are unanimous. Now, if they would make the effort in good temper, could they not, with nearly equal unanimity, frame and pass a law, by means of which to keep good that unanimous oath?

There is some difference of opinion whether this clause should be enforced by national or by state authority, but surely that difference is not a very material one. If the slave is to be surrendered, it can be of but little consequence to him or to others by which authority it is done. And should anyone, in any case, be content that his oath shall go unkept, on a merely unsubstantial controversy as to how it shall be kept?

Again: in any law upon this subject, ought not all the safeguards of liberty known in civilized and humane jurisprudence to be introduced, so that a free man be not, in any case, surrendered as a slave? And might it not be well, at the same time, to provide by law for the enforcement of that clause in the Constitution which guarantees that "the citizens of each state shall be entitled to all privileges and immunities of citizens in the several states?"

I take the official oath today with no mental reservations and with no purpose to construe the Constitution or laws by any hypercritical rules. And while I do not choose now to specify particular acts of Congress as proper to be enforced, I do suggest that it will be much safer for all, both in official and private stations, to conform to and abide by all those acts which stand unrepealed, than to violate any of them, trusting to find impunity in having them held to be unconstitutional.

It is seventy-two years since the first inauguration of a president under our national Constitution. During that period fifteen different and greatly distinguished citizens have, in succession, administered the executive branch of the government. They have conducted it through many perils and, generally, with great success. Yet with all this scope for precedent, I now enter upon the same task for the brief constitutional term of four years under great and peculiar difficulty. A disruption of the federal Union, heretofore only menaced, is now formidably attempted.

I hold that in contemplation of universal law, and of the Constitution, the Union of these states is perpetual. Perpetuity is implied, if not expressed, in the fundamental law of all national governments. It is safe to assert that no government proper ever had a provision in its organic law for its own termination. Continue to execute all the express provisions of our national Constitution and the Union will endure forever—it being impossible to destroy it except by some action not provided for in the instrument itself.

Again: if the United States be not a government proper but an association of states in the nature of contract merely, can it, as a contract, be peaceably unmade by less than all the parties who made it? One party to a contract may violate it—break it, so to speak—but does it not require all to lawfully rescind it?

Descending from these general principles, we find the proposition that, in legal contemplation, the Union is perpetual, confirmed by the history of the Union itself. The Union is much older than the Constitution. It was formed, in fact, by the Articles of Association in 1774. It was matured and continued by the Declaration of Independence in 1776. It was further matured and the faith of all the then thirteen states expressly plighted and engaged that it should be perpetual by the Articles of Confederation in 1778. And finally, in 1787, one of the declared objects for ordaining and establishing the Constitution, was "to form a more perfect union." But if destruction of the Union by one, or by a part only, of the states, be lawfully possible, the Union is less perfect than before the Constitution, having lost the vital element of perpetuity.

It follows from these views that no state, upon its own mere motion, can lawfully get out of the Union—that resolves and ordinances to that effect are legally void, and that acts of violence within any state or states against the authority of the United States, are insurrectionary or revolutionary, according to circumstances.

I therefore consider that, in view of the Constitution and the laws, the Union is unbroken; and, to the extent of my ability, I shall take care, as the Constitution itself expressly enjoins upon me, that the laws of the Union be faithfully executed in all the states. Doing this I deem to be only a simple duty on my part, and I shall perform it, so far as practicable, unless my rightful masters, the American people, shall withhold the requisite means or in some authoritative manner direct the contrary. I trust this will not be regarded as a menace, but only as the declared purpose of the Union that it will constitutionally defend and maintain itself.

In doing this there needs to be no bloodshed or violence, and there shall be none, unless it be forced upon the national authority. The power confided to me will be used to hold, occupy, and possess the property and places belonging to the government and to collect the duties and imposts; but beyond what may be necessary for these objects, there will be no invasion—no using of force against or among the people anywhere. Where hostility to the United States, in any interior locality, shall be so great and so universal as to prevent competent resident citizens from holding the federal offices, there will be no attempt to force obnoxious strangers among the people for that object. While the strict legal right may exist in the government to enforce the exercise of these offices, the attempt to do so would be so irritating and so nearly impracticable with all that I deem it better to forego, for the time, the uses of such offices.

The mails, unless repelled, will continue to be furnished in all parts of the Union. So far as possible, the people everywhere shall have that sense of perfect security which is most favorable to calm thought and reflection. The course here indicated will be followed unless current events and experience shall show a modification or change to be proper, and in every case and exigency, my best discretion will be exercised, according to circumstances actually existing and with a view and a hope of a peaceful solution of the national troubles and the restoration of fraternal sympathies and affections.

That there are persons in one section or another who seek to destroy the Union at all events, and are glad of any pretext to do it, I will neither affirm or deny; but if there be such, I need address no word to them. To those, however, who really love the Union, may I not speak?

Before entering upon so grave a matter as the destruction of our national fabric, with all its benefits, its memories, and its hopes, would it not be wise to ascertain precisely why we do it? Will you hazard so desperate a step, while there is any possibility that any portion of the ills you fly from have no real existence? Will you, while the certain ills you fly to are greater than all the real ones you fly from? Will you risk the commission of so fearful a mistake?

All profess to be content in the Union, if all constitutional rights can be maintained. Is it true, then, that any right, plainly written in the Constitution, has been denied? I think not. Happily the human mind is so constituted that no party can reach to the audacity of doing this. Think, if you can, of a single instance in which a plainly written provision of the Constitution has ever been denied. If, by the mere force of numbers, a majority should deprive a minority of any clearly written constitutional right, it might, in a moral point of view, justify revolution—certainly would, if such right were a vital one. But such is not our case. All the vital rights of minorities, and of individuals, are so plainly assured to them by affirmations and negations, guaranties and prohibitions in the Constitution that controversies never arise concerning them. But no organic law can ever be framed with a provision specifically applicable to every question which may occur in practical administration. No foresight can anticipate nor any document of reasonable length contain express provisions for all possible questions. Shall fugitives from labor be surrendered by national or by state authority? The Constitution does not expressly say. May Congress prohibit slavery in the territories? The Constitution does not expressly say. Must Congress protect slavery in the territories? The Constitution does not expressly say.

From questions of this class spring all our constitutional controversies, and we divide upon them into majorities and minorities. If the minority will not acquiesce, the majority must, or the government must cease. There is no other alternative; for continuing the government, is acquiescence on one side or the other. If a minority, in such case, will secede rather than acquiesce, they make a precedent which, in turn, will divide and ruin them; for a minority of their own will secede from them whenever a majority refuses to be controlled by such minority. For instance, why may not any portion of a new confederacy, a year or two hence, arbitrarily secede again, precisely as portions of the present Union now claim to secede from it? All who cherish disunion sentiments are now being educated to the exact temper of doing this. Is there such perfect identity of interests among the states to compose a new Union, as to produce harmony only, and prevent renewed secession?

Plainly, the central idea of secession is the essence of anarchy. A majority, held in restraint by constitutional checks and limitations, and always changing easily with deliberate changes of popular opinions and sentiments, is the only true sovereign of a free people. Whoever rejects it does of necessity fly to anarchy or to despotism. Unanimity is impossible; the rule of a minority, as a permanent arrangement, is wholly inadmissible; so that, rejecting the majority principle, anarchy, or despotism in some form, is all that is left.

I do not forget the position assumed by some, that constitutional questions are to be decided by the Supreme Court; nor do I deny that such decisions must be binding in any case, upon the parties to a suit, as to the object of that suit, while they are also entitled to very high respect and consideration, in all parallel cases, by all other departments of the government. And while it is obviously possible that such decision may be erroneous in any given case, still the evil effect following it, being limited to that particular case, with the chance that it may be over-ruled, and never become a precedent for other cases, can better be borne than could the evils of a different practice. At the same time the candid citizen must confess that if the policy of the government, upon vital questions, affecting the whole people, is to be irrevocably fixed by decisions of the Supreme Court, the instant they are made, in ordinary litigation between parties, in personal actions, the people will have ceased, to be their own rulers, having, to that extent, practically resigned their government, into the hands of that eminent tribunal. Nor is there, in this view, any assault upon the court, or the judges. It is a duty, from which they may not shrink, to decide cases properly brought before them; and it is no fault of theirs, if others seek to turn their decisions to political purposes.

One section of our country believes slavery is right and ought to be extended, while the other believes it is wrong and ought not to be extended. This is the only substantial dispute. The fugitive slave clause of the Constitution, and the law for the suppression of the foreign slave trade, are each as well enforced, perhaps, as any law can ever be in a community where the moral sense of the people imperfectly supports the law itself. The great body of the people abide by the dry legal obligation in both cases, and a few break over in each. This, I think, cannot be perfectly cured; and it would be worse in both cases after the separation of the sections than before. The foreign slave trade, now imperfectly suppressed, would be ultimately revived without restriction in one section, while fugitive slaves, now only partially surrendered, would not be surrendered at all by the other.

Physically speaking, we cannot separate. We cannot remove our respective sections from each other, nor build an impassable wall between them. A husband and wife may be divorced, and go out of the presence and beyond the reach of each other; but the different parts of our country cannot do this. They cannot but remain face to face, and intercourse, either amicable or hostile, must continue between them. Is it possible then to make that intercourse more advantageous, or more satisfactory, after separation than before? Can aliens make treaties easier than friends can make laws? Can treaties be more faithfully enforced between aliens than laws can among friends? Suppose you go to war, you cannot fight always; and when, after much loss on both sides, and no gain on either, you cease fighting, the identical old questions, as to terms of intercourse, are again upon you.

This country, with its institutions, belongs to the people who inhabit it. Whenever they shall grow weary of the existing government, they can exercise their constitutional right of amending it or their revolutionary right to dismember or overthrow it. I cannot be ignorant of the fact that many worthy and patriotic citizens are desirous of having the national Constitution amended. While I make no recommendation of amendments, I fully recognize the rightful authority of the people over the whole subject, to be exercised in either of the modes prescribed in the instrument itself; and I should, under existing circumstances, favor rather than oppose a fair opportunity being afforded the people to act upon it.

I will venture to add that, to me, the convention mode seems preferable, in that it allows amendments to originate with the people themselves instead of only permitting them to take, or reject, propositions originated by others, not especially chosen for the purpose, and which might not be precisely such as they would wish to either accept or refuse. I understand a proposed amendment to the Constitution—which amendment, however, I have not seen—has passed Congress, to the effect that the federal government shall never interfere with the domestic institutions of the states, including that of persons held to service. To avoid misconstruction of what I have said, I depart from my purpose not to speak of particular amendments so far as to say that, holding such a provision to now be implied constitutional law, I have no objection to its being made express and irrevocable.

The chief magistrate derives all his authority from the people, and they have conferred none upon him to fix terms for the separation of the states. The people themselves can do this also if they choose; but the executive, as such, has nothing to do with it. His duty is to administer the present government as it came to his hands and to transmit it, unimpaired by him, to his successor.

Why should there not be a patient confidence in the ultimate justice of the people? Is there any better, or equal hope, in the world? In our present differences, is either party without faith of being in the right? If the Almighty Ruler of nations, with his eternal truth and justice, be on your side of the North, or on yours of the South, that truth and that justice will surely prevail by the judgment of this great tribunal, the American people.

By the frame of the government under which we live, this same people have wisely given their public servants but little power for mischief; and have, with equal wisdom, provided for the return of that little to their own hands at very short intervals. While the people retain their virtue and vigilance, no administration by any extreme of wickedness or folly can very seriously injure the government in the short space of four years.

My countrymen, one and all, think calmly and well upon this whole subject. Nothing valuable can be lost by taking time. If there be an object to hurry any of you, in hot haste, to a step which you would never take deliberately, that object will be frustrated by taking time; but no good object can be frustrated by it. Such of you as are now dissatisfied still have the old Constitution unimpaired, and, on the sensitive point, the laws of your own framing under it; while the new administration will have no immediate power, if it would, to change either. If it were admitted that you who are dissatisfied, hold the right side in the dispute, there still is no single good reason for precipitate action. Intelligence, patriotism, Christianity, and a firm reliance on Him who has never yet forsaken this favored land, are still competent to adjust, in the best way, all our present difficulty.

In your hands, my dissatisfied fellow countrymen, and not in mine, is the momentous issue of civil war. The government will not assail you. You can have no conflict without being yourselves the aggressors. You have no oath registered in Heaven to destroy the government while I shall have the most solemn one to "preserve, protect and defend" it.

I am loath to close. We are not enemies, but friends. We must not be enemies. Though passion may have strained, it must not break our bonds of affection. The mystic chords of memory, stretching from every battlefield and patriot grave to every living heart and hearthstone, all over this broad land, will yet swell the chorus of the Union, when again touched, as surely they will be, by the better angels of our nature.

ABRAHAM LINCOLN

Emancipation Proclamation

(1863)

"I do order and declare that all persons
held as slaves . . . are, and henceforward
shall be, free"

*While Lincoln and Jackson were quite different—in temperament, in literary
style, in attitudes toward slavery—they shared one thing in common: both held
sweeping views of executive power. As the Civil War exploded into a massive
and bloody conflict, Lincoln frequently acted alone so that he could act quickly.
The Emancipation Proclamation is a good example of his willingness to push the
presidency's limits. In the preliminary document of September 1862, and again
in the final proclamation of January 1863, Lincoln leaned not on Congress or
the courts but on his wartime powers as president.*

Whereas, on the 22nd day of September, in the year of our Lord 1862,
a proclamation was issued by the president of the United States,
containing, among other things, the following, to wit:

"That on the 1st day of January, in the year of our Lord 1863, all
persons held as slaves within any state or designated part of a state, the
people whereof shall then be in rebellion against the United States, shall
be then, thenceforward, and forever free; and the executive government
of the United States, including the military and naval authority thereof,
will recognize and maintain the freedom of such persons, and will do no

act or acts to repress such persons, or any of them, in any efforts they may make for their actual freedom.

"That the executive will, on the 1st day of January aforesaid, by proclamation, designate the states and parts of states, if any, in which the people thereof, respectively, shall then be in rebellion against the United States; and the fact that any state, or the people thereof, shall on that day be, in good faith, represented in the Congress of the United States by members chosen thereto at elections wherein a majority of the qualified voters of such state shall have participated, shall, in the absence of strong countervailing testimony, be deemed conclusive evidence that such State, and the people thereof, are not then in rebellion against the United States."

Now, therefore I, Abraham Lincoln, president of the United States, by virtue of the power in me vested as commander-in-chief of the Army and Navy of the United States in time of actual armed rebellion against authority and government of the United States, and as a fit and necessary war measure for suppressing said rebellion, do, on this 1st day of January, in the year of our Lord 1863, and in accordance with my purpose so to do publicly proclaimed for the full period of one hundred days, from the day first above mentioned, order and designate as the states and parts of states wherein the people thereof respectively, are this day in rebellion against the United States, the following, to wit:

Arkansas, Texas, Louisiana (except the Parishes of St. Bernard, Plaquemines, Jefferson, St. Johns, St. Charles, St. James, Ascension, Assumption, Terrebonne, Lafourche, St. Mary, St. Martin, and Orleans, including the City of New Orleans), Mississippi, Alabama, Florida, Georgia, South Carolina, North Carolina, and Virginia (except the forty-eight counties designated as West Virginia, and also the counties of Berkley, Accomac, Northampton, Elizabeth City, York, Princess Ann, and Norfolk, including the cities of Norfolk and Portsmouth), and which excepted parts are, for the present, left precisely as if this proclamation were not issued.

And by virtue of the power, and for the purpose aforesaid, I do order and declare that all persons held as slaves within said designated states, and parts of states, are, and henceforward shall be free; and that the executive government of the United States, including the military and naval authorities thereof, will recognize and maintain the freedom of said persons.

And I hereby enjoin upon the people so declared to be free to abstain from all violence, unless in necessary self-defense; and I recommend to them that, in all cases when allowed, they labor faithfully for reasonable wages.

And I further declare and make known that such persons of suitable condition will be received into the armed service of the United States to garrison forts, positions, stations, and other places, and to man vessels of all sorts in said service.

And upon this act, sincerely believed to be an act of justice, warranted by the Constitution upon military necessity, I invoke the considerate judgment of mankind, and the gracious favor of Almighty God.

ABRAHAM LINCOLN

Gettysburg Address

(1863)

"Four score and seven years ago"

On November 19, 1863, Lincoln gave this short speech at the dedication of a soldiers' cemetery in Gettysburg. The text, which would become his most famous, echoes with American history. Post–Emancipation Proclamation, it also puts slavery (and not merely preserving the Union) at the center of the soldiers' sacrifice.

Four score and seven years ago our fathers brought forth on this continent a new nation, conceived in liberty and dedicated to the proposition that all men are created equal.

Now we are engaged in a great civil war, testing whether that nation, or any nation so conceived and so dedicated, can long endure. We are met on a great battlefield of that war. We have come to dedicate a portion of that field as a final resting place for those who here gave their lives that that nation might live. It is altogether fitting and proper that we should do this.

But, in a larger sense, we cannot dedicate—we cannot consecrate—we cannot hallow—this ground. The brave men, living and dead, who struggled here have consecrated it far above our poor power to add or detract. The world will little note, nor long remember what we say here, but it can never forget what they did here.

It is for us the living, rather, to be dedicated here to the unfinished work which they who fought here have thus far so nobly advanced. It is rather for us to be here dedicated to the great task remaining before us—that from these honored dead we take increased devotion to that cause for which they gave the last full measure of devotion—that we here highly resolve that these dead shall not have died in vain—that this nation, under God, shall have a new birth of freedom—and that government of the people, by the people, for the people shall not perish from the earth.

ABRAHAM LINCOLN

Second Inaugural Address

(1865)

"With malice toward none"

Lincoln's second inaugural address, delivered on March 4, 1865, did not list recent victories or celebrate the war's approaching end. Instead, Lincoln made one more attempt at unity, arguing that white Americans in the North and South had both contributed to the sin of slavery—and that both had suffered through a conflict longer and bloodier than anyone could have imagined. "War came," Lincoln said. Soon, he hoped, healing would come too.

At this second appearing to take the oath of the presidential office, there is less occasion for an extended address than there was at the first. Then a statement, somewhat in detail, of a course to be pursued, seemed fitting and proper. Now, at the expiration of four years, during which public declarations have been constantly called forth on every point and phase of the great contest which still absorbs the attention and engrosses the energies of the nation, little that is new could be presented. The progress of our arms, upon which all else chiefly depends, is as well known to the public as to myself; and it is, I trust, reasonably satisfactory and encouraging to all. With high hope for the future, no prediction in regard to it is ventured.

On the occasion corresponding to this four years ago, all thoughts were anxiously directed to an impending civil war. All dreaded it—all sought to avert it. While the inaugural address was being delivered from this place, devoted altogether to saving the Union without war, insurgent agents were in the city seeking to destroy it without war—seeking to dissolve the Union and divide effects by negotiation. Both parties deprecated war; but one of them would make war rather than let the nation survive, and the other would accept war rather than let it perish. And the war came.

One-eighth of the whole population were colored slaves, not distributed generally over the Union but localized in the Southern part of it. These slaves constituted a peculiar and powerful interest. All knew that this interest was, somehow, the cause of the war. To strengthen, perpetuate, and extend this interest was the object for which the insurgents would rend the Union, even by war, while the government claimed no right to do more than to restrict the territorial enlargement of it. Neither party expected for the war, the magnitude, or the duration, which it has already attained. Neither anticipated that the cause of the conflict might cease with or even before the conflict itself should cease. Each looked for an easier triumph and a result less fundamental and astounding. Both read the same Bible, and pray to the same God; and each invokes His aid against the other.

It may seem strange that any men should dare to ask a just God's assistance in wringing their bread from the sweat of other men's faces; but let us judge not that we be not judged. The prayers of both could not be answered; that of neither has been answered fully. The Almighty has His own purposes. "Woe unto the world because of offences! for it must needs be that offences come; but woe to that man by whom the offence cometh!" If we shall suppose that American slavery is one of those offences which, in the providence of God, must needs come, but which, having continued through His appointed time, He now wills to remove, and that He gives to both North and South this terrible war as the woe due to those by whom the offence came, shall we discern therein any departure from those divine attributes which the believers in a Living God always ascribe to Him?

Fondly do we hope—fervently do we pray—that this mighty scourge of war may speedily pass away. Yet, if God wills that it continue, until all the wealth piled by the bondsman's two hundred and fifty years of unrequited toil shall be sunk, and until every drop of blood drawn with the lash shall be paid by another drawn with the sword, as was said three thousand years ago, so still it must be said, "The judgments of the Lord are true and righteous altogether."

With malice toward none, with charity for all, with firmness in the right as God gives us to see the right, let us strive on to finish the work we are in, to bind up the nation's wounds, to care for him who shall have borne the battle, and for his widow, and his orphan—to do all which may achieve and cherish a just and a lasting peace among ourselves and with all nations.

ULYSSES S. GRANT

From *Personal Memoirs*

"The sight was more unendurable than encountering the enemy's fire, and I returned to my tree in the rain"

The Civil War changed everything about American life, including the willingness of public figures to tell their stories during their lifetime. Instead of waiting until after their deaths, politicians like James Buchanan and generals like William T. Sherman published their autobiographies quickly—and found audiences eager to read, learn, and debate. The biggest Civil War memoir, and also the best, came from Ulysses S. Grant, who wrote an elegant and personal book while battling a fatal form of cancer. This excerpt covers Grant's 1862 victory at Shiloh, which was one of the war's most brutal battles, with the fighting taking place on Sunday, April 6, and Monday, April 7.

Some two or three miles from Pittsburg Landing was a log meeting-house called Shiloh. It stood on the ridge which divides the waters of Snake and Lick creeks, the former emptying into the Tennessee just north of Pittsburg Landing, and the latter south. This point was the key to our position and was held by Sherman. His division was at that time wholly raw, no part of it ever having been in an engagement; but I thought this deficiency was more than made up by the superiority of the commander. McClernand was on Sherman's left, with troops that had been engaged at Forts Henry and Donelson and were therefore veterans so far as western troops had become such at that stage of the war. Next to McClernand came Prentiss with a raw division, and on the extreme left, Stuart with one brigade of Sherman's division. Hurlbut was in rear of Prentiss, massed and in reserve at the time of the onset. The division of General C. F. Smith was on the right, also in reserve. General Smith was still sick in bed at Savannah, but within hearing of our guns. His services would no doubt have been of inestimable value had his health permitted his presence. The command of his division devolved upon Brigadier General W. H. L. Wallace, a most estimable and able officer; a veteran too, for he had served a year in the Mexican War and had been with his command at Henry and Donelson. Wallace was mortally wounded in the first day's engagement, and with the change of commanders thus necessarily effected in the heat of battle, the efficiency of his division was much weakened.

The position of our troops made a continuous line from Lick Creek on the left to Owl Creek, a branch of Snake Creek, on the right, facing nearly south and possibly a little west. The water in all these streams was very high at the time and contributed to protect our flanks. The enemy was compelled, therefore, to attack directly in front. This he did with great vigor, inflicting heavy losses on the National side, but suffering much heavier on his own.

The Confederate assaults were made with such a disregard of losses on their own side that our line of tents soon fell into their hands. The ground on which the battle was fought was undulating, heavily timbered with scattered clearings, the woods giving some protection to the troops on both sides. There was also considerable underbrush. A number of attempts were made by the enemy to turn our right flank, where Sherman was posted, but every effort was repulsed with heavy loss. But the front attack was kept up so vigorously that, to prevent the success of these attempts to get on our flanks, the National troops were compelled, several times, to take positions to the rear nearer Pittsburg Landing. When the firing ceased at night the National line was all of a mile in rear of the position it had occupied in the morning.

In one of the backward moves, on the 6th, the division commanded by General Prentiss did not fall back with the others. This left his flanks exposed and enabled the enemy to capture him with about 2,200 of his officers and men. General Badeau gives four o'clock of the 6th as about the time this capture took place. He may be right as to the time, but my recollection is that the hour was later. General Prentiss himself gave the hour as half-past five. I was with him, as I was with each of the division commanders that day, several times, and my recollection is that the last time I was with him was about half-past four, when his division was standing up firmly and the General was as cool as if expecting victory. But no matter whether it was four or later, the story that he and his command were surprised and captured in their camps is without any foundation whatever. If it had been true, as currently reported at the time and yet believed by thousands of people, that Prentiss and his division had been captured in their beds, there would not have been an all-day struggle, with the loss of thousands killed and wounded on the Confederate side.

With the single exception of a few minutes after the capture of Prentiss, a continuous and unbroken line was maintained all day from Snake Creek or its tributaries on the right to Lick Creek or the Tennessee on the left above Pittsburg. There was no hour during the day when there was not heavy firing and generally hard fighting at some point on the line, but seldom at all points at the same time. It was a case of Southern dash against Northern pluck and endurance. Three of the five divisions engaged on Sunday were entirely raw, and many of the men had only received their arms on the way from their states to the field. Many of them had arrived but a day or two before and were hardly able to load their muskets according to the manual. Their officers were equally ignorant of their duties. Under these circumstances it is not astonishing that many of the regiments broke at the first fire. In two cases, as I now remember, colonels led their regiments from the field on first hearing the whistle of the enemy's bullets. In these cases the colonels were constitutional cowards, unfit for any military position; but not so the officers and men led out of danger by them. Better troops never went upon a battlefield than many of these officers and men afterwards proved themselves to be, who fled panic-stricken at the first whistle of bullets and shell at Shiloh.

During the whole of Sunday, I was continuously engaged in passing from one part of the field to another, giving directions to division commanders. In thus moving along the line, however, I never deemed it important to stay long with Sherman. Although his troops were then under fire for the first time, their commander, by his constant presence with them, inspired a confidence in officers and men that enabled them to render services on that bloody battlefield worthy of the best of veterans. McClernand was next to Sherman, and the hardest fighting was in front of these two divisions. McClernand told me on that day, the 6th, that he profited much by having so able a commander supporting him. A casualty to Sherman that would have taken him from the field that day would have been a sad one for the troops engaged at Shiloh. And how near we came to this! On the 6th Sherman was shot twice, once in the hand, once in the shoulder, the ball cutting his coat and making a slight wound, and a third ball passed through his hat. In addition to this he had several horses shot during the day.

The nature of this battle was such that cavalry could not be used in front; I therefore formed ours into line in rear, to stop stragglers, of whom there were many. When there would be enough of them to make a show, and after they had recovered from their fright, they would be sent to reinforce some part of the line which needed support, without regard to their companies, regiments, or brigades.

On one occasion during the day I rode back as far as the river and met General Buell, who had just arrived; I do not remember the hour, but at that time there probably were as many as four or five thousand stragglers lying under cover of the river bluff, panic-stricken, most of whom would have been shot where they lay, without resistance, before they would have taken muskets and marched to the front to protect themselves. This meeting between General Buell and myself was on the dispatch-boat used to run between the landing and Savannah. It was brief, and related specially to his getting his troops over the river. As we left the boat together, Buell's attention was attracted by the men lying under cover of the river bank. I saw him berating them and trying to shame them into joining their regiments. He even threatened them with shells from the gunboats nearby. But it was all to no effect. Most of these men afterward proved themselves as gallant as any of those who saved the battle from which they had deserted. I have no doubt that this sight impressed General Buell with the idea that a line of retreat would be a good thing just then. If he had come in by the front instead of through the stragglers in the rear, he would have thought and felt differently. Could he have come through the Confederate rear, he would have witnessed there a scene similar to that at our own. The distant rear of an army engaged in battle is not the best place from which to judge correctly what is going on in front. Later in the war, while occupying the country between the Tennessee and the Mississippi, I learned that the panic in the Confederate lines had not differed much from that within our own. Some of the country people estimated the stragglers from Johnston's army as high as 20,000. Of course this was an exaggeration.

The situation at the close of Sunday was as follows: along the top of the bluff, just south of the log-house which stood at Pittsburg Landing, Colonel J. D. Webster of my staff had arranged twenty or more pieces of artillery facing south or up the river. This line of artillery was on the crest of a hill overlooking a deep ravine opening into the Tennessee. Hurlbut with his division intact was on the right of this artillery, extending west and possibly a little north. McClernand came next in the general line, looking more to the west. His division was complete in its organization and ready for any duty. Sherman came next, his right extending to Snake Creek. His command, like the other two, was complete in its organization and ready, like its chief, for any service it might be called upon to render. All three divisions were, as a matter of course, more or less shattered and depleted in numbers from the terrible battle of the day. The division of W. H. L. Wallace, as much from the disorder arising from changes of division and brigade commanders under heavy fire as from any other cause, had lost its organization and did not occupy a place in the line as a division. Prentiss's command was gone as a division, many of its members having been killed, wounded or captured, but it had rendered valiant services before its final dispersal, and had contributed a good share to the defense of Shiloh.

The right of my line rested near the bank of Snake Creek, a short distance above the bridge which had been built by the troops for the purpose of connecting Crump's Landing and Pittsburg Landing. Sherman had posted some troops in a log-house and outbuildings which overlooked both the bridge over which Wallace was expected and the creek above that point. In this last position Sherman was frequently attacked before night, but held the point until he voluntarily abandoned it to advance in order to make room for Lew Wallace, who came up after dark.

There was, as I have said, a deep ravine in front of our left. The Tennessee River was very high, and there was water to a considerable depth in the ravine. Here the enemy made a last desperate effort to turn our flank, but was repelled. The gunboats *Tyler* and *Lexington*, Gwin and Shirk commanding, with the artillery under Webster, aided the army and effectually checked their further progress. Before any of Buell's troops had reached the west bank of the Tennessee, firing had almost entirely ceased; anything like an attempt on the part of the enemy to advance had absolutely ceased. There was some artillery firing from an unseen enemy, some of his shells passing beyond us; but I do not remember that there was the whistle of a single musket-ball heard. As his troops arrived in the dusk General Buell marched several of his regiments partway down the face of the hill where they fired briskly for some minutes, but I do not think a single man engaged in this firing received an injury. The attack had spent its force.

General Lew Wallace, with 5,000 effective men, arrived after firing had ceased for the day and was placed on the right. Thus night came, Wallace came, and the advance of Nelson's division came; but none—unless night—in time to be of material service to the gallant men who saved Shiloh on that first day against large odds. Buell's loss on the 6th of April was two men killed and one wounded, all members of the 36th Indiana infantry. The Army of the Tennessee lost on that day at least 7,000 men. The presence of two or three regiments of Buell's army on the west bank before firing ceased had not the slightest effect in preventing the capture of Pittsburg Landing.

So confident was I before firing had ceased on the 6th that the next day would bring victory to our arms if we could only take the initiative, that I visited each division commander in person before any reinforcements had reached the field. I directed them to throw out heavy lines of skirmishers in the morning as soon as they could see and push them forward until they found the enemy, following with their entire divisions in supporting distance, and to engage the enemy as soon as found. To Sherman I told the story of the assault at Fort Donelson and said that the same tactics would win at Shiloh. Victory was assured when Wallace arrived, even if there had been no other support. I was glad, however, to see the reinforcements of Buell and credit them with doing all there was for them to do. During the night of the 6th the remainder of Nelson's division, Buell's army, crossed the river and were ready to advance in the morning, forming the left wing. Two other divisions, Crittenden's and McCook's, came up the river from Savannah in the transports and were on the west bank early on the 7th. Buell commanded them in person. My command was thus nearly doubled in numbers and efficiency.

During the night rain fell in torrents and our troops were exposed to the storm without shelter. I made my headquarters under a tree a few hundred yards back from the river bank. My ankle was so much swollen from the fall of my horse the Friday night preceding, and the bruise was so painful, that I could get no rest. The drenching rain would have precluded the possibility of sleep without this additional cause. Some time after midnight, growing restive under the storm and the continuous pain, I moved back to the log-house under the bank. This had been taken as a hospital, and all night wounded men were being brought in, their wounds dressed, a leg or an arm amputated as the case might require, and everything being done to save life or alleviate suffering. The sight was more unendurable than encountering the enemy's fire, and I returned to my tree in the rain.

The advance on the morning of the 7th developed the enemy in the camps occupied by our troops before the battle began, more than a mile back from the most advanced position of the Confederates on the day before. It is known now that they had not yet learned of the arrival of Buell's command. Possibly they fell back so far to get the shelter of our tents during the rain, and also to get away from the shells that were dropped upon them by the gunboats every fifteen minutes during the night.

The position of the Union troops on the morning of the 7th was as follows: General Lew Wallace on the right; Sherman on his left; then McClernand and then Hurlbut. Nelson, of Buell's army, was on our extreme left, next to the river. Crittenden was next in line after Nelson and on his right, McCook followed and formed the extreme right of Buell's command. My old command thus formed the right wing, while the troops directly under Buell constituted the left wing of the army. These relative positions were retained during the entire day, or until the enemy was driven from the field.

In a very short time the battle became general all along the line. This day everything was favorable to the Union side. We had now become the attacking party. The enemy was driven back all day, as we had been the day before, until finally he beat a precipitate retreat. The last point held by him was near the road leading from the landing to Corinth, on the left of Sherman and right of McClernand. About three o'clock, being near that point and seeing that the enemy was giving way everywhere else, I gathered up a couple of regiments, or parts of regiments, from troops nearby, formed them in line of battle and marched them forward, going in front myself to prevent premature or long-range firing. At this point there was a clearing between us and the enemy favorable for charging, although exposed. I knew the enemy were ready to break and only wanted a little encouragement from us to go quickly and join their friends who had started earlier. After marching to within musket-range I stopped and let the troops pass. The command, *Charge*, was given and was executed with loud cheers and with a run, when the last of the enemy broke.

During this second day of the battle I had been moving from right to left and back, to see for myself the progress made. In the early part of the afternoon, while riding with Colonel McPherson and Major Hawkins, then my chief commissary, we got beyond the left of our troops. We were moving along the northern edge of a clearing, very leisurely, toward the river above the landing. There did not appear to be an enemy to our right, until suddenly a battery with musketry opened upon us from the edge of the woods on the other side of the clearing. The shells and balls whistled about our ears very fast for about a minute. I do not think it took us longer than that to get out of range and out of sight. In the sudden start we made, Major Hawkins lost his hat. He did not stop to pick it up. When we arrived at a perfectly safe position we halted to take an account of damages.

McPherson's horse was panting as if ready to drop. On examination it was found that a ball had struck him forward of the flank just back of the saddle, and had gone entirely through. In a few minutes the poor beast dropped dead; he had given no sign of injury until we came to a stop. A ball had struck the metal scabbard of my sword, just below the hilt, and broken it nearly off; before the battle was over it had broken off entirely. There were three of us: one had lost a horse, killed; one a hat; and one a sword-scabbard. All were thankful that it was no worse.

After the rain of the night before and the frequent and heavy rains for some days previous, the roads were almost impassable. The enemy carrying his artillery and supply trains over them in his retreat, made them still worse for troops following. I wanted to pursue, but had not the heart to order the men who had fought desperately for two days, lying in the mud and rain whenever not fighting, and I did not feel disposed to positively order Buell, or any part of his command, to pursue. Although the senior in rank at the time I had been so only a few weeks. Buell was, and had been for some time past, a department commander, while I commanded only a district. I did not meet Buell in person until too late to get troops ready and pursue with effect; but had I seen him at the moment of the last charge I should have at least requested him to follow.

I rode forward several miles the day after the battle, and found that the enemy had dropped much, if not all, of their provisions, some ammunition and the extra wheels of their caissons, lightening their loads to enable them to get off their guns. About five miles out we found their field hospital abandoned. An immediate pursuit must have resulted in the capture of a considerable number of prisoners and probably some guns.

Shiloh was the severest battle fought at the west during the war, and but few in the east equaled it for hard, determined fighting. I saw an open field, in our possession on the second day, over which the Confederates had made repeated charges the day before, so covered with dead that it would have been possible to walk across the clearing, in any direction, stepping on dead bodies, without a foot touching the ground.

Grant adored novels. (At West Point, he read so many that he got demerits for lingering in the library.) This love of fiction shaped Personal Memoirs— *especially Grant's novelistic portraits of other notable figures, including Robert E. Lee, Sherman, and Lincoln. The following excerpts find Grant meeting Lincoln in the spring of 1864 and again in early 1865, along with the general's reaction to Lincoln's assassination on April 14, 1865.*

On the 23rd of March [1864], I was back in Washington, and on the 26th took up my headquarters at Culpeper Courthouse, a few miles south of the headquarters of the Army of the Potomac.

Although hailing from Illinois myself, the state of the president, I never met Mr. Lincoln until called to the capital to receive my commission as lieutenant general. I knew him, however, very well and favorably from the accounts given by officers under me at the west who had known him all their lives. I had also read the remarkable series of debates between Lincoln and Douglas a few years before, when they were rival candidates for the United States Senate. I was then a resident of Missouri and by no means a "Lincoln man" in that contest, but I recognized then his great ability.

In my first interview with Mr. Lincoln alone he stated to me that he had never professed to be a military man or to know how campaigns should be conducted and never wanted to interfere in them; but that procrastination on the part of commanders, and the pressure from the people at the North and Congress, which was always with him, forced him into issuing his series of "Military Orders"—one, two, three, etc. He did not know but they were all wrong and did know that some of them were. All he wanted or had ever wanted was someone who would take the responsibility and act and call on him for all the assistance needed, pledging himself to use all the power of the government in rendering such assistance. Assuring him that I would do the best I could with the means at hand and avoid as far as possible annoying him or the War Department, our first interview ended.

After a few days, about the 2nd of February [1865], I received a dispatch from Washington, directing me to send the [peace] commissioners to Hampton Roads to meet the president and a member of the cabinet. Mr. Lincoln met them there and had an interview of short duration.

It was not a great while after they met that the president visited me at City Point. He spoke of his having met the commissioners, and said he had told them that there would be no use in entering into any negotiations unless they would recognize: first, that the Union as a whole must be forever preserved; and second, that slavery must be abolished. If they were willing to concede these two points, then he was ready to enter into negotiations and was almost willing to hand them a blank sheet of paper with his signature attached for them to fill in the terms upon which they were willing to live with us in the Union and be one people. He always showed a generous and kindly spirit toward the Southern people, and I never heard him abuse an enemy. Some of the cruel things said about President Lincoln, particularly in the North, used to pierce him to the heart; but never in my presence did he evince a revengeful disposition and I saw a great deal of him at City Point, for he seemed glad to get away from the cares and anxieties of the capital.

Right here I might relate an anecdote of Mr. Lincoln. It was on the occasion of his visit to me just after he had talked with the peace commissioners at Hampton Roads. After a little conversation, he asked me if I had seen that overcoat of Stephens's.

I replied that I had.

"Well," said he, "did you see him take it off?"

I said yes.

"Well," said he, "didn't you think it was the biggest shuck and the littlest ear that ever you did see?"

Long afterwards I told this story to the Confederate General J. B. Gordon, at the time a member of the Senate. He repeated it to Stephens, and, as I heard afterwards, Stephens laughed immoderately at the simile of Mr. Lincoln.

It would be impossible for me to describe the feeling that overcame me at the news of . . . the assassination of the president. I knew his goodness of heart, his generosity, his yielding disposition, his desire to have everybody happy, and above all his desire to see all the people of the United States enter again upon the full privileges of citizenship with equality among all. I knew also the feeling that Mr. Johnson had expressed in speeches and conversation against the Southern people, and I feared that his course towards them would be such as to repel and make them unwilling citizens, and if they became such they would remain so for a long while. I felt that reconstruction had been set back, no telling how far.

I immediately arranged for getting a train to take me back to Washington City, but Mrs. Grant was with me; it was after midnight and Burlington was but an hour away. Finding that I could accompany her to our house and return about as soon as they would be ready to take me from the Philadelphia station, I went up with her and returned immediately by the same special train. The joy that I had witnessed among the people in the street and in public places in Washington when I left there had been turned to grief; the city was in reality a city of mourning. I have stated what I believed then the effect of this would be, and my judgment now is that I was right. I believe the South would have been saved from very much of the hardness of feeling that was engendered by Mr. Johnson's course towards them during the first few months of his administration. Be this as it may, Mr. Lincoln's assassination was particularly unfortunate for the entire nation.

Mr. Johnson's course towards the South did engender bitterness of feeling. His denunciations of treason and his ever-ready remark, "Treason is a crime and must be made odious," was repeated to all those men of the South who came to him to get some assurances of safety so that they might go to work at something with the feeling that what they obtained would be secure to them. He uttered his denunciations with great vehemence, and as they were accompanied with no assurances of safety, many Southerners were driven to a point almost beyond endurance.

The president of the United States is in a large degree, or ought to be, a representative of the feeling, wishes, and judgment of those over whom he presides, and the Southerners who read the denunciations of themselves and their people must have come to the conclusion that he uttered the sentiments of the Northern people; whereas, as a matter of fact, but for the assassination of Mr. Lincoln, I believe the great majority of the Northern people, and the soldiers unanimously, would have been in favor of a speedy reconstruction on terms that would be the least humiliating to the people who had rebelled against their government. They believed, I have no doubt, as I did, that besides being the mildest, it was also the wisest policy.

ULYSSES S. GRANT

Statement on the Ratification of the Fifteenth Amendment

(1870)

"A measure of grander importance than any other one act"

As president, Grant worked to achieve Lincoln's vision of a unified North and South. He also worked to secure more rights for newly freed African Americans, including the right for Black men to vote. In his first inaugural address, Grant called for a constitutional amendment guaranteeing that right, and the Fifteenth Amendment was ratified in 1870, though it was hampered in practice by poll taxes and other anti-voting efforts. Still, Grant commemorated its ratification with a short message—and, like Lincoln, he knew to bolster his prose with a reference to a revered historical figure.

It is unusual to notify the two houses of Congress by message of the promulgation, by proclamation of the secretary of state, of the ratification of a constitutional amendment. In view, however, of the vast importance of the Fifteenth Amendment to the Constitution, this day declared a part of that revered instrument, I deem a departure from the usual custom justifiable. A measure which makes at once four million people voters who were heretofore declared by the highest tribunal in the land not citizens of the United States, nor eligible to become so, with the assertion that "at the time of the Declaration of Independence the opinion was fixed and universal in the civilized portion of the white race, regarded as an axiom in morals as well as in politics, that black men had no rights which the white man was bound to respect," is indeed a measure of grander importance than any other one act of the kind from the foundation of our free government to the present day.

Institutions like ours, in which all power is derived directly from the people, must depend mainly upon their intelligence, patriotism, and industry. I call the attention, therefore, of the newly enfranchised race to the importance of their striving in every honorable manner to make themselves worthy of their new privilege. To the race more favored heretofore by our laws I would say, withhold no legal privilege of advancement to the new citizen. The framers of our Constitution firmly believed that a republican government could not endure without intelligence and education generally diffused among the people. The Father of his country, in his Farewell Address, uses this language:

Promote, then, as an object of primary importance, institutions for the general diffusion of knowledge. In proportion as the structure of a government gives force to public opinion, it is essential that public opinion should be enlightened.

In his first annual message to Congress the same views are forcibly presented, and are again urged in his eighth message.

I repeat that the adoption of the Fifteenth Amendment to the Constitution completes the greatest civil change and constitutes the most important event that has occurred since the nation came into life. The change will be beneficial in proportion to the heed that is given to the urgent recommendations of Washington. If these recommendations were important then, with a population of but a few millions, how much more important now, with a population of forty million, and increasing in a rapid ratio. I would therefore call upon Congress to take all the means within their constitutional powers to promote and encourage popular education throughout the country and upon the people everywhere to see to it that all who possess and exercise political rights shall have the opportunity to acquire the knowledge which will make their share in the government a blessing and not a danger. By such means only can the benefits contemplated by this amendment to the Constitution be secured.

From His "Notes for the Benefit of Biographers"

"Pound the damn fool to death, Jim!"

James Garfield was just a congressman when he decided to dictate his auto-biography to an Ohio author. Still, Garfield knew the manuscript, a key part of which is excerpted here, would be a valuable asset. He'd grown up a bookish child, someone who'd read so much about life at sea that he decided to pursue that life himself, landing a job on a canal boat until, one day, he found him-self in a harrowing fight. When Garfield ran for president, in 1880, he was swarmed by the usual array of campaign biographers, and almost all of them told or retold the tale of this fight. In his manuscript, Garfield had given them the story. Now his biographers could supply the lesson—what the fight revealed about their candidate's courage and also his restraint. The biographies kept coming even after Garfield won the White House. One of the last was written by Horatio Alger, but that lateness provided the perfect title: From Canal Boy to President.

I thought there should be some apprenticeship secured before coming upon a real vessel. In a few hours, I had decided what the apprenticeship should be. I would head out, if possible, upon a canal boat.

Going directly to the canal, I asked if they wanted a hand. No place was vacant except that of driver. This was as I would have it. As canaling was at the bottom of sailing, so driving was at the bottom of canaling. I took the job.

Well, that first trip upon the canal boat was one of many adventures. I could not swim and knew almost nothing about the water except what I had read. The consequence was I fell into the canal just fourteen times and had fourteen almost miraculous escapes from drowning. But not with-standing all, I made justly fair progress in the business and at the close of my first round trip I was promoted to bowsman.

On my second trip, at Beaver Point, Pennsylvania, I had my first fight. We were going along smoothly enough, and I was holding the setting pole carelessly against my shoulder. About twenty feet from me stood a great stout boat hand, whom I knew not by any other name than Dave. Dave and I had been especially good friends but he had a quick and ungovernable temper.

Presently, the boat was given a sudden jerk and the sitting pole slipped from my hold and flew with considerable violence in the direction where Dave was standing.

"Look out, Dave!" I called out.

But it was too late and the pole traveled too fast until Dave was struck just amidships. It hurt him somewhat, and he was moreover stung to madness by what he deemed my carelessness.

"I am sorry, Dave—did it hurt you much?" I asked.

But he paid no attention to my inquiry. Rising, he ran towards me muttering horrible oaths, which it had not been my fortune to know. He said something about thrashing the careless rascal, and this brought up my blood in a minute. I knew I had not been careless. I knew that I had not intended to hurt him, and that he had misconstrued the affair angered me. I was a boy of sixteen, to be sure, and he was a man of thirty-five. But as I remember, not a feeling of fear came into my mind. I determined not to be the whipped but, if possible, to whip.

As Dave rushed towards me, with his head down, muttering his oaths, he reminded me of nothing so much as a mad bull, and I determined to treat him accordingly. Remaining perfectly still until he was almost before me, I suddenly jumped aside and as he passed I dealt him a terrible blow just back of and under the left ear.

With great force he fell with his head between two beams in the bot-tom of the boat.

In an instant I was upon him with one hand at his throat and the other clenched, uplifted to strike.

"Pound the damn fool to death, Jim!" called out the voice of the captain. "If he has no more sense not to get mad at an accident, he had ought to die. Why don't you strike? Damn me if I will interfere."

But I didn't strike. I couldn't, some way. It seemed to me that it would be wrong, and besides my anger had subsided. When I saw Dave wholly in my power, I remembered our friendship, too, and so released my hold.

"Sorry, Jim, I was such a fool as to get mad," said Dave, rising. "But that cussed old pole did hurt my shoulder. So give me your hand—good friends, now?"

And he walked off to his post, rubbing his side.

From His State of the Union

(1881)

"There are very many characteristics which go to make a model civil servant"

After Garfield was assassinated, in 1881, Chester Arthur became president. Garfield's killer had complained about getting skipped for a patronage job, and that was one reason legislators began considering reforms to that system. In his first State of the Union, Arthur endorsed the idea. While his written text lacked Lincolnian vigor, Arthur did raise tentative concerns about basing too much of the hiring and promoting on "competitive" exams. Congress finally passed a major reform bill on this issue in 1883.

The assertion that "original appointments should be based upon ascertained fitness" is not open to dispute. But the question how in practice such fitness can be most effectually ascertained is one which has for years excited interest and discussion. The measure which, with slight variations in its details, has lately been urged upon the attention of Congress and the executive has as its principal feature the scheme of competitive examination. Save for certain exceptions, which need not here be specified, this plan would allow admission to the service only in its lowest grade and would accordingly demand that all vacancies in higher positions should be filled by promotion alone. . . .

To a statute which should incorporate all its essential features I should feel bound to give my approval; but whether it would be for the best interests of the public to fix upon an expedient for immediate and extensive application which embraces certain features of the English system, but excludes or ignores others of equal importance, may be seriously doubted, even by those who are impressed, as I am myself, with the grave importance of correcting the evils which inhere in the present methods of appointment. . . .

There are very many characteristics which go to make a model civil servant. Prominent among them are probity, industry, good sense, good habits, good temper, patience, order, courtesy, tact, self-reliance, manly deference to superior officers, and manly consideration for inferiors. The absence of these traits is not supplied by wide knowledge of books, or by promptitude in answering questions, or by any other quality likely to be brought to light by competitive examination.

To make success in such a contest, therefore, an indispensable condition of public employment would very likely result in the practical exclusion of the older applicants, even though they might possess qualifications far superior to their younger and more brilliant competitors.

These suggestions must not be regarded as evincing any spirit of opposition to the competitive plan, which has been to some extent successfully employed already and which may hereafter vindicate the claim of its most earnest supporters, but it ought to be seriously considered whether the application of the same educational standard to persons of mature years and to young men fresh from school and college would not be likely to exalt mere intellectual proficiency above other qualities of equal or greater importance.

Another feature of the proposed system is the selection by promotion of all officers of the government above the lowest grade, except such as would fairly be regarded as exponents of the policy of the executive and the principles of the dominant party.

To afford encouragement to faithful public servants by exciting in their minds the hope of promotion if they are found to merit it is much to be desired.

But would it be wise to adopt a rule so rigid as to permit no other mode of supplying the intermediate walks of the service?

There are many persons who fill subordinate positions with great credit, but lack those qualities which are requisite for higher posts of duty; and, besides, the modes of thought and action of one whose service in a governmental bureau has been long continued are often so cramped by routine procedure as almost to disqualify him from instituting changes required by the public interests. An infusion of new blood from time to time into the middle ranks of the service might be very beneficial in its results.

The subject under discussion is one of grave importance. The evils which are complained of cannot be eradicated at once; the work must be gradual. . . . If Congress should deem it advisable at the present session to establish competitive tests for admission to the service, no doubts such as have been suggested shall deter me from giving the measure my earnest support.

Address at the Statue of Liberty

(1886)

"A stream of light shall pierce the darkness of ignorance"

Presidents are frequently tasked with dedicating monuments, parks, and other public spaces, but few have been as fortunate as Grover Cleveland. On October 28, 1886, Cleveland came to New York to dedicate the Statue of Liberty, a new and towering figure donated by the French and designed by the sculptor Frédéric Auguste Bartholdi. Cleveland answered the occasion with this brief but graceful speech.

The people of the United States accept with gratitude from their brethren of the French republic the grand and completed work of art we here inaugurate.

This token of the affection and consideration of the people of France demonstrates the kinship of republics and conveys to us the assurance that, in our efforts to commend to mankind the excellence of a government resting upon popular will, we still have beyond the American continent a steadfast ally.

We are not here today to bow before the representation of a fierce and warlike god, filled with wrath and vengeance, but we joyously contemplate instead our own deity keeping watch and ward before the open gates of America, and greater than all that have been celebrated in ancient song.

Instead of grasping in her hand thunderbolts of terror and of death, she holds aloft the light which illumines the way to man's enfranchisement.

We will not forget that liberty has here made her home, nor shall her chosen altar be neglected. Willing votaries will constantly keep alive its fires, and these shall gleam upon the shores of our sister republic in the east. Reflected thence and joined with answering rays, a stream of light shall pierce the darkness of ignorance and man's oppression, until liberty enlightens the world.

From *This Country of Ours*

"The White House . . . is an office and a home combined—an evil combination"

After he left the White House, in 1893, Benjamin Harrison wrote a series of articles for the hugely popular Ladies' Home Journal. *Harrison intended the articles to be a patriotic primer, and eventually he gathered them in book form as* This Country of Ours. *While not a full autobiography, Harrison's book provides a fascinating glimpse of the presidency at the end of the nineteenth century—a time when the president had only a handful of aides, when the Oval Office had not yet been established, when the executive branch still felt rather small.*

The "Executive Mansion" is the official designation of the home of the president; the universal popular designation is the "White House." It is an office and a home combined—an evil combination. There is no break in the day—no change of atmosphere. The blacksmith, when the allotted hours of work are over, banks his fire, lays aside his leather apron, washes his grimy hands, and goes home. And he gets a taste of unsmoked morning air before he resumes his work. There is only a door—one that is never locked—between the president's office and what are not very accurately called his private apartments. There should be an executive office building, not too far away, but wholly distinct from the dwelling house. For everyone else in the public service there is an unroofed space between the bedroom and the desk. The Cabinet Room intervenes between the library and the room usually (but not always) used by the president as an office. Presidents Grant, Hayes, and Garfield used the Cabinet Room as an office. President Arthur took the large oval room above the blue room, which had before been a library and private sitting room, for his office, and during his first term Mr. Cleveland so used it. But the room next east of the Cabinet Room was used by Mr. Lincoln, and generally before his time, as the office, and it is now so used. The Cabinet Room is used as a waiting room. The president tries to get to his office in time to examine his mail before his callers begin to arrive, but is often anticipated by senators and representatives who have early committee engagements at the Capitol.

The broad flat desk at which he seats himself is an artistic and historic piece of cabinet work. It is inscribed:

Her Majesty's ship *Resolute*, forming part of the expedition sent in search of Sir John Franklin in 1852, was abandoned in latitude 74° 41' north, longitude 101° 22' west, on 15th May, 1854. She was discovered and extricated in September, 1855, in latitude 67° north, by Captain Buddington, of the United States whaler, *George Henry*. The ship was purchased, fitted out, and sent to England as a gift to her Majesty, Queen Victoria, by the president and people of the United States, as a token of good will and friendship. This table was made from her timbers when she was broken up, and is presented by the queen of Great Britain and Ireland to the president of the United States as a memorial of the courtesy and loving-kindness which dictated the offer of the gift of the *Resolute*.

The office force of the White House is not large. The private secretary (now secretary to the president) is at the head of it. His office is an important one, and discretion is the talent most in demand! He is not a deputy president. There is an assistant secretary, who carries and delivers the messages to Congress and keeps a record of appointments and of bills submitted for the president's approval. There are six clerks, two of whom are executive clerks. One of these is stenographer to the president and has charge of the mail. The other is a purchasing and disbursing officer. Of the other clerks, one acts as stenographer to the private secretary, one is a telegraph operator, and these, with the remaining clerks, assist in the general office work. There is a doorkeeper for the president, and one for the private secretary. These, with four messengers, complete the office force proper.

The mail that comes daily to the Executive Mansion is very large; in the early months of an administration it is enormous, as many as eight hundred letters being sometimes received in a day. But few of these letters reach the president's desk. The mail is sorted by a trusted and confidential clerk; family and personal letters are sent unopened to the persons to whom they are addressed; letters relating to appointments are, as a rule, acknowledged by one of the clerks and referred to the proper department; and only those that relate to the more important appointments and to matters of public interest are sent to the president's desk. No other course is possible, for, if he dealt personally with all his correspondents, the president could do nothing else. As it is, the mail that comes to his desk is large. The information has been spread very widely that the president does not read many letters, and the devices that are employed to make sure that letters will be seen by him are various and amusing. But the secretary soon learns that the letters marked "personal" or "private" are quite as likely to be applications for office or requests for autographs as anything else. Sometimes a formal protest against the private secretary is endorsed on the envelope, as, "This is for the president, not for the one who reads his letters." A correspondent who had forwarded many papers, the acknowledgment of all of which had been accompanied by the assurance that the papers had been referred to the appropriate department, rather pathetically wrote: "Your letters are all worded about the same."

Very many of the letters addressed to the president are trivial, not a few of them impertinent, and some of them angry and threatening. These, if the private secretary is a judicious man, the president never hears of, and the malicious intent of the writer is thwarted. The requests for autographs are scarcely numerable. A card, with an engraving of the Executive Mansion upon it, is provided for that use, and a pile of these cards upon his desk, and another of autograph albums, make their mute appeal to the president nearly every morning. Patches for autograph bed-quilts and lunch-cloths add to the burden. Begging letters, for numbers, take the second place in the president's mail. They come from every part of the land, and relate to every possible subject. There are appeals to aid the writer to get an education, or to pay off a mortgage, or to buy a piano or a pony; and no form of public appeal is absent—to aid the building of churches, to endow schools, to build monuments, and to aid every other good purpose for which men or women or children associate themselves. On one day the requests for specific sums aggregated nine thousand dollars. . . .

Letters can be turned over to clerks, but callers are not to be so disposed of. Unless the president is very early, he will find some callers waiting for him as he passes through the Cabinet Room to his office. The rules, which are displayed on large cards, announce that the president will receive persons having business with him between certain hours, usually from 9:30 or

10 A.M. until 1 P.M., except on Mondays; but the hours and the exception are very little regarded, and it is a rare piece of good fortune during the early months of an administration if the president gets one wholly unin- terrupted hour at his desk each day. His time is so broken into bits that he is often driven to late night work, or to set up a desk in his bedroom, when preparing a message or other paper requiring unbroken attention. Thoughtlessness is the root of all this. "I only want five minutes"—and if he were the only one it could be spared, but his double is at his heels, and the urgent public business is postponed or done at night with a jaded mind.

It may be said that untimely visitors should be excluded, and so they should; but thoughtfulness on their part would be a cure without a smart. The president's messenger brings in the cards or announces orally the names of the visitors, and they are admitted singly, or all are ushered as they arrive, into the president's office as he may direct. He usually receives them standing near his desk—especially when a number are present—and in the order of their official station, if they are public officers. Those not engaged with the president stand back, and the conversation with each, as he is received, is conducted in a low tone that secures some degree of privacy. There are many senators and representatives, often accompanied by friends or constituents, either singly or in delegations, sometimes simply to pay their respects, but more often to urge some appointment.

In the latter case the president listens and seems to the applicant to be painfully reticent. He concludes the brief interview by saying: "Please file your papers in the proper department, and I will consider the matter."

This incident is repeated over and over—perhaps a hundred times in the course of a morning. The business has not been much advanced, if at all. The appointment may not come before the president for action for several months, and in the nature of things he can recall little, if anything, of what was said so long before. He has been told that Mr. A———, an applicant for the post-office at ———, is a dissipated, disreputable man; and that Mr. B———, who wants the same place, possesses all of the virtues, and talents of the highest order; but if the president depended upon his memory these vices and virtues might be wrongly assigned. All this is explained over and over again to applicants and their friends, but the feeling that something is, or may be, gained by a personal interview prevails, and for the first year and a half of an administration the president spends from four to six hours of each day talking about things he will not have to act upon for months, while the things that ought to be done presently are hurtfully postponed.

WILLIAM McKINLEY

From His Address at the Pan-American Exposition

(1901)

"Isolation is no longer possible or desirable"

With its sprawling campus and international spectacle—all of it illuminated by a stunning array of electric lights—the Pan-American Exposition brought millions to Buffalo in 1901. One of the visitors was William McKinley, and he delivered a speech that reflected his surroundings: pro-growth, pro-globalism, and pro-dawn of a new century. It hinted at an America that one day would move past the Monroe Doctrine. It was also the last speech McKinley would ever give, as he was shot the next day by an anarchist and died just over a week later.

Business life, whether among ourselves or with other people, is ever a sharp struggle for success. It will be none the less so in the future. Without competition we would be clinging to the clumsy antiquated processes of farming and manufacture and the methods of business of long ago, and the twentieth would be no further advanced than the eighteenth century. But though commercial competitors we are, commercial enemies we must not be.

The Pan-American Exposition has done its work thoroughly, presenting in its exhibits evidences of the highest skill and illustrating the progress of the human family in the western hemisphere. This portion of the earth has no cause for humiliation for the part it has performed in the march of civilization. It has not accomplished everything from it. It has simply done its best, and without vanity or boastfulness, and recognizing the manifold achievements of others, it invites the friendly rivalry of all the powers in the peaceful pursuits of trade and commerce, and will co-operate with all in advancing the highest and best interests of humanity.

The wisdom and energy of all the nations are none too great for the world's work. The success of art, science, industry, and invention is an international asset and a common glory.

After all, how near one to the other is every part of the world. Modern inventions have brought into close relation widely separated peoples and made them better acquainted. Geographic and political divisions will continue to exist, but distances have been effaced. Swift ships and swift trains are becoming cosmopolitan. They invade fields which a few years ago were impenetrable. The world's products are exchanged as never before, and with increasing transportation facilities come increasing knowledge and larger trade. Prices are fixed with mathematical precision by supply and demand. The world's selling prices are regulated by market and crop reports.

We travel greater distances in a shorter space of time and with more ease than was ever dreamed of by the fathers. Isolation is no longer possible or desirable. The same important news is read, though in different languages, the same day in all Christendom. The telegraph keeps us advised of what is occurring everywhere, and the press foreshadows, with more or less accuracy, the plans and purposes of the nations.

Market prices of products and of securities are hourly known in every commercial mart, and the investments of the people extend beyond their own national boundaries into the remotest parts of the earth. Vast transactions are conducted and international exchanges are made by the tick of the cable. Every event of interest is immediately bulletined. The quick gathering and transmission of news, like rapid transit, are of recent origin and are only made possible by the genius of the inventor and the courage of the investor. It took a special messenger of the government, with every facility known at the time for rapid travel, nineteen days to go from the city of Washington to New Orleans with a message to General Jackson that the war with England had ceased and a treaty of peace had been signed. How different now!

We reached General Miles in Puerto Rico by cable, and he was able, through the military telegraph, to stop his army on the firing line with the message that the United States and Spain had signed a protocol suspending hostilities. We knew almost instantly of the first shots fired at

Santiago, and the subsequent surrender of the Spanish forces was known at Washington within less than an hour of its consummation. The first ship of Cervera's fleet had hardly emerged from that historic harbor when the fact was flashed to our capital, and the swift destruction that followed was announced immediately through the wonderful medium of telegraphy.

So accustomed are we to safe and easy communication with distant lands that its temporary interruption, even in ordinary times, results in loss and inconvenience. We shall never forget the days of anxious waiting and awful suspense when no information was permitted to be sent from Peking, and the diplomatic representatives of the nations in China, cut off from all communication, inside and outside of the walled capital, were surrounded by an angry and misguided mob that threatened their lives; nor the joy that filled the world when a single message from the government of the United States brought through our minister the first news of the safety of the besieged diplomats.

At the beginning of the nineteenth century there was not a mile of steam railroad on the globe. Now there are enough miles to make its circuit many times. Then there was not a line of electric telegraph; now we have a vast mileage traversing all lands and seas. God and man have linked the nations together. No nation can longer be indifferent to any other. And as we are brought more and more in touch with each other the less occasion there is for misunderstandings and the stronger the disposition, when we have differences, to adjust them in the court of arbitration, which is the noblest forum for the settlement of international disputes.

My fellow citizens, trade statistics indicate that this country is in a state of unexampled prosperity. The figures are almost appalling. They show that we are utilizing our fields and forests and mines and that we are furnishing profitable employment to the millions of workingmen through-out the United States, bringing comfort and happiness to their homes and making it possible to lay by savings for old age and disability. That all the people are participating in this great prosperity is seen in every American community and shown by the enormous and unprecedented deposits in our savings banks. Our duty is the care and security of these deposits, and their safe investment demands the highest integrity and the best business capacity of those in charge of these depositories of the people's earnings.

We have a vast and intricate business, built up through years of toil and struggle, in which every part of the country has its stake, and will not permit of either neglect or of undue selfishness. No narrow, sordid policy will subserve it. The greatest skill and wisdom on the part of the manufacturers and producers will be required to hold and increase it. Our industrial enterprises which have grown to such great proportions affect the homes and occupations of the people and the welfare of the country. Our capacity to produce has developed so enormously and our products have so multiplied that the problem of more markets requires our urgent and immediate attention. Only a broad and enlightened policy will keep what we have. No other policy will get more. In these times of marvelous business energy and gain we ought to be looking to the future, strengthening the weak places in our industrial and commercial system, that we may be ready for any storm or strain.

By sensible trade arrangements, which will not interrupt our home production, we shall extend the outlets for our increasing surplus. A system which provides a mutual exchange of commodities, a mutual exchange is manifestly essential to the continued and healthful growth of our export trade. We must not repose in fancied security that we can forever sell everything and buy little or nothing. If such a thing were possible, it would not be best for us or for those with whom we deal. We should take from our customers such of their products as we can use without harm to our industries and labor. Reciprocity is the natural outgrowth of our wonderful industrial development under the domestic policy now firmly established. What we produce beyond our domestic consumption must have a vent abroad. The excess must be relieved through a foreign outlet and we should sell everywhere we can, and buy wherever the buying will enlarge our sales and productions, and thereby make a greater demand for home labor.

The period of exclusiveness is past.

THEODORE ROOSEVELT

From His State of the Union

(1901)

"The great corporations known as trusts are in certain of their features and tendencies hurtful to the general welfare"

Theodore Roosevelt's first State of the Union is a fine example of his ability, as he told MacArthur, "to put into words what is in {the people's} hearts and minds but not their mouths." While Roosevelt begins his written text with a eulogy for McKinley, that eulogy positions the martyred president as a symbol of both a powerful executive branch and the need to regulate America's corporations—two causes that would animate Roosevelt's own administration.

The Congress assembles this year under the shadow of a great calamity. On the 6th of September, President McKinley was shot by an anarchist while attending the Pan-American Exposition at Buffalo and died in that city on the 14th of that month.

Of the last seven elected presidents, he is the third who has been murdered, and the bare recital of this fact is sufficient to justify grave alarm among all loyal American citizens. Moreover, the circumstances of this, the third assassination of an American president, have a peculiarly sinister significance. Both President Lincoln and President Garfield were killed by assassins of types unfortunately not uncommon in history—President Lincoln falling a victim to the terrible passions aroused by four years of civil war, and President Garfield to the revengeful vanity of a disappointed office-seeker. President McKinley was killed by an utterly depraved criminal belonging to that body of criminals who object to all governments, good and bad alike; who are against any form of popular liberty if it is guaranteed by even the most just and liberal laws; and who are as hostile to the upright exponent of a free people's sober will as to the tyrannical and irresponsible despot.

It is not too much to say that at the time of President McKinley's death he was the most widely loved man in all the United States, while we have never had any public man of his position who has been so wholly free from the bitter animosities incident to public life. His political opponents were the first to bear the heartiest and most generous tribute to the broad kindliness of nature, the sweetness and gentleness of character which so endeared him to his close associates. To a standard of lofty integrity in public life he united the tender affections and home virtues which are all-important in the makeup of national character. A gallant soldier in the great war for the Union, he also shone as an example to all our people because of his conduct in the most sacred and intimate of home relations. There could be no personal hatred of him, for he never acted with aught but consideration for the welfare of others. No one could fail to respect him who knew him in public or private life. The defenders of those murderous criminals who seek to excuse their criminality by asserting that it is exercised for political ends, inveigh against wealth and irresponsible power. But for this assassination even this base apology cannot be urged.

President McKinley was a man of moderate means, a man whose stock sprang from the sturdy tillers of the soil, who had himself belonged among the wageworkers, who had entered the Army as a private soldier. Wealth was not struck at when the president was assassinated, but the honest toil which is content with moderate gains after a lifetime of unremitting labor, largely in the service of the public. Still less was power struck at in the sense that power is irresponsible or centered in the hands of any one individual. The blow was not aimed at tyranny or wealth. It was aimed at one of the strongest champions the wageworker has ever had; at one of the most faithful representatives of the system of public rights and representative government who has ever risen to public office. President McKinley filled that political office for which the entire people vote, and no president, not even Lincoln himself, was ever more earnestly anxious to represent the well thought-out wishes of the people; his one anxiety in every crisis was to keep in closest touch with the people—to find out what they thought and to endeavor to give expression to their thought, after having endeavored to guide that thought aright. He had just been reelected to the presidency because the majority of our citizens, the majority of our farmers and wageworkers, believed that he had faithfully upheld their interests for four years. They felt themselves in close and intimate touch with him. . . .

The fundamental rule in our national life—the rule which underlies all others—is that, on the whole, and in the long run, we shall go up or down together. There are exceptions; and in times of prosperity some will prosper far more, and in times of adversity some will suffer far more, than others; but speaking generally, a period of good times means that all share more or less in them, and in a period of hard times all feel the stress to a greater or less degree. It surely ought not to be necessary to enter into any proof of this statement; the memory of the lean years which began in 1893 is still vivid, and we can contrast them with the conditions in this very year which is now closing. Disaster to great business enterprises can never have its effects limited to the men at the top. It spreads throughout, and while it is bad for everybody, it is worst for those farthest down. The capitalist may be shorn of his luxuries, but the wageworker may be deprived of even bare necessities.

The mechanism of modern business is so delicate that extreme care must be taken not to interfere with it in a spirit of rashness or ignorance. Many of those who have made it their vocation to denounce the great industrial combinations which are popularly, although with technical inaccuracy, known as "trusts," appeal especially to hatred and fear. These are precisely the two emotions, particularly when combined with ignorance, which unfit men for the exercise of cool and steady judgment. In facing new industrial conditions, the whole history of the world shows that legislation will generally be both unwise and ineffective unless undertaken after calm inquiry and with sober self-restraint. Much of the legislation directed at the trusts would have been exceedingly mischievous had it not also been entirely ineffective. In accordance with a well-known sociological law, the ignorant or reckless agitator has been the really effective friend of the evils which he has been nominally opposing. In dealing with business interests, for the government to undertake by crude and ill-considered legislation to do what may turn out to be bad, would be to incur the risk of such far-reaching national disaster that it would be preferable to undertake nothing at all. The men who demand the impossible or the undesirable serve as the allies of the forces with which they are nominally at war, for they hamper those who would endeavor to find out in rational fashion what the wrongs really are and to what extent and in what manner it is practicable to apply remedies.

All this is true, and yet it is also true that there are real and grave evils, one of the chief being over-capitalization because of its many baleful consequences; and a resolute and practical effort must be made to correct these evils.

There is a widespread conviction in the minds of the American people that the great corporations known as trusts are in certain of their features and tendencies hurtful to the general welfare. This springs from no spirit of envy or uncharitableness, nor lack of pride in the great industrial achievements that have placed this country at the head of the nations struggling for commercial supremacy. It does not rest upon a lack of intelligent appreciation of the necessity of meeting changing and changed conditions of trade with new methods, nor upon ignorance of the fact that combination of capital in the effort to accomplish great things is necessary when the world's progress demands that great things be done. It is based upon sincere conviction that combination and concentration should be not prohibited, but supervised and within reasonable limits controlled; and in my judgment this conviction is right.

It is no limitation upon property rights or freedom of contract to require that when men receive from government the privilege of doing business under corporate form, which frees them from individual responsibility and enables them to call into their enterprises the capital of the public, they shall do so upon absolutely truthful representations as to the value of the property in which the capital is to be invested. Corporations engaged in interstate commerce should be regulated if they are found to exercise a license working to the public injury. It should be as much the aim of those who seek for social betterment to rid the business world of crimes of cunning as to rid the entire body politic of crimes of violence. Great corporations exist only because they are created and safeguarded by our institutions; and it is therefore our right and our duty to see that they work in harmony with these institutions.

The first essential in determining how to deal with the great industrial combinations is knowledge of the facts—publicity. In the interest of the public, the government should have the right to inspect and examine the workings of the great corporations engaged in interstate business. Publicity is the only sure remedy which we can now invoke. What further remedies are needed in the way of governmental regulation, or taxation, can only be determined after publicity has been obtained, by process of law, and in the course of administration. The first requisite is knowledge, full and complete—knowledge which may be made public to the world.

Artificial bodies, such as corporations and joint stock or other associations depending upon any statutory law for their existence or privileges, should be subject to proper governmental supervision, and full and accurate information as to their operations should be made public regularly at reasonable intervals.

The large corporations, commonly called trusts, though organized in one state, always do business in many states, often doing very little business in the state where they are incorporated. There is utter lack of uniformity in the state laws about them; and as no state has any exclusive interest in or power over their acts, it has in practice proved impossible to get adequate regulation through state action. Therefore, in the interest of the whole people, the nation should, without interfering with the power of the states in the matter itself, also assume power of supervision and regulation over all corporations doing an interstate business. This is especially true where the corporation derives a portion of its wealth from the existence of some monopolistic element or tendency in its business. There would be no hardship in such supervision; banks are subject to it, and in their case it is now accepted as a simple matter of course. Indeed, it is probable that supervision of corporations by the national government need not go so far as is now the case with the supervision exercised over them by so conservative a state as Massachusetts, in order to produce excellent results.

When the Constitution was adopted, at the end of the eighteenth century, no human wisdom could foretell the sweeping changes, alike in industrial and political conditions, which were to take place by the beginning of the twentieth century. At that time it was accepted as a matter of course that the several states were the proper authorities to regulate, so far as was then necessary, the comparatively insignificant and strictly localized corporate bodies of the day. The conditions are now wholly different and wholly different action is called for. I believe that a law can be framed which will enable the national government to exercise control along the lines above indicated; profiting by the experience gained through the passage and administration of the Interstate-Commerce Act. If, however, the judgment of the Congress is that it lacks the constitutional power to pass such an act, then a constitutional amendment should be submitted to confer the power.

There should be created a cabinet officer, to be known as Secretary of Commerce and Industries, as provided in the bill introduced at the last session of the Congress. It should be his province to deal with commerce in its broadest sense, including among many other things whatever concerns labor and all matters affecting the great business corporations and our merchant marine.

The course proposed is one phase of what should be a comprehensive and far-reaching scheme of constructive statesmanship for the purpose of broadening our markets, securing our business interests on a safe basis, and making firm our new position in the international industrial world, while scrupulously safeguarding the rights of wageworker and capitalist, of investor and private citizen, so as to secure equity as between man and man in this republic.

With the sole exception of the farming interest, no one matter is of such vital moment to our whole people as the welfare of the wageworkers. If the farmer and the wageworker are well off, it is absolutely certain that all others will be well off, too.

THEODORE ROOSEVELT

Address on the "New Nationalism"

(1910)

"I stand for the square deal"

When Roosevelt chose not to run in 1908, he made his preferred replacement clear: William Howard Taft. After Taft won, however, he and Roosevelt began to split apart. On August 31, 1910, Roosevelt spoke at the dedication of a new park in Kansas, a park named after the abolitionist John Brown, which ensured the crowd was full of Civil War veterans. With the help of several speechwriters, Roosevelt used the veterans' presence to ground his ideas in history—to reinterpret the past and future of the Republican Party, reclaiming both in the image of not Taft but the far more populist Roosevelt.

We come here today to commemorate one of the epoch-making events of the long struggle for the rights of man—the long struggle for the uplift of humanity. Our country—this great republic—means nothing unless it means the triumph of a real democracy, the triumph of popular government, and, in the long run, of an economic system under which each man shall be guaranteed the opportunity to show the best that there is in him. That is why the history of America is now the central feature of the history of the world; for the world has set its face hopefully toward our democracy, and, O my fellow citizens, each one of you carries on your shoulders not only the burden of doing well for the sake of your country, but the burden of doing well and of seeing that this nation does well for the sake of mankind.

There have been two great crises in our country's history: first, when it was formed, and then, again, when it was perpetuated; and, in the second of these great crises—in the time of stress and strain which culminated in the Civil War, on the outcome of which depended the justification of what had been done earlier, you men of the Grand Army, you men who fought through the Civil War—not only did you justify your generation, but you justified the wisdom of Washington and Washington's colleagues. If this republic had been founded by them only to be split asunder into fragments when the strain came, then the judgment of the world would have been that Washington's work was not worth doing. It was you who crowned Washington's work, as you carried to achievement the high purpose of Abraham Lincoln.

Now, with this second period of our history the name of John Brown will forever be associated, and Kansas was the theatre upon which the first act of the second of our great national life dramas was played. It was the result of the struggle in Kansas which determined that our country should be in deed as well as in name devoted to both union and freedom, that the great experiment of democratic government on a national scale should succeed and not fail. In name we had the Declaration of Independence in 1776, but we gave the lie by our acts to the words of the Declaration of Independence until 1865; and words count for nothing except in so far as they represent acts. This is true everywhere; but, O my friends, it should be truest of all in political life. A broken promise is bad enough in private life. It is worse in the field of politics. No man is worth his salt in public life who makes on the stump a pledge which he does not keep after election; and, if he makes such a pledge and does not keep it, hunt him out of public life. I care for the great deeds of the past chiefly as spurs to drive us onward in the present. I speak of the men of the past partly that they may be honored by our praise of them, but more that they may serve as examples for the future.

It was a heroic struggle; and, as is inevitable with all such struggles, it had also a dark and terrible side. Very much was done of good, and much also of evil; and, as was inevitable in such a period of revolution, often the same man did both good and evil. For our great good fortune as a nation, we, the people of the United States as a whole, can now afford to forget the evil, or, at least, to remember it without bitterness, and to fix our eyes with pride only on the good that was accomplished. Even in ordinary times there are very few of us who do not see the problems of life as through a glass, darkly; and when the glass is clouded by the murk of furious popular passion, the vision of the best and the bravest is dimmed. Looking back, we are all of us now able to do justice to the valor and the disinterestedness and the love of the right, as to each it was given to see the right, shown both by the men of the north and the men of the south in that contest which was finally decided by the attitude of the west. We can admire the heroic valor, the sincerity, the self-devotion shown alike by the men who wore the blue and the men who wore the gray, and our sadness that such men should have to fight one another is tempered by the glad knowledge that ever hereafter their descendants shall be fighting side by side, struggling in peace as well as in war for the uplift of their common country, all alike resolute to raise to the highest pitch of honor and usefulness the nation to which they all belong. As for the veterans of the Grand Army of the Republic, they deserve honor and recognition such as is paid to no other citizens of the republic; for to them the republic owes it all; for to them it owes its very existence. It is because of what you and your comrades did in the dark years that we of today walk, each of us, head erect and proud that we belong not to one of a dozen little squabbling contemptible commonwealths, but to the mightiest nation upon which the sun shines.

I do not speak of this struggle of the past merely from the historic standpoint. Our interest is primarily in the application today of the lessons taught by the contest a half a century ago. It is of little use for us to pay lip-loyalty to the mighty men of the past unless we sincerely endeavor to apply to the problems of the present precisely the qualities which in other crises enabled the men of that day to meet those crises. It is half melancholy and half amusing to see the way in which well-meaning people gather to do honor to the men who, in company with John Brown, and under the lead of Abraham Lincoln, faced and solved the great problems of the nineteenth century, while, at the same time, these same good people nervously shrink from or frantically denounce those who are trying to meet the problems of the twentieth century in the spirit which was accountable for the successful solution of the problems of Lincoln's time.

Of that generation of men to whom we owe so much, the man to whom we owe most is, of course, Lincoln. Part of our debt to him is because he forecast our present struggle and saw the way out. He said: "I hold that while man exists it is his duty to improve not only his own condition, but to assist in ameliorating mankind."

And again: "Labor is prior to, and independent of, capital. Capital is only the fruit of labor, and could never have existed if labor had not first existed. Labor is the superior of capital, and deserves much the higher consideration."

If that remark was original with me, I should be even more strongly denounced as a Communist agitator than I shall be anyhow. It is Lincoln's. I am only quoting it, and that is one side; that is the side the capitalist should hear.

Now, let the working man hear his side: "Capital has its rights, which are as worthy of protection as any other rights. . . . Nor should this lead to a war upon the owners of property. Property is the fruit of labor. . . . Property is desirable, is a positive good in the world."

And then comes a thoroughly Lincoln-like sentence: "Let not him who is houseless pull down the house of another, but let him work diligently and build one for himself, thus by example assuring that his own shall be safe from violence when built."

It seems to me that, in these words, Lincoln took substantially the attitude that we ought to take; he showed the proper sense of proportion in his relative estimates of capital and labor, of human rights and property rights. Above all, in this speech, as in many others, he taught a lesson in wise kindliness and charity, an indispensable lesson to us of today. But this wise kindliness and charity never weakened his arm or numbed his heart. We cannot afford weakly to blind ourselves to the actual conflict which faces us today. The issue is joined, and we must fight or fail.

In every wise struggle for human betterment one of the main objects, and often the only object, has been to achieve in large measure equality of opportunity. In the struggle for this great end, nations rise from barbarism to civilization, and through it people press forward from one stage of enlightenment to the next. One of the chief factors in progress is the destruction of special privilege. The essence of any struggle for healthy liberty has always been, and must always be, to take from some one man or class of men the right to enjoy power, or wealth, or position, or immunity, which has not been earned by service to his or their fellows. That is what you fought for in the Civil War, and that is what we strive for now.

At many stages in the advance of humanity, this conflict between the men who possess more than they have earned and the men who have earned more than they possess is the central condition of progress. In our day it appears as the struggle of freemen to gain and hold the right of self-government as against the special interests, who twist the methods of free government into machinery for defeating the popular will. At every stage, and under all circumstances, the essence of the struggle is to equalize opportunity, destroy privilege, and give to the life and citizenship of every individual the highest possible value both to himself and to the commonwealth. That is nothing new. All I ask in civil life is what you fought for in the Civil War. I ask that civil life be carried on according to the spirit in which the army was carried on.

You never get perfect justice, but the effort in handling the army was to bring to the front the men who could do the job. Nobody grudged promotion to Grant, or Sherman, or Thomas, or Sheridan, because they earned it. The only complaint was when a man got promotion which he did not earn.

Practical equality of opportunity for all citizens, when we achieve it, will have two great results. First, every man will have a fair chance to make of himself all that in him lies, to reach the highest point to which his capacities, unassisted by special privilege of his own and unhampered by the special privilege of others, can carry him and to get for himself and his family substantially what he has earned. Second, equality of opportunity means that the commonwealth will get from every citizen the highest service of which he is capable. No man who carries the burden of the special privileges of another can give to the commonwealth that service to which it is fairly entitled.

I stand for the square deal. But when I say that I am for the square deal, I mean not merely that I stand for fair play under the present rules of the game, but that I stand for having those rules changed so as to work for a more substantial equality of opportunity and of reward for equally good service. One word of warning, which, I think, is hardly necessary in Kansas. When I say I want a square deal for the poor man, I do not mean that I want a square deal for the man who remains poor because he has not got the energy to work for himself. If a man who has had a chance will not make good, then he has got to quit. And you men of the Grand Army, you want justice for the brave man who fought, and punishment for the coward who shirked his work. Is that not so?

Now, this means that our government, national and state, must be freed from the sinister influence or control of special interests. Exactly as the special interests of cotton and slavery threatened our political integrity before the Civil War, so now the great special business interests too often control and corrupt the men and methods of government for their own profit. We must drive the special interests out of politics. That is one of our tasks today. Every special interest is entitled to justice—full, fair, and complete—and, now, mind you, if there were any attempt by mob violence to plunder and work harm to the special interest, whatever it may be, that I most dislike, and the wealthy man, whomsoever he may be, for whom I have the greatest contempt, I would fight for him, and you would if you were worth your salt. He should have justice. For every special interest is entitled to justice, but not one is entitled to a vote in Congress, to a voice on the bench or to representation in any public office. The Constitution guarantees protection to property, and we must make that promise good. But it does not give the right of suffrage to any corporation.

The true friend of property, the true conservative, is he who insists that property shall be the servant and not the master of the commonwealth, who insists that the creature of man's making shall be the servant and not the master of the man who made it. The citizens of the United States must effectively control the mighty commercial forces which they have called into being.

There can be no effective control of corporations while their political activity remains. To put an end to it will be neither a short nor an easy task, but it can be done.

We must have complete and effective publicity of corporate affairs, so that the people may know beyond peradventure whether the corporations obey the law and whether their management entitles them to the confidence of the public. It is necessary that laws should be passed to prohibit the use of corporate funds directly or indirectly for political purposes; it is still more necessary that such laws should be thoroughly enforced. Corporate expenditures for political purposes, and especially such expenditures by public-service corporations, have supplied one of the principal sources of corruption in our political affairs.

It has become entirely clear that we must have government supervision of the capitalization, not only of public-service corporations, including, particularly, railways, but of all corporations doing an interstate business. I do not wish to see the nation forced into the ownership of the railways if it can possibly be avoided, and the only alternative is thoroughgoing and effective legislation which shall be based on a full knowledge of all the facts, including a physical valuation of property. This physical valuation is not needed, or, at least, is very rarely needed, for fixing rates; but it is needed as the basis of honest capitalization.

We have come to recognize that franchises should never be granted except for a limited time and never without proper provision for compensation to the public. It is my personal belief that the same kind and degree of control and supervision which should be exercised over public-service corporations should be extended also to combinations which control necessaries of life, such as meat, oil, or coal, or which deal in them on an important scale. I have no doubt that the ordinary man who has control of them is much like ourselves. I have no doubt he would like to do well, but I want to have enough supervision to help him realize that desire to do well.

I believe that the officers, and, especially, the directors, of corporations should be held personally responsible when any corporation breaks the law.

Combinations in industry are the result of an imperative economic law which cannot be repealed by political legislation. The effort at prohibiting all combination has substantially failed. The way out lies not in attempting to prevent such combinations, but in completely controlling them in the interest of the public welfare. For that purpose the Federal Bureau of Corporations is an agency of first importance. Its powers and, therefore, its efficiency, as well as that of the Interstate Commerce Commission, should be largely increased. We have a right to expect from the Bureau of Corporations and from the Interstate Commerce Commission a very high grade of public service. We should be as sure of the proper conduct of the interstate railways and the proper management of interstate business as we are now sure of the conduct and management of the national banks, and we should have as effective supervision in one case as in the other. The Hepburn Act, and the amendment to the act in the shape in which it finally passed Congress at the last session, represent a long step in advance, and we must go yet further.

There is a widespread belief among our people that, under the methods of making tariffs which have hitherto obtained, the special interests are too influential. Probably this is true of both the big special interests and the little special interests. These methods have put a premium on selfishness, and, naturally, the selfish big interests have gotten more than their smaller, though equally selfish, brothers. The duty of Congress is to provide a method by which the interest of the whole people shall be all that receives consideration. To this end there must be an expert tariff commission, wholly removed from the possibility of political pressure or of improper business influence. Such a commission can find the real difference between cost of production, which is mainly the difference of labor cost here and abroad. As fast as its recommendations are made, I believe in revising one schedule at a time. A general revision of the tariff almost inevitably leads to logrolling and the subordination of the general public interest to local and special interests.

The absence of effective state and especially national restraint upon unfair money-getting has tended to create a small class of enormously wealthy and economically powerful men, whose chief object is to hold and increase their power. The prime need is to change the conditions which enable these men to accumulate power which it is not for the general welfare that they should hold or exercise. We grudge no man a fortune which represents his own power and sagacity, when exercised with entire regard to the welfare of his fellows. Again, comrades over there, take the lesson from your own experience. Not only did you not grudge, but you gloried in the promotion of the great generals who gained their promotion by leading their army to victory. So it is with us. We grudge no man a fortune in civil life if it is honorably obtained and well used. It is not even enough that it should have been gained without doing damage to the community. We should permit it to be gained only so long as the gaining represents benefit to the community. This, I know, implies a policy of a far more active governmental interference with social and economic conditions in this country than we have yet had, but I think we have got to face the fact that such an increase in governmental control is now necessary.

No man should receive a dollar unless that dollar has been fairly earned. Every dollar received should represent a dollar's worth of service rendered—not gambling in stocks, but service rendered. The really big fortune, the swollen fortune, by the mere fact of its size, acquires qualities which differentiate it in kind as well as in degree from what is possessed by men of relatively small means. Therefore, I believe in a graduated income tax on big fortunes, and in another tax which is far more easily collected and far more effective—a graduated inheritance tax on big fortunes, properly safeguarded against evasion, and increasing rapidly in amount with the size of the estate.

The people of the United States suffer from periodical financial panics to a degree substantially unknown to the other nations, which approach us in financial strength. There is no reason why we should suffer what they escape. It is of profound importance that our financial system should be promptly investigated, and so thoroughly and effectively revised as to make it certain that hereafter our currency will no longer fail at critical times to meet our needs.

It is hardly necessary to me to repeat that I believe in an efficient army and a navy large enough to secure for us abroad that respect which is the surest guaranty of peace. A word of special warning to my fellow citizens who are as progressive as I hope I am. I want them to keep up their interest in our international affairs; and I want them also continually to remember Uncle Sam's interests abroad. Justice and fair dealings among nations rest upon principles identical with those which control justice and fair dealing among the individuals of which nations are composed, with the vital exception that each nation must do its own part in international police work. If you get into trouble here, you can call for the police; but if Uncle Sam gets into trouble, he has got to be his own policeman, and I want to see him strong enough to encourage the peaceful aspirations of other peoples in connection with us. I believe in national friendships and heartiest good-will to all nations; but national friendships, like those between men, must be founded on respect as well as on liking, on forbearance as well as upon trust. I should be heartily ashamed of any American who did not try to make the American government act as justly toward the other nations in international relations as he himself would act toward any individual in private relations. I should be heartily ashamed to see us wrong a weaker power, and I should hang my head forever if we tamely suffered wrong from a stronger power.

Of conservation I shall speak more at length elsewhere. Conservation means development as much as it does protection. I recognize the right and duty of this generation to develop and use the natural resources of our land; but I do not recognize the right to waste them or to rob, by wasteful use, the generations that come after us. I ask nothing of the nation except that it so behave as each farmer here behaves with reference to his own children. That farmer is a poor creature who skins the land and leaves it worthless to his children. The farmer is a good farmer who, having enabled the land to support himself and to provide for the education of his children, leaves it to them a little better than he found it himself. I believe the same thing of a nation.

Moreover, I believe that the natural resources must be used for the benefit of all our people and not monopolized for the benefit of the few, and here again is another case in which I am accused of taking a revolutionary attitude. People forget now that one hundred years ago there were public men of good character who advocated the nation selling its public lands in great quantities, so that the nation could get the most money out of it and giving it to the men who could cultivate it for their own uses. We took the proper democratic ground that the land should be granted in small sections to the men who were actually to till it and live on it. Now, with the water power, with the forests, with the mines, we are brought face to face with the fact that there are many people who will go with us in conserving the resources only if they are to be allowed to exploit them for their benefit. That is one of the fundamental reasons why the special interests should be driven out of politics. Of all the questions which can come before this nation, short of the actual preservation of its existence in a great war, there is none which compares in importance with the great central task of leaving this land even a better land for our descendants than it is for us, and training them into a better race to inhabit the land and pass it on. Conservation is a great moral issue, for it involves the patriotic duty of insuring the safety and continuance of the nation. Let me add that the health and vitality of our people are at least as well worth conserving as their forests, waters, lands, and minerals, and in this great work the national government must bear a most important part.

I have spoken elsewhere also of the great task which lies before the farmers of the country to get for themselves and their wives and children not only the benefits of better farming, but also those of better business methods and better conditions of life on the farm. The burden of this great task will fall, as it should, mainly upon the great organizations of the farmers themselves. I am glad it will, for I believe they are all well able to handle it. In particular, there are strong reasons why the Departments of Agriculture of the various states, the United States Department of Agriculture, and the agricultural colleges and experiment stations should extend their work to cover all phases of farm life instead of limiting themselves, as they have far too often limited themselves in the past, solely to the question of the production of crops. And now a special word to the farmer. I want to see him make the farm as fine a farm as it can be made; and let him remember to see that the improvement goes on indoors as well as out; let him remember that the farmer's wife should have her share of thought and attention just as much as the farmer himself.

Nothing is more true than that excess of every kind is followed by reaction, a fact which should be pondered by reformer and reactionary alike. We are face to face with new conceptions of the relations of property to human welfare, chiefly because certain advocates of the rights of property as against the rights of men have been pushing their claims too far. The man who wrongly holds that every human right is secondary to his profit must now give way to the advocate of human welfare, who rightly maintains that every man holds his property subject to the general right of the community to regulate its use to whatever degree the public welfare may require it.

But I think we may go still further. The right to regulate the use of wealth in the public interest is universally admitted. Let us admit also the right to regulate the terms and conditions of labor, which is the chief element of wealth, directly in the interest of the common good. The fundamental thing to do for every man is to give him a chance to reach a place in which he will make the greatest possible contribution to the public welfare. Understand what I say there. Give him a chance, not push him up if he will not be pushed. Help any man who stumbles; if he lies down, it is a poor job to try to carry him, but if he is a worthy man, try your best to see that he gets a chance to show the worth that is in him. No man can be a good citizen unless he has a wage more than sufficient to cover the bare cost of living, and hours of labor short enough so after his day's work is done he will have time and energy to bear his share in the management of the community, to help in carrying the general load.

We keep countless men from being good citizens by the conditions of life by which we surround them. We need comprehensive workman's compensation acts, both state and national laws to regulate child labor and work for women, and, especially, we need in our common schools not merely education in book learning, but also practical training for daily life and work. We need to enforce better sanitary conditions for our workers and to extend the use of safety appliances for workers in industry and commerce, both within and between the states.

Also, friends, in the interest of the working man himself, we need to set our faces like flint against mob violence just as against corporate greed, against violence and injustice and lawlessness by wage-workers just as much as against lawless cunning and greed and selfish arrogance of employers. If I could ask but one thing of my fellow countrymen, my request would be that, whenever they go in for reform, they remember the two sides, and that they always exact justice from one side as much as from the other. I have small use for the public servant who can always see and denounce the corruption of the capitalist but who cannot persuade himself, especially before election, to say a word about lawless mob violence. And I have equally small use for the man, be he a judge on the bench or editor of a great paper or wealthy and influential private citizen, who can see clearly enough and denounce the lawlessness of mob violence, but whose eyes are closed so that he is blind when the question is one of corruption of business on a gigantic scale. Also, remember what I said about excess in reformer and reactionary alike. If the reactionary man who thinks of nothing but the rights of property could have his way, he would bring about a revolution; and one of my chief fears in connection with progress comes because I do not want to see our people, for lack of proper leadership, compelled to follow men whose intentions are excellent but whose eyes are a little too wild to make it really safe to trust them. Here in Kansas there is one paper which habitually denounces me as the tool of Wall Street, and at the same time frantically repudiates the statement that I am a socialist on the ground that that is an unwarranted slander of the socialists.

National efficiency has many factors. It is a necessary result of the principle of conservation widely applied. In the end, it will determine our failure or success as a nation. National efficiency has to do not only with natural resources and with men, but it is equally concerned with institutions. The state must be made efficient for the work which concerns only the people of the state, and the nation for that which concerns all the people. There must remain no neutral ground to serve as a refuge for lawbreakers, and especially for lawbreakers of great wealth who can hire the vulpine legal cunning which will teach them how to avoid both jurisdictions. It is a misfortune when the national legislature fails to do its duty in providing a national remedy, so that the only national activity is the purely negative activity of the judiciary in forbidding the state to exercise power in the premises.

I do not ask for the over-centralization, but I do ask that we work in a spirit of broad and far-reaching nationalism where we work for what concerns our people as a whole. We are all Americans. Our common interests are as broad as the continent. I speak to you here in Kansas exactly as I would speak in New York or Georgia, for the most vital problems are those which affect us all alike. The national government belongs to the whole American people, and where the whole American people are interested, that interest can be guarded effectively only by the national government. The betterment which we seek must be accomplished, I believe, mainly through the national government.

The American people are right in demanding that New Nationalism, without which we cannot hope to deal with new problems. The New Nationalism puts the national need before sectional or personal advantage. It is impatient of the utter confusion that results from local legislatures attempting to treat national issues as local issues. It is still more impatient of the impotence which springs from over division of governmental powers, the impotence which makes it possible for local selfishness or for legal cunning, hired by wealthy special interests, to bring national activities to a deadlock. This New Nationalism regards the executive power as the steward of the public welfare. It demands of the judiciary that it shall be interested primarily in human welfare rather than in property, just as it demands that the representative body shall represent all the people rather than any one class or section of the people.

I believe in shaping the ends of government to protect property as well as human welfare. Normally, and in the long run, the ends are the same; but whenever the alternative must be faced, I am for men and not for property, as you were in the Civil War. I am far from underestimating the importance of dividends, but I rank dividends below human character. Again, I do not have any sympathy with the reformer who says he does not care for dividends. Of course, economic welfare is necessary, for a man must pull his own weight and be able to support his family. I know well that the reformers must not bring upon the people economic ruin, or the reforms themselves will go down in the ruin. But we must be ready to face temporary disaster, whether or not brought on by those who will war against us to the knife. Those who oppose reform will do well to remember that ruin in its worst form is inevitable if our national life brings us nothing better than swollen fortunes for the few and the triumph in both politics and business of a sordid and selfish materialism.

If our political institutions were perfect, they would absolutely prevent the political domination of money in any part of our affairs. We need to make our political representatives more quickly and sensitively responsive to the people whose servants they are. More direct action by the people in their own affairs under proper safeguards is vitally necessary. The direct primary is a step in this direction, if it is associated with a corrupt-services act effective to prevent the advantage of the man willing recklessly and unscrupulously to spend money over his more honest competitor. It is particularly important that all moneys received or expended for campaign purposes should be publicly accounted for, not only after election, but before election as well. Political action must be made simpler, easier, and freer from confusion for every citizen. I believe that the prompt removal of unfaithful or incompetent public servants should be made easy and sure in whatever way experience shall show to be most expedient in any given class of cases.

One of the fundamental necessities in a representative government such as ours is to make certain that the men to whom the people delegate their power shall serve the people by whom they are elected, and not the special interests. I believe that every national officer, elected or appointed, should be forbidden to perform any service or receive any compensation, directly or indirectly, from interstate corporations, and a similar provision could not fail to be useful within the states.

The object of government is the welfare of the people. The material progress and prosperity of a nation are desirable chiefly so long as they lead to the moral and material welfare of all good citizens. Just in proportion as the average man and woman are honest, capable of sound judgment and high ideals, active in public affairs—but, first of all, sound in their home, and the father and mother of healthy children whom they bring up well—just so far, and no farther, we may count our civilization a success. We must have—I believe we have already—a genuine and permanent moral awakening, without which no wisdom of legislation or administration really means anything; and, on the other hand, we must try to secure the social and economic legislation without which any improvement due to purely moral agitation is necessarily evanescent.

Let me again illustrate by a reference to the Grand Army. You could not have won simply as a disorderly and disorganized mob. You needed generals; you needed careful administration of the most advanced type; and a good commissary—the cracker line. You well remember that success was necessary in many different lines in order to bring about general success. You had to have the administration at Washington good, just as you had to have the administration in the field; and you had to have the work of the generals good. You could not have triumphed without the administration and leadership; but it would all have been worthless if the average soldier had not had the right stuff in him. He had to have the right stuff in him, or you could not get it out of him.

In the last analysis, therefore, vitally necessary though it was to have the right kind of organization and the right kind of generalship, it was even more vitally necessary that the average soldier should have the fighting edge, the right character. So it is in our civil life. No matter how honest and decent we are in our private lives, if we do not have the right kind of law and the right kind of administration of the law, we cannot go forward as a nation. That is imperative; but it must be an addition to, and not a substitute for, the qualities that make us good citizens. In the last analysis, the most important elements in any man's career must be the sum of those qualities which, in the aggregate, we speak of as character. If he has not got it, then no law that the wit of man can devise, no administration of the law by the boldest and strongest executive, will avail to help him. We must have the right kind of character—character that makes a man, first of all, a good man in the home, a good father, and a good husband—that makes a man a good neighbor.

You must have that, and, then, in addition, you must have the kind of law and the kind of administration of the law which will give to those qualities in the private citizen the best possible chance for development. The prime problem of our nation is to get the right type of good citizenship, and, to get it, we must have progress, and our public men must be genuinely progressive.

From His Remarks in Milwaukee

(1912)

"The bullet is in me now, so that I cannot make a very long speech"

By 1912, Roosevelt was challenging Taft in the Republican primary. After he lost, Roosevelt jumped to the Progressive Party, often called the Bull Moose Party, so he could run in the general election. Both Roosevelt and Woodrow Wilson, the Democratic nominee, decided to go out on the stump—a sign of how presidential politics was changing. Roosevelt's friends were always noting his superhuman energy, and there is no better proof than the October event where Roosevelt was shot by a would-be assassin and yet still managed to extemporize a ninety-minute campaign speech. Roosevelt's prolixity, which was also noted by his friends, may have saved his life. That night, when he talked about "my manuscript," he held it up to show the crowd the thick sheaf of papers that had sat in his pocket and slowed the bullet before it entered his chest.

Friends, I shall have to ask you to be as quiet as possible. I do not know whether you fully understand I have been shot, but it takes more than that to kill a Bull Moose. But fortunately I had my manuscript, so you see I was going to make a long speech. And, friends, the hole in it is where the bullet went through, and it probably saved the bullet from going into my heart.

The bullet is in me now, so that I cannot make a very long speech. But I will try my best. . . . I am in this cause with my whole heart and soul. I believe in the Progressive movement—a movement for the betterment of mankind, a movement for making life a little easier for all our people, a movement to try to take the burdens off the man and especially the woman in this country who is the most oppressed.

I am absorbed in the success of that movement. I feel uncommonly proud in belonging to that movement. I ask you now this evening to accept what I am saying as absolute truth when I tell you I am not thinking of my own success. I am not thinking of my life or of anything connected with me personally. . . .

In the first place, speaking to you here in Milwaukee, I wish to say that the Progressive Party is making its appeal to all our fellow citizens, without any regard to their creed or to their birthplace.

We do not regard as essential the way in which a man worships his God or where he was born. We regard as essential the matter of spirit and purpose.

In New York, while I was police commissioner, the two men from whom I got the most assistance were Jacob Riis, who was born in Denmark, and Arthur von Briesen, who was born in Germany, both of them as fine examples of the best and highest American citizenship as you could find in any part of this country.

I have just been introduced by one of your own men, Henry Cochems. His grandfather, his father, and that father's brother served in the United States Army, and they entered it four years after they had come to this country from Germany. Two of them left their lives, spent their lives, on the field of battle.

I am all right—I am a little sore. Anybody has a right to be sore with a bullet in him. You would find that if I was in battle I would be leading my men just the same, just the same way I am going to make this speech.

At one time I promoted five men for gallantry on the field of battle. Afterward it happened, in making some inquiries about them, that I found two of them were Protestants, two Catholics, and one a Jew. One Protestant came from Germany, and one was born in Ireland. I did not promote them because of their religion; it just happened that way. If all of them had been Jews, I would have promoted them; or if all had been Protestants, I would have promoted them; or if they had been Catholics. In that regiment, I had a man born in Italy who distinguished himself by gallantry; there was a young fellow who came across when he was a child from Bohemia who likewise distinguished himself; and friends, I assure you that I was incapable of considering any question whatever but the worth of each individual as a fighting man. If he was a good fighting man, then I saw that Uncle Sam got the benefit from it. That is all.

I make the same appeal in our citizenship. I ask in our civic life that we in the same way pay heed only to the man's quality of citizenship—to repudiate as the worst enemy that we can have whoever tries to get us to discriminate for or against any man because of his creed or his birthplace.

From His Autobiography

"The love of books and the love of outdoors, in their highest expressions, have usually gone hand in hand"

Roosevelt was a vigorous author, pumping out reviews, nature articles, political essays, and even books of history and biography like his multivolume The Winning of the West. *Roosevelt was also a vigorous outdoorsman, championing America's parks and frequently leaving his famous home, Sagamore Hill, to hunt around the world. In this chapter from his autobiography, which was published in 1913, Roosevelt argues that these two traits are not opposed—that in fact being a great reader and a great explorer fit together neatly. Roosevelt's autobiography also launched a new tradition; with the partial exceptions of Taft and George H. W. Bush, every president since Roosevelt, providing he left the White House in good health, has gone on to write his memoirs.*

There are men who love out-of-doors who yet never open a book, and other men who love books but to whom the great book of nature is a sealed volume, and the lines written therein blurred and illegible. Nevertheless among those men whom I have known the love of books and the love of outdoors, in their highest expressions, have usually gone hand in hand. It is an affectation for the man who is praising outdoors to sneer at books. Usually the keenest appreciation of what is seen in nature is to be found in those who have also profited by the hoarded and recorded wisdom of their fellow men. Love of outdoor life, love of simple and hardy pastimes, can be gratified by men and women who do not possess large means, and who work hard; and so can love of good books—not of good bindings and of first editions, excellent enough in their way but sheer luxuries—I mean love of reading books, owning them if possible of course, but, if that is not possible, getting them from a circulating library.

Sagamore Hill takes its name from the old Sagamore Mohannis, who, as chief of his little tribe, signed away his rights to the land two centuries and a half ago. The house stands right on the top of the hill, separated by fields and belts of woodland from all other houses, and looks out over the bay and the Sound. We see the sun go down beyond long reaches of land and of water. Many birds dwell in the trees round the house or in the pastures and the woods nearby, and of course in winter gulls, loons, and wild fowl frequent the waters of the bay and the Sound. We love all the seasons; the snows and bare woods of winter; the rush of growing things and the blossom-spray of spring; the yellow grain, the ripening fruits and tasseled corn, and the deep, leafy shades that are heralded by "the green dance of summer"; and the sharp fall winds that tear the brilliant banners with which the trees greet the dying year.

The Sound is always lovely. In the summer nights we watch it from the piazza, and see the lights of the tall Fall River boats as they steam steadily by. Now and then we spend a day on it, the two of us together in the light rowing skiff, or perhaps with one of the boys to pull an extra pair of oars; we land for lunch at noon under wind-beaten oaks on the edge of a low bluff, or among the wild plum bushes on a spit of white sand, while the sails of the coasting schooners gleam in the sunlight, and the tolling of the bell-buoy comes landward across the waters.

Long Island is not as rich in flowers as the valley of the Hudson. Yet there are many. Early in April there is one hillside near us which glows like a tender flame with the white of the bloodroot. About the same time we find the shy mayflower, the trailing arbutus; and although we rarely pick wild flowers, one member of the household always plucks a little bunch of mayflowers to send to a friend working in Panama, whose soul hungers for the Northern spring. Then there are shadblow and delicate anemones, about the time of the cherry blossoms; the brief glory of the apple orchards follows; and then the thronging dogwoods fill the forests with their radiance; and so flowers follow flowers until the springtime splendor closes with the laurel and the evanescent, honey-sweet locust bloom. The late summer flowers follow, the flaunting lilies, and cardinal flowers, and marshmallows, and pale beach rosemary; and the goldenrod and the asters when the afternoons shorten and we again begin to think of fires in the wide fireplaces.

Most of the birds in our neighborhood are the ordinary home friends of the house and the barn, the wood lot and the pasture; but now and then the species make queer shifts. The cheery quail—alas!—are rarely found near us now; and we no longer hear the whippoorwills at night. But some birds visit us now which formerly did not. When I was a boy neither the black-throated green warbler nor the purple finch nested around us, nor were bobolinks found in our fields. The black-throated green warbler is now one of our commonest summer warblers; there are plenty of purple finches; and, best of all, the bobolinks are far from infrequent. I had written about these new visitors to John Burroughs, and once when he came out to see me I was able to show them to him.

When I was president, we owned a little house in western Virginia, a delightful house, to us at least, although only a shell of rough boards. We used sometimes to go there in the fall, perhaps at Thanksgiving, and on these occasions we would have quail and rabbits of our own shooting, and once in a while a wild turkey. We also went there in the spring. Of course many of the birds were different from our Long Island friends. There were mocking-birds, the most attractive of all birds, and blue grosbeaks, and cardinals and summer redbirds, instead of scarlet tanagers, and those wonderful singers the Bewick's wrens, and Carolina wrens. All these I was able to show John Burroughs when he came to visit us; although, by the way, he did not appreciate as much as we did one set of inmates of the cottage—the flying squirrels. We loved having the flying squirrels, father and mother and half-grown young, in their nest among the rafters; and at night we slept so soundly that we did not in the least mind the wild gambols of the little fellows through the rooms, even when, as sometimes happened, they would swoop down to the bed and scuttle across it.

One April I went to Yellowstone Park, when the snow was still very deep, and I took John Burroughs with me. I wished to show him the big game of the park, the wild creatures that have become so astonishingly tame and tolerant of human presence. In the Yellowstone the animals seem always to behave as one wishes them to! It is always possible to see the sheep and deer and antelope, and also the great herds of elk, which are shyer than the smaller beasts. In April we found the elk weak after the short commons and hard living of winter. Once without much difficulty I regularly rounded up a big band of them, so that John Burroughs could look at them. I do not think, however, that he cared to see them as much as I did. The birds interested him more, especially a tiny owl the size of a robin which we saw perched on the top of a tree in mid-afternoon entirely uninfluenced by the sun and making a queer noise like a cork being pulled from a bottle. I was rather ashamed to find how much better his eyes were than mine in seeing the birds and grasping their differences.

When wolf-hunting in Texas, and when bear-hunting in Louisiana and Mississippi, I was not only enthralled by the sport, but also by the strange new birds and other creatures, and the trees and flowers I had not known before. By the way, there was one feast at the White House which stands above all others in my memory—even above the time when I lured Joel Chandler Harris thither for a night, a deed in which to triumph, as all who knew that inveterately shy recluse will testify. This was "the bear-hunters' dinner." I had been treated so kindly by my friends on these hunts, and they were such fine fellows, men whom I was so proud to think of as Americans, that I set my heart on having them at a hunters' dinner at the White House. One December I succeeded; there were twenty or thirty of them, all told, as good hunters, as daring riders, as first-class citizens as could be found anywhere; no finer set of guests ever sat at meat in the White House; and among other game on the table was a black bear, itself contributed by one of these same guests.

When I first visited California, it was my good fortune to see the "big trees," the Sequoias, and then to travel down into the Yosemite, with John Muir. Of course of all people in the world he was the one with whom it was best worthwhile thus to see the Yosemite. He told me that when Emerson came to California he tried to get him to come out and camp with him, for that was the only way in which to see at their best the majesty and charm of the Sierras. But at the time Emerson was getting old and could not go. John Muir met me with a couple of packers and two mules to carry our tent, bedding, and food for a three days' trip. The first night was clear, and we lay down in the darkening aisles of the great Sequoia grove. The majestic trunks, beautiful in color and in symmetry, rose round us like the pillars of a mightier cathedral than ever was conceived even by the fervor of the Middle Ages. Hermit thrushes sang beautifully in the evening, and again, with a burst of wonderful music, at dawn. I was interested and a little surprised to find that, unlike John Burroughs, John Muir cared little for birds or bird songs, and knew little about them. The hermit thrushes meant nothing to him, the trees and the flowers and the cliffs everything. The only birds he noticed or cared for were some that were very conspicuous, such as the water-ousels—always particular favorites of mine too.

The second night we camped in a snowstorm, on the edge of the canyon walls, under the spreading limbs of a grove of mighty silver fir; and next day we went down into the wonderland of the valley itself. I shall always be glad that I was in the Yosemite with John Muir and in the Yellowstone with John Burroughs.

Like most Americans interested in birds and books, I know a good deal about English birds as they appear in books. I know the lark of Shakespeare and Shelley and the Ettrick Shepherd; I know the nightingale of Milton and Keats; I know Wordsworth's cuckoo; I know mavis and merle singing in the merry green wood of the old ballads; I know Jenny Wren and Cock Robin of the nursery books. Therefore I had always much desired to hear the birds in real life; and the opportunity offered in June, 1910, when I spent two or three weeks in England. As I could snatch but a few hours from a very exacting round of pleasures and duties, it was necessary for me to be with some companion who could identify both song and singer. In Sir Edward Grey, a keen lover of outdoor life in all its phases, and a delightful companion, who knows the songs and ways of English birds as very few do know them, I found the best possible guide.

We left London on the morning of June 9, twenty-four hours before I sailed from Southampton. Getting off the train at Basingstoke, we drove to the pretty, smiling valley of the Itchen. Here we tramped for three or four hours, then again drove, this time to the edge of the New Forest, where we first took tea at an inn, and then tramped through the forest to an inn on its other side, at Brockenhurst. At the conclusion of our walk my companion made a list of the birds we had seen, putting an asterisk (*) opposite those which we had heard sing. There were forty-one of the former and twenty-three of the latter, as follows:

*Thrush, *blackbird, *lark, *yellowhammer, *robin, *wren, *golden-crested wren, *goldfinch, *chaffinch, *greenfinch, pied wagtail, sparrow, *dunnock (hedge, accentor), missel thrush, starling, rook, jackdaw, *blackcap, *garden warbler, *willow warbler, *chiffchaff, *wood warbler, tree-creeper, *reed bunting, *sedge warbler, coot, water hen, little grebe (dabchick), tufted duck, wood pigeon, stock dove, *turtle dove, peewit, tit (? coal tit), *cuckoo, *nightjar, *swallow, martin, swift, pheasant, partridge.

The valley of the Itchen is typically the England that we know from novel and story and essay. It is very beautiful in every way, with a rich, civilized, fertile beauty—the rapid brook twisting among its reed beds, the rich green of trees and grass, the stately woods, the gardens and fields, the exceedingly picturesque cottages, the great handsome houses standing in their parks. Birds were plentiful; I know but few places in America where one would see such an abundance of individuals, and I was struck by seeing such large birds as coots, water hens, grebes, tufted ducks, pigeons, and peewits. In places in America as thickly settled as the valley of the Itchen, I should not expect to see any like number of birds of this size; but I hope that the efforts of the Audubon societies and kindred organizations will gradually make themselves felt until it becomes a point of honor not only with the American man, but with the American small boy, to shield and protect all forms of harmless wild life. True sportsmen should take the lead in such a movement, for if there is to be any shooting there must be something to shoot; the prime necessity is to keep, and not kill out, even the birds which in legitimate numbers may be shot. . . .

At Sagamore Hill we love a great many things—birds and trees and books, and all things beautiful, and horses and rifles and children and hard work and the joy of life. We have great fireplaces, and in them the logs roar and crackle during the long winter evenings. The big piazza is for the hot, still afternoons of summer. As in every house, there are things that appeal to the householder because of their associations, but which would not mean much to others. Naturally, any man who has been president and filled other positions, accumulates such things, with scant regard to his own personal merits.

Perhaps our most cherished possessions are a Remington bronze, "The Bronco Buster," given me by my men when the regiment was mustered out, and a big Tiffany silver vase given to Mrs. Roosevelt by the enlisted men of the battleship *Louisiana* after we returned from a cruise on her to Panama. It was a real surprise gift, presented to her in the White House, on behalf of the whole crew, by four as strapping man-of-war's-men as ever swung a turret or pointed a twelve-inch gun. The enlisted men of the army I already knew well—of course I knew well the officers of both army and navy. But the enlisted men of the navy I only grew to know well when I was president. On the *Louisiana*, Mrs. Roosevelt and I once dined at the chief petty officers' mess, and on another battleship, the *Missouri* (when I was in company with Admiral Evans and Captain Cowles), and again on the *Sylph* and on the *Mayflower*, we also dined as guests of the crew. When we finished our trip on the *Louisiana*, I made a short speech to the assembled crew, and at its close one of the petty officers, the very picture of what a man-of-war's-man should look like, proposed three cheers for me in terms that struck me as curiously illustrative of America at her best; he said, "Now then, men, three cheers for Theodore Roosevelt, the typical American citizen!" That was the way in which they thought of the American president—and a very good way, too. It was an expression that would have come naturally only to men in whom the American principles of government and life were ingrained. . . .

The books are everywhere. There are as many in the north room and in the parlor—is drawing-room a more appropriate name than parlor?—as in the library; the gunroom at the top of the house, which incidentally has the loveliest view of all, contains more books than any of the other rooms; and they are particularly delightful books to browse among, just because they have not much relevance to one another, this being one of the reasons why they are relegated to their present abode. But the books have overflowed into all the other rooms too.

I could not name any principle upon which the books have been gathered. Books are almost as individual as friends. There is no earthly use in laying down general laws about them. Some meet the needs of one person, and some of another; and each person should beware of the booklover's besetting sin, of what Mr. Edgar Allan Poe calls "the mad pride of intellectuality," taking the shape of arrogant pity for the man who does not like the same kind of books.

Of course there are books which a man or woman uses as instruments of a profession—law books, medical books, cookery books, and the like. I am not speaking of these, for they are not properly "books" at all; they come in the category of timetables, telephone directories, and other useful agencies of civilized life. I am speaking of books that are meant to be read. Personally, granted that these books are decent and healthy, the one test to which I demand that they all submit is that of being interesting. If the book is not interesting to the reader, then in all but an infinitesimal number of cases it gives scant benefit to the reader. Of course any reader ought to cultivate his or her taste so that good books will appeal to it, and that trash won't. But after this point has once been reached, the needs of each reader must be met in a fashion that will appeal to those needs. Personally the books by which I have profited infinitely more than by any others have been those in which profit was a by-product of the pleasure; that is, I read them because I enjoyed them, because I liked reading them, and the profit came in as part of the enjoyment.

Of course each individual is apt to have some special tastes in which he cannot expect that any but a few friends will share. Now, I am very proud of my big-game library. I suppose there must be many big-game libraries in Continental Europe, and possibly in England, more extensive than mine, but I have not happened to come across any such library in this country. Some of the originals go back to the sixteenth century, and there are copies or reproductions of the two or three most famous hunting books of the Middle Ages, such as the Duke of York's translation of Gaston Phoebus, and the queer book of the Emperor Maximilian. It is only very occasionally that I meet any one who cares for any of these books. On the other hand, I expect to find many friends who will turn naturally to some of the old or the new books of poetry or romance or history to which we of the household habitually turn. Let me add that ours is in no sense a collector's library. Each book was procured because someone of the family wished to read it. We could never afford to take overmuch thought for the outsides of books; we were too much interested in their insides.

Now and then I am asked as to "what books a statesman should read," and my answer is, poetry and novels—including short stories under the head of novels. I don't mean that he should read only novels and modern poetry. If he cannot also enjoy the Hebrew prophets and the Greek dramatists, he should be sorry. He ought to read interesting books on history and government, and books of science and philosophy; and really good books on these subjects are as enthralling as any fiction ever written in prose or verse. Gibbon and Macaulay, Herodotus, Thucydides and Tacitus, the Heimskringla, Froissart, Joinville and Villehardouin, Parkman and Mahan, Mommsen and Ranke—why, there are scores and scores of solid histories, the best in the world, which are as absorbing as the best of all the novels and of as permanent value.

The same thing is true of Darwin and Huxley and Carlyle and Emerson, and parts of Kant, and of volumes like Sutherland's "Growth of the Moral Instinct," or Acton's Essays and Lounsbury's studies—here again I am not trying to class books together, or measure one by another, or enumerate one in a thousand of those worth reading, but just to indicate that any man or woman of some intelligence and some cultivation can in some line or other of serious thought, scientific or historical or philosophical or economic or governmental, find any number of books which are charming to read, and which in addition give that for which his or her soul hungers.

I do not for a minute mean that the statesman ought not to read a great many different books of this character, just as everyone else should read them. But, in the final event, the statesman, and the publicist, and the reformer, and the agitator for new things, and the upholder of what is good in old things, all need more than anything else to know human nature, to know the needs of the human soul; and they will find this nature and these needs set forth as nowhere else by the great imaginative writers, whether of prose or of poetry.

From *Our Chief Magistrate and His Powers*

"There is no undefined residuum of power"

While William Howard Taft did not attempt a full autobiography, he regularly drew on his life when writing about legal or political questions. One lecture, which Taft collected in his 1916 book Our Chief Magistrate and His Powers, *rejected Roosevelt's vision of executive power—his belief that the president is able to do anything as long as it is not explicitly prohibited by Congress or the Constitution. Taft's position, which was also the position of most politicians in this period, is essentially the opposite, as he explains in this excerpt from the lecture he called "The Limitations of the President's Powers."*

The true view of the executive functions is, as I conceive it, that the president can exercise no power which cannot be fairly and reasonably traced to some specific grant of power or justly implied and included within such express grant as proper and necessary to its exercise. Such specific grant must be either in the federal Constitution or in an act of Congress passed in pursuance thereof. There is no undefined residuum of power which he can exercise because it seems to him to be in the public interest, and there is nothing in the Neagle case and its definition of a law of the United States or in other precedents warranting such an inference. The grants of executive power are necessarily in general terms in order not to embarrass the executive within the field of action plainly marked for him, but his jurisdiction must be justified and vindicated by affirmative constitutional or statutory provision, or it does not exist.

There have not been wanting, however, eminent men in high public office holding a different view and who have insisted upon the necessity for an undefined residuum of executive power in the public interest. They have not been confined to the present generation. . . . [But] it is interesting to compare the language of Mr. Roosevelt in his [*Autobiography*] on the subject of "executive powers," in which he says:

> The most important factor in getting the right spirit in my administration, next to insistence upon courage, honesty, and a genuine democracy of desire to serve the plain people, was my insistence upon the theory that the executive power was limited only by specific restrictions and prohibitions appearing in the Constitution or imposed by Congress under its constitutional powers. My view was that every executive officer and above all every executive officer in high position was a steward of the people bound actively and affirmatively to do all he could for the people and not to content himself with the negative merit of keeping his talents undamaged in a napkin. I declined to adopt this view that what was imperatively necessary for the nation could not be done by the president, unless he could find some specific authorization to do it. My belief was that it was not only his right but his duty to do anything that the needs of the nation demanded unless such action was forbidden by the Constitution or by the laws. Under this interpretation of executive power I did and caused to be done many things not previously done by the president and the heads of the departments. I did not usurp power but I did greatly broaden the use of executive power. In other words, I acted for the common well-being of all our people whenever and in whatever measure was necessary, unless prevented by direct constitutional or legislative prohibition.

I may add that Mr. Roosevelt, by way of illustrating his meaning as to the differing usefulness of presidents, divides the presidents into two classes and designates them as "Lincoln presidents" and "Buchanan presidents." In order more fully to illustrate his division of presidents on their merits, he places himself in the Lincoln class of presidents and me in the Buchanan class. The identification of Mr. Roosevelt with Mr. Lincoln might otherwise have escaped notice, because there are many differences between the two, presumably superficial, which would give the impartial student of history a different impression.

It suggests a story which a friend of mine told of his little daughter Mary. As he came walking home after a business day, she ran out from the house to greet him, all aglow with the importance of what she wished to tell him.

She said, "Papa, I am the best scholar in the class."

The father's heart throbbed with pleasure as he inquired, "Why, Mary, you surprise me. When did the teacher tell you? This afternoon?"

"Oh, no," Mary's reply was, "the teacher didn't tell me—I just noticed it myself."

From *Congressional Government*

"The president and his cabinet must wait upon the will of Congress"

Before Woodrow Wilson was a president, he was a professor. He specialized in politics, and his most important book—an authoritative blend of historical detail and present-day diagnosis, a description of American government as it actually functioned—was titled Congressional Government. *That title is a clue to the branch that still held sway in 1885. In this excerpt from the book's fifth chapter, "The Executive," Wilson explains why America's presidents have remained relatively weak. He also hints at how a stronger, centralized government might provide a better solution.*

The business of the president, occasionally great, is usually not much above routine. Most of the time it is *mere* administration, mere obedience of directions from the masters of policy, [Congress's] standing committees. Except in so far as his power of veto constitutes him a part of the legislature, the president might not inconveniently be a permanent officer: the first official of a carefully-graded and impartially regulated civil service system, through whose sure series of merit promotions the youngest clerk might rise even to the chief magistracy. He is part of the official rather than of the political machinery of the government, and his duties call rather for training than for constructive genius. . . . Administration is something that men must learn, not something to skill in which they are born. Americans take to business of all kinds more naturally than any other nation ever did, and the executive duties of government constitute just an exalted kind of business; but even Americans are not presidents in their cradles. . . .

The president is not all of the executive. He cannot get along without the men whom he appoints, with and by the consent and advice of the Senate, and they are really integral parts of that branch of the government which he titularly contains in his one single person. The characters and training of the secretaries are of almost as much importance as his own gifts and antecedents. . . .

There is no influence except the ascendency or tact of the president himself to keep a cabinet in harmony and to dispose it to cooperation, so that it would be very difficult to lay down any rules as to what elements really constitute an executive. Those elements can be determined exactly of only one administration at a time, and of that only after it has closed and someone who knows its secrets has come forward to tell them. We think of Mr. Lincoln rather than of his secretaries when we look back to the policy of the wartime; but we think of Mr. Hamilton rather than of President Washington when we look back to the policy of the first administration. Daniel Webster was bigger than President Fillmore, and President Jackson was bigger than Mr. Secretary Van Buren. It depends for the most part upon the character and training, the previous station of the cabinet officers, whether or not they act as governing factors in administration, just as it depends upon the president's talents and preparatory schooling whether or not he is a mere figure-head. A weak president may prove himself wiser than the convention which nominated him, by overshadowing himself with a cabinet of notables.

From the necessity of the case, however, the president cannot often be really supreme in matters of administration, except as the Speaker of the House of Representatives is supreme in legislation, as appointer of those who are supreme in its several departments. The president is no greater than his prerogative of veto makes him; he is, in other words, powerful rather as a branch of the legislature than as the titular head of the executive. Almost all distinctively executive functions are specifically bestowed upon the heads of the departments. No president, however earnest and industrious, can keep the Navy in a state of creditable efficiency if he have a corrupt or incapable secretary in the Navy Department; he cannot prevent the army from suffering the damage of demoralization if the secretary of war is without either ability, experience, or conscience; there will be corrupt jobs in the Department of Justice, do what he will to correct the methods of a deceived or deceitful attorney general; he cannot secure even-handed equity for the Indian tribes if the secretary of the interior chooses to thwart him; and the secretary of state may do as much mischief behind his back as can the secretary of the treasury. He might master the details and so control the administration of someone of the departments, but he can scarcely oversee them all with any degree of strictness. His knowledge of what they have done or are doing comes, of course, from the secretaries themselves, and his annual messages to Congress are in large part but a recapitulation of the chief contents of the detailed reports which the heads of the departments themselves submit at the same time to the houses.

It is easy, however, to exaggerate the power of the cabinet. . . . The secretaries are in the leading strings of statutes, and all their duties look towards a strict obedience to Congress. Congress made them and can unmake them. It is to Congress that they must render account for the conduct of administration. . . .

It is quite evident that the means which Congress has of controlling the departments and of exercising the searching oversight at which it aims are limited and defective. Its intercourse with the president is restricted to the executive messages, and its intercourse with the departments has no easier channels than private consultations between executive officials and the committees, informal interviews of the ministers with individual members of Congress, and the written correspondence which the cabinet officers from time to time address to the presiding officers of the two houses, at stated intervals, or in response to formal resolutions of inquiry. Congress stands almost helplessly outside of the departments. Even the special, irk-some, ungracious investigations which it from time to time institutes in its spasmodic endeavors to dispel or confirm suspicions of malfeasance or of wanton corruption do not afford it more than a glimpse of the inside of a small province of federal administration. Hostile or designing officials can always hold it at arm's length by dexterous evasions and concealments. It can violently disturb, but it cannot often fathom, the waters of the sea in which the bigger fish of the civil service swim and feed. Its dragnet stirs without cleansing the bottom. Unless it have at the head of the departments capable, fearless men, altogether in its confidence and entirely in sympathy with its designs, it is clearly helpless to do more than affright those officials whose consciences are their accusers.

And it is easy to see how the commands as well as the questions of Congress may be evaded, if not directly disobeyed, by the executive agents. Its committees may command, but they cannot superintend the execution of their commands. The secretaries, though not free enough to have any independent policy of their own, are free enough to be very poor, because very unmanageable, servants. Once installed, their hold upon their offices does not depend upon the will of Congress. If they please the president, and keep upon living terms with their colleagues, they need not seriously regard the displeasure of the houses, unless, indeed, by actual crime, they rashly put themselves in the way of its judicial wrath. If their folly be not too overt and extravagant, their authority may continue theirs till the earth has four times made her annual journey round the sun. They may make daily blunders in administration and repeated mistakes in business, may thwart the plans of Congress in a hundred small, vexatious ways, and yet all the while snap their fingers at its dissatisfaction or displeasure. They are denied the gratification of possessing real power, but they have the satisfaction of being secure in a petty independence which gives them a chance to be tricky and scheming. There are ways and ways of obeying; and if Congress be not pleased, why need they care? Congress did not give them their places, and cannot easily take them away.

Still it remains true that all the big affairs of the departments are conducted in obedience to the direction of the standing committees. The president nominates and, with legislative approval, appoints to the more important offices of the government, and the members of the cabinet have the privilege of advising him as to matters in most of which he has no power of final action without the concurrence of the Senate; but the gist of all policy is decided by legislative, not by executive, will. It can be no great satisfaction to any man to possess the barren privilege of suggesting the best means of managing the every-day routine business of the several bureaus so long as the larger plans which that business is meant to advance are made for him by others who are set over him. If one is commanded to go to this place or to that place, and must go, will he, nill he, it can be but small solace to him that he is left free to determine whether he will ride or walk in going the journey.

The only serious questions are whether or not this so great and real control exerted by Congress can be exercised efficiently and with sufficient responsibility to those whom Congress represents, and whether good government is promoted by the arrangement. . . . Each branch of the government is fitted out with a small section of responsibility, whose limited opportunities afford to the conscience of each many easy escapes. Every suspected culprit may shift the responsibility upon his fellows. Is Congress rated for corrupt or imperfect or foolish legislation? It may urge that it has to follow hastily its committees or do nothing at all but talk; how can it help it if a stupid committee leads it unawares into unjust or fatuous enterprises? Does administration blunder and run itself into all sorts of straits? The secretaries hasten to plead the unreasonable or unwise commands of Congress, and Congress falls to blaming the secretaries. The secretaries aver that the whole mischief might have been avoided if they had only been allowed to suggest the proper measures; and the men who framed the existing measures in their turn avow their despair of good government so long as they must entrust all their plans to the bungling incompetence of men who are appointed by and responsible to somebody else. How is the schoolmaster, the nation, to know which boy needs the whipping?

Moreover, it is impossible to deny that this division of authority and concealment of responsibility are calculated to subject the government to a very distressing paralysis in moments of emergency. There are few, if any, important steps that can be taken by any one branch of the government without the consent or cooperation of some other branch. Congress must act through the president and his cabinet; the president and his cabinet must wait upon the will of Congress. There is no one supreme, ultimate head—whether magistrate or representative body—which can decide at once and with conclusive authority what shall be done at those times when some decision there must be, and that immediately. Of course this lack is of a sort to be felt at all times, in seasons of tranquil rounds of business as well as at moments of sharp crisis, but in times of sudden exigency it might prove fatal—fatal either in breaking down the system or in failing to meet the emergency. Policy cannot be either prompt or straightforward when it must serve many masters. It must either equivocate, or hesitate, or fail altogether. It may set out with clear purpose from Congress, but get waylaid or maimed by the executive.

If there be one principle clearer than another, it is this: that in any business, whether of government or of mere merchandising, somebody must be trusted, in order that when things go wrong it may be quite plain who should be punished. In order to drive trade at the speed and with the success you desire, you must confide without suspicion in your chief clerk, giving him the power to ruin you because you thereby furnish him with a motive for serving you. His reputation, his own honor or disgrace, all his own commercial prospects, hang upon your success. And human nature is much the same in government as in the dry goods trade. Power and strict accountability for its use are the essential constituents of good government.

A sense of highest responsibility, a dignifying and elevating sense of being trusted, together with a consciousness of being in an official station so conspicuous that no faithful discharge of duty can go unacknowledged and unrewarded and no breach of trust undiscovered and unpunished—these are the influences, the only influences, which foster practical, energetic, and trustworthy statesmanship. The best rulers are always those to whom great power is entrusted in such a manner as to make them feel that they will surely be abundantly honored and recompensed for a just and patriotic use of it, and to make them know that nothing can shield them from full retribution for every abuse of it.

From His Lecture on History and Leadership

"The perennial misunderstanding between the men who write and the men who act"

In addition to his research on politics and history, Wilson wrote about literature and the arts. (The title of one of his essay collections: Mere Literature.*) In a fascinating lecture that he delivered several times in the 1890s, Wilson combined these interests to examine the differences between writers and politicians—or the difference, as he put it, between "men who write" and "men who act." This lecture and its dual categories also provide an interesting vantage for considering Wilson himself, since at various points in his career he was one, the other, or both.*

Only those are "leaders of men," in the general eye, who lead in action. The title belongs, if the whole field of the world be justly viewed, no more rightfully to the men who lead in action than to those who lead in silent thought. A book is often quite as quickening a trumpet as any made of brass and sounded in the field. But it is the estimate of the world that bestows their meaning upon words, and that estimate is not often very far from the fact. The men who act stand nearer to the mass of men than do the men who write; and it is at their hands that new thought gets its translation into the crude language of deeds. The very crudity of that language of deeds exasperates the sensibilities of the author, and his exasperation proves the world's point. He may be *back* of the leaders, but he is not the leader. In his thought there is due and studied proportion; all limiting considerations are set in their right places, as guards to ward off misapprehension. Every cadence of right utterance is made to sound in the careful phrases, in the perfect adjustments of sense. Translate the thought into action and all its shadings disappear. It stands out a naked, lusty thing, sure to rasp the sensibilities of every man of fastidious taste. Stripped for action, a thought must always shock those who cultivate the nice fashions of literary dress, as authors do. But it is only when thought does thus stand forth in unabashed force that it can perform deeds of strength in the arena round about which the great public sit as spectators, awarding the prizes by the suffrage of their applause.

Here, unquestionably, we come upon the heart of the perennial misunderstanding between the men who write and the men who act. The men who write love proportion; the men who act must strike out practicable lines of action and neglect proportion. This would seem to explain the well-nigh universal repugnance felt by literary men towards democracy. The arguments which induce popular action must always be broad and obvious arguments. Only a very gross substance of concrete conception can make any impression on the minds of the masses; they must get their ideas very absolutely put and are much readier to receive a half-truth which they can promptly understand than a whole truth which has too many sides to be seen all at once. How can any man whose method is the method of artistic completeness of thought and expression, whose mood is the mood of contemplation, for a moment understand or tolerate the majority whose purpose and practice it is to strike out broad, rough-hewn policies, whose mood is the mood of action? The great stream of freedom, which "broadens down / from precedent to precedent," is not a clear mountain current such as the fastidious man of chastened taste likes to drink from; it is polluted with not a few of the coarse elements of the gross world on its banks; it is heavy with the drainage of a very material universe.

One of the nicest tests of the repugnance felt by the literary nature for the sort of leadership and action which commends itself to the world of common men you may yourself supply. Asking some author of careful, discriminative thought to utter his ideas to a mass meeting, from a platform occupied by "representative citizens." He will shrink from it as he would shrink from being publicly dissected! Even to hear someone else, who is given to apt public speech, re-render his thoughts in oratorical phrase and make them acceptable to a miscellaneous audience is often a mild, sometimes an acute, form of torture for him. If the world would really know his thoughts for what they are, let them go to his written words, con his phrases, join paragraph with paragraph, chapter with chapter; then, the whole form and fashion of his conceptions impressed upon their minds, they will know him as no platform speaker can ever make him known. Of course such preferences greatly limit his audience. Not many out of the multitudes who crowd about him buy his books. But if the few who can understand read and are convinced, will not his thoughts finally leaven the mass?

The true leader of men, it is plain, is equipped by lacking such sensibilities which the literary man, when analyzed, is found to possess as a chief part of his makeup. He lacks that subtle power of sympathy which enables the men who write the great works of the imagination to put their minds under the spell of a thousand individual motives not their own but the living force in several characters they interpret. No popular leader could write fiction. He could not write fiction. He could not conceive [Robert Browning's] *The Ring and the Book*, the impersonation of a half-score points of view. An imaginative realization of other natures and minds than his own is as impossible for him as his own commanding, dominating frame of mind and character is impossible for the sensitive seer whose imagination can give life to a thousand separate characters. Mr. Browning could no more have been a statesman—if statesmen are to be popular leaders also—than Mr. Disraeli could write a novel. Mr. Browning could see from every individual's point of view—no intellectual sympathy came amiss to him. Mr. Disraeli could see from no point of view but his own—and the characters which he put into those works of his which were meant to be novels move as mere puppets to his will, as the men he governed did. They are his mouthpieces simply and are as little like themselves as were the Tory squires in the commons like themselves after they became his chessmen. . . .

That the leader of men must have such sympathetic and penetrative insight as shall enable him to discern quite unerringly the motives which move other men in the mass is of course self-evident; but the insight which he must have is not the Shakespearean insight. It need not pierce the particular secrets of individual men; it need only know what it is that lies waiting to be stirred in the minds and purposes of groups and masses of men. Besides, it is not a sympathy that serves, but a sympathy whose power is to command, to command by knowing its instrument. . . .

The competent leader of men cares little for the interior niceties of other people's characters; he cares much—everything—for the external uses to which they may be put. His will seeks the lines of least resistance, but the whole question with him is a question of the application of force. There are men to be moved; how shall he move them? He supplies the power; others supply only the materials upon which that power operates. The power will fail if it be misapplied; it will be misapplied if it be not suitable both in kind and method to the nature of the materials upon which it is spent; but that nature is, after all, only its means. It is the power which dictates, dominates; the materials yield. Men are as clay in the hands of the consummate leader.

It often happens that the leader displays a sagacity and an insight in the handling of men in the mass which quite baffle the wits of the shrewdest analyst of individual character. Men in the mass differ from men as individuals. A man who knows, and keenly knows, every man in town may yet fail to understand a mob or a mass meeting of his fellow townsmen. Just as the whole tone and method suitable for a public speech are foreign to the tone and method proper in individual, face-to-face dealings with separate men, so is the art of leading different from the art of writing novels. Some of the gifts and qualities which most commend the literary man to success would inevitably doom the would-be leader to failure.

WOODROW WILSON

First Inaugural Address

(1913)

"No one can mistake the purpose for which the nation now seeks to use the Democratic Party"

On March 4, 1913, Wilson delivered his first inaugural address. Its style was pure Wilson, combining a professor's gift for sweeping analysis with a preacher's gift for inspirational uplift. But Wilson also described a national discontent—a frustration with unchecked growth, with stratified cities, with business and industrial interests that cared more about their wealth than their impact on regular Americans. Wilson's solution, as the coming months would make clear, was a more aggressive presidency. The author of Congressional Government *had studied Roosevelt's White House activism. In fact, during Roosevelt's administration, Wilson had revised his views on executive power: "The president," he wrote, "is at liberty, both in law and conscience, to be as big a man as he can."*

There has been a change of government. It began two years ago, when the House of Representatives became Democratic by a decisive majority. It has now been completed. The Senate about to assemble will also be Democratic. The offices of president and vice president have been put into the hands of Democrats. What does the change mean? That is the question that is uppermost in our minds today. That is the question I am going to try to answer, in order, if I may, to interpret the occasion.

It means much more than the mere success of a party. The success of a party means little except when the nation is using that party for a large and definite purpose. No one can mistake the purpose for which the nation now seeks to use the Democratic Party. It seeks to use it to interpret a change in its own plans and point of view. Some old things with which we had grown familiar, and which had begun to creep into the very habit of our thought and of our lives, have altered their aspect as we have latterly looked critically upon them with fresh, awakened eyes, have dropped their disguises and shown themselves alien and sinister. Some new things, as we look frankly upon them, willing to comprehend their real character, have come to assume the aspect of things long believed in and familiar, stuff of our own convictions. We have been refreshed by a new insight into our own life.

We see that in many things that life is very great. It is incomparably great in its material aspects, in its body of wealth, in the diversity and sweep of its energy, in the industries which have been conceived and built up by the genius of individual men and the limitless enterprise of groups of men. It is great, also, very great, in its moral force. Nowhere else in the world have noble men and women exhibited in more striking forms the beauty and the energy of sympathy and helpfulness and counsel in their efforts to rectify wrong, alleviate suffering, and set the weak in the way of strength and hope. We have built up, moreover, a great system of government, which has stood through a long age as in many respects a model for those who seek to set liberty upon foundations that will endure against fortuitous change, against storm and accident. Our life contains every great thing, and contains it in rich abundance.

But the evil has come with the good, and much fine gold has been corroded. With riches has come inexcusable waste. We have squandered a great part of what we might have used and have not stopped to conserve the exceeding bounty of nature, without which our genius for enterprise would have been worthless and impotent, scorning to be careful, shamefully prodigal as well as admirably efficient. We have been proud of our industrial achievements, but we have not hitherto stopped thoughtfully enough to count the human cost, the cost of lives snuffed out, of energies overtaxed and broken, the fearful physical and spiritual cost to the men and women and children upon whom the dead weight and burden of it all has fallen pitilessly the years through. The groans and agony of it all had not yet reached our ears, the solemn, moving undertone of our life, coming up out of the mines and factories and out of every home where the struggle had its intimate and familiar seat. With the great government went many deep secret things which we too long delayed to look into and scrutinize with candid, fearless eyes. The great government we loved has too often been made use of for private and selfish purposes, and those who used it had forgotten the people.

At last a vision has been vouchsafed us of our life as a whole. We see the bad with the good, the debased and decadent with the sound and vital. With this vision we approach new affairs. Our duty is to cleanse, to reconsider, to restore, to correct the evil without impairing the good, to purify and humanize every process of our common life without weakening or sentimentalizing it. There has been something crude and heartless and unfeeling in our haste to succeed and be great. Our thought has been, "Let every man look out for himself, let every generation look out for itself," while we reared giant machinery which made it impossible that any but those who stood at the levers of control should have a chance to look out for themselves. We had not forgotten our morals. We remembered well enough that we had set up a policy which was meant to serve the humblest as well as the most powerful, with an eye single to the standards of justice and fair play, and remembered it with pride. But we were very heedless and in a hurry to be great.

We have come now to the sober second thought. The scales of heedlessness have fallen from our eyes. We have made up our minds to square every process of our national life again with the standards we so proudly set up at the beginning and have always carried at our hearts. Our work is a work of restoration.

We have itemized with some degree of particularity the things that ought to be altered and here are some of the chief items: a tariff which cuts us off from our proper part in the commerce of the world, violates the just principles of taxation, and makes the government a facile instrument in the hand of private interests; a banking and currency system based upon the necessity of the government to sell its bonds fifty years ago and perfectly adapted to concentrating cash and restricting credits; an industrial system which, take it on all its sides, financial as well as administrative, holds capital in leading strings, restricts the liberties and limits the opportunities of labor, and exploits without renewing or conserving the natural resources of the country; a body of agricultural activities never yet given the efficiency of great business undertakings or served as it should be through the instrumentality of science taken directly to the farm or afforded the facilities of credit best suited to its practical needs; watercourses undeveloped, waste places unreclaimed, forests untended, fast disappearing without plan or prospect of renewal, unregarded waste heaps at every mine. We have studied as perhaps no other nation has the most effective means of production, but we have not studied cost or economy as we should either as organizers of industry, as statesmen, or as individuals.

Nor have we studied and perfected the means by which government may be put at the service of humanity in safeguarding the health of the nation, the health of its men and its women and its children as well as their rights in the struggle for existence. This is no sentimental duty. The firm basis of government is justice, not pity. These are matters of justice. There can be no equality or opportunity, the first essential of justice in the body politic, if men and women and children be not shielded in their lives, their very vitality, from the consequences of great industrial and social processes which they cannot alter, control, or singly cope with. Society must see to it that it does not itself crush or weaken or damage its own constituent parts. The first duty of law is to keep sound the society it serves. Sanitary laws, pure food laws, and laws determining conditions of labor which individuals are powerless to determine for themselves are intimate parts of the very business of justice and legal efficiency.

These are some of the things we ought to do and not leave the others undone, the old-fashioned, never-to-be-neglected, fundamental safeguarding of property and of individual right. This is the high enterprise of the new day: to lift everything that concerns our life as a nation to the light that shines from the hearthfire of every man's conscience and vision of the right. It is inconceivable that we should do this as partisans; it is inconceivable we should do it in ignorance of the facts as they are or in blind haste. We shall restore, not destroy. We shall deal with our economic system as it is and as it may be modified, not as it might be if we had a clean sheet of paper to write upon; and step by step we shall make it what it should be, in the spirit of those who question their own wisdom and seek counsel and knowledge, not shallow self-satisfaction or the excitement of excursions whither they cannot tell. Justice, and only justice, shall always be our motto.

And yet it will be no cool process of mere science. The nation has been deeply stirred, stirred by a solemn passion, stirred by the knowledge of wrong, of ideals lost, of government too often debauched and made an instrument of evil. The feelings with which we face this new age of right and opportunity sweep across our heartstrings like some air out of God's own presence, where justice and mercy are reconciled and the judge and the brother are one. We know our task to be no mere task of politics but a task which shall search us through and through, whether we be able to understand our time and the need of our people, whether we be indeed their spokesmen and interpreters, whether we have the pure heart to comprehend and the rectified will to choose our high course of action.

This is not a day of triumph; it is a day of dedication. Here muster, not the forces of party, but the forces of humanity. Men's hearts wait upon us; men's lives hang in the balance; men's hopes call upon us to say what we will do. Who shall live up to the great trust? Who dares fail to try? I summon all honest men, all patriotic, all forward-looking men, to my side. God helping me, I will not fail them, if they will but counsel and sustain me.

WOODROW WILSON

Address on Tariffs

(1913)

"The president of the United States is a person, not a mere department of the government"

A month after his inaugural, Wilson did something radical: he headed to the Capitol Building to address both houses of Congress in person. Ever since Jefferson's initial State of the Union, in 1801, presidents had preferred to send written documents to the legislature. But Wilson understood that speaking in person—on his campaign promise to lower tariffs and, thus, consumer prices—would generate media coverage, build public support, and put pressure on Congress.

I am very glad indeed to have this opportunity to address the two houses directly and to verify for myself the impression that the president of the United States is a person, not a mere department of the government hailing Congress from some isolated island of jealous power, sending messages, not speaking naturally and with his own voice—that he is a human being trying to cooperate with other human beings in a common service. After this pleasant experience, I shall feel quite normal in all our dealings with one another.

I have called the Congress together in extraordinary session because a duty was laid upon the party now in power at the recent elections which it ought to perform promptly, in order that the burden carried by the people under existing law may be lightened as soon as possible and in order, also,

that the business interests of the country may not be kept too long in suspense as to what the fiscal changes are to be to which they will be required
to adjust themselves. It is clear to the whole country that the tariff duties
must be altered. They must be changed to meet the radical alteration in
the conditions of our economic life which the country has witnessed within
the last generation. While the whole face and method of our industrial
and commercial life were being changed beyond recognition the tariff
schedules have remained what they were before the change began, or have
moved in the direction they were given when no large circumstance of our
industrial development was what it is today. Our task is to square them
with the actual facts. The sooner that is done, the sooner we shall escape
from suffering from the facts and the sooner our men of business will be
free to thrive by the law of nature (the nature of free business) instead of
by the law of legislation and artificial arrangement.

We have seen tariff legislation wander very far afield in our day—very
far indeed from the field in which our prosperity might have had a normal
growth and stimulation. No one who looks the facts squarely in the face or
knows anything that lies beneath the surface of action can fail to perceive
the principles upon which recent tariff legislation has been based. We long
ago passed beyond the modest notion of "protecting" the industries of the
country and moved boldly forward to the idea that they were entitled to
the direct patronage of the government. For a long time—a time so long
that the men now active in public policy hardly remember the conditions
that preceded it—we have sought in our tariff schedules to give each group
of manufacturers or producers what they themselves thought that they
needed in order to maintain a practically exclusive market as against the
rest of the world. Consciously or unconsciously, we have built up a set of
privileges and exemptions from competition behind which it was easy by
any, even the crudest, forms of combination to organize monopoly, until
at last nothing is normal, nothing is obliged to stand the tests of efficiency
and economy in our world of big business, but everything thrives by con-
certed arrangement. Only new principles of action will save us from a final
hard crystallization of monopoly and a complete loss of the influences that
quicken enterprise and keep independent energy alive.

It is plain what those principles must be. We must abolish everything
that bears even the semblance of privilege or of any kind of artificial
advantage and put our businessmen and producers under the stimulation
of a constant necessity to be efficient, economical, and enterprising masters of competitive supremacy, better workers and merchants than any in

the world. Aside from the duties laid upon articles which we do not, and probably cannot, produce, therefore, and the duties laid upon luxuries and merely for the sake of the revenues they yield, the object of the tariff duties henceforth laid must be effective competition, the whetting of American wits by contest with the wits of the rest of the world.

It would be unwise to move toward this end headlong, with reckless haste or with strokes that cut at the very roots of what has grown up amongst us by long process and at our own invitation. It does not alter a thing to upset it and break it and deprive it of a chance to change. It destroys it. We must make changes in our fiscal laws, in our fiscal system, whose object is development, a more free and wholesome development, not revolution or upset or confusion. We must build up trade, especially foreign trade. We need the outlet and the enlarged field of energy more than we ever did before. We must build up industry as well and must adopt freedom in the place of artificial stimulation only so far as it will build, not pull down. In dealing with the tariff the method by which this may be done will be a matter of judgment, exercised item by item. To some not accustomed to the excitements and responsibilities of greater freedom our methods may in some respects and at some points seem heroic, but remedies may be heroic and yet be remedies. It is our business to make sure that they are genuine remedies. Our object is clear. If our motive is above just challenge and only an occasional error of judgment is chargeable against us, we shall be fortunate.

We are called upon to render the country a great service in more matters than one. Our responsibility should be met and our methods should be thorough, as thorough as moderate and well considered, based upon the facts as they are and not worked out as if we were beginners. We are to deal with the facts of our own day, with the facts of no other, and to make laws which square with those facts. It is best, indeed it is necessary, to begin with the tariff. I will urge nothing upon you now at the opening of your session which can obscure that first object or divert our energies from that clearly defined duty. At a later time I may take the liberty of calling your attention to reforms which should press close upon the heels of the tariff changes, if not accompany them, of which the chief is the reform of our banking and currency laws, but just now I refrain. For the present, I put these matters on one side and think only of this one thing—of the changes in our fiscal system which may best serve to open once more the free channels of prosperity to a great people whom we would serve to the utmost and throughout both rank and file.

Address on Women's Suffrage

(1916)

"We feel the tide; we rejoice in the strength of it"

America's presidents have given major speeches on many issues and identities, focusing on Black Americans, Native Americans, immigrant Americans, and religious Americans, among others. This diversity makes one deficiency stand out: the lack of speeches focusing on American women, whether on the issues that affect them uniquely or on the fact that, in the end, every issue is a women's issue. This deficiency reflects the same sexism as the presidency's exclusively male makeup (so far). But it also makes the exceptions interesting, such as this address Wilson delivered in the fall of 1916, at a women's suffrage convention presided over by Carrie Chapman Catt. The convention drew thousands of supporters to Atlantic City, New Jersey, the state where Wilson had served as governor. Wilson could have promised to use the considerable powers he had concentrated in the White House. Instead, he offered the crowd historical analysis and a note of hope. Still, that was more than previous presidents had offered them, and they responded with a standing ovation. "When you said you had come here to fight with us," Catt told Wilson from the stage, "you touched our hearts."

I have found it a real privilege to be here tonight and to listen to the addresses which you have heard. Though you may not all of you believe it, I would a great deal rather hear somebody else speak than speak myself; but I should feel that I was omitting a duty if I did not address you tonight and say some of the things that have been in my thoughts as I realized the approach of this evening and the duty that would fall upon me.

The astonishing thing about the movement which you represent is not that it has grown so slowly, but that it has grown so rapidly. No doubt for those who have been a long time in the struggle, like your honored president, it seems a long and arduous path that has been trodden, but when you think of the cumulating force of this movement in recent decades, you must agree with me that it is one of the most astonishing tides in modern history. Two generations ago—no doubt, Madam President will agree with me in saying it—it was a handful of women who were fighting this cause. Now it is a great multitude of women who are fighting it.

And there are some interesting historical connections which I would like to attempt to point out to you. One of the most striking facts about the history of the United States is that at the outset it was a lawyers' history. Almost all of the questions to which America addressed itself, say, a hundred years ago, were legal questions, were questions of method—not questions of what you were going to do with your government, but questions of how you were going to constitute your government; how you were going to balance the powers of the states and the federal government; how you were going to balance the claims of property against the processes of liberty; how you were going to make your governments up so as to balance the parts against each other so that the legislature would check the executive, and the executive the legislature, and the courts both of them put together.

The whole conception of government when the United States became a nation was a mechanical conception of government, and the mechanical conception of government which underlay it was the Newtonian theory of the universe. If you pick up *The Federalist*, some parts of it read like a treatise on astronomy instead of a treatise on government. They speak of the centrifugal and the centripetal forces, and locate the president somewhere in a rotating system. The whole thing is a calculation of power and an adjustment of parts. There was a time when nobody but a lawyer could know enough to run the government of the United States, and a distinguished English publicist once remarked, speaking of the complexity of the American government, that it was no proof of the excellence of the American Constitution that it had been successfully operated because the Americans could run any constitution. But there have been a great many technical difficulties in running it.

And then something happened. A great question arose in this country which, though complicated with legal elements, was at bottom a human question, and nothing but a question of humanity. That was the slavery question. And is it not significant that it was then, and then for the first time, that women became prominent in politics in America? Not many women; those prominent in that day were so few that you can name them over in a brief catalogue, but, nevertheless, they then began to play a part in writing, not only, but in public speech, which was a very novel part for women to play in America.

After the Civil War had settled some of what seemed to be the most difficult legal questions of our system, the life of the nation began not only to unfold but to accumulate. Life in the United States was a comparatively simple matter at the time of the Civil War. There was none of that under-ground struggle which is now so manifest to those who look only a little way beneath the surface. Stories such as Dr. Davis has told tonight were uncommon in those simpler days; the pressure of low wages, the agony of obscure and unremunerated toil, did not exist in America in anything like the same proportions that they exist now. And as our life has unfolded and accumulated, as the contacts of it have become hot, as the populations have assembled in the cities, and the cool spaces of the country have been supplanted by the feverish urban areas, the whole nature of our political questions has been altered. They have ceased to be legal questions. They have more and more become social questions, questions with regard to the relations of human beings to one another—not merely their legal relations, but their moral and spiritual relations to one another.

This has been most characteristic of American life in the last few decades, and as these questions have assumed greater and greater promi-nence, the movement which this association represents has gathered cumu-lative force. So that, if anybody asks himself, "What does this gathering force mean?"—if he knows anything about the history of the country, he knows that it means something that has not only come to stay, but has come with conquering power.

I get a little impatient sometimes about the discussion of the channels and methods by which it is to prevail. It is going to prevail, and that is a very superficial and ignorant view of it which attributes it to mere social unrest. It is not merely because the women are discontented. It is because the women have seen visions of duty, and that is something which we not only cannot resist, but, if we be true Americans, we do not wish to resist. America took its origin in visions of the human spirit, in aspirations for the deepest sort of liberty of the mind and of the heart, and as visions of that sort come up to the sight of those who are spiritually minded in

America, America comes more and more into her birthright and into the perfection of her development.

So that what we have to realize in dealing with forces of this sort is that we are dealing with the substance of life itself. I have felt as I sat here tonight the wholesome contagion of the occasion. Almost every other time that I ever visited Atlantic City, I came to fight somebody. I hardly know how to conduct myself when I have not come to fight against anybody, but with somebody. I have come to suggest, among other things, that when the forces of nature are steadily working and the tide is rising to meet the moon, you need not be afraid that it will not come to its flood. We feel the tide; we rejoice in the strength of it; and we shall not quarrel in the long run as to the method of it. Because, when you are working with masses of men and organized bodies of opinion, you have got to carry the organized body along. The whole art and practice of government consists not in moving individuals, but in moving masses. It is all very well to run ahead and beckon, but, after all, you have got to wait for the body to follow.

I have not come to ask you to be patient, because you have been. But I have come to congratulate you that there was a force behind you that will beyond any peradventure be triumphant, and for which you can afford a little while to wait.

WOODROW WILSON

From His Address on War with Germany

(1917)

"The world must be made safe for democracy"

As president, Wilson also began delivering the State of the Union in person. At his first one, he had predicted a sunny international forecast. ("There is but one cloud upon our horizon," he said, meaning Mexico.) Wilson was wrong—before long, World War I had overwhelmed Europe, with America struggling to balance between supporting its allies and avoiding entering the war. Finally, on April 2, 1917, Wilson again addressed both houses of Congress, asking them to declare war on Germany.

I have called the Congress into extraordinary session because there are serious, very serious, choices of policy to be made and made immediately, which it was neither right nor constitutionally permissible that I should assume the responsibility of making.

On the 3rd of February last, I officially laid before you the extraordinary announcement of the Imperial German Government that on and after the first day of February, it was its purpose to put aside all restraints of law or of humanity and use its submarines to sink every vessel that sought to approach either the ports of Great Britain and Ireland or the western coasts of Europe or any of the ports controlled by the enemies of Germany within the Mediterranean. That had seemed to be the object of the German submarine warfare earlier in the war, but since April of last year the Imperial Government had somewhat restrained the commanders of its undersea craft in conformity with its promise then given to us that passenger boats should not be sunk and that due warning would be given to all other vessels which its submarines might seek to destroy when no resistance was offered or escape attempted, and care taken that their crews were given at least a fair chance to save their lives in their open boats. The precautions taken were meager and haphazard enough, as was proved in distressing instance after instance in the progress of the cruel and unmanly business, but a certain degree of restraint was observed.

The new policy has swept every restriction aside. Vessels of every kind, whatever their flag, their character, their cargo, their destination, their errand, have been ruthlessly sent to the bottom without warning and without thought of help or mercy for those on board, the vessels of friendly neutrals along with those of belligerents. Even hospital ships and ships carrying relief to the sorely bereaved and stricken people of Belgium, though the latter were provided with safe conduct through the proscribed areas by the German government itself and were distinguished by unmistakable marks of identity, have been sunk with the same reckless lack of compassion or of principle.

I was for a little while unable to believe that such things would in fact be done by any government that had hitherto subscribed to the humane practices of civilized nations. International law had its origin in the attempt to set up some law which would be respected and observed upon the seas, where no nation had right of dominion and where lay the free highways of the world. By painful stage after stage has that law been built up, with meager enough results, indeed, after all was accomplished that could be accomplished, but always with a clear view, at least, of what the heart and conscience of mankind demanded.

This minimum of right the German government has swept aside under the plea of retaliation and necessity and because it had no weapons which it could use at sea except these which it is impossible to employ as it is employing them without throwing to the winds all scruples of humanity or of respect for the understandings that were supposed to underlie the intercourse of the world.

I am not now thinking of the loss of property involved, immense and serious as that is, but only of the wanton and wholesale destruction of the lives of noncombatants, men, women, and children, engaged in pursuits which have always, even in the darkest periods of modern history, been deemed innocent and legitimate. Property can be paid for; the lives of peaceful and innocent people cannot be.

The present German submarine warfare against commerce is a warfare against mankind. It is a war against all nations. American ships have been sunk, American lives taken in ways which it has stirred us very deeply to learn of, but the ships and people of other neutral and friendly nations have been sunk and overwhelmed in the waters in the same way. There has been no discrimination. The challenge is to all mankind. Each nation must decide for itself how it will meet it. The choice we make for ourselves must be made with a moderation of counsel and a temperateness of judgment befitting our character and our motives as a nation.

We must put excited feeling away. Our motive will not be revenge or the victorious assertion of the physical might of the nation, but only the vindication of right, of human right, of which we are only a single champion.

When I addressed the Congress on the 26th of February last, I thought that it would suffice to assert our neutral rights with arms, our right to use the seas against unlawful interference, our right to keep our people safe against unlawful violence. But armed neutrality, it now appears, is impracticable. Because submarines are in effect outlaws when used as the German submarines have been used against merchant shipping, it is impossible to defend ships against their attacks as the law of nations has assumed that merchantmen would defend themselves against privateers or cruisers, visible craft giving chase upon the open sea. It is common prudence in such circumstances, grim necessity indeed, to endeavor to destroy them before they have shown their own intention. They must be dealt with upon sight, if dealt with at all.

The German government denies the right of neutrals to use arms at all within the areas of the sea which it has proscribed, even in the defense of rights which no modern publicist has ever before questioned their right to defend. The intimation is conveyed that the armed guards which we have placed on our merchant ships will be treated as beyond the pale of law and subject to be dealt with as pirates would be. Armed neutrality is ineffectual enough at best; in such circumstances and in the face of such pretensions it is worse than ineffectual: it is likely only to produce what it was meant to prevent; it is practically certain to draw us into the war without either the rights or the effectiveness of belligerents.

There is one choice we cannot make, we are incapable of making: we will not choose the path of submission and suffer the most sacred rights of our nation and our people to be ignored or violated. The wrongs against which we now array ourselves are no common wrongs; they cut to the very roots of human life.

With a profound sense of the solemn and even tragical character of the step I am taking and of the grave responsibilities which it involves, but in unhesitating obedience to what I deem my constitutional duty, I advise that the Congress declare the recent course of the Imperial German Government to be in fact nothing less than war against the government and people of the United States. . . .

We are now about to accept gauge of battle with this natural foe to liberty and shall, if necessary, spend the whole force of the nation to check and nullify its pretensions and its power. We are glad, now that we see the facts with no veil of false pretense about them to fight thus for the ultimate peace of the world and for the liberation of its peoples, the German peoples included: for the rights of nations great and small and the privilege of men everywhere to choose their way of life and of obedience. The world must be made safe for democracy. Its peace must be planted upon the tested foundations of political liberty.

We have no selfish ends to serve. We desire no conquest, no dominion. We seek no indemnities for ourselves, no material compensation for the sacrifices we shall freely make. We are but one of the champions of the rights of mankind. We shall be satisfied when those rights have been made as secure as the faith and the freedom of nations can make them. . . .

It is a distressing and oppressive duty, gentlemen of the Congress, which I have performed in thus addressing you. There are, it may be, many months of fiery trial and sacrifice ahead of us. It is a fearful thing to lead this great peaceful people into war, into the most terrible and disastrous of all wars, civilization itself seeming to be in the balance. But the right is more precious than peace, and we shall fight for the things which we have always carried nearest our hearts—for democracy, for the right of those who submit to authority to have a voice in their own governments, for the rights and liberties of small nations, for a universal dominion of right by such a concert of free peoples as shall bring peace and safety to all nations and make the world itself at last free.

To such a task we can dedicate our lives and our fortunes, everything that we are and everything that we have, with the pride of those who know that the day has come when America is privileged to spend her blood and her might for the principles that gave her birth and happiness and the peace which she has treasured. God helping her, she can do no other.

Remarks at Yellowstone Park

(1923)

"We spent this Sabbath day . . . close to God Almighty"

Warren Harding, H. L. Mencken once wrote, "writes the worst English that I have ever encountered. It reminds me of a string of wet sponges; it reminds me of tattered washing on the line." Perhaps that's why Harding was the first president to hire a speechwriter, the journalist Judson Welliver, on his official White House staff. Welliver didn't save Harding from delivering pompous and lengthy speeches, probably because Harding wanted his speeches to sound that way. But even Harding could achieve eloquence—as in these impromptu remarks he gave after visiting Yellowstone in the summer of 1923, during a multiweek tour of the American west.

It is a very great pleasure to be greeted so cordially by so many of you on this Sabbath evening. We have been spending two wonderful days in your vicinity, and we spent this Sabbath day, I believe, quite as close to God Almighty as though we worshipped in temples erected by man, for we spent the day amidst the grandeur, the majesty, and the inspirations of the great Yellowstone National Park. I hope, aye, I believe, that everyone of our party finds himself this Sabbath evening with a greater reverence for the Creator and a deeper desire to be worthy of God's best intent.

The Yellowstone Park is a wonderful place. It is a great possession for you of Montana and the other states which have territory therein; it is a great possession for those who live nearby; it is a great possession for the United States of America. I have been marveling at our experiences of the last two days. During that time we have seen literally a fine cross-section of the citizenship of our land. I believe that during my brief sojourn in the park I have greeted personally travelers from every state in the American union, and, in addition to that, I have had the privilege of greeting citizens of England, of Canada, and of Cuba. Manifestly all the country is beginning to turn its face toward the Yellowstone National Park, and I am glad of it, for there is nothing more helpful, nothing more uplifting, nothing that gives one a greater realization of the wonders of creation than a visit to that great national institution.

I have gathered some interesting impressions from my sojourn in the park, and I wonder if similar impressions have come to you who live nearby. For instance, because of the protection of wildlife in the park, there has been created amongst the wild creatures there an air and feeling of confidence which causes them to experience a sense of security. We saw it everywhere, and as I watched the wild life of the park today, unconcerned and unmindful of the human beings about them, manifesting their confidence in the security of the situation, I thought how helpful it would be to human kind if we could have a like confidence in one another in all the relations of life.

There was another incident that appealed strongly to me. As we were nearing the end of our trip this afternoon and were coming down one of the long grades, our car suddenly approached a mother grouse and a group of little grouse chicks. The excellent driver of the car brought it to too sudden a halt, but he did it out of regard for that young wild life which was not capable of knowing the danger or protecting itself. The driver did not want to destroy one of those little grouse chicks, not much bigger than a hickory nut—I do not know whether or not you are familiar with hickory nuts in this section—and I liked him for what he did. He exhibited one of the finest impulses that animate the heart of man, namely, to spare innocent, defenseless life. The old mother grouse seemed not to know or care, because she did not realize the danger, but our driver did. I should like to see that example more frequently followed in our relationships with one another. Those who know, those who are strong, those who are in a position to command ought always to be ready to protect the weak, the helpless, and those who do not know. I am sure that if we will more faithfully carry out that principle, we shall be even a better people than we are.

If you have been observing our travels you have noted that it is not customary for me to deliver addresses on the Sabbath. I believe in keeping the day holy. I believe, my countrymen, in a religious America, for I know that we shall be a better people as we become a more moral and pious people. I think, however, it will not be unseemly if I say on this occasion, since you are so deeply interested in the National Park, that I should like to have brought to the attention of all America what a wonder state you are and what a wonder spot the park is. I have crossed the Atlantic three times with very great satisfaction, and I have learned valuable lessons from observation in the Old World; it has been my fortune to travel partway across the Pacific; but, knowing the Yellowstone Park as I now do, I have no hesitancy in saying to everybody in America, "You ought to make it a point to see the Yellowstone National Park before you venture beyond the borders of the United States." I know of nothing to compare with it anywhere in the world, and I am glad we are making of it such a success as a national playground.

In addition to being able to visit the park it is good to have the privilege of coming to this wonder section of our country. You of Montana live in a vast and wonderful state. I hope you will never allow it to become too common to you. Not so very long ago I heard the pastor of a Washington church deliver a sermon in which he admonished his congregation never to allow the uncommon things to become common. If I could convey his thought to you, I would urge you never to allow the grandeur of the mountains and the majesty of this great western country to become so common to you that you will lose the ability to appraise the value of their inspiration and worth. You live in a wonderland, indeed, and we who have come from sections further east have been marveling and indulging in the most extravagant comment of admiration and approval.

I speak the plain truth when I say to you that I am rejoiced that I have come to know better your state and the people of your state. It is a fine thing, my countrymen, to know each other better. I love to preach the gospel of understanding. I want you to understand your government, and I think your government ought to understand you. If we can only have understanding in the world and, with that understanding, the practice of the Golden Rule, we shall not only be a peaceful people among ourselves, but we shall always remain at peace with the nations of the earth.

Again let me thank you for the cordiality of this surprising greeting tonight, and accept my very best wishes for a happy and a fortunate future.

CALVIN COOLIDGE

Address to the Massachusetts State Senate

(1914)

"Self-government means self-support"

While on his western tour, in California, Harding had a heart attack and died. That left Calvin Coolidge president—an ascent made mostly possible by Coolidge's talents as a writer. During his time in Massachusetts politics, Coolidge worked obsessively on his speeches, including this one from 1914, when he was president of the state senate. Once he became governor, Coolidge's supporters gathered his best addresses into a book, Have Faith in Massachusetts, *and shared it widely with journalists, politicians, and voters. Coolidge's book got him some presidential buzz at the 1920 Republican Convention—and won him the vice presidential slot, as the* Have Faith *fan who nominated him would later admit. This address demonstrates Coolidge's gifts for concision and aphorism, along with his deep belief in individual liberty.*

This commonwealth is one. We are all members of one body. The welfare of the weakest and the welfare of the most powerful are inseparably bound together. Industry cannot flourish if labor languish. Transportation cannot prosper if manufactures decline. The general welfare cannot be provided for in any one act, but it is well to remember that the benefit of one is the benefit of all, and the neglect of one is the neglect of all. The suspension of one man's dividends is the suspension of another man's pay envelope.

Men do not make laws. They do but discover them. Laws must be justified by something more than the will of the majority. They must rest on the eternal foundation of righteousness. That state is most fortunate in its form of government which has the aptest instruments for the discovery of laws. The latest, most modern, and nearest perfect system that statesmanship has devised is representative government. Its weakness is the weakness of us imperfect human beings who administer it. Its strength is that even such administration secures to the people more blessings than any other system ever produced. No nation has discarded it and retained liberty. Representative government must be preserved.

Courts are established not to determine the popularity of a cause, but to adjudicate and enforce rights. No litigant should be required to submit his case to the hazard and expense of a political campaign. No judge should be required to seek or receive political rewards. The courts of Massachusetts are known and honored wherever men love justice. Let their glory suffer no diminution at our hands. The electorate and judiciary cannot combine. A hearing means a hearing. When the trial of causes goes outside the courtroom, Anglo-Saxon constitutional government ends.

The people cannot look to legislation generally for success. Industry, thrift, character are not conferred by act or resolve. Government cannot relieve from toil. It can provide no substitute for the rewards of service. It can, of course, care for the defective and recognize distinguished merit. The normal must care for themselves. Self-government means self-support.

Man is born into the universe with a personality that is his own. He has a right that is founded upon the constitution of the universe to have property that is his own. Ultimately, property rights and personal rights are the same thing. The one cannot be preserved if the other be violated. Each man is entitled to his rights and the rewards of his service, be they never so large or never so small.

History reveals no civilized people among whom there were not a highly educated class and large aggregations of wealth, represented usually by the clergy and the nobility. Inspiration has always come from above. Diffusion of learning has come down from the university to the common school—the kindergarten is last. No one would now expect to aid the common school by abolishing higher education.

It may be that the diffusion of wealth works in an analogous way. As the little red schoolhouse is built in the college, it may be that the fostering and protection of large aggregations of wealth are the only foundation on which to build the prosperity of the whole people. Large profits mean large payrolls. But profits must be the result of service performed. In no land are there so many and such large aggregations of wealth as here; in no land do they perform larger service; in no land will the work of a day bring so large a reward in material and spiritual welfare.

Have faith in Massachusetts. In some unimportant detail some other states may surpass her, but in the general results there is no place on earth where the people secure, in a larger measure, the blessings of organized government, and nowhere can those functions more properly be termed self-government.

Do the day's work. If it be to protect the rights of the weak, whoever objects, do it. If it be to help a powerful corporation better to serve the people, whatever the opposition, do that. Expect to be called a standpatter, but don't be a standpatter. Expect to be called a demagogue, but don't be a demagogue. Don't hesitate to be as revolutionary as science. Don't hesitate to be as reactionary as the multiplication table. Don't expect to build up the weak by pulling down the strong. Don't hurry to legislate. Give administration a chance to catch up with legislation.

We need a broader, firmer, deeper faith in the people—a faith that men desire to do right, that the commonwealth is founded upon a righteousness which will endure, a reconstructed faith that the final approval of the people is given not to demagogues, slavishly pandering to their selfishness, merchandising with the clamor of the hour, but to statesmen, ministering to their welfare, representing their deep, silent, abiding convictions.

Statutes must appeal to more than material welfare. Wages won't satisfy, be they never so large. Nor houses; nor lands; nor coupons, though they fall thick as the leaves of autumn. Man has a spiritual nature. Touch it, and it must respond as the magnet responds to the pole.

To that, not to selfishness, let the laws of the commonwealth appeal. Recognize the immortal worth and dignity of man. Let the laws of Massachusetts proclaim to her humblest citizen, performing the most menial task, the recognition of his manhood, the recognition that all men are peers, the humblest with the most exalted, the recognition that all work is glorified. Such is the path to equality before the law. Such is the foundation of liberty under the law. Such is the sublime revelation of man's relation to man—democracy.

CALVIN COOLIDGE

Address Welcoming Home Charles Lindbergh

(1927)

"It is the same story of valor and victory by a son of the people that shines through every page of American history"

Given the demands of the modern presidency, Coolidge had to rely on speechwriters in the White House, including Welliver, the Harding holdover. There were simply too many occasions and addresses—and too large an audience with the rise of radio. (Coolidge's first State of the Union was the first to be broadcast over the air.) In this speech, which was also broadcast in 1927, Coolidge welcomes home Charles Lindbergh, fresh off his transatlantic flight, while praising another exciting technology: the airplane.

It was in America that the modern art of flying a heavier-than-air machine was first developed. As the experiments became successful, the airplane was devoted to practical purposes. It has been adapted to commerce in the transportation of passengers and mail and used for national defense by our land and sea forces. Beginning with a limited flying radius, its length has been gradually extended. We have made many flying records. Our Army flyers have circumnavigated the globe. One of our Navy men started from California and flew far enough to have reached Hawaii, but being off his course landed in the water. Another officer of the Navy has flown to the North Pole. Our own country has been traversed from shore to shore in a single flight.

It had been apparent for some time that the next great feat in the air would be a continuous flight from the mainland of America to the mainland of Europe. Two courageous Frenchmen made the reverse attempt and passed to a fate that is as yet unknown. Others were speeding their preparations to make the trial, but it remained for an unknown youth to tempt the elements and win. It is the same story of valor and victory by a son of the people that shines through every page of American history.

Twenty-five years ago there was born in Detroit, Michigan, a boy representing the best traditions of this country, of a stock known for its deeds of adventure and exploration. His father, moved with a desire for public service, was a member of Congress for several terms. His mother, who dowered her son with her own modesty and charm, is with us today. Engaged in the vital profession of school teaching, she has permitted neither money nor fame to interfere with her fidelity to her duties. Too young to have enlisted in the World War, her son became a student at one of the big state universities. His interest in aviation led him to an Army aviation school, and in 1925 he was graduated as an airplane pilot. In November 1926, he had reached the rank of captain in the Officers' Reserve Corps. Making his home in St. Louis, he had joined the 110th Observation Squadron of the Missouri National Guard. Some of his qualities noted by the Army officers who examined him for promotion, as shown by reports in the files of the Militia Bureau of the War Department, are as follows: "Intelligent," "industrious," "energetic," "dependable," "purposeful," "alert," "quick of reaction," "serious," "deliberate," "stable," "efficient," "frank," "modest," "congenial," "a man of good moral habits and regular in all his business transactions." One of the officers expressed his belief that the young man "would successfully complete everything he undertakes." This reads like a prophecy.

Later he became connected with the United States Mail Service, where he exhibited marked ability and from which he is now on leave of absence.

On a morning just three weeks ago yesterday, this wholesome, earnest, fearless, courageous product of America rose into the air from Long Island in a monoplane christened *The Spirit of St. Louis* in honor of his home and that of his supporters. It was no haphazard adventure. After months of most careful preparation, supported by a valiant character, driven by an unconquerable will and inspired by the imagination and the spirit of his Viking ancestors, this reserve officer set wing across the dangerous stretches of the North Atlantic. He was alone. His destination was Paris.

Thirty-three hours and thirty minutes later, in the evening of the second day, he landed at his destination on the French flying field at Le Bourget. He had traveled over 3,600 miles and established a new and remarkable record. The execution of his project was a perfect exhibition of art.

This country will always remember the way in which he was received by the people of France, by their president, and by their government. It was the more remarkable because they were mourning the disappearance of their intrepid countrymen, who had tried to span the Atlantic on a western flight.

Our messenger of peace and good will had broken down another barrier of time and space and brought two great peoples into closer communion. In less than a day and a half he had crossed the ocean over which Columbus had traveled for sixty-nine days, and the Pilgrim fathers for sixty-six days, on their way to the New World. But, above all, in showering applause and honors upon this genial, modest, American youth, with the naturalness, the simplicity, and the poise of true greatness, France had the opportunity to show clearly her good will for America and our people. With like acclaim and evidences of cordial friendship our ambassador without portfolio was received by the rulers, the governments, and the peoples of England and Belgium. From other nations came hearty messages of admiration for him and for his country. For these manifold evidences of friendship we are profoundly grateful.

The absence of self-acclaim, the refusal to become commercialized, which has marked the conduct of this sincere and genuine exemplar of fine and noble virtues, has endeared him to everyone. He has returned unspoiled. Particularly has it been delightful to have him refer to his airplane as somehow possessing a personality and being equally entitled to credit with himself, for we are proud that in every particular this silent partner represented American genius and industry. I am told that more than one hundred separate companies furnished materials, parts, or service in its construction.

And now, my fellow citizens, this young man has returned. He is here. He has brought his unsullied fame home. It is our great privilege to welcome back to his native land on behalf of his own people, who have a deep affection for him and have been thrilled by this splendid achievement, a colonel of the United States Officers' Reserve Corps, an illustrious citizen of our republic, a conqueror of the air and strengthener of the ties which bind us to our sister nations across the sea, and, as president of the United States, I bestow of distinguished flying cross, as a symbol of appreciation for what he is and what he has done, upon Colonel Charles A. Lindbergh.

CALVIN COOLIDGE

From His Autobiography

"It costs a great deal to be president"

As Coolidge prepared to leave Washington, he returned to writing himself, working on a personal essay about the night he became president—and the events that led to him losing two family members soon thereafter. When the essay appeared in a magazine in the spring of 1929, it immediately became the most widely discussed story in America. Coolidge kept writing until he had completed a bestselling autobiography, and readers loved it. Emily Newell Blair, a prominent suffragist, was no fan of Coolidge, but she praised his book. "Nothing could better educate us for choosing our public officials," Blair wrote in a review, "than to read after each administration the ex-president's own interpretation of his life and experience. . . . It would make us understand our national characteristics, our national mind."

It has undoubtedly been the lot of every native boy of the United States to be told that he will someday be President. Nearly every young man who happens to be elected a member of his state legislature is pointed to by his friends and his local newspaper as on the way to the White House.

My own experience in this respect did not differ from that of others. But I never took such suggestions seriously, as I was convinced in my own mind that I was not qualified to fill the exalted office of president.

I had not changed this opinion after the November elections of 1919, when I was chosen governor of Massachusetts for a second term by a majority which had only been exceeded in 1896.

When I began to be seriously mentioned by some of my friends at that time as the Republican candidate for president, it became apparent that there were many others who shared the same opinion as to my fitness which I had so long entertained. But the coming national convention, acting in accordance with an unchangeable determination, took my destiny into its own hands and nominated me for vice president.

Had I been chosen for the first place, I could have accepted it only with a great deal of trepidation, but when the events of August, 1923, bestowed upon me the presidential office, I felt at once that power had been given me to administer it. This was not any feeling of exclusiveness. While I felt qualified to serve, I was also well aware that there were many others who were better qualified. It would be my province to get the benefit of their opinions and advice. It is a great advantage to a president, and a major source of safety to the country, for him to know that he is not a great man. When a man begins to feel that he is the only one who can lead in this republic, he is guilty of treason to the spirit of our institutions.

After President Harding was seriously stricken, although I noticed that some of the newspapers at once sent representatives to be near me at the home of my father in Plymouth, Vermont, the official reports which I received from his bedside soon became so reassuring that I believed all danger past.

On the night of August 2, 1923, I was awakened by my father coming up the stairs calling my name. I noticed that his voice trembled. As the only times I had ever observed that before were when death had visited our family, I knew that something of the gravest nature had occurred.

His emotion was partly due to the knowledge that a man whom he had met and liked was gone, partly to the feeling that must possess all of our citizens when the life of their president is taken from them.

But he must have been moved also by the thought of the many sacrifices he had made to place me where I was, the twenty-five-mile drives in storms and in zero [degree] weather over our mountain roads to carry me to the academy, and all the tenderness and care he had lavished upon me in the thirty-eight years since the death of my mother in the hope that I might sometime rise to a position of importance, which he now saw realized.

He had been the first to address me as president of the United States. It was the culmination of the lifelong desire of a father for the success of his son.

He placed in my hands an official report and told me that President Harding had just passed away. My wife and I at once dressed.

Before leaving the room I knelt down and, with the same prayer with which I have since approached the altar of the church, asked God to bless the American people and give me power to serve them.

My first thought was to express my sympathy for those who had been bereaved and after that was done to attempt to reassure the country with the knowledge that I proposed no sweeping displacement of the men then in office and that there were to be no violent changes in the administration of affairs. As soon as I had dispatched a telegram to Mrs. Harding, I therefore issued a short public statement declaratory of that purpose.

Meantime, I had been examining the Constitution to determine what might be necessary for qualifying by taking the oath of office. It is not clear that any additional oath is required beyond what is taken by the vice president when he is sworn into office. It is the same form as that taken by the president.

Having found this form in the Constitution I had it set up on the typewriter and the oath was administered by my father in his capacity as a notary public, an office he had held for a great many years.

The oath was taken in what we always called the sitting room by the light of the kerosene lamp, which was the most modern form of lighting that had then reached the neighborhood. The Bible which had belonged to my mother lay on the table at my hand. It was not officially used, as it is not the practice in Vermont or Massachusetts to use a Bible in connection with the administration of an oath. . . .

Where succession to the highest office in the land is by inheritance or appointment, no doubt there have been kings who have participated in the induction of their sons into their office, but in republics where the succession comes by an election I do not know of any other case in history where a father has administered to his son the qualifying oath of office which made him the chief magistrate of a nation. It seemed a simple and natural thing to do at the time, but I can now realize something of the dramatic force of the event.

This room was one which was already filled with sacred memories for me. In it my sister and my stepmother passed their last hours. It was associated with my boyhood recollections of my own mother, who sat and reclined there during her long invalid years, though she passed away in an adjoining room where my father was to follow her within three years from this eventful night.

When I started for Washington that morning I turned aside from the main road to make a short devotional visit to the grave of my mother. It had been a comfort to me during my boyhood when I was troubled to be near her last resting place, even in the dead of night. Some way, that morning, she seemed very near to me.

A telegram was sent to my pastor, Dr. Jason Noble Pierce, to meet me on my arrival at Washington that evening, which he did.

I found the cabinet mostly scattered. Some members had been with the late president and some were in Europe. The secretary of state, [Charles Evans] Hughes, and myself at once began the preparation of plans for the funeral.

I issued the usual proclamation.

The Washington services were held in the rotunda of the Capitol, followed by a simple service and interment at Marion, Ohio, which I attended with the cabinet and a large number of officers of the government.

The nation was grief-stricken. Especially noticeable was the deep sympathy everyone felt for Mrs. Harding. Through all this distressing period her bearing won universal commendation. Her attitude of sympathy and affection towards Mrs. Coolidge and myself was an especial consolation to us. . . .

In spite of the remarkable record which had already been made, much remained to be done. While anything that relates to the functions of the government is of enormous interest to me, its economic relations have always had a peculiar fascination for me.

Though these are necessarily predicated on order and peace, yet our people are so thoroughly law-abiding and our foreign relations are so happy that the problem of government action which is to carry its benefits into the homes of all the people becomes almost entirely confined to the realm of economics.

My personal experience with business had been such as comes to a country lawyer.

My official experience with government business had been of a wide range. As mayor, I had charge of the financial affairs of the city of Northampton. As lieutenant governor, I was chairman of the Committee on Finance of the Governor's Council, which had to authorize every cent of the expenditures of the commonwealth before they could be made. As governor, I was chargeable with responsibility both for appropriations and for expenditures.

My fundamental idea of both private and public business came first from my father. He had the strong New England trait of great repugnance at seeing anything wasted. He was a generous and charitable man, but he regarded waste as a moral wrong.

Wealth comes from industry and from the hard experience of human toil. To dissipate it in waste and extravagance is disloyalty to humanity.

This is by no means a doctrine of parsimony. Both men and nations should live in accordance with their means and devote their substance not only to productive industry, but to the creation of the various forms of beauty and the pursuit of culture which give adornments to the art of life.

When I became president it was perfectly apparent that the key by which the way could be opened to national progress was constructive economy. Only by the use of that policy could the high rates of taxation, which were retarding our development and prosperity, be diminished, and the enormous burden of our public debt be reduced.

Without impairing the efficient operation of all the functions of the government, I have steadily and without ceasing pressed on in that direction. This policy has encouraged enterprise, made possible the highest rate of wages which has ever existed, returned large profits, brought to the homes of the people the greatest economic benefits they ever enjoyed, and given to the country as a whole an unexampled era of prosperity. This wellbeing of my country has given me the chief satisfaction of my administration.

One of my most pleasant memories will be the friendly relations which I have always had with the representatives of the press in Washington. I shall always remember that at the conclusion of the first regular conference I held with them at the White House office they broke into hearty applause.

I suppose that in answering their questions I had been fortunate enough to tell them what they wanted to know in such a way that they could make use of it.

While there have been newspapers which supported me, of course there have been others which opposed me, but they have usually been fair. I shall always consider it the highest tribute to my administration that the opposition have based so little of their criticism on what I have really said and done.

I have often said that there was no cause for feeling disturbed at being misrepresented in the press. It would be only when they began to say things detrimental to me which were true that I should feel alarm.

Perhaps one of the reasons I have been a target for so little abuse is because I have tried to refrain from abusing other people.

The words of the president have an enormous weight and ought not to be used indiscriminately.

It would be exceedingly easy to set the country all by the ears and foment hatreds and jealousies, which, by destroying faith and confidence, would help nobody and harm everybody. The end would be the destruction of all progress.

While everyone knows that evils exist, there is yet sufficient good in the people to supply material for most of the comment that needs to be made.

The only way I know to drive out evil from the country is by the constructive method of filling it with good. The country is better off tranquilly considering its blessings and merits, and earnestly striving to secure more of them, than it would be in nursing hostile bitterness about its deficiencies and faults. . . .

I have seen a great many attempts at political strategy in my day and elaborate plans made to encompass the destruction of this or that public man. I cannot now think of any that did not react with overwhelming force upon the perpetrators, sometimes destroying them and sometimes giving their proposed victim an opportunity to demonstrate his courage, strength, and soundness, which increased his standing with the people and raised him to higher office.

There is only one form of political strategy in which I have any confidence, and that is to try to do the right thing and sometimes be able to succeed.

Many people at once began to speak about nominating me to lead my party in the next campaign. I did not take any position in relation to their efforts. Unless the nomination came to me in a natural way, rather than as the result of an artificial campaign, I did not feel it would be of any value.

The people ought to make their choice on a great question of that kind without the influence that could be exerted by a president in office.

After the favorable reception which was given to my [first address to Congress], I stated at the Gridiron Dinner that I should be willing to be a candidate. The convention nominated me the next June by a vote which was practically unanimous.

With the exception of the occasion of my notification, I did not attend any partisan meetings or make any purely political speeches during the campaign. I spoke several times at the dedication of a monument, the observance of the anniversary of a historic event, at a meeting of some commercial body, or before some religious gathering. The campaign was magnificently managed by William M. Butler, and as it progressed the final result became more and more apparent.

My own participation was delayed by the death of my son Calvin, which occurred on the 7th of July. He was a boy of much promise, proficient in his studies with a scholarly mind, who had just turned sixteen.

He had a remarkable insight into things.

The day I became president he had just started to work in a tobacco field. When one of his fellow laborers said to him, "If my father was president I would not work in a tobacco field," Calvin replied, "If my father were your father, you would."

After he was gone someone sent us a letter he had written about the same time to a young man who had congratulated him on being the "first boy" in the land. To this he had replied that he had done nothing and so did not merit the title, which should go to "some boy who had distinguished himself through his own actions."

We do not know what might have happened to him under other circumstances, but if I had not been president he would not have raised a blister on his toe, which resulted in blood poisoning, playing lawn tennis in the [White House's] south grounds.

In his suffering he was asking me to make him well. I could not.

When he went the power and the glory of the presidency went with him.

The ways of Providence are often beyond our understanding. It seemed to me that the world had need of the work that it was probable he could do.

I do not know why such a price was exacted for occupying the White House.

Sustained by the great outpouring of sympathy from all over the nation, my wife and I bowed to the Supreme Will and with such courage as we had went on in the discharge of our duties.

In less than two years my father followed him.

At his advanced age he had overtaxed his strength receiving the thousands of visitors who went to my old home at Plymouth. It was all a great satisfaction to him and he would not have had it otherwise.

When I was there and visitors were kept from the house for a short period, he would be really distressed in the thought that they could not see all they wished, and he would go out where they were himself and mingle among them.

I knew for some weeks that he was passing his last days. I sent to bring him to Washington, but he clung to his old home.

It was a sore trial not to be able to be with him, but I had to leave him where he most wished to be. When his doctors advised me that he could survive only a short time I started to visit him, but he sank to rest while I was on my way.

For my personal contact with him during his last months I had to resort to the poor substitute of the telephone. When I reached home he was gone.

It costs a great deal to be president.

From *The Ordeal of Woodrow Wilson*

"Even when Mr. Wilson did not entirely agree with me, he listened with patience"

Herbert Hoover was a diligent writer. During his 1928 presidential campaign, he gave a speech championing America's tradition of "rugged individualism"— and arguing that it was time to reduce the nation's government and regulations to pre–World War I levels. After his presidency, he wrote many volumes of memoir, including ones that covered his response to a depression that no degree of individualism could fix. But Hoover wrote his most intriguing book late in life, with The Ordeal of Woodrow Wilson *coming out in 1958. Hoover recalled working as Wilson's food administrator during World War I. It's a fascinating example of one president writing about another, joining Grant on Lincoln, John Quincy Adams on his father, and George W. Bush on his father, among others. But it's also an example of a president trying to spin history—to make Wilson seem like a Herbert Hoover Republican.*

I have no need to speak of his great scholarly attainments. They were built into a superior mind. He possessed great clarity of thought, with an ability quickly to reduce problems to their bare bones. His public addresses were often clothed with great eloquence. As a Jeffersonian Democrat, he was a "liberal" of the nineteenth-century cast. His training in history and economics rejected every scintilla of socialism, which today connotes a liberal.

His philosophy of American living was based upon free enterprise, both in social and in economic systems. He held that the economic system must be regulated to prevent monopoly and unfair practices. He believed that federal intervention in the economic or social life of our people was justified only when the task was greater than the states or individuals could perform for themselves.

He yielded with great reluctance to the partial and temporary abandonment of our principles of life during the war because of the multitude of tasks with which the citizen or the states could not cope. But he often expressed to me the hope that our methods of doing so were such that they could be quickly reversed and free enterprise restored.

Coming from an academic ivory tower with only a brief political career, he at times stumbled badly in the thicket of politics. Some of the appointments to which he was persuaded by politicians were bad. However, of the men whom he selected for the conduct of major war activities, few were political appointees and all were men of high ability and integrity.

In evaluating Mr. Wilson's makeup there are a few phenomena to bear in mind. He frequently has been described as "obstinate." In my view this was not true. His mind ran to "moral principles," "justice," and "right." In them he held deep convictions. In some phases of character he partook of the original Presbyterians—what they concluded was right, was thereafter right as against all comers. He often referred with pride to his ancestral inheritance from the Scotch Covenanters of 1638.

The trouble into which he fell with these principles and ideals lay in their conflict with the age-old concepts and aims of nations in Europe. In these conflicts he was at times compelled to choose the lesser of evils. But he was slow to budge. He was not a snob but he had little patience with small minds.

His further difficulty was that at times he became impatient with honest and proper argument against his conclusions, and too often for his own good he construed such argument as personal criticism. He sometimes carried resentment at what he considered personal criticism to the extent of casting loyal and devoted friends into outer darkness. At one time I myself ran into a minor mental barbed-wire entanglement, but without serious results. In my work, even when Mr. Wilson did not entirely agree with me, he listened with patience, and we were always able to find a path ahead. . . .

[During the war,] new agencies had to be created to meet the demands both for supplies for our military forces and for the civilian and military necessities of the Allies. These new agencies, in order to control raw materials, food, coal, imports, exports, and shipping, had many problems in common. Among them was the need, with the huge drain on our supplies, to stimulate production and reduce domestic consumption. With the law of supply and demand upset by the forced drain for the Allies it was also necessary to control domestic prices, distribution, exports, and imports in order to protect supplies for our own people and prevent speculation and profiteering.

These governmental activities were strange in American life, and Congress was tardy, fearful, and often inadequate in conferring the powers upon the president which were vital to enable the civilian agencies to contribute their part in winning the war.

To meet the cry that these were dictatorial powers, the president at the beginning developed the idea that they should be administered by boards, commissions, councils, or committees. I had reported to him mistakes the Allies had made by this sort of organization at the start, and their ultimate but slow recognition that administration must be conducted by a single head. As a matter of fact, a single executive had been the basic concept of organization of our government and our business world ever since the foundation of the republic. I was fortunate in persuading the president that a new term, "administrator," would not connote dictatorship and I, therefore, did not have to go through the unhappy experiences of some of my colleagues.

However, after a few months of stumbling and bitter experience, the president returned to our traditional methods of organization with a single executive in authority, and the boards, commissions, committees, and councils relegated to purely advisory functions.

The president made appointments irrespective of political faiths. No more splendid men could have been found than Bernard M. Baruch, who directed the War Industries Board; Secretary of the Treasury W. G. McAdoo, who was also railway administrator; Harry A. Garfield, who directed the Fuel Administration; [and] Charles M. Schwab, who directed ship construction. . . . Thousands of competent men of all professions answered the president's call as volunteers to staff these new organizations.

In my job I was confronted with a crop failure immediately following the declaration of war, which plagued us from the harvest of 1917 to the harvest of 1918. But despite the difficulties and frustrations, with the loyal support of the housewives, the processors, and the middlemen, we so reduced consumption as to make possible huge exports from what was statistically a vacuum.

Early in my relations with the president, I learned that he preferred a letter or a memorandum to personal interviews whenever it was possible.

Further, where it was necessary to secure his written authority by personal interviews, he liked to have a possible draft document ready to sign. This accounts for the large number of such documents in this text and in my other memoirs—few of which have ever been published.

The following letter is of interest in indicating the president's attitude toward the Allies:

The White House, December 10, 1917

My Dear Mr. Hoover:

I have noticed on one or two of the posters of the Food Administration the words, "Our Allies." I would be very much obliged if you would issue instructions that "Our Associates in the War" is to be substituted. I have been very careful about this myself because we have no allies, and I think I am right in believing that the people of the country are very jealous of any intimation that there are formal alliances. You will understand, of course, that I am implying no criticism. I am only thinking it important that we should all use the same language.

Woodrow Wilson

FRANKLIN D. ROOSEVELT

Review of Claude Bowers's
Jefferson and Hamilton

(1925)

"Is a Jefferson on the horizon?"

In 1925, Franklin D. Roosevelt's political career seemed finished. He had already lost a national election as the Democratic vice presidential nominee, and now he was suffering from sickness and partial paralysis. And yet this incisive book review, published late that year, suggests Roosevelt wasn't done running yet. Roosevelt explored the divide between Hamilton and Jefferson, a divide he defined as between government by economic elites and government for everyday Americans. It's a piece that reveals as much about the reviewer as the book, and Roosevelt ends by posing a question that he and his revived career would soon answer.

I felt like saying "at last" as I read Mr. Claude G. Bowers's thrilling *Jefferson and Hamilton.* Perhaps this feeling is influenced by my personal experiences, but, in the broader sense, I am convinced that it would be a supreme contribution to current thought if the simple historic facts of this book could be learned in the newspaper editorial rooms as well as in the homes and schools of America.

Let me explain the personal side of it. A year ago I took occasion in a letter addressed to more than a thousand Democratic leaders throughout the country to refer in passing to the difference between the Jeffersonian and Hamiltonian ideas for an American method of government, and to apply

256

their fundamental differences to present-day policies of our two great parties. Immediately many editors, including even some of the metropolitan
press, launched sneers at the mere suggestion that Jeffersonianism could,
in any remote manner, bear upon the America of 1925. A materialistic
press reflects a materialistic age, but I still boil inwardly when I think of
these smug writers who, wish being father to the thought, deny that the
forces hostile to control of government by the people which existed in the
crisis of 1790–1800 could still be a threat in our present day and land.

The other personal reason is that for some years I have been, frankly, fed
up with the romantic cult which has, since the publication of a historical
novel, surrounded the name of Alexander Hamilton, and I have longed
to write this very book, which now so much more ably comes from the
delightful and untiring research of Mr. Bowers.

What is more valuable, however, is that in this study of a period which
was, in every way, as important to the preservation of the Union as was the
Civil War itself, a spirit of fairness and calm judgment is shown which
makes the book not merely convincing to the general reader but of permanent value to the advanced student.

For Hamilton emerges still a romantic and fascinating figure, albeit in
his true character of aristocrat and convinced opponent of popular government. And in Jefferson we see not only the savior of the deeper ideals of
the Revolution, but also the man with human failings, the consummate
politician.

The history of the United States may be interesting to some for the
mere fact of events or personalities, but it is of value to us as a whole
because of the application we make of these facts to present problems.
It is in this spirit in which the book must be read: if we obtain from its
pages only the knowledge of the definite establishment of a democratic
republic because of the leadership of Jefferson and his associates, we fail
unless we in addition apply the basic ideals of those days to the later events
in American history and to the often essentially similar problems that still
lie unsolved before us.

In fact what is the chief revelation is not the day-by-day contest of
the first ten years of the constitutional United States, but the constantly
recurring thought of parallel or at least analogous situations existing in
our own generation.

Mr. Bowers's book enters into the midst of the organization of the
government in 1789 after the ratification of the Constitution and the
election of President Washington. I could have wished for an introductory

chapter summarizing the chaos and the groping through which, for six long years, we passed by the grace of God, from the close of war in 1783 to the formation of the federal government. But the scenes in New York during the organizing of the first cabinet and the first Congress hint very clearly of the divergent schools of thought which shortly before had compromised on the Constitution.

What a picture of the New York which was the nation's capital! The country village—seaport, the pigs in the streets, the town pumps, the dark lanes, the profiteers, the taverns and boarding houses. Then the terrific problems awaiting a new experiment in government. Leaders arriving from New England, from the south—men from the commercial centers and from agricultural constituencies—men from communities old and established, men from the frontiers of western New York and Pennsylvania and Virginia and the Carolinas—self-made, self-taught men, and scions of families which for generations had considered themselves the peerage of America.

There were no political parties, yet the line of demarcation was drawn before ever Washington was inaugurated. It is the little things which germinate. The World War had its murder of Sarajevo; the birth of American party battles had rise in the problem of the titles by which the president, the cabinet, and the Congress should be addressed. Next the social climbers, the snobbery, the appointment of Hamilton and Jefferson to the cabinet, the rise of Hamilton to a position of supremacy and with it the control of the infant government by the moneyed class. All still in the stage of experiment, and who, even today, can say that immediate success did not lie in the establishment of the republic's finances and commercial credit? Alexander Hamilton we honor because of his masterstroke for sound money, his genius for finance. Yet we must take into account the scandal of the day, the unconscionable profiteering of his followers—even some in Congress—in that same moneyed class who made veritable fortunes from the stupidity or the need or the lack of inside information on the part of the thousands of veterans, tradesmen, farmers, or frontier settlers away from the larger seaport towns.

Slowly the lines were being formed. Within the cabinet itself Jefferson, a veritable westerner of his day, mistrusting the fondness of Hamilton for this chambers of commerce and his contempt for the opinion of the masses; Hamilton, confident of his power, confident of the power of his leaders among merchants and aristocrats, wholly lacking in understanding or in fear of the rights of what he thought of as the rabble—the poor, the uneducated, the average human being who, even then, made up the mass of his countrymen.

The scene changes to Philadelphia, the next temporary capital. More display, greater snobbery, and increased assurance on the part of the men and women of wealth, of family, of commercial prestige; and, most important, a growth of the pro-British sentiment on the part of these, and an abhorrence for the successes and excesses of the onrushing French Revolution.

It is natural that in this environment the demarcation into parties grew apace. Jefferson, eclipsed in the cabinet by Hamilton, the natural democrat against the natural aristocrat, began then the mobilization of the masses against the autocracy of the few. It was a colossal task. With Hamilton were the organized compact forces of wealth, of birth, of commerce, of the press. With him at heart was Washington, the president. Jefferson could count only on the scattered raw material of the working masses, difficult to reach, more difficult to organize.

So began a warfare by press and pamphlet, skillfully forced by Jefferson and Madison and Freneau, bitterly answered by Hamilton and Ames and Fenno. A drawn battle of wits, perhaps, but every new reader a step toward the goal of Jefferson. A true public opinion was being made possible.

Yet, while the foundation stone was being laid in the education of the raw material, Jefferson found his position as secretary of state more and more impossible. Hamilton, conscious of his supremacy, certain of the sanity and righteousness of his policies, reached out from the Treasury to conduct all the departments. Jefferson, the philosopher, resigned, content to abide his day and from his beloved farm with unseen hand to guide the formation of the famous democratic societies throughout the states.

We are prone to assume that foreign events have played small part in our internal affairs, yet around the wars resulting from the French Revolution were built the principal surface issues of the United States from 1793 to 1800. From the British Orders in Council, and the seizure of American vessels, came the mission of John Jay and the treaty he brought home from London. The fat was in the fire.

At once the followers of the democratic theory found their ammunition. It mattered not that Hamilton was himself disgusted with Jay's surrenders. The treaty was the child of the administration and therefore of the Federalist faction. Scenes of marching mobs, of burning effigies, of bitter personalities filled the year of 1796. They came too late to oust the Federalists from power, but they forced division and distrust into their ranks and the selection of John Adams as president, contrary to the better judgment of Hamilton. Jefferson, next highest in votes, became vice president and again took his place in the nation's capital.

One great and final stand was made by the friends of privilege and of government by strong-arm methods. The Alien and Sedition Laws were passed by what had become a strict party vote; four years of what Mr. Bowers properly calls "hysterics" and a "reign of terror" ensued. Freedom of the press was attacked—in vain; partisan courts flung men into prison—in vain; every criticism of the administration was called treason—in vain.

Jefferson and Giles and Lyon and Madison and Sam Adams and Hancock and Gallatin and all their lieutenants and all their followers were labeled anarchists and atheists and traitors—modern words like *socialist* and *radical* and *bolshevik* had not yet come to men's tongues.

The surge grew in spite of names and jails and appeals to a false patriotism. There was no turning back for the Hamiltonians. Only a mighty gamble could bring success. The XYZ Papers furnished the excuse for a war with France, and Hamilton saw the opportunity to avoid and evade domestic issues of a fundamental character by uniting all against a foreign foe.

His difficulty was the old one—it is hard to acquire much enthusiasm against an enemy which won't fight back. France was exceedingly busy at home keeping out the Coalition Kings, and had no reason or desire for a war against us in any event.

Nevertheless, Hamilton sounded the call to arms, had Washington given the honorary position of commander in chief of the Army and himself the actual command, raised troops and loans, bought equipment, and made a great ado. If there had been an enemy close at hand to attack, the Federalists might have ridden to a continuance in power. But there was no enemy, and soon the fever of the imagined disease abated. In a last effort to sustain the war spirit the unfortunate Hamilton met his fall from leadership at the hands of his Federalist president, John Adams. In the final crisis within his party this old Revolutionary leader, vain, pompous, fat, rose to his last great act of patriotism—he made peace with France.

So the ten years' drama drew to its curtain. Through all the mudslinging, the abuse of power, the deliberate misrepresentation, Jefferson remained the calm philosopher. When troops were asked, it was Jefferson's followers who were the readiest to fall in on country's call. When grave questions of domestic policy arose, it was reserved for certain Federalists of New England to be the first to talk of the dissolution of the Union. Jefferson's faith in mankind was vindicated; his appeal to the intelligence of the average voter bore fruit; his conception of a democratic republic came true.

It seems the irony of fate that in the final balloting for president by Congress it was Hamilton himself who helped his courteous antithesis to the supreme place. An ill-considered revenge was plotted by other federal leaders to keep Jefferson from the presidency by electing Aaron Burr. It gave Hamilton his last public chance. Whether he was actuated more by bitter hatred of the man who was later to kill him, or by the higher resolve to bow to the expressed will of the electorate, matters not. He chose right—and Thomas Jefferson and the principles of a true republic were triumphant.

I have a breathless feeling as I lay down this book—a picture of escape after escape which this nation passed through in those first ten years; a picture of what might have been if the Republic had been finally organized as Alexander Hamilton sought. But I have a breathless feeling, too, as I wonder if, a century and a quarter later, the same contending forces are not again mobilizing. Hamiltons we have today. Is a Jefferson on the horizon?

FRANKLIN D. ROOSEVELT

First Inaugural Address

(1933)

"The only thing we have to fear is fear itself"

On March 4, 1933, Roosevelt became president of a country gripped by depression and despair. Banks were struggling to stay open; unemployment topped 25 percent. In his first inaugural address, Roosevelt previewed his solution to these problems: a far larger federal government, administering what on the campaign trail he had called a "new deal." This inaugural also hints at Roosevelt's preferred path for achieving his New Deal legislation—the biggest expansion yet of executive power.

This is a day of national consecration. And I am certain that my fellow Americans expect that on my induction into the presidency I will address them with a candor and a decision which the present situation of our nation impels.

This is preeminently the time to speak the truth, the whole truth, frankly and boldly. Nor need we shrink from honestly facing conditions in our country today. This great nation will endure as it has endured, will revive and will prosper. So, first of all, let me assert my firm belief that the only thing we have to fear is fear itself—nameless, unreasoning, unjustified terror which paralyzes needed efforts to convert retreat into advance. In every dark hour of our national life, a leadership of frankness and vigor has met with that understanding and support of the people themselves, which is essential to victory. I am convinced that you will again give that support to leadership in these critical days.

In such a spirit, on my part and on yours, we face our common difficulties. They concern, thank God, only material things. Values have shrunken to fantastic levels; taxes have risen; our ability to pay has fallen; government of all kinds is faced by serious curtailment of income; the means of exchange are frozen in the currents of trade; the withered leaves of industrial enterprise lie on every side; farmers find no markets for their produce; the savings of many years in thousands of families are gone. More important, a host of unemployed citizens face the grim problem of existence, and an equally great number toil with little return. Only a foolish optimist can deny the dark realities of the moment.

Yet our distress comes from no failure of substance. We are stricken by no plague of locusts. Compared with the perils which our forefathers conquered because they believed and were not afraid, we have still much to be thankful for. Nature still offers her bounty, and human efforts have multiplied it. Plenty is at our doorstep, but a generous use of it languishes in the very sight of the supply. Primarily this is because rulers of the exchange of mankind's goods have failed through their own stubbornness and their own incompetence, have admitted their failure, and have abdicated. Practices of the unscrupulous moneychangers stand indicted in the court of public opinion, rejected by the hearts and minds of men.

True, they have tried, but their efforts have been cast in the pattern of an outworn tradition. Faced by failure of credit, they have proposed only the lending of more money. Stripped of the lure of profit by which to induce our people to follow their false leadership, they have resorted to exhortations, pleading tearfully for restored confidence. They know only the rules of a generation of self-seekers. They have no vision, and when there is no vision the people perish.

The moneychangers have fled from their high seats in the temple of our civilization. We may now restore that temple to the ancient truths. The measure of the restoration lies in the extent to which we apply social values more noble than mere monetary profit.

Happiness lies not in the mere possession of money; it lies in the joy of achievement, in the thrill of creative effort. The joy and moral stimulation of work no longer must be forgotten in the mad chase of evanescent profits. These dark days will be worth all they cost us if they teach us that our true destiny is not to be ministered unto but to minister to ourselves and to our fellow men.

Recognition of the falsity of material wealth as the standard of success goes hand in hand with the abandonment of the false belief that public office and high political position are to be valued only by the standards of pride of place and personal profit, and there must be an end to a conduct in banking and in business which too often has given to a sacred trust the likeness of callous and selfish wrongdoing. Small wonder that confidence languishes, for it thrives only on honesty, on honor, on the sacredness of obligations, on faithful protection, on unselfish performance; without them it cannot live. Restoration calls, however, not for changes in ethics alone. This nation asks for action, and action now.

Our greatest primary task is to put people to work. This is no unsolvable problem if we face it wisely and courageously. It can be accomplished in part by direct recruiting by the government itself, treating the task as we would treat the emergency of a war, but at the same time, through this employment, accomplishing greatly needed projects to stimulate and reorganize the use of our natural resources.

Hand in hand with this we must frankly recognize the overbalance of population in our industrial centers and, by engaging on a national scale in a redistribution, endeavor to provide a better use of the land for those best fitted for the land. The task can be helped by definite efforts to raise the values of agricultural products and with this the power to purchase the output of our cities. It can be helped by preventing realistically the tragedy of the growing loss through foreclosure of our small homes and our farms. It can be helped by insistence that the federal, state, and local governments act forthwith on the demand that their cost be drastically reduced. It can be helped by the unifying of relief activities which today are often scattered, uneconomical, and unequal. It can be helped by national planning for and supervision of all forms of transportation and of communications and other utilities which have a definitely public character. There are many ways in which it can be helped, but it can never be helped merely by talking about it. We must act and act quickly.

Finally, in our progress toward a resumption of work we require two safeguards against a return of the evils of the old order: there must be a strict supervision of all banking and credits and investments, so that there will be an end to speculation with other people's money; and there must be provision for an adequate but sound currency.

These are the lines of attack. I shall presently urge upon a new Congress, in special session, detailed measures for their fulfillment, and I shall seek the immediate assistance of the several states.

Through this program of action we address ourselves to putting our own national house in order and making income balance outgo. Our international trade relations, though vastly important, are in point of time and necessity secondary to the establishment of a sound national economy. I favor as a practical policy the putting of first things first. I shall spare no effort to restore world trade by international economic readjustment, but the emergency at home cannot wait on that accomplishment.

The basic thought that guides these specific means of national recovery is not narrowly nationalistic. It is the insistence, as a first consideration, upon the interdependence of the various elements in and parts of the United States—a recognition of the old and permanently important manifestation of the American spirit of the pioneer. It is the way to recovery. It is the immediate way. It is the strongest assurance that the recovery will endure.

In the field of world policy, I would dedicate this nation to the policy of the good neighbor: the neighbor who resolutely respects himself and, because he does so, respects the rights of others; the neighbor who respects his obligations and respects the sanctity of his agreements in and with a world of neighbors.

If I read the temper of our people correctly, we now realize as we have never realized before our interdependence on each other—that we cannot merely take but we must give as well; that if we are to go forward, we must move as a trained and loyal army willing to sacrifice for the good of a common discipline, because without such discipline no progress is made, no leadership becomes effective. We are, I know, ready and willing to submit our lives and property to such discipline, because it makes possible a leadership which aims at a larger good. This I propose to offer, pledging that the larger purposes will bind upon us all as a sacred obligation with a unity of duty hitherto evoked only in time of armed strife.

With this pledge taken, I assume unhesitatingly the leadership of this great army of our people dedicated to a disciplined attack upon our common problems.

Action in this image and to this end is feasible under the form of government which we have inherited from our ancestors. Our Constitution is so simple and practical that it is possible always to meet extraordinary needs by changes in emphasis and arrangement without loss of essential form. That is why our constitutional system has proved itself the most superbly enduring political mechanism the modern world has produced. It has met every stress of vast expansion of territory, of foreign wars, of bitter internal strife, of world relations.

It is to be hoped that the normal balance of executive and legislative authority may be wholly adequate to meet the unprecedented task before us. But it may be that an unprecedented demand and need for undelayed action may call for temporary departure from that normal balance of public procedure.

I am prepared under my constitutional duty to recommend the measures that a stricken nation in the midst of a stricken world may require. These measures, or such other measures as the Congress may build out of its experience and wisdom, I shall seek, within my constitutional authority, to bring to speedy adoption.

But in the event that the Congress shall fail to take one of these two courses, and in the event that the national emergency is still critical, I shall not evade the clear course of duty that will then confront me. I shall ask the Congress for the one remaining instrument to meet the crisis—broad executive power to wage a war against the emergency, as great as the power that would be given to me if we were in fact invaded by a foreign foe.

For the trust reposed in me I will return the courage and the devotion that befit the time. I can do no less.

We face the arduous days that lie before us in the warm courage of national unity; with the clear consciousness of seeking old and precious moral values; with the clean satisfaction that comes from the stern performance of duty by old and young alike. We aim at the assurance of a rounded and permanent national life.

We do not distrust the future of essential democracy. The people of the United States have not failed. In their need they have registered a mandate that they want direct, vigorous action. They have asked for discipline and direction under leadership. They have made me the present instrument of their wishes. In the spirit of the gift I take it.

In this dedication of a nation we humbly ask the blessing of God. May He protect each and everyone of us. May He guide me in the days to come.

FRANKLIN D. ROOSEVELT

Fireside Chat on the Banking System

(1933)

"It is your problem no less than it is mine.
Together we cannot fail"

One way Roosevelt expanded executive power was through his fireside chats. In his book review, Roosevelt had noted that Jefferson's coalition was "difficult to reach, more difficult to organize." The radio changed that, and in his intimate and optimistic tone, Roosevelt formed a deep connection with regular Americans inside their homes. In his first chat, on March 12, 1933, the president explained his new banking holiday. But he also appealed to his audience's commitment to unity and hard work.

I want to talk for a few minutes with the people of the United States about banking—with the comparatively few who understand the mechanics of banking, but more particularly with the overwhelming majority who use banks for the making of deposits and the drawing of checks. I want to tell you what has been done in the last few days, why it was done, and what the next steps are going to be. I recognize that the many proclamations from state capitols and from Washington, the legislation, the treasury regulations, etc., couched for the most part in banking and legal terms, should be explained for the benefit of the average citizen. I owe this in particular because of the fortitude and good temper with which everybody has accepted the inconvenience and hardships of the banking holiday. I know that when you understand what we in Washington have been about, I shall continue to have your cooperation as fully as I have had your sympathy and help during the past week.

First of all, let me state the simple fact that when you deposit money in a bank the bank does not put the money into a safe deposit vault. It invests your money in many different forms of credit—bonds, commercial paper, mortgages, and many other kinds of loans. In other words, the bank puts your money to work to keep the wheels of industry and of agriculture turning around. A comparatively small part of the money you put into the bank is kept in currency—an amount which in normal times is wholly sufficient to cover the cash needs of the average citizen. In other words, the total amount of all the currency in the country is only a small fraction of the total deposits in all of the banks.

What, then, happened during the last few days of February and the first few days of March? Because of undermined confidence on the part of the public, there was a general rush by a large portion of our population to turn bank deposits into currency or gold—a rush so great that the soundest banks could not get enough currency to meet the demand. The reason for this was that on the spur of the moment it was, of course, impossible to sell perfectly sound assets of a bank and convert them into cash except at panic prices far below their real value.

By the afternoon of March 3rd, scarcely a bank in the country was open to do business. Proclamations temporarily closing them in whole or in part had been issued by the governors in almost all the states.

It was then that I issued the proclamation providing for the nationwide bank holiday, and this was the first step in the government's reconstruction of our financial and economic fabric.

The second step was the legislation promptly and patriotically passed by the Congress confirming my proclamation and broadening my powers so that it became possible in view of the requirement of time to extend the holiday and lift the ban of that holiday gradually. This law also gave authority to develop a program of rehabilitation of our banking facilities. I want to tell our citizens in every part of the nation that the national Congress—Republicans and Democrats alike—showed by this action a devotion to public welfare and a realization of the emergency and the necessity for speed that it is difficult to match in our history.

The third stage has been the series of regulations permitting the banks to continue their functions to take care of the distribution of food and household necessities and the payment of payrolls.

This bank holiday, while resulting in many cases in great inconvenience, is affording us the opportunity to supply the currency necessary to meet the situation. No sound bank is a dollar worse off than it was when it closed its doors last Monday. Neither is any bank which may turn out not to be in a position for immediate opening. The new law allows the twelve Federal Reserve Banks to issue additional currency on good assets, and thus the banks which reopen will be able to meet every legitimate call. The new currency is being sent out by the Bureau of Engraving and Printing in large volume to every part of the country. It is sound currency because it is backed by actual, good assets.

A question you will ask is this: Why are all the banks not to be reopened at the same time? The answer is simple. Your government does not intend that the history of the past few years shall be repeated. We do not want and will not have another epidemic of bank failures.

As a result, we start tomorrow, Monday, with the opening of banks in the twelve Federal Reserve Bank cities—those banks which on first examination by the Treasury have already been found to be all right. This will be followed on Tuesday by the resumption of all their functions by banks already found to be sound in cities where there are recognized clearinghouses. That means about two hundred and fifty cities of the United States.

On Wednesday and succeeding days, banks in smaller places all through the country will resume business, subject of course to the government's physical ability to complete its survey. It is necessary that the reopening of banks be extended over a period in order to permit the banks to make applications for necessary loans, to obtain currency needed to meet their requirements, and to enable the government to make common sense checkups.

Let me make it clear to you that if your bank does not open the first day you are by no means justified in believing that it will not open. A bank that opens on one of the subsequent days is in exactly the same status as the bank that opens tomorrow.

I know that many people are worrying about state banks, not members of the Federal Reserve System. These banks can and will receive assistance from member banks and from the Reconstruction Finance Corporation. These state banks are following the same course as the national banks except that they get their licenses to resume business from the state authorities, and these authorities have been asked by the secretary of the treasury to permit their good banks to open up on the same schedule as the national banks. I am confident that the state banking departments will be as careful as the national government in the policy relating to the opening of banks and will follow the same broad policy.

It is possible that when the banks resume a very few people who have not recovered from their fear may again begin withdrawals. Let me make it clear that the banks will take care of all needs—and it is my belief that hoarding during the past week has become an exceedingly unfashionable pastime. It needs no prophet to tell you that when the people find that they can get their money—that they can get it when they want it for all legitimate purposes—the phantom of fear will soon be laid. People will again be glad to have their money where it will be safely taken care of and where they can use it conveniently at any time. I can assure you that it is safer to keep your money in a reopened bank than under the mattress.

The success of our whole great national program depends, of course, upon the cooperation of the public—on its intelligent support and use of a reliable system.

Remember that the essential accomplishment of the new legislation is that it makes it possible for banks more readily to convert their assets into cash than was the case before. More liberal provision has been made for banks to borrow on these assets at the Reserve Banks and more liberal provision has also been made for issuing currency on the security of these good assets. This currency is not fiat currency. It is issued only on adequate security, and every good bank has an abundance of such security.

One more point before I close. There will be, of course, some banks unable to reopen without being reorganized. The new law allows the government to assist in making these reorganizations quickly and effectively and even allows the government to subscribe to at least a part of new capital which may be required.

I hope you can see from this elemental recital of what your government is doing that there is nothing complex, or radical, in the process.

We had a bad banking situation. Some of our bankers had shown themselves either incompetent or dishonest in their handling of the people's funds. They had used the money entrusted to them in speculations and unwise loans. This was, of course, not true in the vast majority of our banks, but it was true in enough of them to shock the people for a time into a sense of insecurity and to put them into a frame of mind where they did not differentiate, but seemed to assume that the acts of a comparative few had tainted them all. It was the government's job to straighten out this situation and do it as quickly as possible. And the job is being performed.

I do not promise you that every bank will be reopened or that individual losses will not be suffered, but there will be no losses that possibly could be avoided; and there would have been more and greater losses had we continued to drift. I can even promise you salvation for some at least of the sorely pressed banks. We shall be engaged not merely in reopening sound banks but in the creation of sound banks through reorganization.

It has been wonderful to me to catch the note of confidence from all over the country. I can never be sufficiently grateful to the people for the loyal support they have given me in their acceptance of the judgment that has dictated our course, even though all our processes may not have seemed clear to them.

After all, there is an element in the readjustment of our financial system more important than currency, more important than gold, and that is the confidence of the people. Confidence and courage are the essentials of success in carrying out our plan. You people must have faith; you must not be stampeded by rumors or guesses. Let us unite in banishing fear. We have provided the machinery to restore our financial system; it is up to you to support and make it work.

It is your problem no less than it is mine. Together we cannot fail.

FRANKLIN D. ROOSEVELT

From His Fireside Chat on the War in Europe

(1940)

"We must be the great arsenal of democracy"

While Roosevelt dealt with America's biggest domestic crisis since the Civil War, a global crisis was beginning to emerge: World War II. On December 29, 1940, he gave another fireside chat written with the help of Robert Sherwood, among others. (The White House's speechwriting staff had expanded, just like the rest of the federal government.) Many Americans remained skeptical about assisting the countries battling Germany and Japan, to say nothing of entering another global war. In this chat, Roosevelt explained the urgency of the European situation—and once again appealed to America's commitment to unity and hard work.

This is not a fireside chat on war. It is a talk on national security, because the nub of the whole purpose of your president is to keep you now, and your children later, and your grandchildren much later, out of a last-ditch war for the preservation of American independence and all the things that American independence means to you and to me and to ours.

Tonight, in the presence of a world crisis, my mind goes back eight years to a night in the midst of a domestic crisis. It was a time when the wheels of American industry were grinding to a full stop, when the whole banking system of our country had ceased to function.

I well remember that while I sat in my study in the White House, preparing to talk with the people of the United States, I had before my eyes the picture of all those Americans with whom I was talking. I saw the workmen in the mills, the mines, the factories; the girl behind the counter; the small shopkeeper; the farmer doing his spring plowing; the widows and the old men wondering about their life's savings.

I tried to convey to the great mass of American people what the banking crisis meant to them in their daily lives.

Tonight, I want to do the same thing, with the same people, in this new crisis which faces America. We met the issue of 1933 with courage and realism. We face this new crisis—this new threat to the security of our nation—with the same courage and realism.

Never before since Jamestown and Plymouth Rock has our American civilization been in such danger as now.

For, on September 27, 1940, by an agreement signed in Berlin, three powerful nations, two in Europe and one in Asia, joined themselves together in the threat that if the United States of America interfered with or blocked the expansion program of these three nations—a program aimed at world control—they would unite in ultimate action against the United States.

The Nazi masters of Germany have made it clear that they intend not only to dominate all life and thought in their own country, but also to enslave the whole of Europe and then to use the resources of Europe to dominate the rest of the world.

It was only three weeks ago their leader stated this: "There are two worlds that stand opposed to each other." And then in defiant reply to his opponents, he said this: "Others are correct when they say: With this world we cannot ever reconcile ourselves. . . . I can beat any other power in the world." So said the leader of the Nazis.

In other words, the Axis not merely admits but proclaims that there can be no ultimate peace between their philosophy of government and our philosophy of government.

In view of the nature of this undeniable threat, it can be asserted, properly and categorically, that the United States has no right or reason to encourage talk of peace until the day shall come when there is a clear intention on the part of the aggressor nations to abandon all thought of dominating or conquering the world.

At this moment, the forces of the states that are leagued against all peoples who live in freedom are being held away from our shores. The Germans and the Italians are being blocked on the other side of the Atlantic by the British, and by the Greeks, and by thousands of soldiers and sailors who were able to escape from subjugated countries. In Asia, the Japanese are being engaged by the Chinese nation in another great defense. In the Pacific Ocean is our fleet.

Some of our people like to believe that wars in Europe and in Asia are of no concern to us. But it is a matter of most vital concern to us that European and Asiatic war-makers should not gain control of the oceans which lead to this hemisphere.

One hundred and seventeen years ago, the Monroe Doctrine was conceived by our government as a measure of defense in the face of a threat against this hemisphere by an alliance in continental Europe. Thereafter, we stood on guard in the Atlantic with the British as neighbors. There was no treaty. There was no "unwritten agreement."

And yet, there was the feeling, proven correct by history, that we as neighbors could settle any disputes in peaceful fashion. The fact is that during the whole of this time the western hemisphere has remained free from aggression from Europe or from Asia.

Does anyone seriously believe that we need to fear attack anywhere in the Americas while a free Britain remains our most powerful naval neighbor in the Atlantic? Does anyone seriously believe, on the other hand, that we could rest easy if the Axis powers were our neighbors there?

If Great Britain goes down, the Axis powers will control the continents of Europe, Asia, Africa, Australia, and the high seas—and they will be in a position to bring enormous military and naval resources against this hemisphere. It is no exaggeration to say that all of us, in all the Americas, would be living at the point of a gun—a gun loaded with explosive bullets, economic as well as military.

We should enter upon a new and terrible era in which the whole world, our hemisphere included, would be run by threats of brute force. To survive in such a world, we would have to convert ourselves permanently into a militaristic power on the basis of war economy.

Some of us like to believe that even if Great Britain falls, we are still safe, because of the broad expanse of the Atlantic and of the Pacific.

But the width of those oceans is not what it was in the days of clipper ships. At one point between Africa and Brazil the distance is less than from Washington to Denver, Colorado—five hours for the latest type of bomber. And at the north end of the Pacific Ocean, America and Asia almost touch each other. Even today we have planes that could fly from the British Isles to New England and back again without refueling. And remember that the range of the modern bomber is ever being increased. . . .

Let us no longer blind ourselves to the undeniable fact that the evil forces which have crushed and undermined and corrupted so many others are already within our own gates. Your government knows much about them and every day is ferreting them out.

Their secret emissaries are active in our own and in neighboring countries. They seek to stir up suspicion and dissension to cause internal strife. They try to turn capital against labor, and vice versa. They try to reawaken long slumbering racial and religious enmities which should have no place in this country. They are active in every group that promotes intolerance. They exploit for their own ends our natural abhorrence of war. These trouble-breeders have but one purpose. It is to divide our people into hostile groups and to destroy our unity and shatter our will to defend ourselves.

There are also American citizens, many of them in high places, who, unwittingly in most cases, are aiding and abetting the work of these agents. I do not charge these American citizens with being foreign agents. But I do charge them with doing exactly the kind of work that the dictators want done in the United States.

These people not only believe that we can save our own skins by shutting our eyes to the fate of other nations. Some of them go much further than that. They say that we can and should become the friends and even the partners of the Axis powers. Some of them even suggest that we should imitate the methods of the dictatorships. Americans never can and never will do that. . . .

The history of recent years proves that shootings and chains and concentration camps are not simply the transient tools but the very altars of modern dictatorships. They may talk of a "new order" in the world, but what they have in mind is only a revival of the oldest and the worst tyranny. In that there is no liberty, no religion, no hope.

The proposed "new order" is the very opposite of a United States of Europe or a United States of Asia. It is not a government based upon the consent of the governed. It is not a union of ordinary, self-respecting men and women to protect themselves and their freedom and their dignity from oppression. It is an unholy alliance of power and pelf to dominate and enslave the human race.

The British people and their allies today are conducting an active war against this unholy alliance. Our own future security is greatly dependent on the outcome of that fight. Our ability to "keep out of war" is going to be affected by that outcome.

Thinking in terms of today and tomorrow, I make the direct statement to the American people that there is far less chance of the United States getting into war, if we do all we can now to support the nations defending themselves against attack by the Axis than if we acquiesce in their defeat, submit tamely to an Axis victory, and wait our turn to be the object of attack in another war later on.

If we are to be completely honest with ourselves, we must admit that there is risk in any course we may take. But I deeply believe that the great majority of our people agree that the course that I advocate involves the least risk now and the greatest hope for world peace in the future.

The people of Europe who are defending themselves do not ask us to do their fighting. They ask us for the implements of war, the planes, the tanks, the guns, the freighters which will enable them to fight for their liberty and for our security. Emphatically we must get these weapons to them in sufficient volume and quickly enough, so that we and our children will be saved the agony and suffering of war which others have had to endure.

Let not the defeatists tell us that it is too late. It will never be earlier. Tomorrow will be later than today. . . .

I want to make it clear that it is the purpose of the nation to build now with all possible speed every machine, every arsenal, every factory that we need to manufacture our defense material. We have the men—the skill—the wealth—and above all, the will.

I am confident that if and when production of consumer or luxury goods in certain industries requires the use of machines and raw materials that are essential for defense purposes, then such production must yield, and will gladly yield, to our primary and compelling purpose.

I appeal to the owners of plants—to the managers—to the workers—to our own government employees—to put every ounce of effort into producing these munitions swiftly and without stint. With this appeal I give you the pledge that all of us who are officers of your government will devote ourselves to the same whole-hearted extent to the great task that lies ahead.

As planes and ships and guns and shells are produced, your government, with its defense experts, can then determine how best to use them to defend this hemisphere. The decision as to how much shall be sent abroad and how much shall remain at home must be made on the basis of our overall military necessities.

We must be the great arsenal of democracy. For us this is an emergency as serious as war itself. We must apply ourselves to our task with the same resolution, the same sense of urgency, the same spirit of patriotism and sacrifice as we would show were we at war.

FRANKLIN D. ROOSEVELT

From His State of the Union

(1941)

"Four essential human freedoms"

In his eighth State of the Union, delivered on January 6, 1941, Roosevelt tried to reframe America's obligations to its allies. His reasons were historical, intellectual—and, finally, moral, as he called on Americans to defend "four essential human freedoms," in closing paragraphs he wrote himself.

I address you, the members of the seventy-seventh Congress, at a moment unprecedented in the history of the union. I use the word "unprecedented," because at no previous time has American security been as seriously threatened from without as it is today.

Since the permanent formation of our government under the Constitution, in 1789, most of the periods of crisis in our history have related to our domestic affairs. Fortunately, only one of these—the four-year War Between the States—ever threatened our national unity. Today, thank God, one hundred and thirty million Americans, in forty-eight states, have forgotten points of the compass in our national unity.

It is true that prior to 1914 the United States often had been disturbed by events in other continents. We had even engaged in two wars with European nations and in a number of undeclared wars in the West Indies, in the Mediterranean, and in the Pacific for the maintenance of American rights and for the principles of peaceful commerce. But in no case had a serious threat been raised against our national safety or our continued independence.

What I seek to convey is the historic truth that the United States as a nation has at all times maintained clear, definite opposition to any attempt to lock us in behind an ancient Chinese wall while the procession of civilization went past. Today, thinking of our children and of their children, we oppose enforced isolation for ourselves or for any other part of the Americas.

That determination of ours, extending over all these years, was proved, for example, during the quarter century of wars following the French Revolution.

While the Napoleonic struggles did threaten interests of the United States because of the French foothold in the West Indies and in Louisiana, and while we engaged in the War of 1812 to vindicate our right to peaceful trade, it is nevertheless clear that neither France nor Great Britain nor any other nation was aiming at domination of the whole world.

In like fashion, from 1815 to 1914—ninety-nine years—no single war in Europe or in Asia constituted a real threat against our future or against the future of any other American nation. Except in the Maximilian interlude in Mexico, no foreign power sought to establish itself in this hemisphere, and the strength of the British fleet in the Atlantic has been a friendly strength. It is still a friendly strength.

Even when the World War broke out in 1914, it seemed to contain only small threat of danger to our own American future. But, as time went on, the American people began to visualize what the downfall of democratic nations might mean to our own democracy.

We need not overemphasize imperfections in the Peace of Versailles. We need not harp on failure of the democracies to deal with problems of world reconstruction. We should remember that the Peace of 1919 was far less unjust than the kind of "pacification" which began even before Munich, and which is being carried on under the new order of tyranny that seeks to spread over every continent today. The American people have unalterably set their faces against that tyranny.

Every realist knows that the democratic way of life is at this moment being directly assailed in every part of the world—assailed either by arms, or by secret spreading of poisonous propaganda by those who seek to destroy unity and promote discord in nations that are still at peace.

During sixteen long months this assault has blotted out the whole pattern of democratic life in an appalling number of independent nations, great and small. The assailants are still on the march, threatening other nations, great and small.

Therefore, as your president, performing my constitutional duty to "give to the Congress information of the state of the union," I find it, unhappily, necessary to report that the future and the safety of our country and of our democracy are overwhelmingly involved in events far beyond our borders.

Armed defense of democratic existence is now being gallantly waged in four continents. If that defense fails, all the population and all the resources of Europe, Asia, Africa, and Australia will be dominated by the conquerors. Let us remember that the total of those populations and their resources in those four continents greatly exceeds the sum total of the population and the resources of the whole of the western hemisphere, many times over.

In times like these it is immature—and, incidentally, untrue—for anybody to brag that an unprepared America, single-handed and with one hand tied behind its back, can hold off the whole world.

No realistic American can expect from a dictator's peace international generosity, or return of true independence, or world disarmament, or freedom of expression, or freedom of religion—or even good business. . . .

When the dictators, if the dictators, are ready to make war upon us, they will not wait for an act of war on our part. They did not wait for Norway or Belgium or the Netherlands to commit an act of war. Their only interest is in a new one-way international law, which lacks mutuality in its observance and, therefore, becomes an instrument of oppression.

The happiness of future generations of Americans may well depend upon how effective and how immediate we can make our aid felt. No one can tell the exact character of the emergency situations that we may be called upon to meet. The nation's hands must not be tied when the nation's life is in danger.

We must all prepare to make the sacrifices that the emergency—almost as serious as war itself—demands. Whatever stands in the way of speed and efficiency in defense preparations must give way to the national need.

A free nation has the right to expect full cooperation from all groups. A free nation has the right to look to the leaders of business, of labor, and of agriculture to take the lead in stimulating effort, not among other groups but within their own groups. . . .

In the future days, which we seek to make secure, we look forward to a world founded upon four essential human freedoms.

The first is freedom of speech and expression—everywhere in the world.

The second is freedom of every person to worship God in his own way—everywhere in the world.

The third is freedom from want—which, translated into world terms, means economic understandings which will secure to every nation a healthy peacetime life for its inhabitants, everywhere in the world.

The fourth is freedom from fear—which, translated into world terms, means a world-wide reduction of armaments to such a point and in such a thorough fashion that no nation will be in a position to commit an act of physical aggression against any neighbor, anywhere in the world.

That is no vision of a distant millennium. It is a definite basis for a kind of world attainable in our own time and generation. That kind of world is the very antithesis of the so-called new order of tyranny which the dictators seek to create with the crash of a bomb.

To that new order we oppose the greater conception—the moral order. A good society is able to face schemes of world domination and foreign revolutions alike without fear.

Since the beginning of our American history, we have been engaged in change—in a perpetual peaceful revolution—a revolution which goes on steadily, quietly adjusting itself to changing conditions—without the concentration camp or the quicklime in the ditch. The world order which we seek is the cooperation of free countries, working together in a friendly, civilized society.

This nation has placed its destiny in the hands and heads and hearts of its millions of free men and women, and its faith in freedom under the guidance of God. Freedom means the supremacy of human rights everywhere. Our support goes to those who struggle to gain those rights or keep them. Our strength is our unity of purpose. To that high concept there can be no end save victory.

FRANKLIN D. ROOSEVELT

Address on Pearl Harbor

(1941)

"A date which will live in infamy"

After a long national debate over intervening in World War II, the attack on Pearl Harbor decided it. On December 8, 1941, Roosevelt addressed both houses of Congress, asking them to declare war.

Yesterday, December 7, 1941—a date which will live in infamy—the United States of America was suddenly and deliberately attacked by naval and air forces of the Empire of Japan.

The United States was at peace with that nation and, at the solicitation of Japan, was still in conversation with its government and its emperor looking toward the maintenance of peace in the Pacific. Indeed, one hour after Japanese air squadrons had commenced bombing in the American Island of Oahu, the Japanese ambassador to the United States and his colleague delivered to our secretary of state a formal reply to a recent American message. And while this reply stated that it seemed useless to continue the existing diplomatic negotiations, it contained no threat or hint of war or of armed attack.

It will be recorded that the distance of Hawaii from Japan makes it obvious that the attack was deliberately planned many days or even weeks ago. During the intervening time, the Japanese government has deliberately sought to deceive the United States by false statements and expressions of hope for continued peace.

The attack yesterday on the Hawaiian Islands has caused severe damage to American naval and military forces. I regret to tell you that very many American lives have been lost. In addition American ships have been reported torpedoed on the high seas between San Francisco and Honolulu.

Yesterday the Japanese Government also launched an attack against Malaya.

Last night Japanese forces attacked Hong Kong.

Last night Japanese forces attacked Guam.

Last night Japanese forces attacked the Philippine Islands.

Last night the Japanese attacked Wake Island.

And this morning the Japanese attacked Midway Island.

Japan has, therefore, undertaken a surprise offensive extending throughout the Pacific area. The facts of yesterday and today speak for themselves. The people of the United States have already formed their opinions and well understand the implications to the very life and safety of our nation.

As commander in chief of the Army and Navy, I have directed that all measures be taken for our defense. But always will our whole nation remember the character of the onslaught against us.

No matter how long it may take us to overcome this premeditated invasion, the American people in their righteous might will win through to absolute victory. I believe that I interpret the will of the Congress and of the people when I assert that we will not only defend ourselves to the uttermost, but will make it very certain that this form of treachery shall never again endanger us.

Hostilities exist. There is no blinking at the fact that our people, our territory, and our interests are in grave danger.

With confidence in our armed forces—with the unbounding determination of our people—we will gain the inevitable triumph, so help us God.

I ask that the Congress declare that since the unprovoked and dastardly attack by Japan on Sunday, December 7, 1941, a state of war has existed between the United States and the Japanese Empire.

From *Memoirs*

"Is there anything we can do for you? For you are the one in trouble now"

When the first volume of Harry S. Truman's Memoirs *appeared in 1955, it stunned readers by revealing the burden of the modern presidency: the expanded powers; the expanded government; the international scope; and, most of all, the possibility of nuclear war. "The president cannot be less than a superman," wrote one reviewer, "or the sheer weight of the work will crush him." Truman's book opens with a particularly crushing episode—these pages on the death of Roosevelt and Truman's first hours as president.*

Shortly before five o'clock in the afternoon of Thursday, April 12, 1945, after the Senate adjourned, I went to the office of House Speaker Sam Rayburn. I went there to get an agreement between the speaker and the vice president on certain legislation and to discuss the domestic and world situation generally. As I entered, the speaker told me that Steve Early, the president's press secretary, had just telephoned, requesting me to call the White House.

I returned the call and was immediately connected with Early.

"Please come right over," he told me in a strained voice, "and come in through the main Pennsylvania Avenue entrance."

I turned to Rayburn, explaining that I had been summoned to the White House and would be back shortly. I did not know why I had been called, but I asked that no mention be made of the matter. The president, I thought, must have returned to Washington for the funeral of his friend, Bishop Atwood, the former Episcopal Bishop of Arizona, and I imagined that he wanted me to go over some matters with him before his return to Warm Springs.

On previous occasions when the president had called me to the White House for private talks he had asked me to keep the visits confidential. At such times I had used the east entrance to the White House, and in this way the meetings were kept off the official caller list. Now, however, I told Tom Harty, my government chauffeur, to drive me to the main entrance.

We rode alone, without the usual guards. The Secret Service had assigned three men to work in shifts when I became vice president. However, this guard was reinforced, as a routine practice, during the time President Roosevelt was away on his trip to Yalta and again when he went to Warm Springs. A guard had been placed on duty at my Connecticut Avenue apartment, where I had lived as senator and continued to live as vice president, and another accompanied me wherever I went. These men were capable, efficient, self-effacing, and usually the guard who was on duty met me at my office after the Senate had adjourned. But on this one occasion I slipped away from all of them. Instead of returning from Speaker Rayburn's office to my own before going to the car that was waiting for me, I ran through the basement of the Capitol Building and lost them. This was the only time in eight years that I enjoyed the luxury of privacy by escaping from the ever-present vigil of official protection.

I reached the White House about 5:25 P.M. and was immediately taken in the elevator to the second floor and ushered into Mrs. Roosevelt's study. Mrs. Roosevelt herself, together with Colonel John and Mrs. Anna Roosevelt Boettiger and Mr. Early, were in the room as I entered, and I knew at once that something unusual had taken place. Mrs. Roosevelt seemed calm in her characteristic, graceful dignity. She stepped forward and placed her arm gently about my shoulder.

"Harry," she said quietly, "the president is dead."

For a moment I could not bring myself to speak.

The last news we had had from Warm Springs was that Mr. Roosevelt was recuperating nicely. In fact, he was apparently doing so well that no member of his immediate family, and not even his personal physician, was with him. All this flashed through my mind before I found my voice.

"Is there anything I can do for you?" I asked at last.

I shall never forget her deeply understanding reply.

"Is there anything we can do for you?" she asked. "For you are the one in trouble now."

The greatness and the goodness of this remarkable lady showed even in that moment of sorrow. I was fighting off tears. The overwhelming fact that faced me was hard to grasp. I had been afraid for many weeks that something might happen to this great leader, but now that the worst had happened I was unprepared for it. I did not allow myself to think about it after I became vice president. But I had done a lot of thinking about it at the Chicago convention. I recall wondering whether President Roosevelt himself had had any inkling of his own condition. The only indication I had ever had that he knew he was none too well was when he talked to me just before I set out on my campaign trip for the vice presidency in the fall of 1944. He asked me how I was going to travel, and I told him I intended to cover the country by airplane.

"Don't do that, please," he told me. "Go by train. It is necessary that you take care of yourself."

Sometime later, too, Mrs. Roosevelt had seemed uneasy about the president's loss of appetite. She remarked to me at a dinner shortly after the elections, "I can't get him to eat. He just won't eat."

She was very devoted to the president, as he was to her. Mrs. Roosevelt was also close to the president in his work. In a way, she was his eyes and ears. Her famous trips were taken at his direction and with his approval, and she went on these long, arduous journeys mainly in order to be able to inform and advise him.

But now, as I stood there with her, I was thinking of a letter I had written to my mother and my sister a few hours earlier. They had not received it yet—would not receive it until this terrible news of the president's death had reached them. But once my letter had arrived, they would know how little I had anticipated this overwhelming hour.

Dear Mamma & Mary [I had written]: I am trying to write you a letter today from the desk of the president of the Senate while a windy senator . . . is making a speech on a subject with which he is in no way familiar. The Jr. Sen. from Arizona made a speech on the subject, and he knew what he was talking about. . . .

We are considering the Mexican Treaty on water in the Colorado River and the Rio Grande. It is of vital importance to Southwestern U.S. and northern Mexico. Hope we get it over someday soon.

The senators from California and one from Utah and a very disagreeable one from Nevada (McCarran) are fighting the ratification. I have to sit up here and make parliamentary rulings—some of which are common sense and some of which are not.

Hope you are having a nice spell of weather. We've had a week of beautiful weather but it is raining and misting today. I don't think it's going to last long. Hope not for I must fly to Providence, R.I., Sunday morning.

Turn on your radio tomorrow night at 9:30 your time, and you'll hear Harry make a Jefferson Day address to the nation. I think I'll be on all the networks, so it ought not to be hard to get me. It will be followed by the president, whom I'll introduce.

Hope you are both well and stay that way.

Love to you both.

Write when you can.

Harry

That is what I had written only a few hours earlier, but now the lightning had struck, and events beyond anyone's control had taken command. America had lost a great leader, and I was faced with a terrible responsibility.

It seems to me that for a few minutes we stood silent, and then there was a knock on the study door. Secretary of State Stettinius entered. He was in tears, his handsome face sad and drawn. He had been among the first to be notified, for as secretary of state, who is the keeper of the Great Seal of the United States and all official state papers, it was his official duty to ascertain and to proclaim the passing of the president.

I asked Steve Early, Secretary Stettinius, and Les Biffle, who now had also joined us, to call all the members of the cabinet to a meeting as quickly as possible. Then I turned to Mrs. Roosevelt and asked if there was anything she needed to have done. She replied that she would like to go to Warm Springs at once, and asked whether it would be proper for her to make use of a government plane. I assured her that the use of such a plane was right and proper, and I made certain that one would be placed at her disposal, knowing that a grateful nation would insist on it.

But now a whole series of arrangements had to be made. I went to the president's office at the west end of the White House. I asked Les Biffle to arrange to have a car sent for Mrs. Truman and Margaret, and I called them on the phone myself, telling them what had happened—telling them, too, to come to the White House. I also called Chief Justice Harlan Fiske Stone, and having given him the news, I asked him to come as soon as possible so that he might swear me in. He said that he would come at once. And that is what he did, for he arrived within hardly more than fifteen or twenty minutes.

Others were arriving by now. Speaker Rayburn, House Majority Leader John W. McCormack, and House Minority Leader Joseph W. Martin were among them. I tried personally to reach Senator Alben W. Barkley, Senate majority leader, but I could not locate him. I learned later that word of the president's death had reached him promptly and that he had gone at once to see Mrs. Roosevelt. In fact, he was with her in the White House while the group about me was gathering in the Cabinet Room.

There was no time for formalities and protocol. Among the people there were a score or so of officials and members of Congress. Only three women were present—Mrs. Truman and Margaret and Secretary Frances Perkins.

The Cabinet Room in the White House is not extensive. It is dominated by the huge and odd-shaped table, presented to the president by Jesse Jones, at which the president and the members of the cabinet sit, and by the leather-upholstered armchairs that are arranged around it.

Steve Early, Jonathan Daniels, and others of the president's secretarial staff were searching for a Bible for me to hold when Chief Justice Stone administered the oath of office.

We were in the final days of the greatest war in history—a war so vast that few corners of the world had been able to escape being engulfed by it. There were none who did not feel its effects. In that war the United States had created military forces so enormous as to defy description, yet now, when the nation's greatest leader in that war lay dead, and a simple ceremony was about to acknowledge the presence of his successor in the nation's greatest office, only two uniforms were present. These were worn by Fleet Admiral Leahy and General Fleming, who, as public works administrator, had been given duties that were much more civilian in character than military.

So far as I know, this passed unnoticed at the time, and the very fact that no thought was given to it demonstrates convincingly how firmly the concept of the supremacy of the civil authority is accepted in our land.

By now a Bible had been found. It was placed near where I stood at the end of the great table. Mrs. Truman and Margaret had not joined me for over an hour after I had called them, having gone first to see Mrs. Roosevelt. They were standing side by side now, at my left, while Chief Justice Stone had taken his place before me at the end of the table. Clustered about me and behind were nine members of the cabinet, while Speaker Rayburn and a few other members of Congress took positions behind Chief Justice Stone. There were others present, but not many.

I picked up the Bible and held it in my left hand. Chief Justice Stone raised his right hand and gave the oath as it is written in the Constitution.

With my right hand raised, I repeated it after him: "I, Harry S. Truman, do solemnly swear that I will faithfully execute the office of President of the United States, and will to the best of my ability, preserve, protect and defend the Constitution of the United States."

I dropped my hand.

The clock beneath Woodrow Wilson's portrait marked the time at 7:09.

Less than two hours before, I had come to see the president of the United States, and now, having repeated that simply worded oath, I myself was president.

The ceremony at which I had taken the oath of office had lasted hardly more than a minute, but a delay followed while the inevitable official photographs were taken. Then, after most of those present had gripped my hand—often without a word, so great were their pent-up emotions—and after Mrs. Truman and Margaret had left, everyone else withdrew except the members of the cabinet.

We took our places around the table, though Postmaster General Walker's chair was vacant, for he was ill, and as we did so, Secretary Early entered. The press, he explained, wanted to know if the San Francisco conference on the United Nations would meet, as had been planned, on April 25.

I did not hesitate a second. I told Early that the conference would be held as President Roosevelt had directed. There was no question in my mind that the conference had to take place. It was of supreme importance that we build an organization to help keep the future peace of the world. It was the first decision I made as president.

When Early had left, I spoke to the cabinet. I told them briefly, as I had already told some of them individually, that I would be pleased if all of them would remain in their posts. It was my intention, I said, to continue both the foreign and the domestic policies of the Roosevelt administration. I made it clear, however, that I would be president in my own right and that I would assume full responsibility for such decisions as had to be made. I told them that I hoped they would not hesitate to give me their advice—that I would be glad to listen to them. I left them in no doubt that they could differ with me if they felt it necessary, but that all final policy decisions would be mine. I added that once such decisions had been made I expected them to support me. When there is a change in administration, there are bound to be some changes in the cabinet, but I knew how necessary it was for me to keep an open mind on all the members of the cabinet until we had had an opportunity to work together. Their experience with President Roosevelt and their knowledge were necessary to me in this crisis.

I intended, also, to maintain a similar attitude toward the heads of all the federal agencies. But I had some mental reservations about the heads of certain temporary war agencies.

That first meeting of the cabinet was short, and when it adjourned, the members rose and silently made their way from the room—except for Secretary Stimson.

He asked to speak to me about a most urgent matter. Stimson told me that he wanted me to know about an immense project that was under way—a project looking to the development of a new explosive of almost unbelievable destructive power. That was all he felt free to say at the time, and his statement left me puzzled. It was the first bit of information that had come to me about the atomic bomb, but he gave me no details. It was not until the next day that I was told enough to give me some understanding of the almost incredible developments that were under way and the awful power that might soon be placed in our hands.

> *Truman's* Memoirs *also included personal passages. One of the best is the following, which moves from his Missouri youth to his passion for history. Most presidents have read deeply about the past, and most of them have read it in the same fashion as Truman—with an emphasis on the individual over the social context, and with a conviction that history offers a tool not just for selling their beliefs but for developing and testing those beliefs, too.*

We learned geometry, music, rhetoric, logic, and a smattering of astronomy. History and biography were my favorites. The lives of great men and famous women intrigued me, and I read all I could find about them.

We had an excellent history teacher, Miss Maggie Phelps, and an English teacher, Miss Tillie Brown, who was a genius at making us appreciate good literature. She also made us want to read it.

Our science teacher was Professor W. L. C. Palmer, who became principal of the high school and afterward superintendent of all the schools. He married our mathematics and Latin teacher, Miss Adelia Hardin.

I do not remember a bad teacher in all my experience. They were all different, of course, but they were the salt of the earth. They gave us our high ideals, and they hardly ever received more than forty dollars a month for it.

My debt to history is one which cannot be calculated. I know of no other motivation which so accounts for my awakening interest as a young lad in the principles of leadership and government.

Whether that early interest stemmed partly from some hereditary trait in my natural makeup is something for the psychologists to decide. But I know that the one great external influence which, more than anything else, nourished and sustained that interest in government and public service was the endless reading of history which I began as a boy and which I have kept up ever since.

In school, history was taught by paragraphs. Each great event in history was written up in one paragraph. I made it my business to look up the background of these events and to find out who brought them about. In the process, I became very interested in the men who made world history. The lives of the great administrators of past ages intrigued me, and I soon learned that the really successful ones were few and far between. I wanted to know what caused the successes or the failures of all the famous leaders of history.

The only way to find the answers was to read. I pored over Plutarch's *Lives* time and time again and spent as much time reading Abbott's biographies of famous men. I read the standard histories of ancient Egypt, the Mesopotamian cultures, Greece and Rome, the exploits of Genghis Khan and the stories of oriental civilizations, the accounts of the development of every modern country, and particularly the history of America.

Reading history, to me, was far more than a romantic adventure. It was solid instruction and wise teaching which I somehow felt that I wanted and needed. Even as a youth I felt that I ought to know the facts about the system of government under which I was living, and how it came to be.

It seemed to me that if I could understand the true facts about the growth and development of the United States Government and could know the details of the lives of its presidents and political leaders I would be getting for myself a valuable part of the total education which I hoped to have someday. I know of no surer way to get a solid foundation in political science and public administration than to study the histories of past administrations of the world's most successful system of government.

While still a boy I could see that history had some extremely valuable lessons to teach. I learned from it that a leader is a man who has the ability to get other people to do what they don't want to do, and like it. It takes a leader to put economic, military, and government forces to work so they will operate. I learned that in those periods of history when there was no leadership, society usually grouped through dark ages of one degree or another. I saw that it takes men to make history, or there would be no history. History does not make the man. . . .

I was beginning to realize—forty years before I had any thought of becoming President of the United States—that almost all current events in the affairs of governments and nations have their parallels and precedents in the past. It was obvious to me even then that a clear understanding of administrative problems presupposes a knowledge of similar ones as recorded in history and of their disposition. Long before I ever considered going into public life, I had arrived at the conclusion that no decisions affecting the people should be made impulsively, but on the basis of historical background and careful consideration of the facts as they exist at the time.

History taught me that the leader of any country, in order to assume his responsibilities as a leader, must know the history of not only his own country but of all the other great countries, and that he must make the effort to apply this knowledge to the decisions that have to be made for the welfare of all the people.

HARRY S. TRUMAN

Statement on the Dropping
of the Atomic Bomb

(1945)

"It is a harnessing of the basic power of
the universe"

On August 6, 1945—not quite four months after Truman's conversation with Secretary Stimson, described in his Memoirs—*an American bomber dropped an atomic bomb on the city of Hiroshima. Soon after, the president released this written statement.*

Sixteen hours ago, an American airplane dropped one bomb on Hiroshima, an important Japanese Army base. That bomb had more power than twenty thousand tons of T.N.T. It had more than two thousand times the blast power of the British "Grand Slam," which is the largest bomb ever yet used in the history of warfare.

The Japanese began the war from the air at Pearl Harbor. They have been repaid many fold. And the end is not yet. With this bomb we have now added a new and revolutionary increase in destruction to supplement the growing power of our armed forces. In their present form these bombs are now in production and even more powerful forms are in development.

It is an atomic bomb. It is a harnessing of the basic power of the universe. The force from which the sun draws its power has been loosed against those who brought war to the Far East.

Before 1939, it was the accepted belief of scientists that it was theoretically possible to release atomic energy. But no one knew any practical method of doing it. By 1942, however, we knew that the Germans were working feverishly to find a way to add atomic energy to the other engines of war with which they hoped to enslave the world. But they failed. We may be grateful to Providence that the Germans got the V-1s and V-2s late and in limited quantities and even more grateful that they did not get the atomic bomb at all.

The battle of the laboratories held fateful risks for us as well as the battles of the air, land, and sea, and we have now won the battle of the laboratories as we have won the other battles.

Beginning in 1940, before Pearl Harbor, scientific knowledge useful in war was pooled between the United States and Great Britain, and many priceless helps to our victories have come from that arrangement. Under that general policy the research on the atomic bomb was begun. With American and British scientists working together we entered the race of discovery against the Germans.

The United States had available the large number of scientists of distinction in the many needed areas of knowledge. It had the tremendous industrial and financial resources necessary for the project and they could be devoted to it without undue impairment of other vital war work. In the United States the laboratory work and the production plants, on which a substantial start had already been made, would be out of reach of enemy bombing, while at that time Britain was exposed to constant air attack and was still threatened with the possibility of invasion. For these reasons Prime Minister Churchill and President Roosevelt agreed that it was wise to carry on the project here. We now have two great plants and many lesser works devoted to the production of atomic power. Employment during peak construction numbered 125,000 and over 65,000 individuals are even now engaged in operating the plants. Many have worked there for two and a half years. Few know what they have been producing. They see great quantities of material going in and they see nothing coming out of these plants, for the physical size of the explosive charge is exceedingly small. We have spent two billion dollars on the greatest scientific gamble in history—and won.

But the greatest marvel is not the size of the enterprise, its secrecy, nor its cost, but the achievement of scientific brains in putting together infinitely complex pieces of knowledge held by many men in different fields of science into a workable plan. And hardly less marvelous has been the capacity of industry to design, and of labor to operate, the machines and methods to do things never done before so that the brainchild of many minds came forth in physical shape and performed as it was supposed to do. Both science and industry worked under the direction of the United States Army, which achieved a unique success in managing so diverse a problem in the advancement of knowledge in an amazingly short time. It is doubtful if such another combination could be got together in the world. What has been done is the greatest achievement of organized science in history. It was done under high pressure and without failure.

We are now prepared to obliterate more rapidly and completely every productive enterprise the Japanese have above ground in any city. We shall destroy their docks, their factories, and their communications. Let there be no mistake; we shall completely destroy Japan's power to make war.

It was to spare the Japanese people from utter destruction that the ultimatum of July 26 was issued at Potsdam. Their leaders promptly rejected that ultimatum. If they do not now accept our terms they may expect a rain of ruin from the air, the like of which has never been seen on this earth. Behind this air attack will follow sea and land forces in such numbers and power as they have not yet seen and with the fighting skill of which they are already well aware.

The secretary of war, who has kept in personal touch with all phases of the project, will immediately make public a statement giving further details.

His statement will give facts concerning the sites at Oak Ridge near Knoxville, Tennessee, and at Richland near Pasco, Washington, and an installation near Santa Fe, New Mexico. Although the workers at the sites have been making materials to be used in producing the greatest destructive force in history they have not themselves been in danger beyond that of many other occupations, for the utmost care has been taken of their safety.

The fact that we can release atomic energy ushers in a new era in man's understanding of nature's forces. Atomic energy may in the future supplement the power that now comes from coal, oil, and falling water, but at present it cannot be produced on a basis to compete with them commercially. Before that comes there must be a long period of intensive research.

It has never been the habit of the scientists of this country or the policy of this government to withhold from the world scientific knowledge. Normally, therefore, everything about the work with atomic energy would be made public.

But under present circumstances it is not intended to divulge the technical processes of production or all the military applications, pending further examination of possible methods of protecting us and the rest of the world from the danger of sudden destruction.

I shall recommend that the Congress of the United States consider promptly the establishment of an appropriate commission to control the production and use of atomic power within the United States. I shall give further consideration and make further recommendations to the Congress as to how atomic power can become a powerful and forceful influence towards the maintenance of world peace.

HARRY S. TRUMAN

From His Address
on Greece and Turkey

(1947)

"The free peoples of the world look to us
for support in maintaining their freedoms"

*In the aftermath of World War II, and in the age of the atomic bomb, new
questions emerged about America's foreign policy. Truman provided some answers
in a major speech on March 12, 1947—one that, like a growing number of
presidential speeches, was broadcast on television. Instead of keeping to itself in
times of peace, Truman argued, America should aid other democracies facing
totalitarian threats; instead of the Monroe Doctrine, America should follow the
Truman Doctrine. Many historians have come to see this address as the start of
the Cold War between America and the Soviet Union.*

The gravity of the situation which confronts the world today necessitates my appearance before a joint session of the Congress. The foreign
policy and the national security of this country are involved.

One aspect of the present situation, which I present to you at this time
for your consideration and decision, concerns Greece and Turkey.

The United States has received from the Greek government an urgent
appeal for financial and economic assistance. Preliminary reports from the
American Economic Mission now in Greece and reports from the American

ambassador in Greece corroborate the statement of the Greek government that assistance is imperative if Greece is to survive as a free nation.

I do not believe that the American people and the Congress wish to turn a deaf ear to the appeal of the Greek government.

Greece is not a rich country. Lack of sufficient natural resources has always forced the Greek people to work hard to make both ends meet. Since 1940, this industrious, peace-loving country has suffered invasion, four years of cruel enemy occupation, and bitter internal strife.

When forces of liberation entered Greece, they found that the retreating Germans had destroyed virtually all the railways, roads, port facilities, communications, and merchant marine. More than a thousand villages had been burned. Eighty-five percent of the children were tubercular. Livestock, poultry, and draft animals had almost disappeared. Inflation had wiped out practically all savings.

As a result of these tragic conditions, a militant minority, exploiting human want and misery, was able to create political chaos which, until now, has made economic recovery impossible.

Greece is today without funds to finance the importation of those goods which are essential to bare subsistence. Under these circumstances the people of Greece cannot make progress in solving their problems of reconstruction. Greece is in desperate need of financial and economic assistance to enable it to resume purchases of food, clothing, fuel, and seeds. These are indispensable for the subsistence of its people and are obtainable only from abroad. Greece must have help to import the goods necessary to restore internal order and security so essential for economic and political recovery.

The Greek government has also asked for the assistance of experienced American administrators, economists, and technicians to ensure that the financial and other aid given to Greece shall be used effectively in creating a stable and self-sustaining economy and in improving its public administration. . . .

No government is perfect. One of the chief virtues of a democracy, however, is that its defects are always visible and under democratic processes can be pointed out and corrected. The government of Greece is not perfect. Nevertheless, it represents 85 percent of the members of the Greek parliament who were chosen in an election last year. Foreign observers, including 692 Americans, considered this election to be a fair expression of the views of the Greek people.

The Greek government has been operating in an atmosphere of chaos and extremism. It has made mistakes. The extension of aid by this country does not mean that the United States condones everything that the Greek government has done or will do. We have condemned in the past, and we condemn now, extremist measures of the right or the left. We have in the past advised tolerance, and we advise tolerance now.

Greece's neighbor, Turkey, also deserves our attention.

The future of Turkey as an independent and economically sound state is clearly no less important to the freedom-loving peoples of the world than the future of Greece. The circumstances in which Turkey finds itself today are considerably different from those of Greece. Turkey has been spared the disasters that have beset Greece. And during the war, the United States and Great Britain furnished Turkey with material aid.

Nevertheless, Turkey now needs our support.

Since the war Turkey has sought additional financial assistance from Great Britain and the United States for the purpose of effecting that modernization necessary for the maintenance of its national integrity.

That integrity is essential to the preservation of order in the Middle East.

The British Government has informed us that, owing to its own difficulties, it can no longer extend financial or economic aid to Turkey.

As in the case of Greece, if Turkey is to have the assistance it needs, the United States must supply it. We are the only country able to provide that help.

I am fully aware of the broad implications involved if the United States extends assistance to Greece and Turkey, and I shall discuss these implications with you at this time.

One of the primary objectives of the foreign policy of the United States is the creation of conditions in which we and other nations will be able to work out a way of life free from coercion. This was a fundamental issue in the war with Germany and Japan. Our victory was won over countries which sought to impose their will, and their way of life, upon other nations.

To ensure the peaceful development of nations, free from coercion, the United States has taken a leading part in establishing the United Nations. The United Nations is designed to make possible lasting freedom and independence for all its members. We shall not realize our objectives, however, unless we are willing to help free peoples to maintain their free institutions and their national integrity against aggressive movements that seek to impose upon them totalitarian regimes. This is no more than a frank recognition that totalitarian regimes imposed upon free peoples, by direct or indirect aggression, undermine the foundations of international peace and hence the security of the United States.

The peoples of a number of countries of the world have recently had totalitarian regimes forced upon them against their will. The government of the United States has made frequent protests against coercion and intimidation, in violation of the Yalta agreement, in Poland, Romania, and Bulgaria. I must also state that in a number of other countries there have been similar developments.

At the present moment in world history nearly every nation must choose between alternative ways of life. The choice is too often not a free one.

One way of life is based upon the will of the majority, and is distinguished by free institutions, representative government, free elections, guarantees of individual liberty, freedom of speech and religion, and freedom from political oppression.

The second way of life is based upon the will of a minority forcibly imposed upon the majority. It relies upon terror and oppression, a controlled press and radio, fixed elections, and the suppression of personal freedoms.

I believe that it must be the policy of the United States to support free peoples who are resisting attempted subjugation by armed minorities or by outside pressures.

I believe that we must assist free peoples to work out their own destinies in their own way.

I believe that our help should be primarily through economic and financial aid, which is essential to economic stability and orderly political processes. . . .

I would not recommend it except that the alternative is much more serious. The United States contributed $341,000,000,000 toward winning World War II. This is an investment in world freedom and world peace.

The assistance that I am recommending for Greece and Turkey amounts to little more than 1/10 of 1 percent of this investment. It is only common sense that we should safeguard this investment and make sure that it was not in vain.

The seeds of totalitarian regimes are nurtured by misery and want. They spread and grow in the evil soil of poverty and strife. They reach their full growth when the hope of a people for a better life has died.

We must keep that hope alive.

The free peoples of the world look to us for support in maintaining their freedoms.

If we falter in our leadership, we may endanger the peace of the world—and we shall surely endanger the welfare of this nation.

From *Crusade in Europe*

"Do your best to save them"

On the morning of December 7, 1941—Roosevelt's "date which will live in infamy"—Dwight Eisenhower was a fifty-one-year-old brigadier general. By the end of World War II, he was solely in charge of the Allied Expeditionary Force. After the war, Eisenhower wrote a terrific memoir about his service, Crusade in Europe; *it became a bestseller and a boost when he ran for president in 1952. One of his influences, Eisenhower later said, was Grant's* Personal Memoirs, *and a comparison between it and* Crusade in Europe, *with the latter's accounts of aircraft carriers and globalized scope, shows how much war had changed. Yet the books also overlap in some compelling ways, not only in their literary style— clipped, concrete, clear—but in their subjects' dogged focus on completing their work.*

On the afternoon of December 7, at Fort Sam Houston, Texas, tired out from the long and exhausting staff work of the maneuvers and their aftermath, I went to bed with orders that under no circumstances was I to be disturbed. My dreams were of a two weeks' leave I was going to take, during which my wife and I were going to West Point to spend Christmas with our plebe son, John. But even dreams like this—and my strict orders—could be shattered with impunity by the aide who brought the news that we were at war.

Within an hour of the Pearl Harbor attack, orders began pouring into Third Army Headquarters from the War Department. There were orders for the immediate transfer of anti-aircraft units to the West Coast, where the terrified citizens hourly detected phantom bombers in the sky; orders for the establishment of anti-sabotage measures; orders for careful guarding of industrial plants; orders for reconnaissance along our southern border to prevent the entrance of spies; and orders to ensure the safety of ports along the Gulf of Mexico. There were orders for rushing heavy bodies of troops to the west in anticipation of any attacks the Japanese might contemplate. In turn, General Krueger's headquarters had to send out instructions to a hundred stations as rapidly as they could be prepared and checked. It was a period of intense activity.

Immediacy of movement was the keynote. The normal channels of administration were abandoned; the chain of command was compressed at meetings where all echelons got their instructions in a single briefing; the slow and methodical process of drawing up detailed movement orders that specified to the last jot of equipment what should be taken with the troops, how it should be crated and marked, was ignored. A single telephone call would start an infantry unit across the continent; troops and equipment entrained with nothing in writing to show by what authority they moved. Guns were loaded on flatcars, if flatcars were available; on gondolas if they could be had; in freight cars if nothing else was at hand. The men travelled in *de luxe* Pullmans, in troop sleepers, in modern coaches, and in day cars that had been obsolete and sidetracked in the yards for a generation and were now drafted for emergency troop movements.

I had five days of this. Early in the morning of December 12 the telephone connecting us directly to the War Department in Washington began to jangle. I answered and someone inquired: "Is that you, Ike?"

"Yes."

"The chief says for you to hop a plane and get up here right away. Tell your boss that formal orders will come through later."

The "chief" was [Army chief of staff George] Marshall, and the man at the other end of the line was Colonel Walter Bedell Smith, who was later to become my close friend and chief of staff throughout the European operations.

This message was a hard blow. During the first World War every one of my frantic efforts to get to the scene of action had been defeated—for reasons which had no validity to me except that they all boiled down to "War Department orders." I hoped in any new war to stay with troops. Being ordered to a city where I had already served a total of eight years would mean, I thought, a virtual repetition of my experience in World War I. Heavy-hearted, I telephoned my wife to pack a bag, and within the hour I was headed for the War Department.

I had probably been ordered to Washington, I decided, because of my recently completed tour in the Philippines. Within a matter of hours after their assault on Pearl Harbor, the Japanese had launched against the Philippines an air attack that quickly reduced our inadequate air forces to practical impotence. It was the spot upon which official and public interest was centered, and General Marshall undoubtedly wanted someone on his staff who was reasonably familiar with conditions then current in the islands, who was acquainted with both the Philippines Department of the United States Army and the defense organization of the Philippines Commonwealth, which war had caught halfway in its planned development.

The Commonwealth defense organization dated back to 1935, when General MacArthur was asked by newly elected President Manuel Quezon to plan and build a military force able to defend the islands; on July 4, 1946, when the Commonwealth was to become an independent republic, United States troops were to be withdrawn and armed defense would thereafter be a Philippines function. On General MacArthur's acceptance, a military mission of American officers was formed and I was assigned to it as his senior assistant.

In 1935 we planned to turn out each year during the coming ten, through a program of universal military training, approximately 30,000 soldiers with five and a half months' basic experience. At first we would form units of only platoon size, but within four or five years we hoped to produce regiments and by 1946, with a total of 300,000 men who had the minimum basic training, we would be able to form thirty divisions.

During the same transitional period the Philippines Department of the United States Army, while working closely with the Commonwealth defense force and supplying it with officer and enlisted instructors, arms, and equipment, was planning also for its own part in defense should war come before Philippine independence. In such a contingency it was planned to withdraw our troops on the main island of Luzon into the Bataan Peninsula across from Corregidor so that the two areas would constitute one almost impregnable position where our forces could hold until reinforcements arrived. In 1938, I witnessed a maneuver demonstrating this plan, and shortly after I left the islands it was repeated on a larger scale.

Travelling to Washington on December 12, 1941, I had no clear idea of the progress of fighting in the Philippines. The reports we had received at Fort Sam Houston were fragmentary and obscure. Undoubtedly the Japanese would not dare bypass the islands. But the direction and weight of their assault was still unknown when I arrived at the War Department.

Washington in wartime has been variously described in numbers of pungent epigrams, all signifying chaos. Traditionally the government, including the service departments, has always been as unprepared for war and its all-embracing problems as the country itself, and the incidence of emergency has, under an awakened sense of overwhelming responsibility, resulted in confusion, intensified by a swarming influx of contract seekers and well-meaning volunteers. This time, however, the War Department had achieved a gratifying level of efficiency before the outbreak of war. So far as my own observations during the months I served there would justify a judgment, this was due to the vision and determination of one man, General Marshall. Naturally he had support. He was backed up by the president and by many of our ablest leaders in Congress and in key positions in the administration. But it would have been easy for General Marshall, during 1940–41, to drift along with the current, to let things slide in anticipation of a normal end to a brilliant military career—for he had earned, throughout the professional army, a reputation for brilliance. Instead he had for many months deliberately followed the hard way, determined that at whatever cost to himself or to anyone else the Army should be decently prepared for the conflict which he daily, almost hourly, expected.

I reported to General Marshall early on Sunday morning, December 14, and for the first time in my life talked to him for more than two minutes at a time. It was the fourth time I had ever seen him. Without preamble or waste of time the chief of staff outlined the general situation, naval and military, in the western Pacific.

The Navy informed him that the Pacific Fleet would be unable for some months to participate in major operations. The Navy's carriers remained intact because they had not been at Pearl Harbor at the time of the attack, but supporting vessels for the carriers were so few in number that great restrictions would have to be placed upon their operation. Moreover, at that moment there was no assurance that the Japanese would not quickly launch a major amphibious assault upon Hawaii or possibly even upon the mainland, and the Navy felt that these carriers should be reserved for reconnaissance work and defense, except only when some great emergency demanded from them other employment. The Navy Department had given General Marshall no estimate of the date when they expected the fleet to be sufficiently repaired and strengthened to take offensive action in the Pacific area.

The garrison in Hawaii was so weak that there was general agreement between the War and Navy Departments that its air and ground strength should be reinforced as rapidly as possible and should take priority over other efforts in the Pacific.

At the time of the Japanese attack American army and air forces in the Philippines had reached an aggregate of 30,000, including the Philippine Scouts, formations integrated into the United States Army, but with all enlisted personnel and some of the officers native Filipinos.

United States outfits provided the garrison for Corregidor and its smaller supporting forts. Other American units were organized into the Philippine Divisions which consisted of Philippine Scout units and the 31st Infantry Regiment. National Guard units—three field artillery regiments, one anti-aircraft artillery regiment, one infantry regiment, two tank battalions, and service troops—had recently arrived as reinforcements.

The air strength had been increased during 1941, and on the day of attack there were thirty-five modern bombers, B-17s, stationed in the Philippines. Present also were 220 airplanes of the fighter type, not all of them in operating readiness. General Marshall knew that this air detachment had been hit and badly damaged during the initial Japanese attack, but he had no report upon the circumstances of that action.

There were known to be shortages in essential items of supply, but in the matter of food and normal types of ammunition it was thought there would be little difficulty, provided the garrison was given time to concentrate these at their points of greatest usefulness.

The Navy Yard at Cavite, just outside Manila, had been damaged very severely by Japanese bombers on December 10. That portion of the modest task force comprising the Asiatic Fleet which was disposed at or near Manila consisted mainly of small divisions of submarines. The largest warship in the Asiatic Fleet was the heavy cruiser, *Houston*, at Iloilo.

Against a strong and sustained attack, forces such as these could not hold out indefinitely. All the evidence indicated that the Japanese intended to overrun the Philippines as rapidly as possible, and the problem was to determine what could now be done.

General Marshall took perhaps twenty minutes to describe all this and then abruptly asked, "What should be our general line of action?"

I thought a second and, hoping I was showing a poker face, answered: "Give me a few hours."

"All right," he said, and I was dismissed.

Significantly and characteristically, he did not even hint at one of the most important factors in the problem: the psychological effects of the Philippine battle upon people in the United States and throughout the Pacific. Clearly he felt that anyone stupid enough to overlook this consideration had no business wearing the star of a brigadier-general.

I took my problem to a desk assigned me in the division of the War Department then known as "War Plans," headed by my old friend Brigadier-General Leonard T. Gerow. Obviously, if I were to be of any service to General Marshall in the War Department, I would have to earn his confidence: the logic of this, my first answer, would have to be unimpeachable, and the answer would have to be prompt. A curious echo from the long ago came to my aid.

For three years, soon after the first World War, I served under one of the most accomplished soldiers of our time, Major-General Fox Conner. One of the subjects of which he talked to me most was allied command, its difficulties and its problems. Another was George C. Marshall. Again and again General Conner said to me: "We cannot escape another great war. When we go into that war, it will be in company with allies. Systems of single command will have to be worked out. We must not accept the 'coordination' concept under which Foch was compelled to work. We must insist on individual and single responsibility—leaders will have to learn how to overcome nationalistic considerations in the conduct of campaigns. One man who can do it is Marshall—he is close to being a genius."

With that memory I determined that my answer should be short, emphatic, and based on reasoning in which I honestly believed. No oratory, plausible argument, or glittering generality would impress anyone entitled to be labeled genius by Fox Conner.

The question before me was almost unlimited in its implications, and my qualifications for approaching it were probably those of the average hard-working Army officer of my age. Naturally, I had pursued the military courses of the Army's school system. Soon after completing the War College in 1928, I went to serve as a special assistant in the office of the assistant secretary of war, where my duties were quickly expanded to include confidential work for the chief of staff of the Army.

In these positions I was forced to examine worldwide military matters and to study concretely such subjects as the mobilization and composition of armies, the role of air forces and navies in war, tendencies toward mechanization, and the acute dependence of all elements of military life upon the industrial capacity of the nation. This last was to me of special importance because of my intense belief that large-scale motorization and mechanization and the development of air forces in unprecedented strength would characterize successful military forces of the future. On this subject

I wrote a number of studies and reports. Holding these convictions, I knew that any sane preparation for war involved also sound plans for the prompt mobilization of industry. The years devoted to work of this kind opened up to me an almost new world. During that time I met and worked with many people whose opinions I respected highly, both in military and civil life. Among these an outstanding figure was Mr. Bernard Baruch, for whom my admiration was and is profound. I still believe that if Mr. Baruch's recommendations for universal price fixing and his organizational plans had been completely and promptly adopted in December 1941 this country would have saved billions in money—possibly much in time and therefore in lives.

From tasks such as these I had gone, in 1935, to the Philippines. Now, six years later, I was back in the War Department, the nation was at war, and the Philippines were in deadly danger.

So I began my concentration on General Marshall's question. Our naval situation in the western Pacific, as outlined by the chief of staff, was at that moment completely depressing. The fleet could not attempt any aggressive action far from a secure base and dared not venture with surface vessels into Philippine waters. The clamor of ground and air commanders in Hawaii and on the West Coast for defensive strength—clamors emphasized in hysterical terms by mayors, city councils, and congressmen—would, if answered, have absorbed far more than all United States shipping, troops, and immediately available anti-aircraft force then in existence.

It was painfully clear that the Philippines themselves could not, at that time, be reinforced directly by land and sea forces. Any hope of sending major reinforcements into the islands had to be based upon such future rehabilitation of our Navy as would permit it to operate safely in the Philippines area. At the moment there was no way of estimating when this could be done.

To prolong the duration of the defense while the Navy was undergoing repair, there was the possibility that we could ship to the islands vitally needed items by submarine and blockade runners, and, provided we could keep open the necessary line of communications, something could be shipped by air. Australia was the base nearest to the Philippines that we could hope to establish and maintain, and the necessary line of air communications would therefore follow along the islands intervening between that continent and the Philippines.

If we were to use Australia as a base it was mandatory that we procure a line of communications leading to it. This meant that we must instantly move to save Hawaii, Fiji, New Zealand, and New Caledonia, and we had to make certain of the safety of Australia itself.

It seemed possible, though not probable, that the Netherlands Indies, in some respects the richest area in the world in natural resources, could be denied to the Jap invader, who would soon be desperately in need of Indies oil to continue his offensives. Unless this could be done short-range fighter planes could not be flown into the Philippines, and fighter planes were vital to successful defense.

In spite of difficulties, risks, and fierce competition for every asset we had, a great nation such as ours, no matter how unprepared for war, could not afford cold-bloodedly to turn its back upon our Filipino wards and the many thousand Americans, troops and civilians, in the archipelago. We had to do whatever was remotely possible for the hapless islands, particularly by air support and by providing vital supplies, although the end result might be no more than postponement of disaster. And we simply had to save the air lifeline through Australia, New Zealand, Fiji, and Hawaii.

With these bleak conclusions I marched back to the chief of staff. "General," I said, "it will be a long time before major reinforcements can go to the Philippines, longer than the garrison can hold out with any driblet assistance, if the enemy commits major forces to their reduction. But we must do everything for them that is humanly possible. The people of China, of the Philippines, of the Dutch East Indies will be watching us. They may excuse failure but they will not excuse abandonment. Their trust and friendship are important to us. Our base must be Australia, and we must start at once to expand it and to secure our communications to it. In this last we dare not fail. We must take great risks and spend any amount of money required."

He merely replied: "I agree with you." His tone implied that I had been given the problem as a check to an answer he had already reached. He added: "Do your best to save them."

With that I went to work.

DWIGHT EISENHOWER

From His Address
on the Soviet Union

(1953)

"The cost of one modern heavy bomber is this: a modern brick school in more than thirty cities"

On April 16, 1953—only a few months into his presidency, and only a few weeks after the death of Joseph Stalin—Eisenhower gave one of his most notable speeches, on the escalating Cold War. Eisenhower tried to sketch the differences between America's strategy and the Soviet Union's. But the former general also warned about the shared cost of escalation: not just the possibility of mass deaths, but the certainty of misdirected money and energy. In this excerpt from what came to be known as his "Chance for Peace" or "Cross of Iron" speech, Eisenhower dreams of a different war, a war aimed at "the brute forces of poverty and need."

In this spring of 1953, the free world weighs one question above all others: the chance for a just peace for all peoples.

To weigh this chance is to summon instantly to mind another recent moment of great decision. It came with that yet more hopeful spring of 1945, bright with the promise of victory and of freedom. The hope of all just men in that moment too was a just and lasting peace.

The eight years that have passed have seen that hope waver, grow dim, and almost die. And the shadow of fear again has darkly lengthened across the world.

Today the hope of free men remains stubborn and brave, but it is sternly disciplined by experience. It shuns not only all crude counsel of despair but also the self-deceit of easy illusion. It weighs the chance for peace with sure, clear knowledge of what happened to the vain hope of 1945.

In that spring of victory the soldiers of the Western Allies met the soldiers of Russia in the center of Europe. They were triumphant comrades in arms. Their peoples shared the joyous prospect of building, in honor of their dead, the only fitting monument—an age of just peace. All these war-weary peoples shared too this concrete, decent purpose: to guard vigilantly against the domination ever again of any part of the world by a single, unbridled aggressive power.

This common purpose lasted an instant and perished. The nations of the world divided to follow two distinct roads.

The United States and our valued friends, the other free nations, chose one road.

The leaders of the Soviet Union chose another.

The way chosen by the United States was plainly marked by a few clear precepts, which govern its conduct in world affairs.

First: No people on earth can be held, as a people, to be an enemy, for all humanity shares the common hunger for peace and fellowship and justice.

Second: No nation's security and well-being can be lastingly achieved in isolation but only in effective cooperation with fellow nations.

Third: Any nation's right to a form of government and an economic system of its own choosing is inalienable.

Fourth: Any nation's attempt to dictate to other nations their form of government is indefensible.

And fifth: A nation's hope of lasting peace cannot be firmly based upon any race in armaments but rather upon just relations and honest understanding with all other nations.

In the light of these principles the citizens of the United States defined the way they proposed to follow, through the aftermath of war, toward true peace. This way was faithful to the spirit that inspired the United Nations: to prohibit strife, to relieve tensions, to banish fears. This way was to control and to reduce armaments. This way was to allow all nations to devote their energies and resources to the great and good tasks of healing the war's wounds, of clothing and feeding and housing the needy, of perfecting a just political life, of enjoying the fruits of their own free toil.

The Soviet government held a vastly different vision of the future. In the world of its design, security was to be found, not in mutual trust and mutual aid but in force: huge armies, subversion, rule of neighbor nations. The goal was power superiority at all cost. Security was to be sought by denying it to all others.

The result has been tragic for the world and, for the Soviet Union, it has also been ironic. The amassing of Soviet power alerted free nations to a new danger of aggression. It compelled them in self-defense to spend unprecedented money and energy for armaments. It forced them to develop weapons of war now capable of inflicting instant and terrible punishment upon any aggressor.

It instilled in the free nations—and let none doubt this—the unshakable conviction that, as long as there persists a threat to freedom, they must at any cost remain armed, strong, and ready for the risk of war.

It inspired them—and let none doubt this—to attain a unity of purpose and will beyond the power of propaganda or pressure to break, now or ever.

There remained, however, one thing essentially unchanged and unaffected by Soviet conduct: the readiness of the free nations to welcome sincerely any genuine evidence of peaceful purpose enabling all peoples again to resume their common quest of just peace.

The free nations, most solemnly and repeatedly, have assured the Soviet Union that their firm association has never had any aggressive purpose whatsoever. Soviet leaders, however, have seemed to persuade themselves, or tried to persuade their people, otherwise.

And so it has come to pass that the Soviet Union itself has shared and suffered the very fears it has fostered in the rest of the world. This has been the way of life forged by eight years of fear and force. What can the world, or any nation in it, hope for if no turning is found on this dread road?

The worst to be feared and the best to be expected can be simply stated.

The worst is atomic war.

The best would be this: a life of perpetual fear and tension; a burden of arms draining the wealth and the labor of all peoples; a wasting of strength that defies the American system or the Soviet system or any system to achieve true abundance and happiness for the peoples of this earth.

Every gun that is made, every warship launched, every rocket fired signifies, in the final sense, a theft from those who hunger and are not fed, those who are cold and are not clothed.

This world in arms is not spending money alone. It is spending the sweat of its laborers, the genius of its scientists, the hopes of its children. The cost of one modern heavy bomber is this: a modern brick school in more than thirty cities. It is two electric power plants, each serving a town of 60,000 population. It is two fine, fully equipped hospitals. It is some fifty miles of concrete highway. We pay for a single fighter plane with a half million bushels of wheat. We pay for a single destroyer with new homes that could have housed more than 8,000 people.

This, I repeat, is the best way of life to be found on the road the world has been taking.

This is not a way of life at all, in any true sense. Under the cloud of threatening war, it is humanity hanging from a cross of iron.

These plain and cruel truths define the peril and point the hope that come with this spring of 1953. This is one of those times in the affairs of nations when the gravest choices must be made, if there is to be a turning toward a just and lasting peace. It is a moment that calls upon the governments of the world to speak their intentions with simplicity and with honesty.

It calls upon them to answer the question that stirs the hearts of all sane men: Is there no other way the world may live?

The world knows that an era ended with the death of Joseph Stalin. The extraordinary thirty-year span of his rule saw the Soviet Empire expand to reach from the Baltic Sea to the Sea of Japan, finally to dominate 800 million souls. The Soviet system shaped by Stalin and his predecessors was born of one World War. It survived with stubborn and often amazing courage a second World War. It has lived to threaten a third.

Now a new leadership has assumed power in the Soviet Union. Its links to the past, however strong, cannot bind it completely. Its future is, in great part, its own to make. This new leadership confronts a free world aroused, as rarely in its history, by the will to stay free.

This free world knows, out of the bitter wisdom of experience, that vigilance and sacrifice are the price of liberty. It knows that the defense of Western Europe imperatively demands the unity of purpose and action made possible by the North Atlantic Treaty Organization, embracing a European Defense Community. It knows that Western Germany deserves to be a free and equal partner in this community and that this, for Germany, is the only safe way to full, final unity. It knows that aggression in Korea and in southeast Asia are threats to the whole free community to be met by united action.

This is the kind of free world which the new Soviet leadership confronts. It is a world that demands and expects the fullest respect of its rights and interests. It is a world that will always accord the same respect to all others. So the new Soviet leadership now has a precious opportunity to awaken, with the rest of the world, to the point of peril reached and to help turn the tide of history. Will it do this? . . .

As progress in all these areas strengthens world trust, we could proceed concurrently with the next great work—the reduction of the burden of armaments now weighing upon the world. To this end we would welcome and enter into the most solemn agreements. These could properly include:

1. The limitation, by absolute numbers or by an agreed international ratio, of the sizes of the military and security forces of all nations.
2. A commitment by all nations to set an agreed limit upon that proportion of total production of certain strategic materials to be devoted to military purposes.
3. International control of atomic energy to promote its use for peaceful purposes only and to ensure the prohibition of atomic weapons.
4. A limitation or prohibition of other categories of weapons of great destructiveness.
5. The enforcement of all these agreed limitations and prohibitions by adequate safeguards, including a practical system of inspection under the United Nations.

The details of such disarmament programs are manifestly critical and complex. Neither the United States nor any other nation can properly claim to possess a perfect, immutable formula. But the formula matters less than the faith—the good faith without which no formula can work justly and effectively.

The fruit of success in all these tasks would present the world with the greatest task, and the greatest opportunity, of all. It is this: the dedication of the energies, the resources, and the imaginations of all peaceful nations to a new kind of war. This would be a declared total war not upon any human enemy but upon the brute forces of poverty and need. . . .

This government is ready to ask its people to join with all nations in devoting a substantial percentage of the savings achieved by disarmament to a fund for world aid and reconstruction. The purposes of this great work would be to help other peoples to develop the undeveloped areas of the world, to stimulate profitable and fair world trade, to assist all peoples to know the blessings of productive freedom.

The monuments to this new kind of war would be these: roads and schools, hospitals and homes, food and health.

We are ready, in short, to dedicate our strength to serving the needs, rather than the fears, of the world. We are ready, by these and all such actions, to make of the United Nations an institution that can effectively guard the peace and security of all peoples.

I know of nothing I can add to make plainer the sincere purpose of the United States.

I know of no course, other than that marked by these and similar actions, that can be called the highway of peace.

I know of only one question upon which progress waits. It is this: What is the Soviet Union ready to do?

DWIGHT EISENHOWER

Farewell Address

(1961)

"The military-industrial complex"

On January 17, 1961, with only three days left in his presidency, Eisenhower gave a televised address. It recalled another of his influences in both style and content: Washington and his Farewell Address. While America had avoided a war like the one Eisenhower had warned of in his speech after Stalin's death, his other worry had already come true: both his government and the Soviet Union's were devoting enormous resources to what Eisenhower called the "military-industrial complex." In this address, he asserts once again that a fixation on war can warp a nation's priorities and its soul.

Three days from now, after half a century in the service of our country, I shall lay down the responsibilities of office as, in traditional and solemn ceremony, the authority of the presidency is vested in my successor.

This evening I come to you with a message of leave-taking and farewell, and to share a few final thoughts with you, my countrymen.

Like every other citizen, I wish the new president, and all who will labor with him, Godspeed. I pray that the coming years will be blessed with peace and prosperity for all.

Our people expect their president and the Congress to find essential agreement on issues of great moment, the wise resolution of which will better shape the future of the nation. My own relations with the Congress, which began on a remote and tenuous basis when, long ago, a member of the Senate appointed me to West Point, have since ranged to the intimate during the war and immediate postwar period and, finally, to the mutually interdependent during these past eight years.

In this final relationship, the Congress and the administration have, on most vital issues, cooperated well, to serve the national good rather than mere partisanship, and so have assured that the business of the nation should go forward. So, my official relationship with the Congress ends in a feeling, on my part, of gratitude that we have been able to do so much together.

We now stand ten years past the midpoint of a century that has witnessed four major wars among great nations. Three of these involved our own country. Despite these holocausts, America is today the strongest, the most influential, and most productive nation in the world. Understandably proud of this pre-eminence, we yet realize that America's leadership and prestige depend not merely upon our unmatched material progress, riches, and military strength, but on how we use our power in the interests of world peace and human betterment.

Throughout America's adventure in free government, our basic purposes have been to keep the peace; to foster progress in human achievement; and to enhance liberty, dignity, and integrity among people and among nations. To strive for less would be unworthy of a free and religious people. Any failure traceable to arrogance, or our lack of comprehension or readiness to sacrifice, would inflict upon us grievous hurt both at home and abroad.

Progress toward these noble goals is persistently threatened by the conflict now engulfing the world. It commands our whole attention, absorbs our very beings. We face a hostile ideology—global in scope, atheistic in character, ruthless in purpose, and insidious in method. Unhappily the danger it poses promises to be of indefinite duration. To meet it successfully, there is called for not so much the emotional and transitory sacrifices of crisis, but rather those which enable us to carry forward steadily, surely, and without complaint the burdens of a prolonged and complex struggle—with liberty the stake. Only thus shall we remain, despite every provocation, on our charted course toward permanent peace and human betterment.

Crises there will continue to be. In meeting them, whether foreign or domestic, great or small, there is a recurring temptation to feel that some spectacular and costly action could become the miraculous solution to all current difficulties. A huge increase in newer elements of our defense; development of unrealistic programs to cure every ill in agriculture; a dramatic expansion in basic and applied research—these and many other possibilities, each possibly promising in itself, may be suggested as the only way to the road we wish to travel.

But each proposal must be weighed in the light of a broader consideration: the need to maintain balance in and among national programs—balance between the private and the public economy; balance between cost and hoped for advantage; balance between the clearly necessary and the comfortably desirable; balance between our essential requirements as a nation and the duties imposed by the nation upon the individual; balance between actions of the moment and the national welfare of the future. Good judgment seeks balance and progress; lack of it eventually finds imbalance and frustration.

The record of many decades stands as proof that our people and their government have, in the main, understood these truths and have responded to them well in the face of stress and threat. But threats, new in kind or degree, constantly arise. I mention two only.

A vital element in keeping the peace is our military establishment. Our arms must be mighty, ready for instant action so that no potential aggressor may be tempted to risk his own destruction.

Our military organization today bears little relation to that known by any of my predecessors in peacetime, or indeed by the fighting men of World War II or Korea.

Until the latest of our world conflicts, the United States had no armaments industry. American makers of plowshares could, with time and as required, make swords as well. But now we can no longer risk emergency improvisation of national defense; we have been compelled to create a permanent armaments industry of vast proportions. Added to this, three and a half million men and women are directly engaged in the defense establishment. We annually spend on military security more than the net income of all United States corporations.

This conjunction of an immense military establishment and a large arms industry is new in the American experience. The total influence—economic, political, even spiritual—is felt in every city, every statehouse, every office of the federal government. We recognize the imperative need for this development. Yet we must not fail to comprehend its grave implications. Our toil, resources, and livelihood are all involved; so is the very structure of our society.

In the councils of government, we must guard against the acquisition of unwarranted influence, whether sought or unsought, by the military-industrial complex. The potential for the disastrous rise of misplaced power exists and will persist.

We must never let the weight of this combination endanger our liberties or democratic processes. We should take nothing for granted. Only an alert and knowledgeable citizenry can compel the proper meshing of the huge industrial and military machinery of defense with our peaceful methods and goals, so that security and liberty may prosper together.

Akin to, and largely responsible for the sweeping changes in our industrial-military posture, has been the technological revolution during recent decades. In this revolution, research has become central; it also becomes more formalized, complex, and costly. A steadily increasing share is conducted for, by, or at the direction of the federal government.

Today, the solitary inventor, tinkering in his shop, has been overshadowed by task forces of scientists in laboratories and testing fields. In the same fashion, the free university, historically the fountainhead of free ideas and scientific discovery, has experienced a revolution in the conduct of research. Partly because of the huge costs involved, a government contract becomes virtually a substitute for intellectual curiosity. For every old blackboard there are now hundreds of new electronic computers.

The prospect of domination of the nation's scholars by federal employment, project allocations, and the power of money is ever present—and is gravely to be regarded.

Yet, in holding scientific research and discovery in respect, as we should, we must also be alert to the equal and opposite danger that public policy could itself become the captive of a scientific-technological elite.

It is the task of statesmanship to mold, to balance, and to integrate these and other forces, new and old, within the principles of our democratic system—ever aiming toward the supreme goals of our free society.

Another factor in maintaining balance involves the element of time. As we peer into society's future, we—you and I, and our government—must avoid the impulse to live only for today, plundering, for our own ease and convenience, the precious resources of tomorrow. We cannot mortgage the material assets of our grandchildren without risking the loss also of their political and spiritual heritage. We want democracy to survive for all generations to come, not to become the insolvent phantom of tomorrow.

Down the long lane of the history yet to be written, America knows that this world of ours, ever growing smaller, must avoid becoming a community of dreadful fear and hate and be, instead, a proud confederation of mutual trust and respect.

Such a confederation must be one of equals. The weakest must come to the conference table with the same confidence as do we, protected as we are by our moral, economic, and military strength. That table, though scarred by many past frustrations, cannot be abandoned for the certain agony of the battlefield.

Disarmament, with mutual honor and confidence, is a continuing imperative. Together we must learn how to compose differences, not with arms but with intellect and decent purpose. Because this need is so sharp and apparent I confess that I lay down my official responsibilities in this field with a definite sense of disappointment. As one who has witnessed the horror and the lingering sadness of war—as one who knows that another war could utterly destroy this civilization which has been so slowly and painfully built over thousands of years—I wish I could say tonight that a lasting peace is in sight.

Happily, I can say that war has been avoided. Steady progress toward our ultimate goal has been made. But so much remains to be done. As a private citizen, I shall never cease to do what little I can to help the world advance along that road.

So—in this, my last good night to you as your president—I thank you for the many opportunities you have given me for public service in war and peace. I trust that in that service you find some things worthy; as for the rest of it, I know you will find ways to improve performance in the future.

You and I—my fellow citizens—need to be strong in our faith that all nations, under God, will reach the goal of peace with justice. May we be ever unswerving in devotion to principle, confident but humble with power, diligent in pursuit of the nation's great goals.

To all the peoples of the world, I once more give expression to America's prayerful and continuing aspiration: We pray that peoples of all faiths, all races, all nations, may have their great human needs satisfied; that those now denied opportunity shall come to enjoy it to the full; that all who yearn for freedom may experience its spiritual blessings; that those who have freedom will understand, also, its heavy responsibilities; that all who are insensitive to the needs of others will learn charity; that the scourges of poverty, disease, and ignorance will be made to disappear from the earth; and that, in the goodness of time, all peoples will come to live together in a peace guaranteed by the binding force of mutual respect and love.

From an Essay on Writing Autobiography

★

"Anyone engaged in writing a memoir should recognize that his place in history is by no means going to be established by his own words"

After exiting the White House, Eisenhower turned to his presidential memoirs, published across two volumes in 1963 and 1965. These volumes were important, if uneven, and afterward Eisenhower's publisher urged him to write an essay about his writing process. While the president put it through several drafts, this essay was never officially published. Yet it remains an insightful piece—for Eisenhower's analysis of what political memoirs should be, and for his explanation of why they so often make for uneven reads.

By definition a memoir is a personal account—whether short and specific, or long and general—primarily concerned with decisions and events in which the author was a participant and of incidents with which he has been personally familiar. No matter how much outside material may be included to prove authenticity or increase reader interest, the account is written from his special viewpoint. This is what makes the memoir different from other documents and gives it value. It reveals—unless it is a mere recitation of dry data and statistics—the attitudes and processes of a particular mind; usually these revelations are more intimate than is found in his other writings and speeches.

Many historians and biographers have expressed their opinions about General Grant and have written exhaustively on every known facet of his career, but only General Grant could describe how *he felt* when he encountered frustrations or achieved triumphs. Only he could help us share the weight of responsibility resting upon him at any moment or give us an inkling of the factors he thought to be overriding in making memorable decisions. As one example: Some writers on the Civil War expressed astonishment upon learning from their research that, before the Battle of Shiloh, when the greater part of Grant's army was lying idle at Pittsburg Landing close to a large Confederate force, he did not take the logical precautionary measure of requiring his troops to entrench. The public had no inkling of his reasons until his memoir was published. In it he explained why he did nothing. "The fact is, I regarded the campaign we were engaged in as an offensive one and had no idea that the enemy would leave strong entrenchments to take the initiative when he knew he would be attacked where he was if he remained." Here is a personal confession of a false assumption, one that resulted in a tactical surprise of the Union army by General Albert Sidney Johnston's Confederate forces. It proved most embarrassing to Grant's army and could have destroyed his career.

Biographies rarely achieve completeness. Unless there could be a competent Boswell constantly by his side, no biography about a truly busy man could scarcely be expected to be an all-inclusive analysis of a personality and the motivations for his words and actions. Possibly one of the reasons we find, already in print, so many books about the late President Kennedy is that each writer saw his subject from a limited angle.

One indefensible attitude assumed by some authors is to claim, or imply, a far closer association and friendship with the individual or activity they write about, than they actually have had. This is pure chicanery and I suppose that almost every man who has ever had his name widely publicized has been victimized by it, at least to some extent. Had President Kennedy lived to complete his public service and later to prepare a memoir, it is certain that the public's understanding of the man, his character, his accomplishments and failures would be fuller and more balanced.

Just as a personal memoir can arouse the suspicion of "self-serving" so can a biography display the same defect; this is particularly true of those written by contemporaries. A desire to "catch the market" can be, for some, more persuasive than a hope of being useful to history. It seems that time alone provides the maturing processes out of which eventually develops a picture of satisfactory clarity, truth, and objectivity.

Yet a record of personal experiences can have several useful purposes, none of which is basically to amuse or entrance. If the story is about conflict, the conscientious reporter does not seek to contrive such tense situations as are dreamed up by gifted historical novelists like Ryan, Collins, Lapierre, and others. Even did he possess a portion of their ability in dramatic composition, he would defeat his basic purpose if he should try to exploit such a capacity because he is, in fact, a recorder of actions and events as seen from his personal viewpoint. The drama, if any, should be provided by the naked facts he relates and by his response to them.

A British professor, reviewing a book by my old friend Harold Macmillan, noted that personal accounts by individuals who have been prominent in public life invariably make dreary reading. Aside from the former prime minister, he cited the writings of Herbert Hoover, Harry Truman, and myself. I think he is right, absolutely.

But what author of this kind of book is aiming primarily at sprightly expression and beauty of language? He does not pretend to compete, nor need he, with a Washington Irving, a Churchill, or a Mark Twain.

A memoir should, I think, strive to clarify or correct accounts that the writer believes to be distorted or false. Some biographers of Washington have been almost idolatrous and have related numerous stories about him that are palpably apocryphal. In contrast, numerous periodicals published during his second administration incessantly described him in the most unfavorable and bitter terms, picturing him as a tyrant seeking avidly to perpetuate personal power. So, if we read only the contemporary publications, or the later writers who tried to idealize or destroy him, we would never gain a true appreciation of his worth and character. But his own letters and speeches have helped scholars of a later era to assure a logical evaluation of this foremost of all Americans.

A memoir might well present a personal interpretation of past actions that for reasons of state could not then be revealed. Moreover, I suppose that most autobiographers are, to some extent, and sometimes against their own preferences, induced to emphasize incidents that have occasioned widespread comment in the public press, particularly when these have involved disagreements or prolonged arguments. Certainly I would far rather write about those incidents and occasions that, during my long association with Winston Churchill, demonstrate the remarkable degree to which we saw eye to eye in examining a multitude of difficult military and political problems and about the satisfaction I had in the knowledge of his friendship and confidence, than dwell upon the few instances when we found ourselves at loggerheads. But these latter occasions have commanded the attention of some authors and have almost compelled me to write at various times to explain their origin, the conflicting considerations involved, and the resulting decisions.

I suspect that few men in public service are self-inspired to undertake the preparation of a lengthy memoir. Frequently, however, publishers or personal friends—believing that the public should be given the man's own story because it can probably do something to satisfy public curiosity or help fill gaps that otherwise would exist in the history of the period—persuade him to write about his experiences. To achieve this constructive purpose, truthful and thorough explanation must be his guide, though he might try to enhance reader interest by incorporating amusing and informative anecdotes.

So, I repeat, the British critic's comment is indubitably correct, but it is no ways pertinent. In gastronomical terms, he complains of the lack of caviar and salad in the menu, while the restaurant offers a diet of bread, meat, and potatoes. Or, indulging in a more artistic metaphor, a personal memoir is not intended to suggest to the reader a collection of masterpieces in painting; rather it strives to be a series of word photographs, presented, if necessary, not in color but in black and white. Even so, few of these pictures can be wholly new; a public figure's exposure to the world's publicity media during the dramatic periods of his life precludes any possibility that his story will be completely fresh; but it will certainly help round out the accounts of mere observers. It will supply a different angle from which may be seen his important experiences.

An important point, I think, is that anyone engaged in writing a memoir should recognize that his place in history is by no means going to be established by his own words. This will be done by later writers who will have the perspective provided by time. But he can make sure that such perspective will include his own honest views and interpretations. Unless historians sense this essential ingredient of honesty, then whatever the memoir contains will likely be disregarded.

From *Why England Slept*

"Democracy, which is built primarily for peace, is at a disadvantage"

In the summer of 1940, when John F. Kennedy was twenty-three, he published his first book, Why England Slept. *His father was delighted. "You would be surprised," he told his son, "how a book that really makes the grade with high-class people stands you in good stead for years to come." Kennedy's book certainly made the grade, analyzing the worsening situation in Europe and suggesting that Hitler's rise had less to do with democracy's leaders than with the problems inherent to democracy itself. It also helped Kennedy for years to come. When he ran for Congress, in 1946, his campaign based its slogan—"The New Generation Offers a Leader"—on one of the many positive responses to his book.*

In 1930 and 1931, we blamed all the evils that this country was then suffering, from the drought to the world depression, on Herbert Hoover. If we had continued to hold those beliefs, we would never have learned anything from that experience. We would have dismissed it as being a question of leadership and would have done nothing to prevent such an experience from happening again. It is, therefore, because I believe England's experience holds such a vital lesson for us, that I have sought to get away from the scapegoat idea.

For England has been a testing ground. It has been a case of a democratic form of government, with a capitalistic economy, trying to compete with the new totalitarian system, based on an economy of rigid state control.

For a country whose government and economic structure is similar to England's and which may some day be similarly in competition with a dictatorship, there should be a valuable lesson. . . .

In regard to capitalism, we observe first that it was obedience to its principles that contributed so largely to England's failure. It has been estimated in authoritative circles that Hitler has spent anywhere from $50,000,000,000 to $100,000,000,000 in building up Germany's armaments. He ran Germany's debt to skyrocket heights and saved Germany from suffering violent inflation only by rigid state control.

How, therefore, could England have hoped to match his effort? When England's governmental revenue was less than $5,000,000,000 a year, she could not hope to do so over a very long period of time without going bankrupt. She, too, would have had to initiate rigid state control to prevent inflation and that would have been the end of capitalism and democracy. It may be argued that she could have sold her investments in other countries. But if she had done that, with the unfavorable balance of trade which she had had in the last few years, she could not have continued to pay for her imports. It would have meant ruin either way, and so naturally England was unwilling, *until she knew war was imminent*, to take the risk of making huge expenditures. America has gotten a taste of the same problem with her appropriations of around $13,000,000,000 this year. If she has to keep up this type of effort, or in fact anything remotely similar for seven or eight years, it will mean either a violent cut in relief expenditures, which will cause social unrest, or a great danger of inflation. And we are much richer than England. This then is a factor that must be considered in discussing Britain's effort, and in evaluating the ability of a capitalist economy to compete with a dictatorship.

How much did democracy's weakness contribute to England's present position? In the first place, democracy is essentially peace-loving; the people don't want to go to war. When they do go, it is with a very firm conviction, because they must believe deeply and strongly in their cause before they consent. This gives them an advantage over a totalitarian system, where the people may find themselves in a war in which they only half believe. Nevertheless, the hatred of war is, in this day of modern warfare, a great disadvantage. It takes years to prepare for modern mechanized warfare. It takes months of training for men to be able to handle the new machines. Democracy's spirit alone cannot make up this difference. This has been brutally proved by recent events. The result is that people, because of their hatred of war, will not permit armaments to be built. They are so determined to stay out that they cannot look ahead to the day when they will find occasion to fight. Woodrow Wilson was elected on a platform of "He kept us out of war," and yet, shortly after, America was at war with Germany. Nowadays, however, simply a sudden willingness to go to war will not prepare you for war. The plans have to be made years in advance, and it is extremely difficult to get support for this in a democracy.

This had an important effect on England's efforts. The people for a long time would not have tolerated any great armaments program. Even though Churchill vigorously pointed out the dangers, the people were much more ready to put their confidence in those who favored a strong peace policy. The result of this attitude is that a democracy will always be behind a dictatorship. In a dictatorship, a vigorous armaments program can be carried on, even though the people are deeply hostile to the idea of going to war. The rigidly controlled state press can then build up a war psychology at any time. In contrast, in a democracy the cry of "war-monger" will discourage any politician who advocates a vigorous arms policy. This leaves armaments with few supporters.

There is no lobby for armaments as there is for relief or for agriculture. No group backed by millions of votes can persuade the representatives of the people that this is what the people want. The business lobby will oppose armament, as it did in the Congress of American Industry Proclamation and that of the American Chamber of Commerce in 1938.

The lobbies of agriculture and relief will oppose it, as it would mean taking money from their cause for something in which they are not directly interested. This happened in our Congress in the first part of 1940.

And so armaments must stand purely on the ground of military necessity, and it is difficult for the average legislator to look far into the future; he is primarily concerned with the immediate problems.

I say, therefore, that democracy's weaknesses are great in competing with a totalitarian system. Democracy is the superior form of government, because it is based on a respect for man as a reasonable being. *For the long run*, then, democracy is superior. But for the short run, democracy has great weaknesses. When it competes with a system of government which cares nothing for permanency, a system built primarily for war, democracy, which is built primarily for peace, is at a disadvantage. And democracy must recognize its weaknesses; it must learn to safeguard its institutions if it hopes to survive.

In England we can see vividly where democracy failed. In the case of the A.R.P., for example, the government failed to get volunteers until after Munich had driven home the seriousness of the situation. But Germany had 12,000,000 members by 1936. She needed no such shock to build up this vital defense measure. Should England have forced people to join? Yes, if the A.R.P. is considered the vital thing. No, if the democratic system is considered the important factor, as freedom of the individual is in essence democracy.

Again we witnessed the struggle between the national government and the local government as to who should bear the burden of the cost of the A.R.P. Should the government have forced the local authorities to provide their quotas? Freedom of local governments from centralized control is one of the cornerstones upon which we have erected our democracy.

Should the trade union have been forced to cooperate with the government long before May of 1940? Should strikes have been outlawed, labor standards disregarded, men forced to go into trades and do work to which they were opposed? The smashing of the trade union is symbolic of fascism. The right of labor to strike, the right to decent wages and decent hours have been what democracy has boasted is fundamental to its success.

Much of the cause of England's failure may be attributed to the leaders. The great advantage a democracy is presumed to have over a dictatorship is that ability and not brute force is the qualification for leadership. Therefore, if a democracy cannot produce able leaders, its chance for survival is slight.

I say, therefore, that many of the very factors intrinsic in democracy resulted in England's falling further and further behind. For democracy and capitalism are institutions which are geared for a world at peace. It is our problem to find a method of protecting them in a world at war.

Address to the Greater Houston Ministerial Association

(1960)

"I believe in an America where the separation of church and state is absolute"

By the time Kennedy ran for president, in 1960, he had perfected a hybrid style, balancing weighty books and speeches with glamorous magazine covers and television hits. He turned to the first approach to tackle one of his campaign's biggest potential problems: Kennedy's own Catholicism. In this address that he gave on September 12 to the Greater Houston Ministerial Association, Kennedy connects his beliefs to America's history and higher ideals—to the tradition of separating church and state that stretched back to Jefferson.

While the so-called religious issue is necessarily and properly the chief topic here tonight, I want to emphasize from the outset that we have far more critical issues to face in the 1960 election: the spread of Communist influence, until it now festers ninety miles off the coast of Florida; the humiliating treatment of our president and vice president by those who no longer respect our power; the hungry children I saw in West Virginia, the old people who cannot pay their doctor bills, the families forced to give up their farms—an America with too many slums, with too few schools, and too late to the moon and outer space.

These are the real issues which should decide this campaign. And they are not religious issues—for war and hunger and ignorance and despair know no religious barriers.

But because I am a Catholic, and no Catholic has ever been elected president, the real issues in this campaign have been obscured—perhaps deliberately, in some quarters less responsible than this. So it is apparently necessary for me to state once again not what kind of church I believe in, for that should be important only to me, but what kind of America I believe in.

I believe in an America where the separation of church and state is absolute—where no Catholic prelate would tell the president (should he be Catholic) how to act, and no Protestant minister would tell his parishioners for whom to vote; where no church or church school is granted any public funds or political preference; and where no man is denied public office merely because his religion differs from the president who might appoint him or the people who might elect him.

I believe in an America that is officially neither Catholic, Protestant, nor Jewish—where no public official either requests or accepts instructions on public policy from the Pope, the National Council of Churches, or any other ecclesiastical source; where no religious body seeks to impose its will directly or indirectly upon the general populace or the public acts of its officials; and where religious liberty is so indivisible that an act against one church is treated as an act against all.

For while this year it may be a Catholic against whom the finger of suspicion is pointed, in other years it has been, and may someday be again, a Jew, or a Quaker, or a Unitarian, or a Baptist. It was Virginia's harassment of Baptist preachers, for example, that helped lead to Jefferson's statute of religious freedom. Today I may be the victim—but tomorrow it may be you, until the whole fabric of our harmonious society is ripped at a time of great national peril.

Finally, I believe in an America where religious intolerance will someday end—where all men and all churches are treated as equal; where every man has the same right to attend or not attend the church of his choice; where there is no Catholic vote, no anti-Catholic vote, no bloc voting of any kind; and where Catholics, Protestants, and Jews, at both the lay and pastoral level, will refrain from those attitudes of disdain and division which have so often marred their works in the past and promote instead the American ideal of brotherhood.

That is the kind of America in which I believe. And it represents the kind of presidency in which I believe—a great office that must neither be humbled by making it the instrument of any one religious group nor tarnished by arbitrarily withholding its occupancy from the members of any one religious group. I believe in a president whose religious views are his own private affair, neither imposed by him upon the nation or imposed by the nation upon him as a condition to holding that office.

I would not look with favor upon a president working to subvert the First Amendment's guarantees of religious liberty. Nor would our system of checks and balances permit him to do so—and neither do I look with favor upon those who would work to subvert Article VI of the Constitution by requiring a religious test, even by indirection, for it. If they disagree with that safeguard they should be out openly working to repeal it.

I want a chief executive whose public acts are responsible to all groups and obligated to none—who can attend any ceremony, service, or dinner his office may appropriately require of him; and whose fulfillment of his presidential oath is not limited or conditioned by any religious oath, ritual, or obligation.

This is the kind of America I believe in—and this is the kind I fought for in the South Pacific, and the kind my brother died for in Europe. No one suggested then that we might have a "divided loyalty," that we did "not believe in liberty," or that we belonged to a disloyal group that threatened the "freedoms for which our forefathers died."

And in fact this is the kind of America for which our forefathers died— when they fled here to escape religious test oaths that denied office to members of less favored churches; when they fought for the Constitution, the Bill of Rights, and the Virginia Statute of Religious Freedom; and when they fought at the shrine I visited today, the Alamo. For side by side with Bowie and Crockett died McCafferty and Bailey and Carey—but no one knows whether they were Catholics or not, for there was no religious test at the Alamo.

I ask you tonight to follow in that tradition—to judge me on the basis of my record of fourteen years in Congress; on my declared stands against an Ambassador to the Vatican, against unconstitutional aid to parochial schools, and against any boycott of the public schools (which I have attended myself); instead of judging me on the basis of these pamphlets and publications we all have seen that carefully select quotations out of context from the statements of Catholic church leaders, usually in other countries, frequently in other centuries, and always omitting, of course, the statement of the American Bishops in 1948 which strongly endorsed church-state separation, and which more nearly reflects the views of almost every American Catholic.

I do not consider these other quotations binding upon my public acts— why should you? But let me say, with respect to other countries, that I am wholly opposed to the state being used by any religious group, Catholic or Protestant, to compel, prohibit, or persecute the free exercise of any other religion. And I hope that you and I condemn with equal fervor those nations which deny their presidency to Protestants and those which deny it to Catholics. And rather than cite the misdeeds of those who differ, I would cite the record of the Catholic Church in such nations as Ireland and France—and the independence of such statesmen as Adenauer and De Gaulle.

But let me stress again that these are my views—for, contrary to common newspaper usage, I am not the Catholic candidate for president. I am the Democratic Party's candidate for president who happens also to be a Catholic. I do not speak for my church on public matters, and the church does not speak for me.

Whatever issue may come before me as president—in birth control, divorce, censorship, gambling, or any other subject—I will make my decision in accordance with these views, in accordance with what my conscience tells me to be the national interest, and without regard to outside religious pressures or dictates. And no power or threat of punishment could cause me to decide otherwise.

But if the time should ever come—and I do not concede any conflict to be even remotely possible—when my office would require me to either violate my conscience or violate the national interest, then I would resign the office, and I hope any conscientious public servant would do the same.

But I do not intend to apologize for these views to my critics of either Catholic or Protestant faith—nor do I intend to disavow either my views or my Church in order to win this election.

If I should lose on the real issues, I shall return to my seat in the Senate, satisfied that I had tried my best and was fairly judged. But if this election is decided on the basis that forty million Americans lost their chance of being president on the day they were baptized, then it is the whole nation that will be the loser—in the eyes of Catholics and non-Catholics around the world, in the eyes of history, and in the eyes of our own people.

But if, on the other hand, I should win the election, then I shall devote every effort of mind and spirit to fulfilling the oath of the presidency—practically identical, I might add, to the oath I have taken for fourteen years in the Congress. For, without reservation, I can "solemnly swear that I will faithfully execute the office of president of the United States, and will to the best of my ability preserve, protect, and defend the Constitution . . . so help me God."

JOHN F. KENNEDY

Inaugural Address

(1961)

"Ask not what your country can do for you; ask what you can do for your country"

Kennedy's most important collaborator—political, intellectual, and literary—was Theodore Sorensen. Sorensen helped produce Kennedy's second book, Profiles in Courage, *which played a vital role in lifting him to the presidency. The two collaborated again on the inaugural address Kennedy delivered on January 20, 1961. Like the book, the address is grounded in history and a call for political courage.*

We observe today not a victory of party but a celebration of freedom—symbolizing an end as well as a beginning, signifying renewal as well as change. For I have sworn before you and Almighty God the same solemn oath our forebears prescribed nearly a century and three quarters ago.

The world is very different now. For man holds in his mortal hands the power to abolish all forms of human poverty and all forms of human life. And yet the same revolutionary beliefs for which our forebears fought are still at issue around the globe—the belief that the rights of man come not from the generosity of the state but from the hand of God.

We dare not forget today that we are the heirs of that first revolution. Let the word go forth from this time and place, to friend and foe alike, that the torch has been passed to a new generation of Americans—born in this century, tempered by war, disciplined by a hard and bitter peace, proud of our ancient heritage, and unwilling to witness or permit the slow undoing of those human rights to which this nation has always been committed and to which we are committed today at home and around the world.

Let every nation know, whether it wishes us well or ill, that we shall pay any price, bear any burden, meet any hardship, support any friend, oppose any foe to assure the survival and the success of liberty.

This much we pledge—and more.

To those old allies whose cultural and spiritual origins we share, we pledge the loyalty of faithful friends. United, there is little we cannot do in a host of cooperative ventures. Divided, there is little we can do—for we dare not meet a powerful challenge at odds and split asunder.

To those new states whom we welcome to the ranks of the free, we pledge our word that one form of colonial control shall not have passed away merely to be replaced by a far more iron tyranny. We shall not always expect to find them supporting our view. But we shall always hope to find them strongly supporting their own freedom—and to remember that, in the past, those who foolishly sought power by riding the back of the tiger ended up inside.

To those peoples in the huts and villages of half the globe struggling to break the bonds of mass misery, we pledge our best efforts to help them help themselves, for whatever period is required—not because the Communists may be doing it, not because we seek their votes, but because it is right. If a free society cannot help the many who are poor, it cannot save the few who are rich.

To our sister republics south of our border, we offer a special pledge—to convert our good words into good deeds in a new alliance for progress, to assist free men and free governments in casting off the chains of poverty. But this peaceful revolution of hope cannot become the prey of hostile powers. Let all our neighbors know that we shall join with them to oppose aggression or subversion anywhere in the Americas. And let every other power know that this hemisphere intends to remain the master of its own house.

To that world assembly of sovereign states, the United Nations, our last best hope in an age where the instruments of war have far outpaced the instruments of peace, we renew our pledge of support—to prevent it from becoming merely a forum for invective, to strengthen its shield of the new and the weak, and to enlarge the area in which its writ may run.

Finally, to those nations who would make themselves our adversary, we offer not a pledge but a request: that both sides begin anew the quest for peace before the dark powers of destruction, unleashed by science, engulf all humanity in planned or accidental self-destruction.

We dare not tempt them with weakness. For only when our arms are sufficient beyond doubt can we be certain beyond doubt that they will never be employed.

But neither can two great and powerful groups of nations take comfort from our present course—both sides overburdened by the cost of modern weapons, both rightly alarmed by the steady spread of the deadly atom, yet both racing to alter that uncertain balance of terror that stays the hand of mankind's final war.

So let us begin anew—remembering on both sides that civility is not a sign of weakness, and sincerity is always subject to proof. Let us never negotiate out of fear. But let us never fear to negotiate.

Let both sides explore what problems unite us instead of belaboring those problems which divide us.

Let both sides, for the first time, formulate serious and precise proposals for the inspection and control of arms—and bring the absolute power to destroy other nations under the absolute control of all nations.

Let both sides seek to invoke the wonders of science instead of its terrors. Together let us explore the stars, conquer the deserts, eradicate disease, tap the ocean depths, and encourage the arts and commerce.

Let both sides unite to heed in all corners of the earth the command of Isaiah—to "undo the heavy burdens . . . (and) let the oppressed go free."

And if a beachhead of cooperation may push back the jungle of suspicion, let both sides join in creating a new endeavor—not a new balance of power but a new world of law, where the strong are just and the weak secure and the peace preserved.

All this will not be finished in the first one hundred days. Nor will it be finished in the first one thousand days, nor in the life of this administration, nor even perhaps in our lifetime on this planet. But let us begin.

In your hands, my fellow citizens, more than mine, will rest the final success or failure of our course. Since this country was founded, each generation of Americans has been summoned to give testimony to its national loyalty. The graves of young Americans who answered the call to service surround the globe.

Now the trumpet summons us again—not as a call to bear arms, though arms we need—not as a call to battle, though embattled we are—but a call to bear the burden of a long twilight struggle, year in and year out, "rejoicing in hope, patient in tribulation"—a struggle against the common enemies of man: tyranny, poverty, disease, and war itself.

Can we forge against these enemies a grand and global alliance, north and south, east and west, that can assure a more fruitful life for all mankind? Will you join in that historic effort?

In the long history of the world, only a few generations have been granted the role of defending freedom in its hour of maximum danger. I do not shrink from this responsibility—I welcome it. I do not believe that any of us would exchange places with any other people or any other generation. The energy, the faith, the devotion which we bring to this endeavor will light our country and all who serve it—and the glow from that fire can truly light the world.

And so, my fellow Americans: ask not what your country can do for you; ask what you can do for your country.

My fellow citizens of the world: ask not what America will do for you, but what together we can do for the freedom of man.

Finally, whether you are citizens of America or citizens of the world, ask of us here the same high standards of strength and sacrifice which we ask of you. With a good conscience our only sure reward, with history the final judge of our deeds, let us go forth to lead the land we love, asking His blessing and His help but knowing that, here on earth, God's work must truly be our own.

JOHN F. KENNEDY

Address on Communism and Germany

(1963)

"Ich bin ein Berliner"

In the summer of 1963, Kennedy traveled to West Berlin, which had been isolated by the recently erected Berlin Wall. He spoke to a crowd of more than one hundred thousand people, but the president's audience was equally his Cold War opponent, the Soviet Union. Despite a series of diplomatic mishaps, including the Bay of Pigs invasion, Kennedy emphasized America's resolve, using his speech's setting to draw clear lines between Communism and capitalism.

Two thousand years ago the proudest boast was "civis Romanus sum." Today, in the world of freedom, the proudest boast is "Ich bin ein Berliner."

There are many people in the world who really don't understand, or say they don't, what is the great issue between the free world and the Communist world. Let them come to Berlin. There are some who say that Communism is the wave of the future. Let them come to Berlin. And there are some who say in Europe and elsewhere we can work with the Communists. Let them come to Berlin. And there are even a few who say that it is true that Communism is an evil system, but it permits us to make economic progress. "Lass' sie nach Berlin kommen." Let them come to Berlin.

Freedom has many difficulties and democracy is not perfect, but we have never had to put a wall up to keep our people in, to prevent them from leaving us. I want to say on behalf of my countrymen, who live many miles away on the other side of the Atlantic, who are far distant from you, that they take the greatest pride that they have been able to share with you, even from a distance, the story of the last eighteen years. I know of no town, no city, that has been besieged for eighteen years that still lives with the vitality and the force, and the hope and the determination of the city of West Berlin.

While the wall is the most obvious and vivid demonstration of the failures of the Communist system, for all the world to see, we take no satisfaction in it, for it is, as your mayor has said, an offense not only against history but an offense against humanity, separating families, dividing husbands and wives and brothers and sisters, and dividing a people who wish to be joined together.

What is true of this city is true of Germany—real, lasting peace in Europe can never be assured as long as one German out of four is denied the elementary right of free men, and that is to make a free choice. In eighteen years of peace and good faith, this generation of Germans has earned the right to be free, including the right to unite their families and their nation in lasting peace, with good will to all people. You live in a defended island of freedom, but your life is part of the main. So let me ask you, as I close, to lift your eyes beyond the dangers of today to the hopes of tomorrow; beyond the freedom merely of this city of Berlin, or your country of Germany, to the advance of freedom everywhere; beyond the wall to the day of peace with justice; beyond yourselves and ourselves to all mankind.

Freedom is indivisible, and when one man is enslaved, all are not free. When all are free, then we can look forward to that day when this city will be joined as one and this country and this great continent of Europe in a peaceful and hopeful globe. When that day finally comes, as it will, the people of West Berlin can take sober satisfaction in the fact that they were in the front lines for almost two decades.

All free men, wherever they may live, are citizens of Berlin. And, therefore, as a free man, I take pride in the words "Ich bin ein Berliner."

JOHN F. KENNEDY

Address at Amherst College

(1963)

"When power leads men towards arrogance,
poetry reminds him of his limitations"

*On October 26, 1963—some months after Robert Frost's death, but only a few
weeks before Kennedy's own—the president came to Amherst College to speak at
the groundbreaking for a library named after the poet. It gave Kennedy a chance
to revisit the theme of Woodrow Wilson and John Quincy Adams: the vexed
relationship between Americans who write and Americans who act.*

Many years ago, Woodrow Wilson said, what good is a political party
unless it is serving a great national purpose? And what good is a
private college or university unless it is serving a great national purpose?
The library being constructed today, this college, itself—all of this, of
course, was not done merely to give this school's graduates an advantage, an economic advantage, in the life struggle. It does do that. But in
return for that, in return for the great opportunity which society gives
the graduates of this and related schools, it seems to me incumbent upon
this and other schools' graduates to recognize their responsibility to the
public interest.

Privilege is here, and with privilege goes responsibility. And I think,
as your president said, that it must be a source of satisfaction to you that
this school's graduates have recognized it. I hope that the students who

are here now will also recognize it in the future. Although Amherst has been in the forefront of extending aid to needy and talented students, private colleges, taken as a whole, draw 50 percent of their students from the wealthiest 10 percent of our nation. And even state universities and other public institutions derive 25 percent of their students from this group. In March 1962, persons of 18 years or older who had not completed high school made up 46 percent of the total labor force, and such persons comprised 64 percent of those who were unemployed. And in 1958, the lowest fifth of the families in the United States had 4 ½ percent of the total personal income, the highest fifth, 44 ½ percent.

There is inherited wealth in this country and also inherited poverty. And unless the graduates of this college and other colleges like it who are given a running start in life—unless they are willing to put back into our society those talents, the broad sympathy, the understanding, the compassion—unless they are willing to put those qualities back into the service of the great republic, then obviously the presuppositions upon which our democracy are based are bound to be fallible.

The problems which this country now faces are staggering, both at home and abroad. We need the service, in the great sense, of every educated man or woman to find ten million jobs in the next two and a half years, to govern our relations—a country which lived in isolation for 150 years, and is now suddenly the leader of the free world—to govern our relations with over one hundred countries, to govern those relations with success so that the balance of power remains strong on the side of freedom, to make it possible for Americans of all different races and creeds to live together in harmony, to make it possible for a world to exist in diversity and freedom. All this requires the best of all of us.

Therefore, I am proud to come to this college, whose graduates have recognized this obligation and to say to those who are now here that the need is endless, and I am confident that you will respond.

Robert Frost said:

Two roads diverged in a wood, and I—
I took the one less traveled by,
And that has made all the difference.

I hope that road will not be the less traveled by, and I hope your commitment to the great republic's interest in the years to come will be worthy of your long inheritance since your beginning.

This day devoted to the memory of Robert Frost offers an opportunity for reflection, which is prized by politicians as well as by others, and even by poets. For Robert Frost was one of the granite figures of our time in America. He was supremely two things: an artist and an American.

A nation reveals itself not only by the men it produces but also by the men it honors, the men it remembers. In America, our heroes have customarily run to men of large accomplishments. But today this college and country honors a man whose contribution was not to our size but to our spirit, not to our political beliefs but to our insight, not to our self-esteem but to our self-comprehension. In honoring Robert Frost, we therefore can pay honor to the deepest sources of our national strength. That strength takes many forms, and the most obvious forms are not always the most significant. The men who create power make an indispensable contribution to the nation's greatness, but the men who question power make a contribution just as indispensable, especially when that questioning is disinterested, for they determine whether we use power or power uses us.

Our national strength matters, but the spirit which informs and controls our strength matters just as much. This was the special significance of Robert Frost. He brought an unsparing instinct for reality to bear on the platitudes and pieties of society. His sense of the human tragedy fortified him against self-deception and easy consolation. "I have been," he wrote, "one acquainted with the night." And because he knew the midnight as well as the high noon, because he understood the ordeal as well as the triumph of the human spirit, he gave his age strength with which to overcome despair. At bottom, he held a deep faith in the spirit of man, and it is hardly an accident that Robert Frost coupled poetry and power, for he saw poetry as the means of saving power from itself. When power leads men towards arrogance, poetry reminds him of his limitations. When power narrows the areas of man's concern, poetry reminds him of the richness and diversity of his existence. When power corrupts, poetry cleanses. For art establishes the basic human truth which must serve as the touchstone of our judgment.

The artist, however faithful to his personal vision of reality, becomes the last champion of the individual mind and sensibility against an intrusive society and an officious state. The great artist is thus a solitary figure. He has, as Frost said, a lover's quarrel with the world. In pursuing his perceptions of reality, he must often sail against the currents of his time. This is not a popular role. If Robert Frost was much honored in his lifetime, it was because a good many preferred to ignore his darker truths. Yet in retrospect, we see how the artist's fidelity has strengthened the fiber of our national life.

If sometimes our great artists have been the most critical of our society, it is because their sensitivity and their concern for justice, which must motivate any true artist, makes him aware that our nation falls short of its highest potential. I see little of more importance to the future of our country and our civilization than full recognition of the place of the artist.

If art is to nourish the roots of our culture, society must set the artist free to follow his vision wherever it takes him. We must never forget that art is not a form of propaganda; it is a form of truth. And as Mr. MacLeish once remarked of poets, there is nothing worse for our trade than to be in style. In free society art is not a weapon and it does not belong to the spheres of polemic and ideology. Artists are not engineers of the soul. It may be different elsewhere. But democratic society—in it, the highest duty of the writer, the composer, the artist is to remain true to himself and to let the chips fall where they may. In serving his vision of the truth, the artist best serves his nation. And the nation which disdains the mission of art invites the fate of Robert Frost's hired man, the fate of having "nothing to look backward to with pride, and nothing to look forward to with hope."

I look forward to a great future for America, a future in which our country will match its military strength with our moral restraint, its wealth with our wisdom, its power with our purpose. I look forward to an America which will not be afraid of grace and beauty, which will protect the beauty of our natural environment, which will preserve the great old American houses and squares and parks of our national past, and which will build handsome and balanced cities for our future.

I look forward to an America which will reward achievement in the arts as we reward achievement in business or statecraft. I look forward to an America which will steadily raise the standards of artistic accomplishment and which will steadily enlarge cultural opportunities for all of our citizens. And I look forward to an America which commands respect throughout the world not only for its strength but for its civilization as well. And I look forward to a world which will be safe not only for democracy and diversity but also for personal distinction.

Robert Frost was often skeptical about projects for human improvement, yet I do not think he would disdain this hope. As he wrote during the uncertain days of the Second War:

Take human nature altogether since time began . . .
And it must be a little more in favor of man,
Say a fraction of one percent at the very least . . .
Our hold on this planet wouldn't have so increased.

Because of Mr. Frost's life and work, because of the life and work of this college, our hold on this planet has increased.

LYNDON B. JOHNSON

From His State of the Union

(1964)

"This administration today, here and now,
declares unconditional war on poverty in
America"

*When Lyndon B. Johnson gave his first State of the Union, on January 8, 1964,
it had been just over six weeks since Kennedy's assassination. "Let us carry forward
the plans and programs of John Fitzgerald Kennedy," the new president said,
"not because of our sorrow or sympathy, but because they are right." Johnson ran
through a number of plans and programs, including ones for reducing the defense
budget and pushing for civil rights. But the speech's most memorable passages,
excerpted here, came when Johnson proposed a "war on poverty"—a war he would
later wage through his "Great Society" legislation.*

This administration today, here and now, declares unconditional war
on poverty in America. I urge this Congress and all Americans to join
with me in that effort.

It will not be a short or easy struggle, no single weapon or strategy
will suffice, but we shall not rest until that war is won. The richest nation
on earth can afford to win it. We cannot afford to lose it. One thousand
dollars invested in salvaging an unemployable youth today can return
$40,000 or more in his lifetime.

Poverty is a national problem, requiring improved national organization and support. But this attack, to be effective, must also be organized at the state and the local level and must be supported and directed by state and local efforts.

For the war against poverty will not be won here in Washington. It must be won in the field, in every private home, in every public office, from the courthouse to the White House.

The program I shall propose will emphasize this cooperative approach to help that one-fifth of all American families with incomes too small to even meet their basic needs.

Our chief weapons in a more pinpointed attack will be better schools, and better health, and better homes, and better training, and better job opportunities to help more Americans, especially young Americans, escape from squalor and misery and unemployment rolls where other citizens help to carry them.

Very often a lack of jobs and money is not the cause of poverty, but the symptom. The cause may lie deeper in our failure to give our fellow citizens a fair chance to develop their own capacities, in a lack of education and training, in a lack of medical care and housing, in a lack of decent communities in which to live and bring up their children.

But whatever the cause, our joint federal-local effort must pursue poverty, pursue it wherever it exists—in city slums and small towns, in sharecropper shacks or in migrant worker camps, on Indian reservations, among whites as well as negroes, among the young as well as the aged, in the boom towns and in the depressed areas.

Our aim is not only to relieve the symptom of poverty, but to cure it and, above all, to prevent it. No single piece of legislation, however, is going to suffice.

We will launch a special effort in the chronically distressed areas of Appalachia.

We must expand our small but our successful area redevelopment program.

We must enact youth employment legislation to put jobless, aimless, hopeless youngsters to work on useful projects.

We must distribute more food to the needy through a broader food stamp program.

We must create a National Service Corps to help the economically handicapped of our own country as the Peace Corps now helps those abroad.

We must modernize our unemployment insurance and establish a high-level commission on automation. If we have the brainpower to invent these machines, we have the brainpower to make certain that they are a boon and not a bane to humanity.

We must extend the coverage of our minimum wage laws to more than two million workers now lacking this basic protection of purchasing power.

We must, by including special school aid funds as part of our education program, improve the quality of teaching, training, and counseling in our hardest hit areas.

We must build more libraries in every area and more hospitals and nursing homes under the Hill-Burton Act, and train more nurses to staff them.

We must provide hospital insurance for our older citizens financed by every worker and his employer under Social Security, contributing no more than $1 a month during the employee's working career to protect him in his old age in a dignified manner without cost to the Treasury, against the devastating hardship of prolonged or repeated illness.

We must, as a part of a revised housing and urban renewal program, give more help to those displaced by slum clearance, provide more housing for our poor and our elderly, and seek as our ultimate goal in our free enterprise system a decent home for every American family.

We must help obtain more modern mass transit within our communities as well as low-cost transportation between them.

Above all, we must release $11 billion of tax reduction into the private spending stream to create new jobs and new markets in every area of this land.

These programs are obviously not for the poor or the underprivileged alone. Every American will benefit by the extension of social security to cover the hospital costs of their aged parents. Every American community will benefit from the construction or modernization of schools, libraries, hospitals, and nursing homes, from the training of more nurses, and from the improvement of urban renewal in public transit.

LYNDON B. JOHNSON

Address on Voting Rights

(1965)

"We shall overcome"

On March 7, 1965—better known as "Bloody Sunday"—civil rights marchers were beaten and teargassed by police in Selma, Alabama. In response, Johnson called for a new bill that would meet one of the marchers' demands: making good on the promise of Grant's Fifteenth Amendment and guaranteeing Black Americans the right to vote. Johnson applied the full power of the executive branch, crafting legislation, cajoling individual lawmakers, and pushing the issue in a primetime address that was broadcast on March 15. At several points in the speech, Johnson repeats a line from a hymn the marchers had sung in Selma: "We shall overcome."

I speak tonight for the dignity of man and the destiny of democracy.
I urge every member of both parties, Americans of all religions and of all colors, from every section of this country, to join me in that cause.

At times history and fate meet at a single time in a single place to shape a turning point in man's unending search for freedom. So it was at Lexington and Concord. So it was a century ago at Appomattox. So it was last week in Selma, Alabama.

There, long-suffering men and women peacefully protested the denial of their rights as Americans. Many were brutally assaulted. One good man, a man of God, was killed.

There is no cause for pride in what has happened in Selma. There is no cause for self-satisfaction in the long denial of equal rights of millions of

Americans. But there is cause for hope and for faith in our democracy in what is happening here tonight.

For the cries of pain and the hymns and protests of oppressed people have summoned into convocation all the majesty of this great government—the government of the greatest nation on earth.

Our mission is at once the oldest and the most basic of this country: to right wrong, to do justice, to serve man.

In our time we have come to live with moments of great crisis. Our lives have been marked with debate about great issues—issues of war and peace, issues of prosperity and depression. But rarely in any time does an issue lay bare the secret heart of America itself. Rarely are we met with a challenge not to our growth or abundance, our welfare or our security, but rather to the values and the purposes and the meaning of our beloved nation.

The issue of equal rights for American negroes is such an issue. And should we defeat every enemy, should we double our wealth and conquer the stars and still be unequal to this issue, then we will have failed as a people and as a nation.

For with a country as with a person, "What is a man profited, if he shall gain the whole world, and lose his own soul?"

There is no negro problem. There is no southern problem. There is no northern problem. There is only an American problem. And we are met here tonight as Americans—not as Democrats or Republicans—we are met here as Americans to solve that problem.

This was the first nation in the history of the world to be founded with a purpose. The great phrases of that purpose still sound in every American heart, north and south: "All men are created equal"—"government by consent of the governed"—"give me liberty or give me death." Well, those are not just clever words, or those are not just empty theories. In their name Americans have fought and died for two centuries, and tonight around the world they stand there as guardians of our liberty, risking their lives.

Those words are a promise to every citizen that he shall share in the dignity of man. This dignity cannot be found in a man's possessions; it cannot be found in his power or in his position. It really rests on his right to be treated as a man equal in opportunity to all others. It says that he shall share in freedom—he shall choose his leaders, educate his children, and provide for his family according to his ability and his merits as a human being.

To apply any other test—to deny a man his hopes because of his color or race, his religion or the place of his birth—is not only to do injustice, it is to deny America and to dishonor the dead who gave their lives for American freedom.

Our fathers believed that if this noble view of the rights of man was to flourish, it must be rooted in democracy. The most basic right of all was the right to choose your own leaders. The history of this country, in large measure, is the history of the expansion of that right to all of our people.

Many of the issues of civil rights are very complex and most difficult. But about this there can and should be no argument. Every American citizen must have an equal right to vote. There is no reason which can excuse the denial of that right. There is no duty which weighs more heavily on us than the duty we have to ensure that right.

Yet the harsh fact is that in many places in this country men and women are kept from voting simply because they are negroes.

Every device of which human ingenuity is capable has been used to deny this right. The negro citizen may go to register only to be told that the day is wrong, or the hour is late, or the official in charge is absent. And if he persists, and if he manages to present himself to the registrar, he may be disqualified because he did not spell out his middle name or because he abbreviated a word on the application.

And if he manages to fill out an application he is given a test. The registrar is the sole judge of whether he passes this test. He may be asked to recite the entire Constitution, or explain the most complex provisions of state law. And even a college degree cannot be used to prove that he can read and write.

For the fact is that the only way to pass these barriers is to show a white skin.

Experience has clearly shown that the existing process of law cannot overcome systematic and ingenious discrimination. No law that we now have on the books—and I have helped to put three of them there—can ensure the right to vote when local officials are determined to deny it.

In such a case our duty must be clear to all of us. The Constitution says that no person shall be kept from voting because of his race or his color. We have all sworn an oath before God to support and to defend that Constitution. We must now act in obedience to that oath.

Wednesday, I will send to Congress a law designed to eliminate illegal barriers to the right to vote.

The broad principles of that bill will be in the hands of the Democratic and Republican leaders tomorrow. After they have reviewed it, it will come here formally as a bill. I am grateful for this opportunity to come here tonight at the invitation of the leadership to reason with my friends, to give them my views, and to visit with my former colleagues.

I have had prepared a more comprehensive analysis of the legislation which I had intended to transmit to the clerk tomorrow but which I will submit to the clerks tonight. But I want to really discuss with you now briefly the main proposals of this legislation.

This bill will strike down restrictions to voting in all elections—federal, state, and local—which have been used to deny negroes the right to vote. This bill will establish a simple, uniform standard which cannot be used, however ingenious the effort, to flout our Constitution. It will provide for citizens to be registered by officials of the United States Government if the state officials refuse to register them. It will eliminate tedious, unnecessary lawsuits which delay the right to vote. Finally, this legislation will ensure that properly registered individuals are not prohibited from voting.

I will welcome the suggestions from all of the members of Congress—I have no doubt that I will get some—on ways and means to strengthen this law and to make it effective. But experience has plainly shown that this is the only path to carry out the command of the Constitution.

To those who seek to avoid action by their national government in their own communities, who want to and who seek to maintain purely local control over elections, the answer is simple: Open your polling places to all your people. Allow men and women to register and vote whatever the color of their skin. Extend the rights of citizenship to every citizen of this land.

There is no constitutional issue here. The command of the Constitution is plain.

There is no moral issue. It is wrong—deadly wrong—to deny any of your fellow Americans the right to vote in this country.

There is no issue of states' rights or national rights. There is only the struggle for human rights.

I have not the slightest doubt what will be your answer.

The last time a president sent a civil rights bill to the Congress it contained a provision to protect voting rights in federal elections. That civil rights bill was passed after eight long months of debate. And when that bill came to my desk from the Congress for my signature, the heart of the voting provision had been eliminated.

This time, on this issue, there must be no delay, no hesitation, and no compromise with our purpose.

We cannot, we must not, refuse to protect the right of every American to vote in every election that he may desire to participate in. And we ought not and we cannot and we must not wait another eight months before we get a bill. We have already waited a hundred years and more, and the time for waiting is gone.

So I ask you to join me in working long hours—nights and weekends, if necessary—to pass this bill. And I don't make that request lightly. For from the window where I sit, with the problems of our country, I recognize that outside this chamber is the outraged conscience of a nation, the grave concern of many nations, and the harsh judgment of history on our acts.

But even if we pass this bill, the battle will not be over. What happened in Selma is part of a far larger movement which reaches into every section and state of America. It is the effort of American negroes to secure for themselves the full blessings of American life.

Their cause must be our cause too. Because it is not just negroes, but really it is all of us who must overcome the crippling legacy of bigotry and injustice. And we shall overcome.

As a man whose roots go deeply into Southern soil, I know how agonizing racial feelings are. I know how difficult it is to reshape the attitudes and the structure of our society.

But a century has passed, more than a hundred years, since the negro was freed. And he is not fully free tonight.

It was more than a hundred years ago that Abraham Lincoln, a great president of another party, signed the Emancipation Proclamation, but emancipation is a proclamation and not a fact.

A century has passed, more than a hundred years, since equality was promised. And yet the negro is not equal.

A century has passed since the day of promise. And the promise is unkept.

The time of justice has now come. I tell you that I believe sincerely that no force can hold it back. It is right in the eyes of man and God that it should come. And when it does, I think that day will brighten the lives of every American.

For negroes are not the only victims. How many white children have gone uneducated, how many white families have lived in stark poverty, how many white lives have been scarred by fear, because we have wasted our energy and our substance to maintain the barriers of hatred and terror?

So I say to all of you here, and to all in the nation tonight, that those who appeal to you to hold on to the past do so at the cost of denying you your future.

This great, rich, restless country can offer opportunity and education and hope to all: black and white, north and south, sharecropper and city dweller. These are the enemies: poverty, ignorance, disease. They are the enemies and not our fellow man, not our neighbor. And these enemies too—poverty, disease, and ignorance—we shall overcome.

Now let none of us in any sections look with prideful righteousness on the troubles in another section, or on the problems of our neighbors. There is really no part of America where the promise of equality has been fully kept. In Buffalo as well as in Birmingham, in Philadelphia as well as in Selma, Americans are struggling for the fruits of freedom.

This is one nation. What happens in Selma or in Cincinnati is a matter of legitimate concern to every American. But let each of us look within our own hearts and our own communities, and let each of us put our shoulder to the wheel to root out injustice wherever it exists.

As we meet here in this peaceful, historic chamber tonight, men from the south, some of whom were at Iwo Jima, men from the north who have carried Old Glory to far corners of the world and brought it back without a stain on it, men from the east and from the west, are all fighting together without regard to religion, or color, or region, in Vietnam. Men from every region fought for us across the world twenty years ago.

And in these common dangers and these common sacrifices the south made its contribution of honor and gallantry no less than any other region of the great republic—and in some instances, a great many of them, more.

And I have not the slightest doubt that good men from everywhere in this country, from the Great Lakes to the Gulf of Mexico, from the Golden Gate to the harbors along the Atlantic, will rally together now in this cause to vindicate the freedom of all Americans. For all of us owe this duty; and I believe that all of us will respond to it.

Your president makes that request of every American.

The real hero of this struggle is the American negro. His actions and protests, his courage to risk safety and even to risk his life, have awakened the conscience of this nation. His demonstrations have been designed to call attention to injustice, designed to provoke change, designed to stir reform.

He has called upon us to make good the promise of America. And who among us can say that we would have made the same progress were it not for his persistent bravery and his faith in American democracy.

For at the real heart of battle for equality is a deep-seated belief in the democratic process. Equality depends not on the force of arms or tear gas but upon the force of moral right; not on recourse to violence but on respect for law and order.

There have been many pressures upon your president and there will be others as the days come and go. But I pledge you tonight that we intend to fight this battle where it should be fought: in the courts, and in the Congress, and in the hearts of men.

We must preserve the right of free speech and the right of free assembly. But the right of free speech does not carry with it, as has been said, the right to holler fire in a crowded theater. We must preserve the right to free assembly, but free assembly does not carry with it the right to block public thoroughfares to traffic.

We do have a right to protest, and a right to march under conditions that do not infringe the constitutional rights of our neighbors. And I intend to protect all those rights as long as I am permitted to serve in this office.

We will guard against violence, knowing it strikes from our hands the very weapons which we seek—progress, obedience to law, and belief in American values.

In Selma, as elsewhere, we seek and pray for peace. We seek order. We seek unity. But we will not accept the peace of stifled rights, or the order imposed by fear, or the unity that stifles protest. For peace cannot be purchased at the cost of liberty.

In Selma tonight, as in every—and we had a good day there—as in every city, we are working for just and peaceful settlement. We must all remember that after this speech I am making tonight, after the police and the FBI and the marshals have all gone, and after you have promptly passed this bill, the people of Selma and the other cities of the nation must still live and work together. And when the attention of the nation has gone elsewhere they must try to heal the wounds and to build a new community.

This cannot be easily done on a battleground of violence, as the history of the south itself shows. It is in recognition of this that men of both races have shown such an outstandingly impressive responsibility in recent days—last Tuesday, again today.

The bill that I am presenting to you will be known as a civil rights bill. But in a larger sense, most of the program I am recommending is a civil rights program. Its object is to open the city of hope to all people of all races.

Because all Americans just must have the right to vote. And we are going to give them that right.

All Americans must have the privileges of citizenship regardless of race. And they are going to have those privileges of citizenship regardless of race.

But I would like to caution you and remind you that to exercise these privileges takes much more than just legal right. It requires a trained mind and a healthy body. It requires a decent home, and the chance to find a job, and the opportunity to escape from the clutches of poverty.

Of course, people cannot contribute to the nation if they are never taught to read or write, if their bodies are stunted from hunger, if their sickness goes untended, if their life is spent in hopeless poverty just drawing a welfare check.

So we want to open the gates to opportunity. But we are also going to give all our people, black and white, the help that they need to walk through those gates.

My first job after college was as a teacher in Cotulla, Texas, in a small Mexican-American school. Few of them could speak English, and I couldn't speak much Spanish. My students were poor, and they often came to class without breakfast, hungry. They knew even in their youth the pain of prejudice. They never seemed to know why people disliked them. But they knew it was so, because I saw it in their eyes. I often walked home late in the afternoon, after the classes were finished, wishing there was more that I could do. But all I knew was to teach them the little that I knew, hoping that it might help them against the hardships that lay ahead.

Somehow you never forget what poverty and hatred can do when you see its scars on the hopeful face of a young child.

I never thought then, in 1928, that I would be standing here in 1965. It never even occurred to me in my fondest dreams that I might have the chance to help the sons and daughters of those students and to help people like them all over this country.

But now I do have that chance—and I'll let you in on a secret—I mean to use it. And I hope that you will use it with me.

This is the richest and most powerful country which ever occupied the globe. The might of past empires is little compared to ours. But I do not want to be the president who built empires, or sought grandeur, or extended dominion.

I want to be the president who educated young children to the wonders of their world. I want to be the president who helped to feed the hungry and to prepare them to be taxpayers instead of taxeaters.

I want to be the president who helped the poor to find their own way and who protected the right of every citizen to vote in every election.

I want to be the president who helped to end hatred among his fellow men and who promoted love among the people of all races and all regions and all parties.

I want to be the president who helped to end war among the brothers of this earth.

And so at the request of your beloved speaker and the senator from Montana; the majority leader, the senator from Illinois; the minority leader, Mr. McCulloch; and other members of both parties, I came here tonight—not as President Roosevelt came down one time in person to veto a bonus bill, not as President Truman came down one time to urge the passage of a railroad bill—but I came down here to ask you to share this task with me and to share it with the people that we both work for. I want this to be the Congress, Republicans and Democrats alike, which did all these things for all these people.

Beyond this great chamber, out yonder in fifty states, are the people that we serve. Who can tell what deep and unspoken hopes are in their hearts tonight as they sit there and listen? We all can guess, from our own lives, how difficult they often find their own pursuit of happiness, how many problems each little family has. They look most of all to themselves for their futures. But I think that they also look to each of us.

Above the pyramid on the great seal of the United States it says—in Latin—"God has favored our undertaking."

God will not favor everything that we do. It is rather our duty to divine His will. But I cannot help believing that He truly understands and that He really favors the undertaking that we begin here tonight.

LYNDON B. JOHNSON

From His Dictations for
The Vantage Point

"Dallas has always been a nightmare for me"

The gap between presidential memoirs and their authentic and human authors is often enormous—something one can see by placing Johnson's dictations to his ghostwriters next to his final, sanitized book, The Vantage Point. *In the dictation transcripts, excerpted here, the ex-president chatted about Kennedy's underwear and the many times he felt slighted, including by Kennedy's brother, Robert F. Kennedy. In the book, Johnson forced his ghostwriters to reduce this material to boring summaries like this: "The president had reminded me on several occasions that Massachusetts, New York, and Texas were going to have to bear the burden of financing the 1964 presidential campaign." Why didn't the real Johnson make it into* The Vantage Point? *Because he—and most other modern presidents—worried more about their books being "statesmanlike" than about them being entertaining, honest, or revealing.*

Dallas has always been a nightmare for me. I've never discussed it, and I don't want to think about it anymore than I have to.

I was elected to the Senate in 1941 when I was thirty-three years old. That election was stolen from me in Dallas; they kept counting votes until W. Lee O'Daniel won. He was a nonentity and a flour salesman.

We went to Dallas in [my] 1960 campaign. We were met by Alger and Tower. They had whipped up a lot of mink-coat, fascist-type women.

354

I was regarded as left wing in Texas. There was a great revulsion that I had joined the ticket with the Pope of Rome.

There is a lot of bigotry in Texas.

In 1960 I knew I couldn't get nominated. But there were lots who didn't think so. When I accepted the vice president spot I went to Dallas to speak, and the revulsion expressed itself. They spit on us. They knocked Mrs. Johnson's hat off and said a lot of ugly things. That is pretty commonplace now, but it was new to us then. And it was in Dallas that we learned it. . . .

I never wanted to go to Dallas in 1960, and things didn't get any better there by 1963.

Kennedy thought our [re]election was in danger. I knew it was. His purpose was to raise a million dollars and get enough identification with Texas to carry the state.

The popular image of Texas is of billionaires and people with dollar bills coming out of their ears. He wanted to raise one million dollars. I guess two or three times he talked to me about it and said, "We've got that four-million-dollar debt to pay off." . . .

Kennedy suggested that we come to Texas on my birthday [August 27]. The vice president's relationship to a president is like the wife to the husband—you don't tell him off in public. Kennedy mentioned four or five places he wanted to come to. Well, I've never raised a dime in Dallas in my life—never even carried Dallas. He felt each of those places could contribute $400,000.

[Texas governor John] Connally spoke up firm, clear, straightforward: "Mr. President, that would be the worst thing you could do. For the first thing, with you going in four or five places, everyone would say you are just interested in getting money. In the second place, that weekend at the end of August would be a bad weekend. All the rich folks will be up in Colorado cooling off, and all the poor people will be in Galveston and down around the Gulf Coast."

Kennedy wouldn't take issue with him. He said, "I guess that's right."

The next thing, I heard Connally was in [Washington] at the Mayflower. It was about October 15. . . . Connally told Kennedy, "Don't say anything about money. Make whatever speech you want to make anywhere in Texas and then just give one fundraiser in Austin."

Apparently, Kennedy agreed. Then we all went to work to raise money. Kennedy put Bill Moyers in charge.

The president told me to take one 707—and he'd take the other—when we came down to Texas. We had a good meeting in San Antonio. It was hot, but it was pleasant.

Then we went to Houston. . . . I remember two things mainly about the Houston meeting. One: when we got off the plane, the reception committee said Mrs. Johnson and I could ride in such and such a car. So we got in and when we did, someone said, "Senator [Ralph] Yarborough is supposed to ride here." So someone ran up to him and said, "You're supposed to ride in this car." Yarborough said no, he'd ride with Albert Thomas. Thomas was very anxious to be with Kennedy. Thomas jumped on the Secret Service car following the president. Then we came along. Yarborough rode with Thomas part of the way, not with us.

I didn't care, but the newspaper boys went wild. It was the biggest ever since De Gaulle farted. There were headlines the next morning and all kinds of queries to [press secretary Pierre] Salinger: "Was it true that Yarborough would not ride with the vice president?"

Shortly after we got to the hotel, Kennedy called and said, "I wish you would come down and have a drink with me." He had only his shorts on.

Kennedy had a scotch and water or whatever it was he drank. I had a scotch and soda. He told me, "They've asked Jackie to speak at the [League of United Latin American Citizens], and I want to know something about it." I told him it was an excellent organization. I said I would be glad to go with her. It was a fine thing for her to do.

Kennedy said he had been told about the incident with Yarborough. He said, "I told my staff people, tell him he either rides in the car or he doesn't ride."

I said, "Mr. President, it doesn't make any difference."

He said, "Well, I just told them to tell him that."

The Manchester book [*The Death of a President*] has it that we were heard to say loud words. Well, there weren't any. . . . Manchester's book was Bobby's announcement for the presidency. It was part of a calculated effort to destroy me. . . .

I went downstairs with Mrs. Kennedy and then afterwards we went to the Thomas dinner. Then to Fort Worth.

I got up early the next morning for breakfast. Mrs. Kennedy didn't want to go to that breakfast. Her stomach was just not conditioned to raucous Texans so early in the morning. At the breakfast, President Kennedy said it took Mrs. Kennedy longer to get ready and he made his reference to

himself and to me—"No one ever could make anything out of us, anyway."
Then Mrs. Kennedy made her entrance and she sat by me.

When Kennedy left he said, "Come by my room." A lot has been said
about the difference between those two rooms. Well, everyone knows that
the president gets whatever room or whatever suite he wants. One of these
suites was modernized and the other was old-fashioned. They put me in the
Will Rogers suite because Kennedy's Secret Service had picked the other.

I went up there. I had my baby sister and brother-in-law with me. She
lived in Fort Worth.

Kennedy was once again in his shorts. He called me to come in. He
was putting on his shirt, walking around and talking. He put his arms in
his shirt. That was the way he always dressed. He would put on his shorts
and then put on his shirt. I would always dress the other way; put on my
shorts, then put on my trousers. I had been raised to cover up that part of
me first. I told my sister to wait in the hall.

He said, "How did you like that about us not taking any time to get
ready?" He was looking for a compliment or a laugh about his little wit-
ticism. Presidents always look for that kind of thing, and people always
give it to them. . . .

We got to Dallas, got off the plane. Then I shook hands with the
Kennedys when they got off their plane. Yarborough got into our car, and
everything was very nice. We started to go down to the center. I was very
impressed and very pleased with the crowds.

Then we heard shots. It never occurred to me that it was an assassination or a killing. I just thought it was firecrackers or a car backfiring. I
had heard those all my life. Any politician—any man in public life—gets
used to that kind of sound. The first time I knew that there was anything
unusual was when the car lunged. My grandson, when he saw his nurse
go off in a plane, said, "Oga zoom." . . . That car took off in Dallas—it
zoomed.

And at the same time, this great big old boy from Georgia [Rufus
Youngblood] said, "Down!" And he got on top of me. I knew then this was
no normal operation. Something came over the radio. No—I don't know
whether I really heard this or whether I've just read it and it impressed
me so much that I assume I heard it. Anyhow it said, "We're getting out
of here." . . .

Youngblood put his body on me. He did that all the way to the hospital.
When I got there and got out of that car, I had been crushed.

I was under orders from him all the way. In situations like that, they're in command, and you don't question them. "In this door—to the right—here." Just like it had been planned, every step of the way. When they're good—and Youngblood was good—they're the best you can find.

Mrs. Johnson wanted to see Mrs. Kennedy. And Nellie Connally. Then from there on, there were frequent conversations, and pretty soon they came back and said he was dead.

From His "Checkers" Remarks

(1952)

*"Well, that's about it. That's what we have.
And that's what we owe"*

Johnson was right—a vice president shouldn't tell off his president in public. He shouldn't drag him into a campaign finance scandal, either, but that's exactly what Richard Nixon did in the fall of 1952. As Eisenhower's VP nominee, Nixon had been stumping across the country when reports emerged of a private slush fund, a fund Nixon was rumored to have used for personal expenses. Nixon decided to respond with an unprecedented television appeal, going around the press and speaking directly to tens of millions of voters. The broadcast, which came to be known as the "Checkers" speech, was an enormous success—because Nixon emphasized the confessional notes, but also because he emphasized the "common man" ones as well.

I come before you tonight as a candidate for the vice presidency and as a man whose honesty and integrity has been questioned.

Now, the usual political thing to do when charges are made against you is to either ignore them or to deny them without giving details. I believe we've had enough of that in the United States, particularly with the present administration in Washington, DC. To me the office of the vice presidency of the United States is a great office, and I feel that the people have got to have confidence in the integrity of the men who run for that office and who might obtain it.

I have a theory, too, that the best and only answer to a smear or to an honest misunderstanding of the facts is to tell the truth. And that's why I am here tonight. I want to tell you my side of the case. I'm sure that you have read the charge, and you've heard it, that I, Senator Nixon, took $18,000 from a group of my supporters.

Now, was that wrong? And let me say that it was wrong. I am saying it, incidentally, that it was wrong, just not illegal, because it isn't a question of whether it was legal or illegal—that isn't enough. The question is, was it morally wrong? I say that it was morally wrong if any of that $18,000 went to Senator Nixon, for my personal use. I say that it was morally wrong if it was secretly given and secretly handled. And I say that it was morally wrong if any of the contributors got special favors for the contributions that they made.

And now to answer those questions let me say this: not one cent of the $18,000 or any other money of that type ever went to me for my personal use. Every penny of it was used to pay for political expenses that I did not think should be charged to the taxpayers of the United States. It was not a secret fund. . . .

Some of you will say, and rightly, "Well, what did you use the fund for, Senator? Why did you have to have it?" Let me tell you in just a word how a Senate office operates. First of all, a senator gets $15,000 a year in salary. He gets enough money to pay for one trip a year, a round trip, that is, for himself and his family between his home and Washington, DC. And then he gets an allowance to handle the people that work in his office to handle his mail. And the allowance for my state of California is enough to hire 13 people. And let me say, incidentally, that that allowance is not paid to the senator. It is paid directly to the individuals that the senator puts on his payroll. But all of these people and all of these allowances are for strictly official business; business, for example, when a constituent writes in and wants you to go down to the Veteran's Administration and get some information about his GI policy—items of that type, for example. But there are other expenses that are not covered by the government. And I think I can best discuss those expenses by asking you some questions.

Do you think that when I or any other senator makes a political speech, has it printed, should charge the printing of that speech and the mailing of that speech to the taxpayers? Do you think, for example, when I or any other senator makes a trip to his home state to make a purely political speech, that the cost of that trip should be charged to the taxpayers? Do you think when a senator makes political broadcasts or political television broadcasts, radio or television, that the expense of those broadcasts should be charged to the taxpayers? Well, I know what your answer is. It's the same answer that audiences give me whenever I discuss this particular problem: The answer is no. The taxpayers shouldn't be required to finance items which are not official business but which are primarily political business.

Well, then the question arises, you say, "Well, how do you pay for these and how can you do it legally?" And there are several ways that it can be done, incidentally, and it is done legally in the United States Senate and in the Congress. The first way is to be a rich man. I don't happen to be a rich man, so I couldn't use that one. Another way that is used is to put your wife on the payroll. Let me say, incidentally, that my opponent, my opposite number for the vice presidency on the Democratic ticket, does have his wife on the payroll and has had her on his payroll for the past ten years. Now let me just say this: That's his business, and I'm not critical of him for doing that. You will have to pass judgment on that particular point.

But I have never done that for this reason: I have found that there are so many deserving stenographers and secretaries in Washington that needed the work that I just didn't feel it was right to put my wife on the payroll. My wife's sitting over here. She is a wonderful stenographer. She used to teach stenography and she used to teach shorthand in high school. That was when I met her. And I can tell you folks that she's worked many hours at night and many hours on Saturdays and Sundays in my office, and she's done a fine job, and I am proud to say tonight that in the six years I have been in the House and the Senate of the United States, Pat Nixon has never been on the government payroll.

What are other ways that these finances can be taken care of? Some who are lawyers, and I happen to be a lawyer, continue to practice law, but I haven't been able to do that. I am so far away from California that I have been so busy with my senatorial work that I have not engaged in any legal practice, and, also, as far as law practice is concerned, it seemed to me that the relationship between an attorney and the client was so personal that you couldn't possibly represent a man as an attorney and then have an unbiased view when he presented his case to you in the event that he had one before government.

And so I felt that the best way to handle these necessary political expenses of getting my message to the American people and the speeches I made—the speeches I had printed for the most part concerned this one message of exposing this administration, the Communism in it, the corruption in it—the only way that I could do that was to accept the aid which people in my home state of California, who contributed to my campaign and who continued to make these contributions after I was elected, were glad to make. . . .

Some of you may say, "Well, that is all right, Senator, that's your explanation, but have you got any proof?" And I'd like to tell you this evening that just an hour ago we received an independent audit of this entire fund. I suggested to Governor Sherman Adams, who is the chief of staff of the Dwight Eisenhower campaign, that an independent audit and legal report be obtained, and I have that audit in my hands. It's an audit made by the Price, Waterhouse, & Co. firm, and the legal opinion by Gibson, Dunn, & Crutcher, lawyers in Los Angeles. . . .

There are some that will say, "Well, maybe you were able, Senator, to fake the thing. How can we believe what you say? After all, is there a possibility that maybe you got some sums in cash? Is there a possibility that you might have feathered your own nest?" And so now, what I am going to do—and incidentally this is unprecedented in the history of American politics—I am going at this time to give to this television and radio audience a complete financial history: everything I've earned, everything I've spent, everything I own. And I want you to know the facts.

I'll have to start early. I was born in 1913. Our family was one of modest circumstances, and most of my early life was spent in a store out in East Whittier. It was a grocery store, one of those family enterprises. The only reason we were able to make it go was because my mother and dad had five boys, and we all worked in the store. I worked my way through college and, to a great extent, through law school. And then in 1940, probably the best thing that ever happened to me happened. I married Pat, who is sitting over here. We had a rather difficult time after we were married, like so many of the young couples who may be listening to us. I practiced law. She continued to teach school.

Then, in 1942, I went into the service. Let me say that my service record was not a particularly unusual one. I went to the South Pacific. I guess I'm entitled to a couple of battle stars. I got a couple of letters of commendation. But I was just there when the bombs were falling. And then I returned—returned to the United States, and in 1946, I ran for the Congress. When we came out of the war—Pat and I—Pat during the war had worked as a stenographer, and in a bank, and as an economist for a government agency—and when we came out, the total of our savings, from both my law practice, her teaching, and all the time I was in the war, the total for that entire period was just a little less than $10,000—every cent of that, incidentally, was in government bonds. Well that's where we start, when I go into politics.

Now, what have I earned since I went into politics? Well, here it is. I've jotted it down. Let me read the notes. First of all, I have had my salary as a congressman and as a senator. Second, I have received a total in this past six years of $1,600 from estates which were in my law firm at the time that I severed my connection with it. And, incidentally, as I said before, I have not engaged in any legal practice and have not accepted any fees from business that came into the firm after I went into politics. I have made an average of approximately $1,500 a year from nonpolitical speaking engagements and lectures.

And then, fortunately, we have inherited a little money. Pat sold her interest in her father's estate for $3,000, and I inherited $1,500 from my grandfather. We lived rather modestly. For four years we lived in an apartment in Park Fairfax, in Alexandria, Virginia. The rent was $80 a month. And we saved for the time that we could buy a house. Now, that was what we took in. What did we do with this money? What do we have today to show for it? This will surprise you because it is so little, I suppose, as standards generally go of people in public life.

First of all, we've got a house in Washington, which cost $41,000 and on which we owe $20,000. We have a house in Whittier, California, which cost $13,000 and on which we owe $3,000. My folks are living there at the present time. I have just $4,000 in life insurance, plus my GI policy, which I've never been able to convert and which will run out in two years. I have no life insurance whatever on Pat. I have no life insurance on our two youngsters, Tricia and Julie. I own a 1950 Oldsmobile car. We have our furniture. We have no stocks and bonds of any type. We have no interest of any kind, direct or indirect, in any business. Now, that's what we have. What do we owe?

Well in addition to the mortgage, the $20,000 mortgage on the house in Washington, the $10,000 one on the house in Whittier, I owe $4,500 to the Riggs Bank in Washington, DC, with interest [of] 4.5 percent. I owe $3,500 to my parents, and the interest on that loan, which I pay regularly, because it's a part of the savings they made through the years they were working so hard—I pay regularly 4 percent interest. And then I have a $500 loan, which I have on my life insurance.

Well, that's about it. That's what we have. And that's what we owe. It isn't very much. But Pat and I have the satisfaction that every dime that we've got is honestly ours. I should say this, that Pat doesn't have a mink coat. But she does have a respectable Republican cloth coat, and I always tell her she'd look good in anything.

One other thing I probably should tell you, because if I don't they'll probably be saying this about me, too. We did get something, a gift, after the election. A man down in Texas heard Pat on the radio mention the fact that our two youngsters would like to have a dog. And believe it or not, the day before we left on this campaign trip we got a message from Union Station in Baltimore, saying they had a package for us. We went down to get it. You know what it was? It was a little cocker spaniel dog, in a crate that he had sent all the way from Texas, black and white, spotted, and our little girl Tricia, the six-year-old, named it Checkers. And you know, the kids, like all kids, love the dog, and I just want to say this, right now, that regardless of what they say about it, we're gonna keep it.

It isn't easy to come before a nationwide audience and bare your life, as I've done. But I want to say some things before I conclude, that I think most of you will agree on. Mr. Mitchell, the Chairman of the Democratic National Committee, made this statement that if a man couldn't afford to be in the United States Senate, he shouldn't run for the Senate. And I just want to make my position clear. I don't agree with Mr. Mitchell when he says that only a rich man should serve his government in the United States Senate or in the Congress. I don't believe that represents the thinking of the Democratic Party, and I know that it doesn't represent the thinking of the Republican Party.

I believe that it's fine that a man like Governor [Adlai] Stevenson, who inherited a fortune from his father, can run for president. But I also feel that it's essential in this country of ours that a man of modest means can also run for president.

RICHARD NIXON

Draft of His Statement if Apollo 11 Crashed

(1969)

"There is hope for mankind in their sacrifice"

America's archives contain many speeches that were never given—because something happened, or because something didn't, or because a president changed his mind. There was Washington's one-term farewell, for instance, or the statement Eisenhower drafted taking responsibility for D-Day's potential failure. One of the best such texts was written during the summer of 1969, when William Safire sketched this statement for Nixon—a eulogy the president could read for the astronauts of Apollo 11 in case they didn't make it home. The title of Safire's memo: "In Case of Moon Disaster."

Fate has ordained that the men who went to the moon to explore in peace will stay on the moon to rest in peace.

These brave men, Neil Armstrong and Edwin Aldrin, know that there is no hope for their recovery. But they also know that there is hope for mankind in their sacrifice.

These two men are laying down their lives in mankind's most noble goal: the search for truth and understanding.

They will be mourned by their families and friends; they will be mourned by their nation; they will be mourned by the people of the world; they will be mourned by a Mother Earth that dared send two of her sons into the unknown.

In their exploration, they stirred the people of the world to feel as one; in their sacrifice, they bind more tightly the brotherhood of man.

In ancient days, men looked at stars and saw their heroes in the constellations. In modern times, we do much the same, but our heroes are epic men of flesh and blood.

Others will follow, and surely find their way home. Man's search will not be denied. But these men were the first, and they will remain the foremost in our hearts.

For every human being who looks up at the moon in the nights to come will know that there is some corner of another world that is forever mankind.

RICHARD NIXON

From His Address on Vietnam

(1969)

"The great silent majority"

The summer of 1969 was marked not only by a (successful) moon landing but by massive protests against the Vietnam War. On November 3, Nixon gave a speech detailing his new strategy for the war: "Vietnamization." Still, he sold it with his old "Checkers"-style techniques, theatrically promising to tell the truth and drawing contrasts between the protestors and the people who owned cocker spaniels and cloth coats—the Americans Nixon called, in a durable phrase (and an even more durable concept), the "silent majority."

Tonight I want to talk to you on a subject of deep concern to all Americans and to many people in all parts of the world—the war in Vietnam.

I believe that one of the reasons for the deep division about Vietnam is that many Americans have lost confidence in what their government has told them about our policy. The American people cannot and should not be asked to support a policy which involves the overriding issues of war and peace unless they know the truth about that policy.

Tonight, therefore, I would like to answer some of the questions that I know are on the minds of many of you listening to me. How and why did America get involved in Vietnam in the first place? How has this administration changed the policy of the previous administration? What has really happened in the negotiations in Paris and on the battlefront in Vietnam? What choices do we have if we are to end the war? What are the prospects for peace?

367

Now, let me begin by describing the situation I found when I was inaugurated on January 20.

—The war had been going on for four years.
—31,000 Americans had been killed in action.
—The training program for the South Vietnamese was behind schedule.
—540,000 Americans were in Vietnam with no plans to reduce the number.
—No progress had been made at the negotiations in Paris, and the United States had not put forth a comprehensive peace proposal.
—The war was causing deep division at home and criticism from many of our friends as well as our enemies abroad.

In view of these circumstances there were some who urged that I end the war at once by ordering the immediate withdrawal of all American forces.

From a political standpoint this would have been a popular and easy course to follow. After all, we became involved in the war while my predecessor was in office. I could blame the defeat which would be the result of my action on him and come out as the peacemaker. Some put it to me quite bluntly: This was the only way to avoid allowing Johnson's war to become Nixon's war.

But I had a greater obligation than to think only of the years of my administration and of the next election. I had to think of the effect of my decision on the next generation and on the future of peace and freedom in America and in the world.

Let us all understand that the question before us is not whether some Americans are for peace and some Americans are against peace. The question at issue is not whether Johnson's war becomes Nixon's war. The great question is: How can we win America's peace?

Well, let us turn now to the fundamental issue. Why and how did the United States become involved in Vietnam in the first place?

Fifteen years ago North Vietnam, with the logistical support of Communist China and the Soviet Union, launched a campaign to impose a Communist government on South Vietnam by instigating and supporting a revolution.

In response to the request of the government of South Vietnam, President Eisenhower sent economic aid and military equipment to assist the people of South Vietnam in their efforts to prevent a Communist takeover. Seven years ago, President Kennedy sent 16,000 military personnel to Vietnam as combat advisers. Four years ago, President Johnson sent American combat forces to South Vietnam. . . .

It has become clear that the obstacle in negotiating an end to the war is not the president of the United States. It is not the South Vietnamese government.

The obstacle is the other side's absolute refusal to show the least willingness to join us in seeking a just peace. And it will not do so while it is convinced that all it has to do is to wait for our next concession, and our next concession after that one, until it gets everything it wants.

There can now be no longer any question that progress in negotiation depends only on Hanoi's deciding to negotiate, to negotiate seriously.

I realize that this report on our efforts on the diplomatic front is discouraging to the American people, but the American people are entitled to know the truth—the bad news as well as the good news—where the lives of our young men are involved.

Now let me turn, however, to a more encouraging report on another front.

At the time we launched our search for peace I recognized we might not succeed in bringing an end to the war through negotiation. I, therefore, put into effect another plan to bring peace—a plan which will bring the war to an end regardless of what happens on the negotiating front.

It is in line with a major shift in U.S. foreign policy which I described in my press conference at Guam on July 25. Let me briefly explain what has been described as the Nixon Doctrine—a policy which not only will help end the war in Vietnam, but which is an essential element of our program to prevent future Vietnams.

We Americans are a do-it-yourself people. We are an impatient people. Instead of teaching someone else to do a job, we like to do it ourselves. And this trait has been carried over into our foreign policy.

In Korea and again in Vietnam, the United States furnished most of the money, most of the arms, and most of the men to help the people of those countries defend their freedom against Communist aggression.

Before any American troops were committed to Vietnam, a leader of another Asian country expressed this opinion to me when I was traveling in Asia as a private citizen. He said: "When you are trying to assist another nation defend its freedom, U.S. policy should be to help them fight the war but not to fight the war for them."

Well, in accordance with this wise counsel, I laid down in Guam three principles as guidelines for future American policy toward Asia:

—First, the United States will keep all of its treaty commitments.

—Second, we shall provide a shield if a nuclear power threatens the freedom of a nation allied with us or of a nation whose survival we consider vital to our security.

—Third, in cases involving other types of aggression, we shall furnish military and economic assistance when requested in accordance with our treaty commitments. But we shall look to the nation directly threatened to assume the primary responsibility of providing the manpower for its defense.

After I announced this policy, I found that the leaders of the Philippines, Thailand, Vietnam, South Korea, and other nations which might be threatened by Communist aggression, welcomed this new direction in American foreign policy.

The defense of freedom is everybody's business—not just America's business. And it is particularly the responsibility of the people whose freedom is threatened. In the previous administration, we Americanized the war in Vietnam. In this administration, we are Vietnamizing the search for peace. . . .

My fellow Americans, I am sure you can recognize from what I have said that we really only have two choices open to us if we want to end this war.

—I can order an immediate, precipitate withdrawal of all Americans from Vietnam without regard to the effects of that action.

—Or we can persist in our search for a just peace through a negotiated settlement if possible, or through continued implementation of our plan for Vietnamization if necessary—a plan in which we will withdraw all of our forces from Vietnam on a schedule in accordance with our program, as the South Vietnamese become strong enough to defend their own freedom.

I have chosen this second course. It is not the easy way. It is the right way. It is a plan which will end the war and serve the cause of peace—not just in Vietnam but in the Pacific and in the world.

In speaking of the consequences of a precipitate withdrawal, I mentioned that our allies would lose confidence in America.

Far more dangerous, we would lose confidence in ourselves. Oh, the immediate reaction would be a sense of relief that our men were coming home. But as we saw the consequences of what we had done, inevitable remorse and divisive recrimination would scar our spirit as a people.

We have faced other crises in our history and have become stronger by rejecting the easy way out and taking the right way in meeting our challenges. Our greatness as a nation has been our capacity to do what had to be done when we knew our course was right.

I recognize that some of my fellow citizens disagree with the plan for peace I have chosen. Honest and patriotic Americans have reached different conclusions as to how peace should be achieved.

In San Francisco a few weeks ago, I saw demonstrators carrying signs reading: "Lose in Vietnam, bring the boys home."

Well, one of the strengths of our free society is that any American has a right to reach that conclusion and to advocate that point of view. But as president of the United States, I would be untrue to my oath of office if I allowed the policy of this nation to be dictated by the minority who hold that point of view and who try to impose it on the nation by mounting demonstrations in the street.

For almost two hundred years, the policy of this nation has been made under our Constitution by those leaders in the Congress and the White House elected by all of the people. If a vocal minority, however fervent its cause, prevails over reason and the will of the majority, this nation has no future as a free society. . . .

I know it may not be fashionable to speak of patriotism or national destiny these days. But I feel it is appropriate to do so on this occasion

Two hundred years ago this nation was weak and poor. But even then, America was the hope of millions in the world. Today we have become the strongest and richest nation in the world. And the wheel of destiny has turned so that any hope the world has for the survival of peace and freedom will be determined by whether the American people have the moral stamina and the courage to meet the challenge of free world leadership.

Let historians not record that when America was the most powerful nation in the world we passed on the other side of the road and allowed the last hopes for peace and freedom of millions of people to be suffocated by the forces of totalitarianism.

And so tonight—to you, the great silent majority of my fellow Americans—I ask for your support.

I pledged in my campaign for the presidency to end the war in a way that we could win the peace. I have initiated a plan of action which will enable me to keep that pledge.

The more support I can have from the American people, the sooner that pledge can be redeemed; for the more divided we are at home, the less likely the enemy is to negotiate at Paris.

Let us be united for peace. Let us also be united against defeat. Because let us understand: North Vietnam cannot defeat or humiliate the United States. Only Americans can do that.

GERALD FORD

Address on Taking
the Oath of Office

(1974)

"Our long national nightmare is over"

On August 8, 1974, President Nixon announced he was stepping down. "I have never been a quitter," he promised in his resignation speech, but his Watergate scandal—and, in a rare victory for the modern legislative branch, the threat of impeachment—had changed his mind. The next day, Gerald Ford took the oath of office. The economy was faltering; Vietnam was hovering; the American people were angry and cynical. In a brief address, Ford tried to acknowledge these issues—but also to announce that he and his administration would be moving forward.

The oath that I have taken is the same oath that was taken by George Washington and by every president under the Constitution. But I assume the presidency under extraordinary circumstances never before experienced by Americans. This is an hour of history that troubles our minds and hurts our hearts.

Therefore, I feel it is my first duty to make an unprecedented compact with my countrymen. Not an inaugural address, not a fireside chat, not a campaign speech—just a little straight talk among friends. And I intend it to be the first of many.

I am acutely aware that you have not elected me as your president by your ballots, and so I ask you to confirm me as your president with your prayers. And I hope that such prayers will also be the first of many.

If you have not chosen me by secret ballot, neither have I gained office by any secret promises. I have not campaigned either for the presidency or the vice presidency. I have not subscribed to any partisan platform. I am indebted to no man, and only to one woman—my dear wife—as I begin this very difficult job.

I have not sought this enormous responsibility, but I will not shirk it. Those who nominated and confirmed me as vice president were my friends and are my friends. They were of both parties, elected by all the people and acting under the Constitution in their name. It is only fitting then that I should pledge to them and to you that I will be the president of all the people.

Thomas Jefferson said the people are the only sure reliance for the preservation of our liberty. And down the years, Abraham Lincoln renewed this American article of faith asking, "Is there any better way or equal hope in the world?"

I intend, on Monday next, to request of the Speaker of the House of Representatives and the president pro tempore of the Senate the privilege of appearing before the Congress to share with my former colleagues and with you, the American people, my views on the priority business of the nation and to solicit your views and their views. And may I say to the speaker and the others, if I could meet with you right after these remarks, I would appreciate it.

Even though this is late in an election year, there is no way we can go forward except together and no way anybody can win except by serving the people's urgent needs. We cannot stand still or slip backwards. We must go forward now together.

To the peoples and the governments of all friendly nations, and I hope that could encompass the whole world, I pledge an uninterrupted and sincere search for peace. America will remain strong and united, but its strength will remain dedicated to the safety and sanity of the entire family of man, as well as to our own precious freedom.

I believe that truth is the glue that holds government together, not only our government but civilization itself. That bond, though strained, is unbroken at home and abroad.

In all my public and private acts as your president, I expect to follow my instincts of openness and candor with full confidence that honesty is always the best policy in the end.

My fellow Americans, our long national nightmare is over.

Our Constitution works; our great republic is a government of laws and not of men. Here the people rule. But there is a higher Power, by whatever name we honor Him, who ordains not only righteousness but love, not only justice but mercy.

As we bind up the internal wounds of Watergate, more painful and more poisonous than those of foreign wars, let us restore the golden rule to our political process, and let brotherly love purge our hearts of suspicion and of hate.

In the beginning, I asked you to pray for me. Before closing, I ask again your prayers, for Richard Nixon and for his family. May our former president, who brought peace to millions, find it for himself. May God bless and comfort his wonderful wife and daughters, whose love and loyalty will forever be a shining legacy to all who bear the lonely burdens of the White House.

I can only guess at those burdens, although I have witnessed at close hand the tragedies that befell three presidents and the lesser trials of others.

With all the strength and all the good sense I have gained from life, with all the confidence my family, my friends, and my dedicated staff impart to me, and with the good will of countless Americans I have encountered in recent visits to forty states, I now solemnly reaffirm my promise I made to you last December 6th: to uphold the Constitution, to do what is right as God gives me to see the right, and to do the very best I can for America.

God helping me, I will not let you down.

JIMMY CARTER

From *An Hour Before Daylight*

"I didn't know of any rural families that had
electric lights until the rural-electrification
program came along"

Jimmy Carter is one of America's most prolific presidential authors. His Why
Not the Best? *helped drive his long-shot campaign in* 1976, *and his presidential memoirs appeared a year after he left office, in* 1982. *Out of Carter's dozens
of books, however, the best is easily* An Hour Before Daylight, *published in*
2001 *and excerpted here. It's a memoir but a highly personal one—an account of
Carter growing up in rural Georgia that, in its lean but detail-rich prose, recalls
Coolidge's* Autobiography *and its account of growing up in rural Vermont.*

The first thing I remember clearly was when I was four years old and
my father took us out to show us our new home on the farm. There
were four of us, including my sister, Gloria, who was two years younger
than I. The front door was locked when we got there, and Daddy realized
that he had forgotten the key. He tried to raise one of the windows that
opened onto the front porch, but a wooden bar on the inside let it come up
only about six inches. So he slid me through the crack and I came around
to unlock the door from the inside. The approval of my father for my first
useful act has always been one of my most vivid memories.

Our house was typical of those occupied by middle-income landowners
of the time. Set back about fifty feet from the dirt road, it was square,
painted tan to match the dust, and had a broad front porch and split-shingle

roof. The rooms were laid out in "shotgun" style, with a hall that went down the middle of the house dividing the living room, dining room, and kitchen on the left side from three bedrooms on the right. We also had a screened porch that extended across the back of the house, where we worked and stored things such as well water, corn for the chickens, and extra wood to keep it dry. The front porch was where our family congregated in warm weather, which was about nine months of the year. We had a swing suspended from the ceiling and some rocking chairs out there, and Daddy often used the slightly sloping floor for a quick nap after dinner and before going back to work in the afternoon. I relished lying beside him as a little boy, long before I could do useful work in the fields.

There is little doubt that I now recall those days with more fondness than they deserve. We drew water from a well in the yard, and every day of the year we had the chore of keeping extra bucketfuls in the kitchen and on the back porch, combined with the constant wood-sawing and chopping to supply the cooking stove and fireplaces. In every bedroom was a slop jar (chamber pot) that was emptied each morning into the outdoor privy, about twenty yards from our back door. This small shack had a large hole for adults and a lower and smaller one for children; we wiped with old newspapers or pages torn from Sears, Roebuck catalogues. These were much better facilities than those I knew when I was with the other families on the place, who squatted behind bushes and wiped with corncobs or leaves.

It was a great day for our family in 1935 when Daddy purchased from a mail-order catalogue and erected a windmill with a high wooden tank and pipes that provided running water for the kitchen and a bathroom with toilet. We even had a rudimentary shower made from a large tin can with its bottom perforated by nail holes. One extra benefit was that the top platform of the windmill, up near the fan blades, gave a good view of the nearby fields.

Our house was surrounded by a white-sanded yard, which we had to sweep frequently to remove fowl and animal droppings and leaves from our pecan, magnolia, mulberry, and chinaberry trees. Most of our brush brooms were made of small saplings or limbs of dogwood, which were resilient and long-lasting. Several times a year we took a two-mule wagon about three miles to a pit and loaded it with fresh sand, which was scattered on the yard to give it a new white surface. Behind our house and surrounded by fenced fields were a small garage (never used for a car), a smokehouse, a chicken house, and a large woodpile.

Our artificial light came from kerosene lamps, and it was considered almost sinful to leave one burning in an unoccupied room. The only exception was in the front living room, where we had an Aladdin lamp about five feet high whose asbestos wick miraculously provided illumination bright enough for reading in a wide area. We turned this flame way down when we went to eat a meal, both to conserve fuel and to avoid the lamp's tendency to flame up and blacken the fragile wick with thick soot. When this happened—a mishap for which someone always had to be identified as the culprit—we had to endure an extended period of careful flame control while we waited in near darkness for the soot to burn off enough for us to read again.

One significant difference between my parents was their reading habits. Daddy mostly limited his reading to the daily and weekly newspapers and farm journals, but he also owned a small library, which I still have, that included Halliburton's *Royal Road to Romance*, a collection of A. Conan Doyle's Sherlock Holmes stories, and a complete set of Edgar Rice Burroughs's *Tarzan* books, each carefully signed and numbered by my father to indicate their proper sequence. By contrast, my mother read constantly and encouraged us children to do the same. Since we stayed busy most of the time, Mama and I always had a magazine or book to read while eating our meals, and this became a lifetime habit for my own family and me. The only exception was Sunday dinner, which, for some reason, had too formal an atmosphere for literature at the table. At night, at suppertime, there was no such restraint. . . .

I've often wondered why we were so infatuated with the land, and I think there is a strong tie to the Civil War, or, as we called it, the War Between the States. Although I was born more than half a century after the war was over, it was a living reality in my life. I grew up in one of the families whose people could not forget that we had been conquered, while most of our neighbors were black people whose grandparents had been liberated in the same conflict. Our two races, although inseparable in our daily lives, were kept apart by social custom, misinterpretation of Holy Scriptures, and the unchallenged law of the land as mandated by the United States Supreme Court.

It seemed natural for white folks to cherish our Southern heritage and cling to our way of life, partially because the close ties among many of our local families went back another hundred years before the war, when our Scotch-Irish ancestors had come to Georgia from the British Isles or moved south and west, mostly from Virginia and the Carolinas. We were bound together by blood kinship as well as by lingering resentment against those who had defeated us. A frequent subject of discussion around my grandparents' homes was the damage the "damn Yankees" had done to the South during Reconstruction years.

Many older Georgians still remembered vividly the anger and embarrassment of their parents, who had to live under the domination of carpetbaggers and their Southern allies, who were known as scalawags. My grandfather Gordy was thirteen years old when what he saw as the Northern oppressors finally relinquished political and economic control of the state in 1876, eleven years after the conflict ended. My mother was the only one in her family who ever spoke up to defend Abraham Lincoln. I don't remember ever hearing slavery mentioned, only the unwarranted violation of states' rights and the intrusion of the federal government in the private lives of citizens. Folks never considered that the real tragedy of Reconstruction was its failure to establish social justice for the former slaves. The intense bitterness was mostly confined to our older relatives, who couldn't understand the desire of some of us younger ones to look more into the future—or at least the present—instead of just the past. . . .

I didn't know of any rural families that had electric lights until the rural-electrification program came along in the late 1930s. We had a large battery-powered radio in the front room that we used sparingly, and only at night, as we all sat around looking at it during *Amos and Andy*, *Fibber McGee and Molly*, *Jack Benny*, or *Little Orphan Annie*. When its power failed, we would sometimes bring in the battery from the pickup truck to keep it playing for a special event. I recall some rare baseball games re-created by the announcer from telegraph reports, a few boxing matches, and the late night in 1936 when Alfred Landon was chosen as the Republican nominee for president. The voting went on so long that the battery in our house gave out, and we took the radio outside and set it on the hood of the pickup until the convention made its choice, hours after midnight.

The most memorable radio broadcast was in 1938, the night of the return match between heavyweight boxers Joe Louis and Max Schmeling. The German champion had defeated the black American two years earlier, and the world's attention was focused on the return bout. For our community, this fight had heavy racial overtones, with almost unanimous support at our all-white school for the European over the American. A delegation of our black neighbors came to ask Daddy if they could listen to the broadcast, and we put the radio in the window so the assembled crowd in the yard could hear it. The fight ended abruptly, in the first round, with

Louis almost killing Schmeling. There was no sound from outside—or inside—the house. We heard a quiet "Thank you, Mr. Earl," and then our visitors walked silently out of the yard, crossed the road and the railroad tracks, entered the tenant house, and closed the door. Then all hell broke loose, and their celebration lasted all night. Daddy was tight-lipped, but all the mores of our segregated society had been honored.

JIMMY CARTER

Address on the Energy Crisis

(1979)

"The threat is nearly invisible in ordinary ways. It is a crisis of confidence"

In the summer of 1979, the nation was struggling—with economic stagnation, with lines at the gas pump, with a sense that America's optimism was on E. On July 15, Carter decided to confront these problems in a primetime address. While the result has often been labeled his "malaise" speech, Carter did not use that word. Still, he tried to describe America's malaise and to prod the country to reflect on its concealed causes—tried to deliver a presidential sermon in the style of Lincoln and Wilson, although in the end Carter's attempt did not help his cause.

Good evening. This is a special night for me. Exactly three years ago, on July 15, 1976, I accepted the nomination of my party to run for president of the United States. I promised you a president who is not isolated from the people, who feels your pain, and who shares your dreams and who draws his strength and his wisdom from you.

During the past three years I've spoken to you on many occasions about national concerns: the energy crisis, reorganizing the government, our nation's economy, and issues of war and especially peace. But over those years the subjects of the speeches, the talks, and the press conferences have become increasingly narrow, focused more and more on what the isolated world of Washington thinks is important. Gradually, you've heard more and more about what the government thinks or what the government should be doing and less and less about our nation's hopes, our dreams, and our vision of the future.

Ten days ago I had planned to speak to you again about a very important subject—energy. For the fifth time I would have described the urgency of the problem and laid out a series of legislative recommendations to the Congress. But as I was preparing to speak, I began to ask myself the same question that I now know has been troubling many of you. Why have we not been able to get together as a nation to resolve our serious energy problem?

It's clear that the true problems of our nation are much deeper—deeper than gasoline lines or energy shortages, deeper even than inflation or recession. And I realize more than ever that as president I need your help. So, I decided to reach out and listen to the voices of America.

I invited to Camp David people from almost every segment of our society—business and labor, teachers and preachers, governors, mayors, and private citizens. And then I left Camp David to listen to other Americans, men and women like you. It has been an extraordinary ten days, and I want to share with you what I've heard.

First of all, I got a lot of personal advice. Let me quote a few of the typical comments that I wrote down.

This from a southern governor: "Mr. President, you are not leading this nation—you're just managing the government."

"You don't see the people enough anymore."

"Some of your cabinet members don't seem loyal. There is not enough discipline among your disciples."

"Don't talk to us about politics or the mechanics of government, but about an understanding of our common good."

"Mr. President, we're in trouble. Talk to us about blood and sweat and tears."

"If you lead, Mr. President, we will follow."

Many people talked about themselves and about the condition of our nation. This from a young woman in Pennsylvania: "I feel so far from government. I feel like ordinary people are excluded from political power."

And this from a young Chicano: "Some of us have suffered from recession all our lives."

"Some people have wasted energy, but others haven't had anything to waste."

And this from a religious leader: "No material shortage can touch the important things like God's love for us or our love for one another."

And I like this one particularly from a black woman who happens to be the mayor of a small Mississippi town: "The big-shots are not the only ones who are important. Remember, you can't sell anything on Wall Street unless someone digs it up somewhere else first."

This kind of summarized a lot of other statements: "Mr. President, we are confronted with a moral and a spiritual crisis."

Several of our discussions were on energy, and I have a notebook full of comments and advice. I'll read just a few.

"We can't go on consuming forty percent more energy than we produce. When we import oil we are also importing inflation plus unemployment."

"We've got to use what we have. The Middle East has only five percent of the world's energy, but the United States has twenty-four percent."

And this is one of the most vivid statements: "Our neck is stretched over the fence and [the Organization of Petroleum Exporting Countries] has a knife."

"There will be other cartels and other shortages. American wisdom and courage right now can set a path to follow in the future."

This was a good one: "Be bold, Mr. President. We may make mistakes, but we are ready to experiment."

And this one from a labor leader got to the heart of it: "The real issue is freedom. We must deal with the energy problem on a war footing."

And the last that I'll read: "When we enter the moral equivalent of war, Mr. President, don't issue us BB guns."

These ten days confirmed my belief in the decency and the strength and the wisdom of the American people, but it also bore out some of my longstanding concerns about our nation's underlying problems.

I know, of course, being president, that government actions and legislation can be very important. That's why I've worked hard to put my campaign promises into law—and I have to admit, with just mixed success. But after listening to the American people I have been reminded again that all the legislation in the world can't fix what's wrong with America. So, I want to speak to you first tonight about a subject even more serious than energy or inflation. I want to talk to you right now about a fundamental threat to American democracy.

I do not mean our political and civil liberties. They will endure. And I do not refer to the outward strength of America, a nation that is at peace tonight everywhere in the world, with unmatched economic power and military might.

The threat is nearly invisible in ordinary ways. It is a crisis of confidence. It is a crisis that strikes at the very heart and soul and spirit of our national will. We can see this crisis in the growing doubt about the meaning of our own lives and in the loss of a unity of purpose for our nation.

The erosion of our confidence in the future is threatening to destroy the social and the political fabric of America.

The confidence that we have always had as a people is not simply some romantic dream or a proverb in a dusty book that we read just on the Fourth of July. It is the idea which founded our nation and has guided our development as a people. Confidence in the future has supported everything else—public institutions and private enterprise, our own families, and the very Constitution of the United States. Confidence has defined our course and has served as a link between generations. We've always believed in something called progress. We've always had a faith that the days of our children would be better than our own.

Our people are losing that faith, not only in government itself but in the ability as citizens to serve as the ultimate rulers and shapers of our democracy. As a people we know our past and we are proud of it. Our progress has been part of the living history of America, even the world. We always believed that we were part of a great movement of humanity itself called democracy, involved in the search for freedom, and that belief has always strengthened us in our purpose. But just as we are losing our confidence in the future, we are also beginning to close the door on our past.

In a nation that was proud of hard work, strong families, close-knit communities, and our faith in God, too many of us now tend to worship self-indulgence and consumption. Human identity is no longer defined by what one does, but by what one owns. But we've discovered that owning things and consuming things does not satisfy our longing for meaning. We've learned that piling up material goods cannot fill the emptiness of lives which have no confidence or purpose.

The symptoms of this crisis of the American spirit are all around us. For the first time in the history of our country a majority of our people believe that the next five years will be worse than the past five years. Two-thirds of our people do not even vote. The productivity of American workers is actually dropping, and the willingness of Americans to save for the future has fallen below that of all other people in the western world.

As you know, there is a growing disrespect for government and for churches and for schools, the news media, and other institutions. This is not a message of happiness or reassurance, but it is the truth and it is a warning.

These changes did not happen overnight. They've come upon us gradually over the last generation, years that were filled with shocks and tragedy.

We were sure that ours was a nation of the ballot, not the bullet, until the murders of John Kennedy and Robert Kennedy and Martin Luther King Jr. We were taught that our armies were always invincible and our causes were always just, only to suffer the agony of Vietnam. We respected the presidency as a place of honor until the shock of Watergate.

We remember when the phrase "sound as a dollar" was an expression of absolute dependability, until ten years of inflation began to shrink our dollar and our savings. We believed that our nation's resources were limitless until 1973, when we had to face a growing dependence on foreign oil.

These wounds are still very deep. They have never been healed.

Looking for a way out of this crisis, our people have turned to the federal government and found it isolated from the mainstream of our nation's life. Washington, DC, has become an island. The gap between our citizens and our government has never been so wide. The people are looking for honest answers, not easy answers; clear leadership, not false claims and evasiveness and politics as usual.

What you see too often in Washington and elsewhere around the country is a system of government that seems incapable of action. You see a Congress twisted and pulled in every direction by hundreds of well-financed and powerful special interests. You see every extreme position defended to the last vote, almost to the last breath by one unyielding group or another. You often see a balanced and a fair approach that demands sacrifice, a little sacrifice from everyone, abandoned like an orphan without support and without friends.

Often you see paralysis and stagnation and drift. You don't like it, and neither do I. What can we do?

First of all, we must face the truth, and then we can change our course. We simply must have faith in each other, faith in our ability to govern ourselves, and faith in the future of this nation. Restoring that faith and that confidence to America is now the most important task we face. It is a true challenge of this generation of Americans.

One of the visitors to Camp David last week put it this way: "We've got to stop crying and start sweating, stop talking and start walking, stop cursing and start praying. The strength we need will not come from the White House, but from every house in America."

We know the strength of America. We are strong. We can regain our unity. We can regain our confidence. We are the heirs of generations who survived threats much more powerful and awesome than those that challenge us now. Our fathers and mothers were strong men and women who shaped a new society during the Great Depression, who fought world wars, and who carved out a new charter of peace for the world.

We ourselves are the same Americans who just ten years ago put a man on the moon. We are the generation that dedicated our society to the pursuit of human rights and equality. And we are the generation that will win the war on the energy problem and in that process rebuild the unity and confidence of America.

We are at a turning point in our history. There are two paths to choose. One is a path I've warned about tonight, the path that leads to fragmentation and self-interest. Down that road lies a mistaken idea of freedom, the right to grasp for ourselves some advantage over others. That path would be one of constant conflict between narrow interests ending in chaos and immobility. It is a certain route to failure.

All the traditions of our past, all the lessons of our heritage, all the promises of our future point to another path, the path of common purpose and the restoration of American values. That path leads to true freedom for our nation and ourselves. We can take the first steps down that path as we begin to solve our energy problem.

Energy will be the immediate test of our ability to unite this nation, and it can also be the standard around which we rally. On the battlefield of energy we can win for our nation a new confidence, and we can seize control again of our common destiny.

In little more than two decades we've gone from a position of energy independence to one in which almost half the oil we use comes from foreign countries, at prices that are going through the roof. Our excessive dependence on OPEC has already taken a tremendous toll on our economy and our people. This is the direct cause of the long lines which have made millions of you spend aggravating hours waiting for gasoline. It's a cause of the increased inflation and unemployment that we now face. This intolerable dependence on foreign oil threatens our economic independence and the very security of our nation.

The energy crisis is real. It is worldwide. It is a clear and present danger to our nation. These are facts and we simply must face them.

What I have to say to you now about energy is simple and vitally important.

Point one: I am tonight setting a clear goal for the energy policy of the United States. Beginning this moment, this nation will never use more foreign oil than we did in 1977—never. From now on, every new addition to our demand for energy will be met from our own production and our own conservation. The generation-long growth in our dependence on foreign oil will be stopped dead in its tracks right now and then reversed as we move through the 1980s, for I am tonight setting the further goal of cutting our dependence on foreign oil by one-half by the end of the next decade—a saving of over 4.5 million barrels of imported oil per day.

Point two: To ensure that we meet these targets, I will use my presidential authority to set import quotas. I'm announcing tonight that for 1979 and 1980, I will forbid the entry into this country of one drop of foreign oil more than these goals allow. These quotas will ensure a reduction in imports even below the ambitious levels we set at the recent Tokyo summit.

Point three: To give us energy security, I am asking for the most massive peacetime commitment of funds and resources in our nation's history to develop America's own alternative sources of fuel—from coal, from oil shale, from plant products for gasohol, from unconventional gas, from the sun.

I propose the creation of an energy security corporation to lead this effort to replace 2.5 million barrels of imported oil per day by 1990. The corporation will issue up to $5 billion in energy bonds, and I especially want them to be in small denominations so that average Americans can invest directly in America's energy security.

Just as a similar synthetic rubber corporation helped us win World War II, so will we mobilize American determination and ability to win the energy war. Moreover, I will soon submit legislation to Congress calling for the creation of this nation's first solar bank, which will help us achieve the crucial goal of twenty percent of our energy coming from solar power by the year 2000.

These efforts will cost money, a lot of money, and that is why Congress must enact the windfall profits tax without delay. It will be money well spent. Unlike the billions of dollars that we ship to foreign countries to pay for foreign oil, these funds will be paid by Americans to Americans. These funds will go to fight, not to increase, inflation and unemployment.

Point four: I'm asking Congress to mandate, to require as a matter of law, that our nation's utility companies cut their massive use of oil by 50 percent within the next decade and switch to other fuels, especially coal, our most abundant energy source.

Point five: To make absolutely certain that nothing stands in the way of achieving these goals, I will urge Congress to create an energy mobilization board which, like the War Production Board in World War II, will have the responsibility and authority to cut through the red tape, the delays, and the endless roadblocks to completing key energy projects.

We will protect our environment. But when this nation critically needs a refinery or a pipeline, we will build it.

Point six: I'm proposing a bold conservation program to involve every state, county, and city and every average American in our energy battle. This effort will permit you to build conservation into your homes and your lives at a cost you can afford.

I ask Congress to give me authority for mandatory conservation and for standby gasoline rationing. To further conserve energy, I'm proposing tonight an extra $10 billion over the next decade to strengthen our public transportation systems. And I'm asking you for your good and for your nation's security to take no unnecessary trips, to use carpools or public transportation whenever you can, to park your car one extra day per week, to obey the speed limit, and to set your thermostats to save fuel. Every act of energy conservation like this is more than just common sense—I tell you it is an act of patriotism.

Our nation must be fair to the poorest among us, so we will increase aid to needy Americans to cope with rising energy prices. We often think of conservation only in terms of sacrifice. In fact, it is the most painless and immediate way of rebuilding our nation's strength. Every gallon of oil each one of us saves is a new form of production. It gives us more freedom, more confidence, that much more control over our own lives.

So, the solution of our energy crisis can also help us to conquer the crisis of the spirit in our country. It can rekindle our sense of unity, our confidence in the future, and give our nation and all of us individually a new sense of purpose.

You know we can do it. We have the natural resources. We have more oil in our shale alone than several Saudi Arabias. We have more coal than any nation on Earth. We have the world's highest level of technology. We have the most skilled work force, with innovative genius, and I firmly believe that we have the national will to win this war.

I do not promise you that this struggle for freedom will be easy. I do not promise a quick way out of our nation's problems, when the truth is that the only way out is an all-out effort. What I do promise you is that I will lead our fight, and I will enforce fairness in our struggle, and I will ensure honesty. And above all, I will act.

We can manage the short-term shortages more effectively and we will, but there are no short-term solutions to our long-range problems. There is simply no way to avoid sacrifice.

Twelve hours from now I will speak again in Kansas City, to expand and to explain further our energy program. Just as the search for solutions to our energy shortages has now led us to a new awareness of our nation's deeper problems, so our willingness to work for those solutions in energy can strengthen us to attack those deeper problems.

I will continue to travel this country, to hear the people of America. You can help me to develop a national agenda for the 1980s. I will listen and I will act. We will act together. These were the promises I made three years ago, and I intend to keep them.

Little by little we can and we must rebuild our confidence. We can spend until we empty our treasuries, and we may summon all the wonders of science. But we can succeed only if we tap our greatest resources— America's people, America's values, and America's confidence.

I have seen the strength of America in the inexhaustible resources of our people. In the days to come, let us renew that strength in the struggle for an energy secure nation.

In closing, let me say this: I will do my best, but I will not do it alone. Let your voice be heard. Whenever you have a chance, say something good about our country. With God's help and for the sake of our nation, it is time for us to join hands in America. Let us commit ourselves together to a rebirth of the American spirit. Working together with our common faith we cannot fail.

From *Where's the Rest of Me?*

"I loved three things: drama, politics, and sports, and I'm not sure they always come in that order"

Ronald Reagan has often been dismissed as an intellectual lightweight—an "amiable dunce." Yet his political rise depended on his own reading, writing, and spinning, with there being no better instance of these efforts than his first book, Where's the Rest of Me? *Beginning with its opening pages, which are excerpted here, the memoir mixes corny conceits, raw confessions, and savvy political positioning, all of it pepped up by Hollywood gossip. It took Reagan and his ghostwriter a lot of work to get the mix right. (An early draft opened with an even odder Virgilian conceit: "I sing of men in Eureka, Illinois, and of gods in Hollywood, California. . . .") But the book appeared at a crucial moment in 1965, just as Reagan was pivoting from a fading career as an actor to a promising one as a candidate for California governor.*

The story begins with the close-up of a bottom in a small town called Tampico in Illinois, on February 6, 1911. My face was blue from screaming, my bottom was red from whacking, and my father claimed afterward that he was white when he said shakily, "For such a little bit of a fat Dutchman, he makes a hell of a lot of noise, doesn't he?"

"I think he's perfectly wonderful," said my mother weakly. "Ronald Wilson Reagan."

Those were their first opinions of me. As far as I know, they never changed during their lifetimes. As for myself, ever since my birth my nickname has been "Dutch" and I have been particularly fond of the colors that were exhibited—red, white, and blue. I have not been uncomfortable on the various occasions when I have had an overwhelming impulse to brandish them. I have heard more than one psychiatrist say that we imbibe our ideals from our mother's milk. Then, I must say, my breastfeeding was the home of the brave baby and the free bosom. I was the hungriest person in the house but I only got chubby when I exercised in the crib; any time I wasn't gnawing on the bars, I was worrying with my thumb in my mouth—habits which have symbolically persisted throughout my life.

In those early days I was sure I was living the whole life of Reagan. When any Irishman, who generally knows quite well how to live, believes that, he is usually right. It was not until thirty years later that I found part of my existence was missing. It came with the making of a picture called *King's Row* for Warner Brothers in 1941. In this I played the role that first made me a motion picture star.

It certainly was one of my best pictures. Based on the novel of the same name by Henry Bellamann, it was a slightly sordid but moving yarn about the antics in a small town, something I had more than a slight acquaintance with. I took the part of Drake McHugh, the gay blade who cut a swathe among the ladies. I had inherited a good deal of money, the story ran, but the head of the bank had absconded with it. On my upper-crust uppers, I made the most of it.

My key scene was to be played in a bed. This environment was the result of the plot which had me injured in an accident in the railroad yards. Taken to a sadistic doctor (who disapproved of my dating his daughter and felt it was his duty to punish me), I recovered consciousness in an upstairs bedroom. I found that the doctor had amputated both my legs at the hips.

It was the portrayal of this moment of total shock which made the scene rough to play. Coming from unconsciousness to full realization of what had happened in a few seconds, it presented me with the most challenging acting problem in my career. Worst of all, I had to give my reaction in a line of no more than five words.

A whole actor would find such a scene difficult; giving it the necessary dramatic impact as half an actor was murderous. I felt I had neither the experience nor the talent to fake it. I simply had to find out how it really felt, short of actual amputation.

I rehearsed the scene before mirrors, in corners of the studio, while driving home, in the men's rooms of restaurants, before selected friends. At night I would wake up staring at the ceiling and automatically mutter the line before I went back to sleep. I consulted physicians and psychologists; I even talked to people who were so disabled, trying to brew in myself the cauldron of emotions a man must feel who wakes up one sunny morning to find half of himself gone.

I got a lot of answers. I supplied some more for myself. None of mine agreed with any of theirs. Theirs did not agree with each other. I was stumped. I commenced to panic as the day for shooting came nearer.

The night before I could not sleep. I appeared wan and worn on the sound stage, still not knowing how to read the line. Without hope, with makeup pasted on and in my nightshirt, I wandered over to the set to see what it looked like. I found the prop men had arranged a neat deception. Under the gay patchwork quilt, they had cut a hole in the mattress and put a supporting box beneath. I stared at it for a minute. Then, obeying an overpowering impulse, I climbed into the rig. I spent almost that whole hour in stiff confinement, contemplating my torso and the smooth undisturbed flat of the covers where my legs should have been.

Gradually the affair began to terrify me. In some weird way, I felt something horrible had happened to my body. Then gradually I became aware that the crew had quietly assembled, the camera was in position, and the set all lighted. Sam Wood, the director, stood beside me, watching me sweat.

"Want to shoot it?" he said in a low voice.

"No rehearsal?" I begged. Somehow I knew this one had to be for real.

God rest his soul—fine director that he was, he just turned to the crew and said, "Let's make it."

There were cries of "Lights!" and "Quiet, please!" I lay back and closed my eyes, as tense as a fiddle-string. I heard Sam's low voice call, "Action!" There was the sharp *clack* which signaled the beginning of the scene. I opened my eyes dazedly, looked around, slowly let my gaze travel downward. I can't describe even now my feeling as I tried to reach for where my legs should be. "Randy!" I screamed. Ann Sheridan (bless her), playing Randy, burst through the door. She wasn't in the shot and normally wouldn't have been on hand until we turned the camera around to get her entrance, but she knew it was one of those scenes where a fellow actor needed all the help he could get, and at that moment, in my mind, she was Randy answering my call. I asked the question—the words that had been haunting me for so many weeks—"Where's the rest of me?"

There was no retake. It was a good scene and it came out that way in the picture. Perhaps I never did quite as well again in a single shot. The reason was that I had put myself, as best I could, in the body of another fellow. Five years later, under different circumstances than make-believe, I had to ask myself the same question. And since that time, no single line in my career has been so effective in explaining to me what an actor's life must be.

So much of our profession is taken up with pretending, with the interpretation of never-never roles, that an actor must spend at least half his waking hours in fantasy, in rehearsal or shooting. If he is only an actor, I feel, he is much like I was in *King's Row*, only half a man—no matter how great his talents. I regard acting with the greatest affection; it has made my life for me. But I realize it tends to become an island of exaggerated importance. During my career on the screen I have commanded excellent salaries, some admiration, fan mail, and a reputation—and my world contracted into not much more than a sound stage, my home, and occasional nights on the town. The circle of my friends closed in. The demands of my work—sometimes as much as fourteen hours a day—cut me off even from my brother Neil, who lived within half a mile of my apartment.

I began to feel like a shut-in invalid, nursed by publicity. I have always liked space, the feeling of freedom, a broad range of friends, and variety (not excluding the publication). Now I had become a semi-automaton "creating" a character another had written, doing what still another person told me to do on the set. Seeing the rushes, I could barely believe the colored shadow on the screen was myself.

Possibly this was the reason I decided to find the rest of me. I loved three things: drama, politics, and sports, and I'm not sure they always come in that order. In all three of them I came out of the monastery of movies into the world. In sports, though I could no longer play top football, I could still swim or ride horseback or simply watch. In motion pictures or television, I could do more than a competent job. In politics, I found myself in the middle of the biggest tohubohu of my life.

As a first-line Irishman, I relished it. There seems to be something blarney-green in the blood of most Sons of the Old Sod—as proved by the recent political history of the country—that gives zest to the shillelagh psyche. I had been lauded as a star in sports and had been praised in movies:

in politics I found myself misrepresented, cursed, vilified, denounced, and libeled. Yet it was by far the most fascinating part of my life.

I suppose my desire to mix into public life was the result of cross-bred genes from both my father and mother. My father was John Edward Reagan (always pronounced Ra-gan), a first-generation black Irishman. He loved shoes. He sold them as a clerk, managed shoe departments and his own stores. He even studied correspondence courses about how to sell more sabots, and spent hours analyzing the bones of the foot. He was a man who might have made a brilliant career out of selling but he lived in a time—and with a weakness—that made him a frustrated man.

I was eleven years old the first time I came home to find my father flat on his back on the front porch and no one there to lend a hand but me. He was drunk, dead to the world. I stood over him for a minute or two. I wanted to let myself in the house and go to bed and pretend he wasn't there. Oh, I wasn't ignorant of his weakness. I don't know at what age I knew what the occasional absences or the loud voices in the night meant, but up till now my mother, Nelle, or my brother handled the situation, and I was a child in bed with the privilege of pretending sleep.

But someplace along the line to each of us, I suppose, must come that first moment of accepting responsibility. If we don't accept it (and some don't), then we must just grow older without quite growing up. I felt myself fill with grief for my father at the same time I was feeling sorry for myself. Seeing his arms spread out as if he were crucified—as indeed he was—his hair soaked with melting snow, snoring as he breathed, I could feel no resentment against him.

That was Nelle's doing. With all the tragedy that was hers because of his occasional bouts with the dark demon in the bottle, she told Neil and myself over and over that alcoholism was a sickness—that we should love and help our father and never condemn him for something that was beyond his control.

I bent over him, smelling the sharp odor of whiskey from the speakeasy. I got a fistful of his overcoat. Opening the door, I managed to drag him inside and get him to bed. In a few days he was the bluff, hearty man I knew and loved and will always remember.

Jack (we all called him by his nickname) was a handsome man—tall, swarthy, and muscular, filled with contradictions of character. A sentimental Democrat who believed fervently in the rights of the workingman—I recall him cursing vehemently about the battle at Herrin in 1922, where twenty-six persons were killed in a massacre brought about by a coalmine strike—he never lost his conviction that the individual must stand on his own feet. Once he caught me fighting in the schoolyard, surrounded by a circle of eggers-on. He stopped the fight, tongue-lashed the crowd—then lifted me a foot in the air with the flat side of his boot. "Not because you were fighting," he said, "but because you weren't winning."

That was my first sample of adult injustice. I *had* been winning.

RONALD REAGAN

First Inaugural Address

(1981)

"Government is not the solution to our problem; government is the problem"

Reagan wrote almost all of his speeches before he ran for president, and in the White House his speechwriters stuck to his established style: conversational, hopeful, and studded with stories and anecdotes, some of which were more historical than others. In his first inaugural address, which he delivered on January 20, 1981, Reagan traded Carter's collective "crisis of confidence" for an America brimming with optimism and individualism.

To a few of us here today, this is a solemn and most momentous occasion, and yet in the history of our nation it is a commonplace occurrence. The orderly transfer of authority as called for in the Constitution routinely takes place, as it has for almost two centuries, and few of us stop to think how unique we really are. In the eyes of many in the world, this every-four-year ceremony we accept as normal is nothing less than a miracle.

Mr. President, I want our fellow citizens to know how much you did to carry on this tradition. By your gracious cooperation in the transition process, you have shown a watching world that we are a united people pledged to maintaining a political system which guarantees individual liberty to a greater degree than any other, and I thank you and your people for all your help in maintaining the continuity which is the bulwark of our republic.

The business of our nation goes forward. These United States are confronted with an economic affliction of great proportions. We suffer from the longest and one of the worst sustained inflations in our national history. It distorts our economic decisions, penalizes thrift, and crushes the struggling young and the fixed-income elderly alike. It threatens to shatter the lives of millions of our people.

Idle industries have cast workers into unemployment, human misery, and personal indignity. Those who do work are denied a fair return for their labor by a tax system which penalizes successful achievement and keeps us from maintaining full productivity.

But great as our tax burden is, it has not kept pace with public spending. For decades we have piled deficit upon deficit, mortgaging our future and our children's future for the temporary convenience of the present. To continue this long trend is to guarantee tremendous social, cultural, political, and economic upheavals.

You and I, as individuals, can, by borrowing, live beyond our means, but for only a limited period of time. Why, then, should we think that collectively, as a nation, we're not bound by that same limitation? We must act today in order to preserve tomorrow. And let there be no misunderstanding: We are going to begin to act, beginning today.

The economic ills we suffer have come upon us over several decades. They will not go away in days, weeks, or months, but they will go away. They will go away because we as Americans have the capacity now, as we've had in the past, to do whatever needs to be done to preserve this last and greatest bastion of freedom.

In this present crisis, government is not the solution to our problem; government is the problem. From time to time we've been tempted to believe that society has become too complex to be managed by self-rule; that government by an elite group is superior to government for, by, and of the people. Well, if no one among us is capable of governing himself, then who among us has the capacity to govern someone else? All of us together, in and out of government, must bear the burden. The solutions we seek must be equitable, with no one group singled out to pay a higher price.

We hear much of special interest groups. Well, our concern must be for a special interest group that has been too long neglected. It knows no sectional boundaries or ethnic and racial divisions, and it crosses political party lines. It is made up of men and women who raise our food, patrol our streets, man our mines and factories, teach our children, keep our homes, and heal us when we're sick—professionals, industrialists, shopkeepers, clerks, cabbies, and truck drivers. They are, in short, "We the people," this breed called Americans.

Well, this administration's objective will be a healthy, vigorous, growing economy that provides equal opportunities for all Americans, with no barriers born of bigotry or discrimination. Putting America back to work means putting all Americans back to work. Ending inflation means freeing all Americans from the terror of runaway living costs. All must share in the productive work of this "new beginning," and all must share in the bounty of a revived economy. With the idealism and fair play which are the core of our system and our strength, we can have a strong and prosperous America, at peace with itself and the world.

So, as we begin, let us take inventory. We are a nation that has a government—not the other way around. And this makes us special among the nations of the earth. Our government has no power except that granted it by the people. It is time to check and reverse the growth of government, which shows signs of having grown beyond the consent of the governed.

It is my intention to curb the size and influence of the federal establishment and to demand recognition of the distinction between the powers granted to the federal government and those reserved to the states or to the people. All of us need to be reminded that the federal government did not create the states; the states created the federal government.

Now, so there will be no misunderstanding, it's not my intention to do away with government. It is rather to make it work—work with us, not over us; to stand by our side, not ride on our back. Government can and must provide opportunity, not smother it; foster productivity, not stifle it.

If we look to the answer as to why for so many years we achieved so much, prospered as no other people on earth, it was because here in this land we unleashed the energy and individual genius of man to a greater extent than has ever been done before. Freedom and the dignity of the individual have been more available and assured here than in any other place on earth. The price for this freedom at times has been high, but we have never been unwilling to pay that price.

It is no coincidence that our present troubles parallel and are proportionate to the intervention and intrusion in our lives that result from unnecessary and excessive growth of government. It is time for us to realize that we're too great a nation to limit ourselves to small dreams. We're not, as some would have us believe, doomed to an inevitable decline. I do not believe in a fate that will fall on us no matter what we do. I do believe in a fate that will fall on us if we do nothing. So, with all the creative energy at our command, let us begin an era of national renewal. Let us renew our determination, our courage, and our strength. And let us renew our faith and our hope.

We have every right to dream heroic dreams. Those who say that we're in a time when there are not heroes, they just don't know where to look. You can see heroes every day going in and out of factory gates. Others, a handful in number, produce enough food to feed all of us and then the world beyond. You meet heroes across a counter, and they're on both sides of that counter. There are entrepreneurs with faith in themselves and faith in an idea who create new jobs, new wealth and opportunity. They're individuals and families whose taxes support the government and whose voluntary gifts support church, charity, culture, art, and education. Their patriotism is quiet, but deep. Their values sustain our national life.

Now, I have used the words "they" and "their" in speaking of these heroes. I could say "you" and "your," because I'm addressing the heroes of whom I speak—you, the citizens of this blessed land. Your dreams, your hopes, your goals are going to be the dreams, the hopes, and the goals of this administration, so help me God.

We shall reflect the compassion that is so much a part of your makeup. How can we love our country and not love our countrymen; and loving them, reach out a hand when they fall, heal them when they're sick, and provide opportunity to make them self-sufficient so they will be equal in fact and not just in theory?

Can we solve the problems confronting us? Well, the answer is an unequivocal and emphatic "yes." To paraphrase Winston Churchill, I did not take the oath I've just taken with the intention of presiding over the dissolution of the world's strongest economy.

In the days ahead I will propose removing the roadblocks that have slowed our economy and reduced productivity. Steps will be taken aimed at restoring the balance between the various levels of government. Progress may be slow, measured in inches and feet, not miles, but we will progress. It is time to reawaken this industrial giant, to get government back within its means, and to lighten our punitive tax burden. And these will be our first priorities, and on these principles there will be no compromise.

On the eve of our struggle for independence a man who might have been one of the greatest among the Founding Fathers, Dr. Joseph Warren, president of the Massachusetts Congress, said to his fellow Americans, "Our country is in danger, but not to be despaired of. . . . On you depend the fortunes of America. You are to decide the important questions upon which rests the happiness and the liberty of millions yet unborn. Act worthy of yourselves."

Well, I believe we, the Americans of today, are ready to act worthy of ourselves, ready to do what must be done to ensure happiness and liberty for ourselves, our children, and our children's children. And as we renew ourselves here in our own land, we will be seen as having greater strength throughout the world. We will again be the exemplar of freedom and a beacon of hope for those who do not now have freedom.

To those neighbors and allies who share our freedom, we will strengthen our historic ties and assure them of our support and firm commitment. We will match loyalty with loyalty. We will strive for mutually beneficial relations. We will not use our friendship to impose on their sovereignty, for our own sovereignty is not for sale.

As for the enemies of freedom, those who are potential adversaries, they will be reminded that peace is the highest aspiration of the American people. We will negotiate for it, sacrifice for it; we will not surrender for it, now or ever.

Our forbearance should never be misunderstood. Our reluctance for conflict should not be misjudged as a failure of will. When action is required to preserve our national security, we will act. We will maintain sufficient strength to prevail if need be, knowing that if we do so we have the best chance of never having to use that strength.

Above all, we must realize that no arsenal or no weapon in the arsenals of the world is so formidable as the will and moral courage of free men and women. It is a weapon our adversaries in today's world do not have. It is a weapon that we as Americans do have. Let that be understood by those who practice terrorism and prey upon their neighbors.

I'm told that tens of thousands of prayer meetings are being held on this day, and for that I'm deeply grateful. We are a nation under God, and I believe God intended for us to be free. It would be fitting and good, I think, if on each inaugural day in future years it should be declared a day of prayer.

This is the first time in our history that this ceremony has been held, as you've been told, on this west front of the Capitol. Standing here, one faces a magnificent vista, opening up on this city's special beauty and history. At the end of this open mall are those shrines to the giants on whose shoulders we stand.

Directly in front of me, the monument to a monumental man, George Washington, father of our country. A man of humility who came to greatness reluctantly. He led America out of revolutionary victory into infant nationhood. Off to one side, the stately memorial to Thomas Jefferson. The Declaration of Independence flames with his eloquence. And then, beyond the Reflecting Pool, the dignified columns of the Lincoln Memorial. Whoever would understand in his heart the meaning of America will find it in the life of Abraham Lincoln.

Beyond those monuments to heroism is the Potomac River, and on the far shore the sloping hills of Arlington National Cemetery, with its row upon row of simple white markers bearing crosses or Stars of David. They add up to only a tiny fraction of the price that has been paid for our freedom.

Each one of those markers is a monument to the kind of hero I spoke of earlier. Their lives ended in places called Belleau Wood, The Argonne, Omaha Beach, Salerno, and halfway around the world on Guadalcanal, Tarawa, Pork Chop Hill, the Chosin Reservoir, and in a hundred rice paddies and jungles of a place called Vietnam.

Under one such marker lies a young man, Martin Treptow, who left his job in a small-town barbershop in 1917 to go to France with the famed Rainbow Division. There, on the western front, he was killed trying to carry a message between battalions under heavy artillery fire.

We are told that on his body was found a diary. On the flyleaf under the heading, "My Pledge," he had written these words: "America must win this war. Therefore I will work, I will save, I will sacrifice, I will endure, I will fight cheerfully and do my utmost, as if the issue of the whole struggle depended on me alone."

The crisis we are facing today does not require of us the kind of sacrifice that Martin Treptow and so many thousands of others were called upon to make. It does require, however, our best effort and our willingness to believe in ourselves and to believe in our capacity to perform great deeds, to believe that together with God's help we can and will resolve the problems which now confront us.

And after all, why shouldn't we believe that? We are Americans.

RONALD REAGAN

Address on the *Challenger* Explosion

(1986)

"Nothing ends here; our hopes and our journeys continue"

On the morning of January 28, 1986, the Challenger *space shuttle and its crew disintegrated in a fiery explosion, just after takeoff. Reagan's State of the Union had been scheduled for that night. Instead, the president gave the following address, mourning the crew and connecting them to America's history of exploration.*

Ladies and gentlemen, I'd planned to speak to you tonight to report on the state of the union, but the events of earlier today have led me to change those plans. Today is a day for mourning and remembering. Nancy and I are pained to the core by the tragedy of the shuttle *Challenger*. We know we share this pain with all of the people of our country. This is truly a national loss.

Nineteen years ago, almost to the day, we lost three astronauts in a terrible accident on the ground. But we've never lost an astronaut in flight; we've never had a tragedy like this. And perhaps we've forgotten the courage it took for the crew of the shuttle. But they, the *Challenger* Seven, were aware of the dangers, but overcame them and did their jobs brilliantly. We mourn seven heroes: Michael Smith, Dick Scobee, Judith Resnik, Ronald McNair, Ellison Onizuka, Gregory Jarvis, and Christa McAuliffe. We mourn their loss as a nation together.

For the families of the seven, we cannot bear, as you do, the full impact of this tragedy. But we feel the loss, and we're thinking about you so very much. Your loved ones were daring and brave, and they had that special grace, that special spirit that says, "Give me a challenge, and I'll meet it with joy." They had a hunger to explore the universe and discover its truths. They wished to serve, and they did. They served all of us.

We've grown used to wonders in this century. It's hard to dazzle us. But for twenty-five years the United States space program has been doing just that. We've grown used to the idea of space, and perhaps we forget that we've only just begun. We're still pioneers. They, the members of the *Challenger* crew, were pioneers.

And I want to say something to the schoolchildren of America who were watching the live coverage of the shuttle's takeoff. I know it is hard to understand, but sometimes painful things like this happen. It's all part of the process of exploration and discovery. It's all part of taking a chance and expanding man's horizons. The future doesn't belong to the fainthearted; it belongs to the brave. The *Challenger* crew was pulling us into the future, and we'll continue to follow them.

I've always had great faith in and respect for our space program, and what happened today does nothing to diminish it. We don't hide our space program. We don't keep secrets and cover things up. We do it all up front and in public. That's the way freedom is, and we wouldn't change it for a minute.

We'll continue our quest in space. There will be more shuttle flights and more shuttle crews and, yes, more volunteers, more civilians, more teachers in space. Nothing ends here; our hopes and our journeys continue. I want to add that I wish I could talk to every man and woman who works for NASA or who worked on this mission and tell them: "Your dedication and professionalism have moved and impressed us for decades. And we know of your anguish. We share it."

There's a coincidence today. On this day, three hundred and ninety years ago, the great explorer Sir Francis Drake died aboard ship off the coast of Panama. In his lifetime the great frontiers were the oceans, and a historian later said, "He lived by the sea, died on it, and was buried in it." Well, today we can say of the *Challenger* crew: Their dedication was, like Drake's, complete.

The crew of the space shuttle *Challenger* honored us by the manner in which they lived their lives. We will never forget them, nor the last time we saw them, this morning, as they prepared for their journey and waved goodbye and "slipped the surly bonds of earth" to "touch the face of God."

RONALD REAGAN

From His Address at Germany's Brandenburg Gate

(1987)

"Mr. Gorbachev, tear down this wall!"

On June 12, 1987, Reagan gave his own speech in Berlin. While his other speeches did arguably more to shape the Cold War—"the ash heap of history," "the evil empire"—this one gave Reagan his most memorable line, when he told his Soviet counterpart, Mikhail Gorbachev, to tear down the Berlin Wall. According to Reagan's speechwriter, Peter Robinson, the line barely made it in. When drafts of the speech circulated at various levels of government, as drafts of this sort of speech always do, an army of diplomats urged the White House to cut it. But Reagan liked the line. "It's going to drive the State Department boys crazy," he told an aide on the ride to the wall, "but I'm going to leave it in."

Twenty-four years ago, President John F. Kennedy visited Berlin, speaking to the people of this city and the world at the city hall. Well, since then two other presidents have come, each in his turn, to Berlin. And today I, myself, make my second visit to your city.

We come to Berlin, we American presidents, because it's our duty to speak, in this place, of freedom. But I must confess, we're drawn here by other things as well: by the feeling of history in this city, more than five hundred years older than our own nation; by the beauty of the Grunewald and the Tiergarten; most of all, by your courage and determination. Perhaps the composer Paul Lincke understood something about American presidents. You see, like so many presidents before me, I come here today because wherever I go, whatever I do: "Ich hab noch einen Koffer in Berlin." [*I still have a suitcase in Berlin.*]

Our gathering today is being broadcast throughout Western Europe and North America. I understand that it is being seen and heard as well in the east. To those listening throughout Eastern Europe, I extend my warmest greetings and the good will of the American people. To those listening in East Berlin, a special word: Although I cannot be with you, I address my remarks to you just as surely as to those standing here before me. For I join you, as I join your fellow countrymen in the west, in this firm, this unalterable belief: Es gibt nur ein Berlin. [*There is only one Berlin.*]

Behind me stands a wall that encircles the free sectors of this city, part of a vast system of barriers that divides the entire continent of Europe. From the Baltic, south, those barriers cut across Germany in a gash of barbed wire, concrete, dog runs, and guard towers. Farther south, there may be no visible, no obvious wall. But there remain armed guards and checkpoints all the same—still a restriction on the right to travel, still an instrument to impose upon ordinary men and women the will of a totalitarian state. Yet it is here in Berlin where the wall emerges most clearly, here, cutting across your city, where the news photo and the television screen have imprinted this brutal division of a continent upon the mind of the world. Standing before the Brandenburg Gate, every man is a German, separated from his fellow men. Every man is a Berliner, forced to look upon a scar.

President [Richard] von Weizsacker has said: "The German question is open as long as the Brandenburg Gate is closed." Today I say: As long as this gate is closed, as long as this scar of a wall is permitted to stand, it is not the German question alone that remains open, but the question of freedom for all mankind. Yet I do not come here to lament. For I find in Berlin a message of hope, even in the shadow of this wall, a message of triumph.

In this season of spring in 1945, the people of Berlin emerged from their air raid shelters to find devastation. Thousands of miles away, the people of the United States reached out to help. And in 1947 Secretary of State—as you've been told—George Marshall announced the creation of what would become known as the Marshall Plan. Speaking precisely 40 years ago this month, he said: "Our policy is directed not against any country or doctrine, but against hunger, poverty, desperation, and chaos."

In the Reichstag a few moments ago, I saw a display commemorating this fortieth anniversary of the Marshall Plan. I was struck by the sign on a burned-out, gutted structure that was being rebuilt. I understand that Berliners of my own generation can remember seeing signs like it dotted throughout the western sectors of the city. The sign read simply: "The Marshall Plan is helping here to strengthen the free world." A strong, free world in the west, that dream became real. Japan rose from ruin to become an economic giant. Italy, France, Belgium—virtually every nation in Western Europe saw political and economic rebirth; the European Community was founded.

In West Germany and here in Berlin, there took place an economic miracle, the Wirtschaftswunder. Adenauer, Erhard, Reuter, and other leaders understood the practical importance of liberty—that just as truth can flourish only when the journalist is given freedom of speech, so prosperity can come about only when the farmer and businessman enjoy economic freedom. The German leaders reduced tariffs, expanded free trade, lowered taxes. From 1950 to 1960 alone, the standard of living in West Germany and Berlin doubled.

Where four decades ago there was rubble, today in West Berlin there is the greatest industrial output of any city in Germany—busy office blocks, fine homes and apartments, proud avenues, and the spreading lawns of parkland. Where a city's culture seemed to have been destroyed, today there are two great universities, orchestras and an opera, countless theaters, and museums. Where there was want, today there's abundance—food, clothing, automobiles—the wonderful goods of the Ku'damm. From devastation, from utter ruin, you Berliners have, in freedom, rebuilt a city that once again ranks as one of the greatest on earth. The Soviets may have had other plans. But, my friends, there were a few things the Soviets didn't count on: Berliner Herz, Berliner Humor, ja, und Berliner Schnauze. [*Berliner heart, Berliner humor, yes, and a Berliner schnauze.*]

In the 1950s, Khrushchev predicted: "We will bury you." But in the west today, we see a free world that has achieved a level of prosperity and well-being unprecedented in all human history. In the Communist world, we see failure, technological backwardness, declining standards of health, even want of the most basic kind—too little food. Even today, the Soviet Union still cannot feed itself. After these four decades, then, there stands before the entire world one great and inescapable conclusion: freedom leads to prosperity. Freedom replaces the ancient hatreds among the nations with comity and peace. Freedom is the victor.

And now the Soviets themselves may, in a limited way, be coming to understand the importance of freedom. We hear much from Moscow about a new policy of reform and openness. Some political prisoners have been released. Certain foreign news broadcasts are no longer being jammed. Some economic enterprises have been permitted to operate with greater freedom from state control. Are these the beginnings of profound changes in the Soviet state? Or are they token gestures, intended to raise false hopes in the west, or to strengthen the Soviet system without changing it? We welcome change and openness, for we believe that freedom and security go together, that the advance of human liberty can only strengthen the cause of world peace.

There is one sign the Soviets can make that would be unmistakable, that would advance dramatically the cause of freedom and peace. General Secretary Gorbachev, if you seek peace, if you seek prosperity for the Soviet Union and Eastern Europe, if you seek liberalization: Come here to this gate. Mr. Gorbachev, open this gate! Mr. Gorbachev, tear down this wall!

I understand the fear of war and the pain of division that afflict this continent—and I pledge to you my country's efforts to help overcome these burdens. To be sure, we in the west must resist Soviet expansion, so we must maintain defenses of unassailable strength. Yet we seek peace, so we must strive to reduce arms on both sides. Beginning ten years ago, the Soviets challenged the western alliance with a grave new threat, hundreds of new and more deadly SS-20 nuclear missiles, capable of striking every capital in Europe. The western alliance responded by committing itself to a counter-deployment unless the Soviets agreed to negotiate a better solution—namely, the elimination of such weapons on both sides. For many months, the Soviets refused to bargain in earnestness. As the alliance, in turn, prepared to go forward with its counter-deployment, there were difficult days—days of protests like those during my 1982 visit to this city—and the Soviets later walked away from the table.

But through it all, the alliance held firm. And I invite those who protested then—I invite those who protest today—to mark this fact: Because we remained strong, the Soviets came back to the table. And because we remained strong, today we have within reach the possibility, not merely of limiting the growth of arms, but of eliminating, for the first time, an entire class of nuclear weapons from the face of the Earth. As I speak, NATO ministers are meeting in Iceland to review the progress of our proposals for eliminating these weapons. At the talks in Geneva, we have also proposed deep cuts in strategic offensive weapons. And the western allies have likewise made far-reaching proposals to reduce the danger of conventional war and to place a total ban on chemical weapons.

While we pursue these arms reductions, I pledge to you that we will maintain the capacity to deter Soviet aggression at any level at which it might occur. And in cooperation with many of our allies, the United States is pursuing the Strategic Defense Initiative research to base deterrence not on the threat of offensive retaliation, but on defenses that truly defend—on systems, in short, that will not target populations, but shield them. By these means we seek to increase the safety of Europe and all the world. But we must remember a crucial fact: east and west do not mistrust each other because we are armed; we are armed because we mistrust each other. And our differences are not about weapons but about liberty. When President Kennedy spoke at the City Hall those 24 years ago, freedom was encircled, Berlin was under siege. And today, despite all the pressures upon this city, Berlin stands secure in its liberty. And freedom itself is transforming the globe. . . .

In these four decades, as I have said, you Berliners have built a great city. You've done so in spite of threats—the Soviet attempts to impose the East-mark, the blockade. Today the city thrives in spite of the challenges implicit in the very presence of this wall. What keeps you here? Certainly there's a great deal to be said for your fortitude, for your defiant courage. But I believe there's something deeper, something that involves Berlin's whole look and feel and way of life—not mere sentiment. No one could live long in Berlin without being completely disabused of illusions. Something instead, that has seen the difficulties of life in Berlin but chose to accept them, that continues to build this good and proud city in contrast to a surrounding totalitarian presence that refuses to release human energies or aspirations. Something that speaks with a powerful voice of affirmation, that says yes to this city, yes to the future, yes to freedom. In a word, I would submit that what keeps you in Berlin is love—love both profound and abiding.

Perhaps this gets to the root of the matter, to the most fundamental distinction of all between east and west. The totalitarian world produces backwardness because it does such violence to the spirit, thwarting the human impulse to create, to enjoy, to worship. The totalitarian world finds even symbols of love and of worship an affront. Years ago, before the East Germans began rebuilding their churches, they erected a secular structure: the television tower at Alexander Platz. Virtually ever since, the authorities have been working to correct what they view as the tower's one major flaw, treating the glass sphere at the top with paints and chemicals of every kind. Yet even today when the sun strikes that sphere—that sphere that towers over all Berlin—the light makes the sign of the cross. There in Berlin, like the city itself, symbols of love, symbols of worship, cannot be suppressed.

As I looked out a moment ago from the Reichstag, that embodiment of German unity, I noticed words crudely spray-painted upon the wall, perhaps by a young Berliner, "This wall will fall. Beliefs become reality." Yes, across Europe, this wall will fall. For it cannot withstand faith; it cannot withstand truth. The wall cannot withstand freedom.

GEORGE H. W. BUSH

Address on the Gulf War

(1990)

"America will stand by her friends"

*On August 2, 1990, Saddam Hussein and Iraq invaded Kuwait. Six days later,
George H. W. Bush deployed fresh American troops to the Middle East—and gave
an Oval Office address explaining why. Bush linked his decision to international
strategies that stretched back to Franklin D. Roosevelt. But he also called this
"a new era." With the Cold War winding down, America turned its attention to
the Middle East and its oil. By building coalitions and delivering speeches like
this one, Bush started a process that would soon lead to Operation Desert Storm.*

In the life of a nation, we're called upon to define who we are and what
we believe. Sometimes these choices are not easy. But today as president,
I ask for your support in a decision I've made to stand up for what's right
and condemn what's wrong, all in the cause of peace.

At my direction, elements of the 82nd Airborne Division, as well as
key units of the United States Air Force, are arriving today to take up
defensive positions in Saudi Arabia. I took this action to assist the Saudi
Arabian government in the defense of its homeland. No one commits
America's armed forces to a dangerous mission lightly, but after perhaps
unparalleled international consultation and exhausting every alternative,
it became necessary to take this action. Let me tell you why.

Less than a week ago, in the early morning hours of August 2nd, Iraqi
armed forces, without provocation or warning, invaded a peaceful Kuwait.

Facing negligible resistance from its much smaller neighbor, Iraq's tanks stormed in blitzkrieg fashion through Kuwait in a few short hours. With more than 100,000 troops, along with tanks, artillery, and surface-to-surface missiles, Iraq now occupies Kuwait. This aggression came just hours after Saddam Hussein specifically assured numerous countries in the area that there would be no invasion. There is no justification whatsoever for this outrageous and brutal act of aggression.

A puppet regime imposed from the outside is unacceptable. The acquisition of territory by force is unacceptable. No one, friend or foe, should doubt our desire for peace; and no one should underestimate our determination to confront aggression.

Four simple principles guide our policy. First, we seek the immediate, unconditional, and complete withdrawal of all Iraqi forces from Kuwait. Second, Kuwait's legitimate government must be restored to replace the puppet regime. And third, my administration, as has been the case with every president from President Roosevelt to President Reagan, is committed to the security and stability of the Persian Gulf. And fourth, I am determined to protect the lives of American citizens abroad.

Immediately after the Iraqi invasion, I ordered an embargo of all trade with Iraq and, together with many other nations, announced sanctions that both freeze all Iraqi assets in this country and protected Kuwait's assets. The stakes are high. Iraq is already a rich and powerful country that possesses the world's second largest reserves of oil and over a million men under arms. It's the fourth largest military in the world. Our country now imports nearly half the oil it consumes and could face a major threat to its economic independence. Much of the world is even more dependent upon imported oil and is even more vulnerable to Iraqi threats.

We succeeded in the struggle for freedom in Europe because we and our allies remain stalwart. Keeping the peace in the Middle East will require no less. We're beginning a new era. This new era can be full of promise, an age of freedom, a time of peace for all peoples. But if history teaches us anything, it is that we must resist aggression or it will destroy our freedoms. Appeasement does not work. As was the case in the 1930s, we see in Saddam Hussein an aggressive dictator threatening his neighbors. Only fourteen days ago, Saddam Hussein promised his friends he would not invade Kuwait. And four days ago, he promised the world he would withdraw. And twice we have seen what his promises mean—his promises mean nothing.

In the last few days, I've spoken with political leaders from the Middle East, Europe, Asia, and the Americas, and I've met with Prime Minister

Thatcher, Prime Minister Mulroney, and NATO Secretary General Woerner. And all agree that Iraq cannot be allowed to benefit from its invasion of Kuwait.

We agree that this is not an American problem or a European problem or a Middle East problem—it is the world's problem. And that's why, soon after the Iraqi invasion, the United Nations Security Council, without dissent, condemned Iraq, calling for the immediate and unconditional withdrawal of its troops from Kuwait. The Arab world, through both the Arab League and the Gulf Cooperation Council, courageously announced its opposition to Iraqi aggression. Japan, the United Kingdom, and France, and other governments around the world have imposed severe sanctions. The Soviet Union and China ended all arms sales to Iraq.

And this past Monday, the United Nations Security Council approved for the first time in twenty-three years mandatory sanctions under Chapter VII of the United Nations Charter. These sanctions, now enshrined in international law, have the potential to deny Iraq the fruits of aggression while sharply limiting its ability to either import or export anything of value, especially oil.

I pledge here today that the United States will do its part to see that these sanctions are effective and to induce Iraq to withdraw without delay from Kuwait.

But we must recognize that Iraq may not stop using force to advance its ambitions. Iraq has massed an enormous war machine on the Saudi border capable of initiating hostilities with little or no additional preparation. Given the Iraqi government's history of aggression against its own citizens, as well as its neighbors, to assume Iraq will not attack again would be unwise and unrealistic.

And therefore, after consulting with King Fahd, I sent Secretary of Defense Dick Cheney to discuss cooperative measures we could take. Following those meetings, the Saudi government requested our help, and I responded to that request by ordering U.S. air and ground forces to deploy to the Kingdom of Saudi Arabia.

Let me be clear: The sovereign independence of Saudi Arabia is of vital interest to the United States. This decision, which I shared with the congressional leadership, grows out of the longstanding friendship and security relationship between the United States and Saudi Arabia. U.S. forces will work together with those of Saudi Arabia and other nations to preserve the integrity of Saudi Arabia and to deter further Iraqi aggression. Through their presence, as well as through training and exercises, these multinational forces will enhance the overall capability of Saudi armed forces to defend the Kingdom.

I want to be clear about what we are doing and why. America does not seek conflict, nor do we seek to chart the destiny of other nations. But America will stand by her friends. The mission of our troops is wholly defensive. Hopefully, they will not be needed long. They will not initiate hostilities, but they will defend themselves, the Kingdom of Saudi Arabia, and other friends in the Persian Gulf.

We are working around the clock to deter Iraqi aggression and to enforce U.N. sanctions. I'm continuing my conversations with world leaders. Secretary of Defense Cheney has just returned from valuable consultations with President Mubarak of Egypt and King Hassan of Morocco. Secretary of State Baker has consulted with his counterparts in many nations, including the Soviet Union, and today he heads for Europe to consult with President Ozal of Turkey, a staunch friend of the United States. And he'll then consult with the NATO Foreign Ministers.

I will ask oil-producing nations to do what they can to increase production in order to minimize any impact that oil flow reductions will have on the world economy. And I will explore whether we and our allies should draw down our strategic petroleum reserves. Conservation measures can also help; Americans everywhere must do their part. And one more thing: I'm asking the oil companies to do their fair share. They should show restraint and not abuse today's uncertainties to raise prices.

Standing up for our principles will not come easy. It may take time and possibly cost a great deal. But we are asking no more of anyone than of the brave young men and women of our Armed Forces and their families. And I ask that in the churches around the country prayers be said for those who are committed to protect and defend America's interests.

Standing up for our principle is an American tradition. As it has so many times before, it may take time and tremendous effort, but most of all, it will take unity of purpose. As I've witnessed throughout my life in both war and peace, America has never wavered when her purpose is driven by principle. And on this August day, at home and abroad, I know she will do no less.

BILL CLINTON

Address at the Memorial for the Oklahoma City Bombing

(1995)

> "You have lost too much, but you have not lost everything. And you have certainly not lost America, for we will stand with you for as many tomorrows as it takes"

As president, Bill Clinton excelled at describing policy ideas in a punchy fashion—in promising to "end welfare as we know it" and to "save Social Security first." (As those examples suggest, Clinton also excelled at triangulation.) Still, his White House's rhetorical high point occurred during a tragedy. On April 23, 1995, four days after the Oklahoma City bombing, Clinton traveled to that city for a memorial service. Like Reagan after the Challenger *disaster, Clinton found the words to comfort a nation beset by grief.*

To the families of those who have been lost and wounded, to the people of Oklahoma City who have endured so much, and the people of this wonderful state, to all of you who are here as our fellow Americans—I am honored to be here today to represent the American people. But I have to tell you that Hillary and I also come as parents, as husband and wife, as people who were your neighbors for some of the best years of our lives.

Today our nation joins with you in grief. We mourn with you. We share your hope against hope that some may still survive. We thank all those who have worked so heroically to save lives and to solve this crime, those here in Oklahoma and those who are all across this great land and many who left their own lives to come here to work hand in hand with you.

We pledge to do all we can to help you heal the injured, to rebuild this city, and to bring to justice those who did this evil.

This terrible sin took the lives of our American family: innocent children, in that building only because their parents were trying to be good parents as well as good workers; citizens in the building going about their daily business; and many there who served the rest of us, who worked to help the elderly and the disabled, who worked to support our farmers and our veterans, who worked to enforce our laws and to protect us. Let us say clearly, they served us well, and we are grateful. But for so many of you they were also neighbors and friends. You saw them at church or the PTA meetings, at the civic clubs, at the ballpark. You know them in ways that all the rest of America could not.

And to all the members of the families here present who have suffered loss, though we share your grief, your pain is unimaginable, and we know that. We cannot undo it. That is God's work.

Our words seem small beside the loss you have endured. But I found a few I wanted to share today. I've received a lot of letters in these last terrible days. One stood out because it came from a young widow and a mother of three whose own husband was murdered with over two hundred other Americans when Pan Am 103 was shot down. Here is what that woman said I should say to you today:

The anger you feel is valid, but you must not allow yourselves to be consumed by it. The hurt you feel must not be allowed to turn into hate but instead into the search for justice. The loss you feel must not paralyze your own lives. Instead, you must try to pay tribute to your loved ones by continuing to do all the things they left undone, thus ensuring they did not die in vain.

Wise words from one who also knows.

You have lost too much, but you have not lost everything. And you have certainly not lost America, for we will stand with you for as many tomorrows as it takes.

If ever we needed evidence of that, I could only recall the words of Governor and Mrs. Keating. If anybody thinks that Americans are mostly mean and selfish, they ought to come to Oklahoma. If anybody thinks Americans have lost the capacity for love and caring and courage, they ought to come to Oklahoma.

To all my fellow Americans beyond this hall, I say, one thing we owe those who have sacrificed is the duty to purge ourselves of the dark forces which gave rise to this evil. They are forces that threaten our common peace, our freedom, our way of life.

Let us teach our children that the God of comfort is also the God of righteousness. Those who trouble their own house will inherit the wind. Justice will prevail.

Let us let our own children know that we will stand against the forces of fear. When there is talk of hatred, let us stand up and talk against it. When there is talk of violence, let us stand up and talk against it. In the face of death, let us honor life. As St. Paul admonished us, let us not be overcome by evil but overcome evil with good.

Yesterday, Hillary and I had the privilege of speaking with some children of other federal employees, children like those who were lost here. And one little girl said something we will never forget. She said we should all plant a tree in memory of the children. So this morning before we got on the plane to come here, at the White House, we planted that tree in honor of the children of Oklahoma. It was a dogwood with its wonderful spring flower and its deep, enduring roots. It embodies the lesson of the Psalms that the life of a good person is like a tree whose leaf does not wither.

My fellow Americans, a tree takes a long time to grow, and wounds take a long time to heal. But we must begin. Those who are lost now belong to God. Some day we will be with them. But until that happens, their legacy must be our lives.

BILL CLINTON

From His Address on the Progressive Tradition

(2000)

"What does the nation mean? What does it mean to be an American?"

Another of Clinton's punchy policy descriptions, delivered during his 1996 State of the Union, was that "the era of big government is over." And yet, near the end of his second term, Clinton attended a conference at Princeton University on the history of progressivism. While the president was there to receive the Whig-Cliosophic Society's James Madison Award, he also gave a speech arguing that his administration fit into that progressive history. Like most presidents, Clinton was a passionate student of the past, regularly reading late into the night, even in the White House. ("It would almost always be biography," one aide recalled, "almost always something in relation to the presidency.") To connect his policies to Wilson's and Roosevelt's, however, Clinton had to invoke not progressive ideals but progressive methods—making his own case for an active presidency along the way.

You know, James Madison is a very important figure to every American and every president who cares, in particular, about the framework and history of the Constitution. But it's interesting to me that he actually participated in debates here in the eighteenth century, including one with Aaron Burr, where Madison was the Whig and Burr was the Clio. It was that debate that produced a memorable line that is too often attributed to me: The era of Whig Government is over.

I must say, when I first saw the program for this conference, I felt some ambivalence. The student in me wanted to come here and stay for the whole thing. But the politician in me wondered what in the living daylights I was doing here. I'm supposed to lead off a group of people whose books I have read, who know more about the subject I'm supposed to address than I ever will.

I can say that I had some unique experience in carrying on the progressive tradition. I always felt that the work we did the last eight years made us the heir of Theodore Roosevelt and Woodrow Wilson—Al Gore and me, our entire administration. And I have a fascination with that period of history.

I own a lot of Theodore Roosevelt's books in the first edition, including a fascinating account of how he organized the Rough Riders. I've also got a wonderful book that Owen Wister, the writer of westerns, wrote about his friendship with Theodore Roosevelt, when, like many of you, they were undergraduates together at Harvard. The other day I acquired Joseph Tumulty's book—he was Woodrow Wilson's private secretary—about his relationship with President Wilson, both as governor and as president. It's a fascinating account of the time, by someone who was admittedly biased but still had a unique perspective.

So I've thought a lot about this period. And I suppose as a politician, I should give myself the leeway of quoting Theodore Roosevelt, who said in his speech on the New Nationalism, "I do not speak merely from a historical standpoint. It is of little use for us to pay lip service to the mighty men of the past, unless we sincerely endeavor to apply those qualities to the problems of the present."

It is in that spirit that I would like to say a few words today, about the progressive tradition, about what it means for today and how it is part, I believe, of a larger ongoing debate in American history about the whole idea of America. What does the nation mean? What does it mean to be an American?

The progressives thought we could only keep faith with the past by keeping faith with the future. Their time had much in common with ours, and therefore, our responsibilities have much in common with theirs, to preserve what is enduring but to adapt our nation time and again to what is new.

Woodrow Wilson said, "It behooves us once again to stand face to face with our ideals, to renew our enthusiasm, to reckon again our duties, to take fresh views of our aims, and fresh courage for their pursuit." These words ring with relevance for your time. Not simply because we stand at the dawn of a new century, as Wilson and Roosevelt did, but because this time, like theirs, is characterized by swift and stunning change.

Like the industrial revolution, this information revolution is a true seismic shift. It alters forever the way we work, live, relate to each other and those beyond our borders. The consequences of the digital chip, nano-technology, the internet, and the sequencing of the human genome will be every bit as profound, if not more profound, than those of the telephone, the assembly line, and the vast migration of Americans to the cities and the opening of America to its first great wave of immigrants.

But these are only the most obvious parallels between the Progressive Era and what I call this time, the last time I came to Princeton, a New Progressive Era. I also believe in a larger sense the Progressive Era and this time represent two of the five pivotal points in American history, when we have been called upon to reaffirm and to redefine not just the role of government for new times but the very idea of the American nation.

That debate has gone on from the beginning. First there was the debate which George Washington, Alexander Hamilton, and John Marshall won over Thomas Jefferson and his friends, about whether we were preeminently going to be one nation or a just a little bit stronger confederation of states. I have to say out of deference to Mr. Jefferson that after he became president, I suspect he was glad he lost the argument, as he sent out Lewis and Clark, imposed the infamous embargo, and bought Louisiana, which at the time cost the equivalent of one full year's budget of the federal government.

Can you imagine what would happen if I came to the Congress and said, "Have I got a deal for you—just $1.9 trillion. What difference does it make?"

The second great debate we had about the idea of the nation occurred obviously in the days leading up to and during and immediately after the Civil War, when Abraham Lincoln saved the Union by moving it closer to the true ideals of the Declaration of Independence and, as Gary Wills has so brilliantly argued, literally redefining the Constitution closer toward those ideals, in the Gettysburg Address.

The third great point was in the Progressive Era, when Woodrow Wilson and Theodore Roosevelt presided over an America fully entering the industrial revolution.

Then the fourth time was during the New Deal, the Second World War, and its immediate aftermath with the dawn of the Cold War, when

Franklin Roosevelt and Harry Truman gave us our first comprehensive social safety net and an institutionalized commitment to American leadership for peace and freedom in the world.

Now, at the dawn of this global information age, Al Gore and I have been working to adapt all of the domestic and foreign policies of the United States to these sweeping changes in science and technology, in social diversity and pluralism, and in increasing global interdependence.

History has taught Americans not to stand passively in the face of change. What the progressive presidents understood so clearly, from Teddy Roosevelt to Wilson to FDR and Truman to Kennedy and Johnson, is the understanding that America either will shape change or be shaped by it. As I've already said, I believe the time in which we live bears the most resemblance to the Progressive Era. But there are also elements of those other great hinge points in American history in this time, too.

You can see it in the fight we had with the Republican Congress that led to the shutdown of the government. You can see it in our efforts to build one America across all the lines that divide us. You can see it in our struggle to end genocide and ethnic cleansing in the Balkans and to build binding ties to Africa, Latin American, and Asian nations with whom we have not been closely aligned in the past.

The central lesson of the progressive is that you either have to shape change consistent with your values, or you will be shaped by it in ways that make it more difficult for you to live by your values. To retreat from responsibility is to invite instability. To embrace the obligation of leadership has consistently under progressive times led to better lives for all Americans.

Wilson and Roosevelt made an enemy of outdated orthodoxy, replacing them with what Teddy's famous cousin Franklin Roosevelt called "bold, persistent experimentation." As many of the scholars here have argued, and doubtless will argue with greater clarity than I can, the progressive legacy is not primarily a set of programs that no longer have great relevance to us but a vital set of principles—the idea that new conditions demand a new approach to government.

When Teddy Roosevelt became president, few Americans looked to him, to his office, or even to their government to solve their problems. At the end of the nineteenth century, the White House was weak; the Congress was at the mercy of special interests. Roosevelt's genius was to redefine the role of government and the role of the president, to protect the public interest, and to act as an accountable agent of change. This is an ideal as old as Madison, but Roosevelt and Wilson gave it new meaning for a new era. What is its meaning today?

When I ran for president in 1992, our government was discredited. In fact, you could hardly run for president unless you had something bad to say about the government. Indeed, part of the political genius of the ascendency of President Reagan and his associates was to attain power by discrediting the very idea of government. They basically were able to say things like, "Government couldn't run a bake sale. The government would mess up a two-car parade." And they found huge majorities of Americans sort of nodding their heads.

Those in the progressive tradition, I believe, had given them some ammunition by clinging to old programs, bureaucracies, and approaches that no longer worked. Then the conservatives used the failures as an excuse to do nothing on the domestic front. Some of our leaders literally made a virtue of their endless capacity to tell the American people how bad the government was. And then when those who were reacting against the progressive tradition took power, they seemed determined to prove it by digging us a huge budgetary hole, quadrupling the nation's debt in twelve years. So our economy sank; our society became considerably more divided; and predictably, public confidence in our democratic government collapsed.

That's why, when I ran in 1992, I said that it would be necessary to change our party, change our national leadership, and change our nation. Al Gore and I believed that we had to find a new way, something now popularly called around the world "a third way," a way back to enduring values, a way beyond a government profoundly indifferent to people's problems, a way forward to meet the challenges of today and tomorrow.

We committed to reinvent government so it could function as it does best in an information society, as a catalyst, a partner to the private sector in creating opportunity, jobs, and hope and providing our citizens with the tools they need to make the most of their own lives. That, too, of course, is a principle as old as our republic: opportunity for all.

And whether we're talking about the information age, the industrial age, or the turn from the eighteenth to the nineteenth century, economic growth and opportunity have always gone hand in hand. That's why we set out to build an economic strategy that would work for this time, rooted in fiscal discipline, investment in our people and our future, and expanding our economic ties with the rest of the world. Well, lucky for us, or I wouldn't be here talking today, it's worked out pretty well.

We've gone from record deficits to record surpluses. Our economy has created twenty-two million jobs. We're in the midst of the longest economic expansion in history. But in the progressive tradition, to use President Kennedy's words, the rising economy is lifting all boats. The Census Bureau reports that in the last year, typical household income rose to the highest level ever recorded, breaking $40,000 for the first time—up since 1993 by $6,300, after inflation. The poverty rate has fallen to 11.8 percent, the lowest in twenty years. Senior poverty is below 10 percent for the first time ever. Child poverty dropped by the largest amount since 1966. Hispanic and African American poverty are the lowest since separate statistics have been kept. Since 1993, seven million Americans have moved out of poverty, over two million last year alone.

Now, a century ago, economic growth was generated by large industrial organizations, popularly called the trust then. Today, economic growth is largely generated by big ideas, which is why there are so many young people like you making a fortune in dot-com companies.

The antitrust provisions and worker provisions that were developed in the Progressive Era to make the economy work and to give more people a chance to share in it still matter today. And they have been built on, modified, and changed, but they still matter today. But today we need even more focus on boosting ideas and innovation, creating the conditions for prosperity, and again, giving everybody the tools they need to succeed in a very different and, in some ways, much less organized world.

You can see our efforts there, just for example in the Telecommunications Act of 1996, where the vice president and I fought for the E-rate so that the poorest schools and hospitals and libraries could all afford to be hooked into the internet and where we fought for a framework that favored competition from new companies over giving all the business of the new information economy to existing big enterprises. Again, it's worked reasonably well. There are hundreds of thousands of new jobs, thousands of new companies out there, and it's an example of how we tried to change the laws and the framework to meet what was best for opportunity for the largest number of Americans, and to give all of our people, especially our young people, the tools they need to take advantage of the age in which we live.

So, in that sense, the nature of opportunity, a constant value, is changing. At the time our nation was founded, opportunity most of all meant the freedom to carve a farm and an existence out of the forest frontier. In the industrial age, the progressives saw that it meant something different. It meant a high school education, a vocational training, preserving competition, protecting American workers from abuses, and keeping children out of the workplace when appropriate.

Today it means mastering new tools and technologies, being able to think broadly, adjust quickly, and being able to keep learning for a lifetime. This morning, for example, at the White House, I met with House and Senate Democrats to push the Congress again to adopt our educational proposals, because I think they are more than ever before at the core of the concept of opportunity and at the core of our ability to keep changing and building an ever more progressive society.

Even though we balanced the budget these last eight years and run a surplus and we've eliminated hundreds of programs, we've also doubled investment in education and training. More than ten million Americans this year will take advantage of the HOPE scholarship and lifelong learning tax credit. We reorganized the student loan program to save students $8 billion in student loan repayments since 1993. We raised the minimum wage, an old tool that I think is still very important in new times. . . .

I am very glad that more and more Americans are sharing in our prosperity. But the other thing I want to say is that still a lot of folks have been left behind. Most of them live in inner cities or small rural towns or on or around Native American reservations. And one of the big challenges now to sort of perfect this progressive movement is to figure out how to bring those people into the circle of opportunity.

I hope very much that, before I leave office, the Congress will pass the new markets initiative that I worked on with the Speaker of the House in a bipartisan fashion. I won't go through all the details, but essentially what it says is we ought to give wealthy Americans with money the same incentives to invest in poor areas in America we provide to invest in poor areas around the world, because we believe that we can do this. And we ought to put the infrastructure there.

For those of you who have never been on an American Indian reservation, let me tell you, just for example, at the Pine Ridge Reservation in South Dakota, one of the most historic parts of American history, the home of the Lakota Sioux, who were the tribe led by an Indian chief named Crazy Horse that dispatched General Custer in the late nineteenth century—the unemployment rate is 73 percent.

I was at Shiprock in northern New Mexico, one of the most beautiful places in our country, the other day at the Navajo Reservation, where the unemployment rate is over 50 percent; 70 percent of the people don't have telephones in their homes. I was introduced by a young woman who won a contest, an academic contest at her school, the prize was a computer, and she couldn't log on to the internet because there was not a phone line in her home. In our country, at our level of wealth, that is unconscionable. And this cannot rightly be called a full Progressive Era until we have addressed these challenges.

We still have to be constantly, restlessly searching for ways to expand the circle of opportunity. This, too, is a principle rooted firmly in the Progressive Era but also in our nation's founding. Remember what the Framers said: they were committed to forming "a more perfect union." They never said the union would be perfect, that we would ever reach complete harmony in our living with our ideals, but that we had a constant, endless lifetime obligation to perfect the union.

If I could leave any of you with a thought that I hope you will have in your mind as you, as citizens, go to the polls, and then as you, as citizens, build your own lives, it is that we get a chance like we've got today maybe once every fifty years, maybe even more seldom, where we have both prosperity, social progress, coupled with national self-confidence and the absence of serious crisis at home or threat abroad, to really imagine the future we would like to build and then go about building it. . . .

The whole idea of the Progressive Era was that everybody should be treated with dignity; everybody deserves certain minimal things in life; that the power of government should be arrayed against private power, so that individual people who are equal under the law, all had at least a fair chance at life. In this era, I often say, in my sort of Arkansas way, that everybody counts; everybody ought to have a chance; and we all do better when we work together. That's what I believe.

That, I think, is an enduring truth of the American dream, going back to the Founders, going back to all the voluntary societies that de Tocqueville chronicled so eloquently, almost two hundred years ago. In this time, we can have a Progressive Era that outlasts the one you came here to study, if we are faithful to its values, if we understand we have to change even more rapidly and perhaps even more profoundly than they did, and if we acknowledge that a precondition of true independence, in the old-fashioned American way in this very new age, is having some humility and compassion and understanding of our interdependence, which is founded on an acknowledgment, an acceptance, a celebration of our common humanity.

That, after all, is what led to the Declaration of Independence and the Constitution. It's what led Abraham Lincoln to lay down his life to hold the country together. And it's what gave us the Progressive Era, the sense that we all matter, that we were all connected, and that we were all entitled, each in our own way, to have a chance to play a part in the endless effort to create "a more perfect union."

The progressives have been important to America. They have redefined the idea of a nation in ways that were sorely needed. But you are in the middle of what could be the longest and most significant Progressive Era in American history. I ask you to study the one that happened before but to fully live the one that is unfolding before your eyes.

GEORGE W. BUSH

Remarks at the Islamic Center in Washington, DC

(2001)

"Terror is not the true faith of Islam"

In the days after a tragedy or disaster, Americans look to their president for leadership. The impromptu remarks George W. Bush made on September 17, 2001, are a fine example of such leadership. After visiting a mosque in Washington, DC, Bush called for religious tolerance. He reminded Americans of their desire to live up to their values—especially in the middle of a disorienting crisis like 9/11.

We've just had wide-ranging discussions on the matter at hand. Like the good folks standing with me, the American people were appalled and outraged at last Tuesday's attacks. And so were Muslims all across the world. Both Americans, our Muslim friends and citizens, taxpaying citizens, and Muslims in nations were just appalled and could not believe what we saw on our TV screens.

These acts of violence against innocents violate the fundamental tenets of the Islamic faith. And it's important for my fellow Americans to understand that.

The English translation is not as eloquent as the original Arabic, but let me quote from the Koran itself: "In the long run, evil in the extreme will be the end of those who do evil. For that they rejected the signs of Allah and held them up to ridicule."

The face of terror is not the true faith of Islam. That's not what Islam is all about. Islam is peace. These terrorists don't represent peace. They represent evil and war.

When we think of Islam, we think of a faith that brings comfort to a billion people around the world—billions of people find comfort and solace and peace—and that's made brothers and sisters out of every race.

America counts millions of Muslims amongst our citizens, and Muslims make an incredibly valuable contribution to our country. Muslims are doctors, lawyers, law professors, members of the military, entrepreneurs, shopkeepers, moms and dads. And they need to be treated with respect. In our anger and emotion, our fellow Americans must treat each other with respect.

Women who cover their heads in this country must feel comfortable going outside their homes. Moms who wear cover must not be intimidated in America. That's not the America I know. That's not the America I value. I've been told that some fear to leave; some don't want to go shopping for their families; some don't want to go about their ordinary daily routines because, by wearing cover, they're afraid they'll be intimidated. That should not and that will not stand in America.

Those who feel like they can intimidate our fellow citizens to take out their anger don't represent the best of America. They represent the worst of humankind, and they should be ashamed of that kind of behavior.

This is a great country. It's a great country because we share the same values of respect and dignity and human worth. And it is my honor to be meeting with leaders who feel just the same way I do. They're outraged; they're sad. They love America just as much as I do.

BARACK OBAMA

Address at the Democratic National Convention

(2004)

"In no other country on earth is my story even possible"

When Barack Obama became a star in 2004—and when he started running for president not even three years later—he did so on the power of his personal story. Obama told that story in his career-making keynote at that year's Democratic National Convention, but he'd been revising it for more than a decade. In his 1995 memoir, Dreams from My Father, Obama had explored and refined the ideas that would drive his future campaigns, including the value of seeking common ground; of rejecting apathy for hard work and hope; and of believing people could change, starting with himself. In Dreams, Obama captured his own cynicism as a college student: "I don't believe that what happens to a kid in Soweto," he'd told a classmate after giving his first political speech, "makes much difference to the people we were talking to." By 2004, Obama was thrilling a far larger audience with the promise that the fate of a kid in Chicago could and must matter to all of them—"even if it's not my child."

On behalf of the great state of Illinois, crossroads of a nation, land of Lincoln, let me express my deep gratitude for the privilege of address-ing this convention. Tonight is a particular honor for me because, let's face it, my presence on this stage is pretty unlikely. My father was a foreign student, born and raised in a small village in Kenya. He grew up herding goats, went to school in a tin-roof shack. His father, my grandfather, was a cook, a domestic servant to the British.

But my grandfather had larger dreams for his son. Through hard work and perseverance my father got a scholarship to study in a magical place: America, which stood as a beacon of freedom and opportunity to so many who had come before.

While studying here, my father met my mother. She was born in a town on the other side of the world, in Kansas. Her father worked on oil rigs and farms through most of the Depression. The day after Pearl Harbor he signed up for duty, joined Patton's army, and marched across Europe. Back home, my grandmother raised their baby and went to work on a bomber assembly line. After the war, they studied on the GI Bill, bought a house through FHA, and later moved west all the way to Hawaii in search of opportunity.

And they, too, had big dreams for their daughter, a common dream, born of two continents.

My parents shared not only an improbable love; they shared an abiding faith in the possibilities of this nation. They would give me an African name, Barack, or "blessed," believing that in a tolerant America your name is no barrier to success. They imagined me going to the best schools in the land, even though they weren't rich, because in a generous America you don't have to be rich to achieve your potential. They are both passed away now. Yet, I know that, on this night, they look down on me with pride.

I stand here today, grateful for the diversity of my heritage, aware that my parents' dreams live on in my precious daughters. I stand here knowing that my story is part of the larger American story, that I owe a debt to all of those who came before me, and that in no other country on earth is my story even possible.

Tonight, we gather to affirm the greatness of our nation, not because of the height of our skyscrapers, or the power of our military, or the size of our economy. Our pride is based on a very simple premise, summed up in a declaration made over two hundred years ago: "We hold these truths to be self-evident: that all men are created equal; that they are endowed by their Creator with certain inalienable rights; that among these are life, liberty, and the pursuit of happiness."

That is the true genius of America, a faith in the simple dreams of its people, the insistence on small miracles. That we can tuck in our children at night and know they are fed and clothed and safe from harm. That we can say what we think, write what we think, without hearing a sudden knock on the door. That we can have an idea and start our own business without paying a bribe or hiring somebody's son. That we can participate in the political process without fear of retribution, and that our votes will be counted—or at least, most of the time.

This year, in this election, we are called to reaffirm our values and commitments, to hold them against a hard reality and see how we are measuring up to the legacy of our forbearers and the promise of future generations.

And fellow Americans—Democrats, Republicans, independents—I say to you tonight: we have more work to do. More to do for the workers I met in Galesburg, Illinois, who are losing their union jobs at the Maytag plant that's moving to Mexico and now are having to compete with their own children for jobs that pay seven bucks an hour. More to do for the father I met who was losing his job and choking back tears, wondering how he would pay $4,500 a month for the drugs his son needs without the health benefits he counted on. More to do for the young woman in East St. Louis, and thousands more like her, who has the grades, has the drive, has the will, but doesn't have the money to go to college.

Don't get me wrong. The people I meet in small towns and big cities, in diners and office parks, they don't expect government to solve all their problems. They know they have to work hard to get ahead, and they want to. Go into the collar counties around Chicago, and people will tell you they don't want their tax money wasted by a welfare agency or the Pentagon. Go into any inner-city neighborhood, and folks will tell you that government alone can't teach kids to learn. They know that parents have to parent, that children can't achieve unless we raise their expectations and turn off the television sets and eradicate the slander that says a black youth with a book is acting white. No, people don't expect government to solve all their problems. But they sense, deep in their bones, that with just a change in priorities, we can make sure that every child in America has a decent shot at life and that the doors of opportunity remain open to all. They know we can do better. And they want that choice.

In this election, we offer that choice. Our party has chosen a man to lead us who embodies the best this country has to offer. That man is John Kerry. John Kerry understands the ideals of community, faith, and sacrifice, because they've defined his life. From his heroic service in Vietnam to his years as prosecutor and lieutenant governor, through two decades in the United States Senate, he has devoted himself to this country. Again and again, we've seen him make tough choices when easier ones were available. His values and his record affirm what is best in us.

John Kerry believes in an America where hard work is rewarded. So instead of offering tax breaks to companies shipping jobs overseas, he'll offer them to companies creating jobs here at home. John Kerry believes in an America where all Americans can afford the same health coverage our politicians in Washington have for themselves. John Kerry believes in energy independence, so we aren't held hostage to the profits of oil companies or the sabotage of foreign oil fields. John Kerry believes in the constitutional freedoms that have made our country the envy of the world, and he will never sacrifice our basic liberties nor use faith as a wedge to divide us. And John Kerry believes that in a dangerous world, war must be an option, but it should never be the first option.

A while back, I met a young man named Shamus at the VFW Hall in East Moline, Illinois. He was a good-looking kid, six-two or six-three, clear-eyed, with an easy smile. He told me he'd joined the Marines and was heading to Iraq the following week. As I listened to him explain why he'd enlisted, his absolute faith in our country and its leaders, his devotion to duty and service, I thought this young man was all any of us might hope for in a child. But then I asked myself: Are we serving Shamus as well as he was serving us?

I thought of more than nine hundred servicemen and -women, sons and daughters, husbands and wives, friends and neighbors, who will not be returning to their hometowns. I thought of families I had met who were struggling to get by without a loved one's full income, or whose loved ones had returned with a limb missing or with nerves shattered, but who still lacked long-term health benefits because they were reservists. When we send our young men and women into harm's way, we have a solemn obligation not to fudge the numbers or shade the truth about why they're going; to care for their families while they're gone; to tend to the soldiers upon their return; and to never ever go to war without enough troops to win the war, secure the peace, and earn the respect of the world.

Now, let me be clear. We have real enemies in the world. These enemies must be found. They must be pursued and they must be defeated. John Kerry knows this. And just as Lieutenant Kerry did not hesitate to risk his life to protect the men who served with him in Vietnam, President Kerry will not hesitate one moment to use our military might to keep America safe and secure.

John Kerry believes in America. And he knows it's not enough for just some of us to prosper. For alongside our famous individualism, there's another ingredient in the American saga: a belief that we are connected as one people.

If there's a child on the south side of Chicago who can't read, that matters to me, even if it's not my child. If there's a senior citizen somewhere who can't pay for her prescription and has to choose between medicine and the rent, that makes my life poorer, even if it's not my grandmother. If there's an Arab-American family being rounded up without benefit of an attorney or due process, that threatens my civil liberties. It's that fundamental belief—I am my brother's keeper, I am my sister's keeper—that makes this country work. It's what allows us to pursue our individual dreams, yet still come together as a single American family.

"E pluribus unum." Out of many, one.

Yet even as we speak, there are those who are preparing to divide us, the spin masters and negative ad peddlers who embrace the politics of anything goes. Well, I say to them tonight, there's not a liberal America and a conservative America—there's the United States of America. There's not a black America and white America and Latino America and Asian America—there's the United States of America.

The pundits like to slice and dice our country into red states and blue states: red states for Republicans, blue states for Democrats. But I've got news for them, too. We worship an awesome God in the blue states, and we don't like federal agents poking around our libraries in the red states. We coach Little League in the blue states and have gay friends in the red states. There are patriots who opposed the war in Iraq and patriots who supported it. We are one people, all of us pledging allegiance to the Stars and Stripes, all of us defending the United States of America.

In the end, that's what this election is about. Do we participate in a politics of cynicism or a politics of hope? John Kerry calls on us to hope. John Edwards calls on us to hope. I'm not talking about blind optimism here—the almost willful ignorance that thinks unemployment will go away if we just don't talk about it, or the health care crisis will solve itself if we just ignore it. No, I'm talking about something more substantial. It's the hope of slaves sitting around a fire, singing freedom songs; the hope of immigrants setting out for distant shores; the hope of a young naval lieutenant bravely patrolling the Mekong Delta; the hope of a millworker's son who dares to defy the odds; the hope of a skinny kid with a funny name who believes that America has a place for him, too.

Hope in the face of difficulty. Hope in the face of uncertainty. The audacity of hope! In the end, that is God's greatest gift to us, the bedrock of this nation. A belief in things not seen. A belief that there are better days ahead.

I believe we can give our middle class relief and provide working families with a road to opportunity. I believe we can provide jobs to the jobless, homes to the homeless, and reclaim young people in cities across America from violence and despair. I believe that as we stand on the crossroads of history, we can make the right choices, and meet the challenges that face us.

America! Tonight, if you feel the same energy I do, the same urgency I do, the same passion I do, the same hopefulness I do—if we do what we must do, then I have no doubt that all across the country, from Florida to Oregon, from Washington to Maine, the people will rise up in November, and John Kerry will be sworn in as president, and John Edwards will be sworn in as vice president, and this country will reclaim its promise, and out of this long political darkness a brighter day will come.

BARACK OBAMA

Address on the
Reverend Wright Controversy

(2008)

"These people are a part of me. And they
are a part of America, this country that
I love"

*One of the most difficult moments during Obama's presidential campaign came
in the spring of 2008, when controversial videos surfaced of his pastor, Jeremiah
Wright. ("Not God bless America," Wright said in one sermon. "God damn
America.") On March 18, Obama confronted the subject in a major speech. There
were echoes of Kennedy confronting his Catholicism, though the combination of
religion and race made Obama's challenge far more complex. While the campaign
and controversy guaranteed a huge audience, Obama tried to tell a layered story
that returned to his favorite themes, and it made an enormous impact. The next
week, a Pew poll found that more than half of American adults had watched
the speech, helping Obama move past the Wright controversy to win the primary
and then the general election in the fall.*

"We the people, in order to form a more perfect union": two hundred
and twenty-one years ago, in a hall that still stands across the
street, a group of men gathered and, with these simple words, launched
America's improbable experiment in democracy. Farmers and scholars,

statesmen and patriots who had traveled across an ocean to escape tyranny and persecution finally made real their declaration of independence at a Philadelphia convention that lasted through the spring of 1787.

The document they produced was eventually signed but ultimately unfinished. It was stained by this nation's original sin of slavery, a question that divided the colonies and brought the convention to a stalemate until the founders chose to allow the slave trade to continue for at least twenty more years, and to leave any final resolution to future generations.

Of course, the answer to the slavery question was already embedded within our Constitution—a Constitution that had at its very core the ideal of equal citizenship under the law; a Constitution that promised its people liberty, and justice, and a union that could be and should be perfected over time.

And yet words on a parchment would not be enough to deliver slaves from bondage, or provide men and women of every color and creed their full rights and obligations as citizens of the United States. What would be needed were Americans in successive generations who were willing to do their part—through protests and struggle, on the streets and in the courts, through a civil war and civil disobedience and always at great risk—to narrow that gap between the promise of our ideals and the reality of their time.

This was one of the tasks we set forth at the beginning of this campaign—to continue the long march of those who came before us, a march for a more just, more equal, more free, more caring, and more prosperous America. I chose to run for the presidency at this moment in history because I believe deeply that we cannot solve the challenges of our time unless we solve them together—unless we perfect our union by understanding that we may have different stories, but we hold common hopes; that we may not look the same and we may not have come from the same place, but we all want to move in the same direction, towards a better future for our children and our grandchildren.

This belief comes from my unyielding faith in the decency and generosity of the American people. But it also comes from my own American story.

I am the son of a black man from Kenya and a white woman from Kansas. I was raised with the help of a white grandfather who survived a Depression to serve in Patton's Army during World War II and a white grandmother who worked on a bomber assembly line at Fort Leavenworth while he was overseas. I've gone to some of the best schools in America and lived in one of the world's poorest nations. I am married to a black

American who carries within her the blood of slaves and slaveowners—an inheritance we pass on to our two precious daughters. I have brothers, sisters, nieces, nephews, uncles, and cousins of every race and every hue, scattered across three continents, and for as long as I live, I will never forget that in no other country on earth is my story even possible.

It's a story that hasn't made me the most conventional candidate. But it is a story that has seared into my genetic makeup the idea that this nation is more than the sum of its parts—that out of many, we are truly one.

Throughout the first year of this campaign, against all predictions to the contrary, we saw how hungry the American people were for this message of unity. Despite the temptation to view my candidacy through a purely racial lens, we won commanding victories in states with some of the whitest populations in the country. In South Carolina, where the Confederate Flag still flies, we built a powerful coalition of African Americans and white Americans.

This is not to say that race has not been an issue in the campaign. At various stages in the campaign, some commentators have deemed me either "too black" or "not black enough." We saw racial tensions bubble to the surface during the week before the South Carolina primary. The press has scoured every exit poll for the latest evidence of racial polarization, not just in terms of white and black but black and brown, as well.

And yet, it has only been in the last couple of weeks that the discussion of race in this campaign has taken a particularly divisive turn.

On one end of the spectrum, we've heard the implication that my candidacy is somehow an exercise in affirmative action, that it's based solely on the desire of wide-eyed liberals to purchase racial reconciliation on the cheap. On the other end, we've heard my former pastor, Reverend Jeremiah Wright, use incendiary language to express views that have the potential not only to widen the racial divide, but views that denigrate both the greatness and the goodness of our nation, that rightly offend white and black alike.

I have already condemned, in unequivocal terms, the statements of Reverend Wright that have caused such controversy. For some, nagging questions remain. Did I know him to be an occasionally fierce critic of American domestic and foreign policy? Of course. Did I ever hear him make remarks that could be considered controversial while I sat in church? Yes. Did I strongly disagree with many of his political views? Absolutely—just as I'm sure many of you have heard remarks from your pastors, priests, or rabbis with which you strongly disagreed.

But the remarks that have caused this recent firestorm weren't simply controversial. They weren't simply a religious leader's effort to speak out against perceived injustice. Instead, they expressed a profoundly distorted view of this country—a view that sees white racism as endemic and that elevates what is wrong with America above all that we know is right with America; a view that sees the conflicts in the Middle East as rooted primarily in the actions of stalwart allies like Israel instead of emanating from the perverse and hateful ideologies of radical Islam.

As such, Reverend Wright's comments were not only wrong but divisive—divisive at a time when we need unity; racially charged at a time when we need to come together to solve a set of monumental problems: two wars, a terrorist threat, a falling economy, a chronic health care crisis, and potentially devastating climate change, problems that are neither black or white or Latino or Asian but rather problems that confront us all.

Given my background, my politics, and my professed values and ideals, there will no doubt be those for whom my statements of condemnation are not enough. Why associate myself with Reverend Wright in the first place, they may ask? Why not join another church? And I confess that if all that I knew of Reverend Wright were the snippets of those sermons that have run in an endless loop on the television and YouTube, or if Trinity United Church of Christ conformed to the caricatures being peddled by some commentators, there is no doubt that I would react in much the same way.

But the truth is, that isn't all that I know of the man. The man I met more than twenty years ago is a man who helped introduce me to my Christian faith, a man who spoke to me about our obligations to love one another, to care for the sick and lift up the poor. He is a man who served his country as a U.S. Marine, who has studied and lectured at some of the finest universities and seminaries in the country, and who for over thirty years led a church that serves the community by doing God's work here on Earth—by housing the homeless, ministering to the needy, providing day care services and scholarships and prison ministries, and reaching out to those suffering from HIV/AIDS.

In my first book, *Dreams from My Father*, I described the experience of my first service at Trinity:

> People began to shout, to rise from their seats and clap and cry out, a forceful wind carrying the reverend's voice up into the rafters. . . . And in that single note—hope!—I heard something else; at the foot of that cross, inside the thousands of churches across the city, I imagined the

stories of ordinary black people merging with the stories of David and Goliath, Moses and Pharaoh, the Christians in the lion's den, Ezekiel's field of dry bones. Those stories—of survival, and freedom, and hope—became our story, my story; the blood that had spilled was our blood, the tears our tears; until this black church, on this bright day, seemed once more a vessel carrying the story of a people into future generations and into a larger world. Our trials and triumphs became at once unique and universal, black and more than black; in chronicling our journey, the stories and songs gave us a means to reclaim memories that we didn't need to feel shame about . . . memories that all people might study and cherish—and with which we could start to rebuild.

That has been my experience at Trinity. Like other predominantly black churches across the country, Trinity embodies the black community in its entirety—the doctor and the welfare mom, the model student and the former gang-banger. Like other black churches, Trinity's services are full of raucous laughter and sometimes bawdy humor. They are full of dancing, clapping, screaming, and shouting that may seem jarring to the untrained ear. The church contains in full the kindness and cruelty, the fierce intelligence and the shocking ignorance, the struggles and successes, the love and, yes, the bitterness and bias that make up the black experience in America.

And this helps explain, perhaps, my relationship with Reverend Wright. As imperfect as he may be, he has been like family to me. He strengthened my faith, officiated my wedding, and baptized my children. Not once in my conversations with him have I heard him talk about any ethnic group in derogatory terms or treat whites with whom he interacted with anything but courtesy and respect. He contains within him the contradictions—the good and the bad—of the community that he has served diligently for so many years.

I can no more disown him than I can disown the black community. I can no more disown him than I can my white grandmother—a woman who helped raise me, a woman who sacrificed again and again for me, a woman who loves me as much as she loves anything in this world, but a woman who once confessed her fear of black men who passed by her on the street and who on more than one occasion has uttered racial or ethnic stereotypes that made me cringe.

These people are a part of me. And they are a part of America, this country that I love.

Some will see this as an attempt to justify or excuse comments that are simply inexcusable. I can assure you it is not. I suppose the politically safe thing would be to move on from this episode and just hope that it fades into the woodwork. We can dismiss Reverend Wright as a crank or a demagogue, just as some have dismissed Geraldine Ferraro, in the aftermath of her recent statements, as harboring some deep-seated racial bias.

But race is an issue that I believe this nation cannot afford to ignore right now. We would be making the same mistake that Reverend Wright made in his offending sermons about America—to simplify and stereotype and amplify the negative to the point that it distorts reality.

The fact is that the comments that have been made and the issues that have surfaced over the last few weeks reflect the complexities of race in this country that we've never really worked through—a part of our union that we have yet to perfect. And if we walk away now, if we simply retreat into our respective corners, we will never be able to come together and solve challenges like health care, or education, or the need to find good jobs for every American.

Understanding this reality requires a reminder of how we arrived at this point. As William Faulkner once wrote, "The past isn't dead and buried. In fact, it isn't even past." We do not need to recite here the history of racial injustice in this country. But we do need to remind ourselves that so many of the disparities that exist in the African-American community today can be directly traced to inequalities passed on from an earlier generation that suffered under the brutal legacy of slavery and Jim Crow.

Segregated schools were, and are, inferior schools; we still haven't fixed them, fifty years after *Brown v. Board of Education*, and the inferior education they provided, then and now, helps explain the pervasive achievement gap between today's black and white students.

Legalized discrimination—where blacks were prevented, often through violence, from owning property, or loans were not granted to African-American business owners, or black homeowners could not access FHA mortgages, or blacks were excluded from unions, or the police force, or fire departments—meant that black families could not amass any meaningful wealth to bequeath to future generations. That history helps explain the wealth and income gap between black and white, and the concentrated pockets of poverty that persists in so many of today's urban and rural communities.

A lack of economic opportunity among black men, and the shame and frustration that came from not being able to provide for one's family,

contributed to the erosion of black families—a problem that welfare policies for many years may have worsened. And the lack of basic services in so
many urban black neighborhoods—parks for kids to play in, police walking
the beat, regular garbage pick-up, and building code enforcement—all
helped create a cycle of violence, blight, and neglect that continue to
haunt us.

This is the reality in which Reverend Wright and other African-
Americans of his generation grew up. They came of age in the late fifties
and early sixties, a time when segregation was still the law of the land and
opportunity was systematically constricted. What's remarkable is not how
many failed in the face of discrimination, but rather how many men and
women overcame the odds, how many were able to make a way out of no
way for those like me who would come after them.

But for all those who scratched and clawed their way to get a piece of
the American Dream, there were many who didn't make it—those who
were ultimately defeated, in one way or another, by discrimination. That
legacy of defeat was passed on to future generations—those young men
and increasingly young women who we see standing on street corners
or languishing in our prisons, without hope or prospects for the future.
Even for those blacks who did make it, questions of race, and racism,
continue to define their worldview in fundamental ways. For the men
and women of Reverend Wright's generation, the memories of humiliation and doubt and fear have not gone away; nor has the anger and the
bitterness of those years. That anger may not get expressed in public, in
front of white co-workers or white friends. But it does find voice in the
barbershop or around the kitchen table. At times, that anger is exploited
by politicians, to gin up votes along racial lines, or to make up for a
politician's own failings.

And occasionally it finds voice in the church on Sunday morning, in
the pulpit and in the pews. The fact that so many people are surprised to
hear that anger in some of Reverend Wright's sermons simply reminds us
of the old truism that the most segregated hour in American life occurs
on Sunday morning. That anger is not always productive; indeed, all too
often it distracts attention from solving real problems; it keeps us from
squarely facing our own complicity in our condition and prevents the
African-American community from forging the alliances it needs to bring
about real change. But the anger is real; it is powerful; and to simply wish
it away, to condemn it without understanding its roots, only serves to widen
the chasm of misunderstanding that exists between the races.

In fact, a similar anger exists within segments of the white community. Most working- and middle-class white Americans don't feel that they have been particularly privileged by their race. Their experience is the immigrant experience—as far as they're concerned, no one's handed them anything, they've built it from scratch. They've worked hard all their lives, many times only to see their jobs shipped overseas or their pension dumped after a lifetime of labor. They are anxious about their futures and feel their dreams slipping away; in an era of stagnant wages and global competition, opportunity comes to be seen as a zero-sum game, in which your dreams come at my expense. So when they are told to bus their children to a school across town; when they hear that an African American is getting an advantage in landing a good job or a spot in a good college because of an injustice that they themselves never committed; when they're told that their fears about crime in urban neighborhoods are somehow prejudiced, resentment builds over time.

Like the anger within the black community, these resentments aren't always expressed in polite company. But they have helped shape the political landscape for at least a generation. Anger over welfare and affirmative action helped forge the Reagan Coalition. Politicians routinely exploited fears of crime for their own electoral ends. Talk show hosts and conservative commentators built entire careers unmasking bogus claims of racism while dismissing legitimate discussions of racial injustice and inequality as mere political correctness or reverse racism.

Just as black anger often proved counterproductive, so have these white resentments distracted attention from the real culprits of the middle-class squeeze—a corporate culture rife with inside dealing, questionable accounting practices, and short-term greed; a Washington dominated by lobbyists and special interests; economic policies that favor the few over the many. And yet, to wish away the resentments of white Americans, to label them as misguided or even racist, without recognizing they are grounded in legitimate concerns—this too widens the racial divide and blocks the path to understanding.

This is where we are right now. It's a racial stalemate we've been stuck in for years. Contrary to the claims of some of my critics, black and white, I have never been so naïve as to believe that we can get beyond our racial divisions in a single election cycle, or with a single candidacy—particularly a candidacy as imperfect as my own.

But I have asserted a firm conviction—a conviction rooted in my faith in God and my faith in the American people—that working together we can move beyond some of our old racial wounds, and that in fact we have no choice if we are to continue on the path of a more perfect union.

For the African-American community, that path means embracing the burdens of our past without becoming victims of our past. It means continuing to insist on a full measure of justice in every aspect of American life. But it also means binding our particular grievances—for better health care, and better schools, and better jobs—to the larger aspirations of all Americans: the white woman struggling to break the glass ceiling, the white man who's been laid off, the immigrant trying to feed his family. And it means taking full responsibility for our own lives—by demanding more from our fathers, and spending more time with our children, and reading to them, and teaching them that while they may face challenges and discrimination in their own lives, they must never succumb to despair or cynicism; they must always believe that they can write their own destiny.

Ironically, this quintessentially American—and yes, conservative—notion of self-help found frequent expression in Reverend Wright's sermons. But what my former pastor too often failed to understand is that embarking on a program of self-help also requires a belief that society can change.

The profound mistake of Reverend Wright's sermons is not that he spoke about racism in our society. It's that he spoke as if our society was static; as if no progress has been made; as if this country—a country that has made it possible for one of his own members to run for the highest office in the land and build a coalition of white and black, Latino and Asian, rich and poor, young and old—is still irrevocably bound to a tragic past. But what we know—what we have seen—is that America can change. That is the true genius of this nation. What we have already achieved gives us hope—the audacity to hope—for what we can and must achieve tomorrow.

In the white community, the path to a more perfect union means acknowledging that what ails the African-American community does not just exist in the minds of black people, that the legacy of discrimination—and current incidents of discrimination, while less overt than in the past—are real and must be addressed. Not just with words, but with deeds—by investing in our schools and our communities; by enforcing our civil rights laws and ensuring fairness in our criminal justice system; by providing this generation with ladders of opportunity that were unavailable for previous generations. It requires all Americans to realize that your dreams do not have to come at the expense of my dreams; that investing in the health, welfare, and education of black and brown and white children will ultimately help all of America prosper.

In the end, then, what is called for is nothing more, and nothing less, than what all the world's great religions demand—that we do unto others as we would have them do unto us. Let us be our brother's keeper, Scripture tells us. Let us be our sister's keeper. Let us find that common stake we all have in one another, and let our politics reflect that spirit as well.

For we have a choice in this country. We can accept a politics that breeds division, and conflict, and cynicism. We can tackle race only as spectacle, as we did in the OJ trial, or in the wake of tragedy, as we did in the aftermath of Katrina, or as fodder for the nightly news. We can play Reverend Wright's sermons on every channel, every day, and talk about them from now until the election and make the only question in this campaign whether or not the American people think that I somehow believe or sympathize with his most offensive words. We can pounce on some gaffe by a Hillary supporter as evidence that she's playing the race card, or we can speculate on whether white men will all flock to John McCain in the general election regardless of his policies.

We can do that.

But if we do, I can tell you that in the next election, we'll be talking about some other distraction. And then another one. And then another one. And nothing will change.

That is one option. Or, at this moment, in this election, we can come together and say, "Not this time." This time we want to talk about the crumbling schools that are stealing the future of black children and white children and Asian children and Hispanic children and Native American children. This time we want to reject the cynicism that tells us that these kids can't learn; that those kids who don't look like us are somebody else's problem. The children of America are not those kids, they are our kids, and we will not let them fall behind in a twenty-first-century economy. Not this time.

This time we want to talk about how the lines in the emergency room are filled with whites and blacks and Hispanics who do not have health care; who don't have the power on their own to overcome the special interests in Washington, but who can take them on if we do it together.

This time we want to talk about the shuttered mills that once provided a decent life for men and women of every race, and the homes for sale that once belonged to Americans from every religion, every region, every walk of life. This time we want to talk about the fact that the real problem is not that someone who doesn't look like you might take your job; it's that the corporation you work for will ship it overseas for nothing more than a profit.

This time we want to talk about the men and women of every color and creed who serve together, and fight together, and bleed together under the same proud flag. We want to talk about how to bring them home from a war that never should've been authorized and never should've been waged, and we want to talk about how we'll show our patriotism by caring for them and their families and giving them the benefits they have earned.

I would not be running for president if I didn't believe with all my heart that this is what the vast majority of Americans want for this country. This union may never be perfect, but generation after generation has shown that it can always be perfected. And today, whenever I find myself feeling doubtful or cynical about this possibility, what gives me the most hope is the next generation—the young people whose attitudes and beliefs and openness to change have already made history in this election.

There is one story in particular that I'd like to leave you with today—a story I told when I had the great honor of speaking on Dr. King's birthday at his home church, Ebenezer Baptist, in Atlanta.

There is a young, twenty-three-year-old white woman named Ashley Baia who organized for our campaign in Florence, South Carolina. She had been working to organize a mostly African-American community since the beginning of this campaign, and one day she was at a roundtable discussion where everyone went around telling their story and why they were there.

And Ashley said that when she was nine years old, her mother got cancer. And because she had to miss days of work, she was let go and lost her health care. They had to file for bankruptcy, and that's when Ashley decided that she had to do something to help her mom.

She knew that food was one of their most expensive costs, and so Ashley convinced her mother that what she really liked and really wanted to eat more than anything else was mustard and relish sandwiches. Because that was the cheapest way to eat.

She did this for a year until her mom got better, and she told everyone at the roundtable that the reason she joined our campaign was so that she could help the millions of other children in the country who want and need to help their parents, too.

Now Ashley might have made a different choice. Perhaps somebody told her along the way that the source of her mother's problems were blacks who were on welfare and too lazy to work, or Hispanics who were coming into the country illegally. But she didn't. She sought out allies in her fight against injustice.

Anyway, Ashley finishes her story and then goes around the room and asks everyone else why they're supporting the campaign. They all have different stories and reasons. Many bring up a specific issue. And finally they come to this elderly black man who's been sitting there quietly the entire time. And Ashley asks him why he's there. And he does not bring up a specific issue. He does not say health care or the economy. He does not say education or the war. He does not say that he was there because of Barack Obama. He simply says to everyone in the room, "I am here because of Ashley."

"I'm here because of Ashley." By itself, that single moment of recognition between that young white girl and that old black man is not enough. It is not enough to give health care to the sick, or jobs to the jobless, or education to our children.

But it is where we start. It is where our union grows stronger. And as so many generations have come to realize over the course of the two hundred and twenty-one years since a band of patriots signed that document in Philadelphia, that is where the perfection begins.

BARACK OBAMA

Statement on the Sandy Hook Elementary School Shooting

(2012)

"They had their entire lives ahead of them—
birthdays, graduations, weddings, kids of
their own"

On December 14, 2012, Obama read a brief statement about the Sandy Hook Elementary School shooting. While his statement was compassionate and concise, it was Obama's delivery—the footage of his voice cracking, his fingers flicking away tears—that captured the heartbreak so many Americans felt.

This afternoon, I spoke with Governor Malloy and FBI Director Mueller. I offered Governor Malloy my condolences on behalf of the nation and made it clear he will have every single resource that he needs to investigate this heinous crime, care for the victims, counsel their families.

We've endured too many of these tragedies in the past few years. And each time I learn the news, I react not as a president but as anybody else would—as a parent. And that was especially true today. I know there's not a parent in America who doesn't feel the same overwhelming grief that I do.

The majority of those who died today were children—beautiful little kids between the ages of five and ten years old. They had their entire lives ahead of them—birthdays, graduations, weddings, kids of their own.

Among the fallen were also teachers—men and women who devoted their lives to helping our children fulfill their dreams.

So our hearts are broken today for the parents and grandparents, sisters and brothers of these little children, and for the families of the adults who were lost.

Our hearts are broken for the parents of the survivors, as well, for as blessed as they are to have their children home tonight, they know that their children's innocence has been torn away from them too early and there are no words that will ease their pain.

As a country, we have been through this too many times. Whether it is an elementary school in Newtown, or a shopping mall in Oregon, or a temple in Wisconsin, or a movie theater in Aurora, or a street corner in Chicago, these neighborhoods are our neighborhoods and these children are our children. And we're going to have to come together and take meaningful action to prevent more tragedies like this, regardless of the politics.

This evening, Michelle and I will do what I know every parent in America will do, which is hug our children a little tighter, and we'll tell them that we love them, and we'll remind each other how deeply we love one another. But there are families in Connecticut who cannot do that tonight, and they need all of us right now. In the hard days to come, that community needs us to be at our best as Americans, and I will do everything in my power as president to help, because while nothing can fill the space of a lost child or loved one, all of us can extend a hand to those in need—to remind them that we are there for them, that we are praying for them, that the love they felt for those they lost endures not just in their memories but also in ours.

May God bless the memory of the victims and, in the words of Scripture, heal the brokenhearted and bind up their wounds.

BARACK OBAMA

Address on the Marches from Selma to Montgomery

(2015)

"It was not a clash of armies but a clash
of wills, a contest to determine the true
meaning of America"

*Fifty years after Bloody Sunday, Obama returned to Selma to commemorate the
event with some of the original marchers, including Congressman John Lewis.
Obama eschewed the specifics of, say, Johnson's "We Shall Overcome" speech,
choosing instead to tell a broader story about America's history and identity.
Obama, ever the writer, called his country a "work in progress," and this speech
is Obama's most developed statement on what it means to be an American and
whether that meaning has changed.*

It is a rare honor in this life to follow one of your heroes. And John Lewis
is one of my heroes.

Now, I have to imagine that when a younger John Lewis woke up that
morning fifty years ago and made his way to Brown Chapel, heroics were
not on his mind. A day like this was not on his mind. Young folks with
bedrolls and backpacks were milling about. Veterans of the movement
trained newcomers in the tactics of nonviolence, the right way to protect
yourself when attacked. A doctor described what tear gas does to the body

while marchers scribbled down instructions for contacting their loved ones. The air was thick with doubt, anticipation, and fear. And they comforted themselves with the final verse of the final hymn they sung:

No matter what may be the test, God will take care of you;
Lean, weary one, upon His breast, God will take care of you.

And then, his knapsack stocked with an apple, a toothbrush, and a book on government—all you need for a night behind bars—John Lewis led them out of the church on a mission to change America.

There are places and moments in America where this nation's destiny has been decided. Many are sites of war—Concord and Lexington, Appomattox, Gettysburg. Others are sites that symbolize the daring of America's character—Independence Hall and Seneca Falls, Kitty Hawk and Cape Canaveral.

Selma is such a place. In one afternoon, fifty years ago, so much of our turbulent history—the stain of slavery and anguish of civil war; the yoke of segregation and tyranny of Jim Crow; the death of four little girls in Birmingham and the dream of a Baptist preacher—all that history met on this bridge.

It was not a clash of armies but a clash of wills, a contest to determine the true meaning of America. And because of men and women like John Lewis, Joseph Lowery, Hosea Williams, Amelia Boynton, Diane Nash, Ralph Abernathy, C. T. Vivian, Andrew Young, Fred Shuttlesworth, Dr. Martin Luther King Jr., and so many others, the idea of a just America and a fair America, an inclusive America and a generous America—that idea ultimately triumphed.

Now, as is true across the landscape of American history, we cannot examine this moment in isolation. The march on Selma was part of a broader campaign that spanned generations, the leaders that day part of a long line of heroes.

We gather here to celebrate them. We gather here to honor the courage of ordinary Americans willing to endure billy clubs and the chastening rod, tear gas and the trampling hoof—men and women who despite the gush of blood and splintered bone would stay true to their North Star and keep marching towards justice.

They did as Scripture instructed: "Rejoice in hope, be patient in tribulation, be constant in prayer." And in the days to come, they went back again and again. When the trumpet call sounded for more to join, the people came—black and white, young and old, Christian and Jew, waving the American flag and singing the same anthems full of faith and hope. A white newsman, Bill Plante, who covered the marches then and who is with us here today, quipped that the growing number of white people lowered the quality of the singing. To those who marched, though, those old gospel songs must have never sounded so sweet.

In time, their chorus would well up and reach President Johnson. And he would send them protection, and speak to the nation, echoing their call for America and the world to hear: "We shall overcome." What enormous faith these men and women had. Faith in God, but also faith in America.

The Americans who crossed this bridge, they were not physically imposing. But they gave courage to millions. They held no elected office. But they led a nation. They marched as Americans who had endured hundreds of years of brutal violence, countless daily indignities—but they didn't seek special treatment, just the equal treatment promised to them almost a century before.

What they did here will reverberate through the ages. Not because the change they won was preordained, not because their victory was complete, but because they proved that nonviolent change is possible, that love and hope can conquer hate.

As we commemorate their achievement, we are well-served to remember that at the time of the marches, many in power condemned rather than praised them. Back then, they were called Communists, or half-breeds, or outside agitators, sexual and moral degenerates, and worse—they were called everything but the name their parents gave them. Their faith was questioned. Their lives were threatened. Their patriotism challenged.

And yet what could be more American than what happened in this place? What could more profoundly vindicate the idea of America than plain and humble people—the unsung, the downtrodden, the dreamers not of high station, not born to wealth or privilege, not of one religious tradition but many—coming together to shape their country's course?

What greater expression of faith in the American experiment than this; what greater form of patriotism is there than the belief that America is not yet finished, that we are strong enough to be self-critical, that each successive generation can look upon our imperfections and decide that it is in our power to remake this nation to more closely align with our highest ideals?

That's why Selma is not some outlier in the American experience. That's why it's not a museum or a static monument to behold from a distance. It is instead the manifestation of a creed written into our founding documents: "We the People . . . in order to form a more perfect union." "We hold these truths to be self-evident, that all men are created equal."

These are not just words. They're a living thing, a call to action, a road map for citizenship and an insistence in the capacity of free men and women to shape our own destiny. For founders like Franklin and Jefferson, for leaders like Lincoln and FDR, the success of our experiment in self-government rested on engaging all of our citizens in this work. And that's what we celebrate here in Selma. That's what this movement was all about, one leg in our long journey toward freedom.

The American instinct that led these young men and women to pick up the torch and cross this bridge is the same instinct that moved patriots to choose revolution over tyranny. It's the same instinct that drew immigrants from across oceans and the Rio Grande, the same instinct that led women to reach for the ballot and workers to organize against an unjust status quo, the same instinct that led us to plant a flag at Iwo Jima and on the surface of the moon.

It's the idea held by generations of citizens who believed that America is a constant work in progress, who believed that loving this country requires more than singing its praises or avoiding uncomfortable truths. It requires the occasional disruption, the willingness to speak out for what's right and shake up the status quo.

That's what makes us unique and cements our reputation as a beacon of opportunity. Young people behind the Iron Curtain would see Selma and eventually tear down a wall. Young people in Soweto would hear Bobby Kennedy talk about ripples of hope and eventually banish the scourge of apartheid. Young people in Burma went to prison rather than submit to military rule. From the streets of Tunis to the Maidan in Ukraine, this generation of young people can draw strength from this place, where the powerless could change the world's greatest superpower and push their leaders to expand the boundaries of freedom.

They saw that idea made real in Selma, Alabama. They saw it made real in America.

Because of campaigns like this, a Voting Rights Act was passed. Political, economic, and social barriers came down, and the change these men and women wrought is visible here today in the presence of African Americans who run boardrooms, who sit on the bench, who serve in elected office from small towns to big cities, from the Congressional Black Caucus to the Oval Office.

Because of what they did, the doors of opportunity swung open not just for African Americans, but for every American. Women marched through those doors. Latinos marched through those doors. Asian-Americans, gay Americans, and Americans with disabilities came through those doors. Their endeavors gave the entire South the chance to rise again, not by reasserting the past but by transcending the past.

What a glorious thing, Dr. King might say. What a solemn debt we owe.

Which leads us to ask, just how might we repay that debt?

First and foremost, we have to recognize that one day's commemoration, no matter how special, is not enough. If Selma taught us anything, it's that our work is never done—the American experiment in self-government gives work and purpose to each generation.

Selma teaches us, as well, that action requires that we shed our cynicism. For when it comes to the pursuit of justice, we can afford neither complacency nor despair.

Just this week, I was asked whether I thought the Department of Justice's Ferguson report shows that, with respect to race, little has changed in this country. I understand the question, for the report's narrative was woefully familiar. It evoked the kind of abuse and disregard for citizens that spawned the civil rights movement. But I rejected the notion that nothing's changed. What happened in Ferguson may not be unique, but it's no longer endemic, or sanctioned by law and custom; and before the civil rights movement, it most surely was.

We do a disservice to the cause of justice by intimating that bias and discrimination are immutable or that racial division is inherent to America. If you think nothing's changed in the past fifty years, ask somebody who lived through the Selma or Chicago or L.A. of the fifties. Ask the female CEO who once might have been assigned to the secretarial pool if nothing's changed. Ask your gay friend if it's easier to be out and proud in America now than it was thirty years ago. To deny this progress—our progress—would be to rob us of our own agency, our capacity, our responsibility to do what we can to make America better.

Of course, a more common mistake is to suggest Ferguson is an isolated incident, that racism is banished, that the work that drew men and women to Selma is complete and that whatever racial tensions remain are a consequence of those seeking to play the "race card" for their own purposes. We don't need the Ferguson report to know that's not true. We just need to open our eyes, and ears, and hearts, to know that this nation's racial history still casts its long shadow upon us. We know the march is not yet over, the race is not yet won, and that reaching that blessed destination where we are judged by the content of our character requires admitting as much.

"We are capable of bearing a great burden," James Baldwin wrote, "once we discover that the burden is reality and arrive where reality is."

There's nothing America can't handle if we actually look squarely at the problem. And this is work for all Americans, and not just some. Not just whites. Not just blacks. If we want to honor the courage of those who marched that day, then all of us are called to possess their moral imagination. All of us will need to feel, as they did, the fierce urgency of now. All of us need to recognize, as they did, that change depends on our actions, our attitudes, the things we teach our children. And if we make such effort, no matter how hard it may seem, laws can be passed, and consciences can be stirred, and consensus can be built.

With such an effort, we can make sure our criminal justice system serves all and not just some. Together, we can raise the level of mutual trust that policing is built on—the idea that police officers are members of the communities they risk their lives to protect, and citizens in Ferguson and New York and Cleveland just want the same thing young people here marched for—the protection of the law. Together, we can address unfair sentencing, and overcrowded prisons, and the stunted circumstances that rob too many boys of the chance to become men and rob the nation of too many men who could be good dads, and workers, and neighbors.

With effort, we can roll back poverty and the roadblocks to opportunity. Americans don't accept a free ride for anyone, nor do we believe in equality of outcomes. But we do expect equal opportunity, and if we really mean it, if we're willing to sacrifice for it, then we can make sure every child gets an education suitable to this new century, one that expands imaginations and lifts their sights and gives them skills. We can make sure every person willing to work has the dignity of a job, and a fair wage, and a real voice, and sturdier rungs on that ladder into the middle class.

With effort, we can protect the foundation stone of our democracy for which so many marched across this bridge—and that is the right to vote. Right now, in 2015, fifty years after Selma, there are laws across this country designed to make it harder for people to vote. As we speak, more of such laws are being proposed. Meanwhile, the Voting Rights Act, the culmination of so much blood and sweat and tears, the product of so much sacrifice in the face of wanton violence, stands weakened, its future subject to partisan rancor.

How can that be? The Voting Rights Act was one of the crowning achievements of our democracy, the result of Republican and Democratic effort. President Reagan signed its renewal when he was in office. President Bush signed its renewal when he was in office. One hundred members of Congress have come here today to honor people who were willing to die for the right it protects. If we want to honor this day, let these hundred go back to Washington, and gather four hundred more, and together pledge to make it their mission to restore the law this year.

Of course, our democracy is not the task of Congress alone, or the courts alone, or the president alone. If every new voter suppression law was struck down today, we'd still have one of the lowest voting rates among free peoples. Fifty years ago, registering to vote here in Selma and much of the South meant guessing the number of jellybeans in a jar or bubbles on a bar of soap. It meant risking your dignity, and sometimes your life. What is our excuse today for not voting? How do we so casually discard the right for which so many fought? How do we so fully give away our power, our voice, in shaping America's future? Why are we pointing to somebody else when we could take the time just to go to the polling places? We give away our power.

Fellow marchers, so much has changed in fifty years. We've endured war and fashioned peace. We've seen technological wonders that touch every aspect of our lives, and take for granted convenience our parents might scarcely imagine. But what has not changed is the imperative of citizenship, that willingness of a twenty-six-year-old deacon, or a Unitarian minister, or a young mother of five, to decide they loved this country so much that they'd risk everything to realize its promise.

That's what it means to love America. That's what it means to believe in America. That's what it means when we say America is exceptional.

For we were born of change. We broke the old aristocracies, declaring ourselves entitled not by bloodline, but endowed by our Creator with certain inalienable rights. We secure our rights and responsibilities through a system of self-government, of and by and for the people. That's why we argue and fight with so much passion and conviction, because we know our efforts matter. We know America is what we make of it.

Look at our history. We are Lewis and Clark and Sacajawea—pioneers who braved the unfamiliar, followed by a stampede of farmers and miners, entrepreneurs and hucksters. That's our spirit. That's who we are.

We are Sojourner Truth and Fannie Lou Hamer, women who could do as much as any man and then some; and we're Susan B. Anthony, who shook the system until the law reflected that truth. That's our character.

We're the immigrants who stowed away on ships to reach these shores, the huddled masses yearning to breathe free—Holocaust survivors, Soviet defectors, the Lost Boys of Sudan. We are the hopeful strivers who cross the Rio Grande because they want their kids to know a better life. That's how we came to be.

We're the slaves who built the White House and the economy of the South. We're the ranch hands and cowboys who opened up the west, and countless laborers who laid rail, and raised skyscrapers, and organized for workers' rights.

We're the fresh-faced GIs who fought to liberate a continent, and we're the Tuskegee Airmen, Navajo code-talkers, and Japanese-Americans who fought for this country even as their own liberty had been denied. We're the firefighters who rushed into those buildings on 9/11, and the volunteers who signed up to fight in Afghanistan and Iraq.

We are the gay Americans whose blood ran on the streets of San Francisco and New York, just as blood ran down this bridge.

We are storytellers, writers, poets, and artists who abhor unfairness, and despise hypocrisy, and give voice to the voiceless, and tell truths that need to be told.

We are the inventors of gospel and jazz and the blues, bluegrass and country, hip-hop and rock and roll, our very own sounds with all the sweet sorrow and reckless joy of freedom.

We are Jackie Robinson, enduring scorn and spiked cleats and pitches coming straight to his head, and stealing home in the World Series anyway.

We are the people Langston Hughes wrote of, who "build our temples for tomorrow, strong as we know how." We are the people Emerson wrote of, "who for truth and honor's sake stand fast and suffer long," who are "never tired, so long as we can see far enough."

That's what America is. Not stock photos or airbrushed history or feeble attempts to define some of us as more American than others. We respect the past, but we don't pine for it. We don't fear the future; we grab for it. America is not some fragile thing; we are large, in the words of Whitman, containing multitudes. We are boisterous and diverse and full of energy, perpetually young in spirit. That's why someone like John Lewis at the ripe age of twenty-five could lead a mighty march.

And that's what the young people here today and listening all across the country must take away from this day. You are America. Unconstrained by habits and convention. Unencumbered by what is, and ready to seize what ought to be. For everywhere in this country, there are first steps to be taken, and new ground to cover, and bridges to be crossed. And it is you, the young and fearless at heart, the most diverse and educated generation in our history, who the nation is waiting to follow.

Because Selma shows us that America is not the project of any one person.

Because the single most powerful word in our democracy is the word "We." We The People. We Shall Overcome. Yes We Can. It is owned by no one. It belongs to everyone. Oh, what a glorious task we are given, to continually try to improve this great nation of ours.

Fifty years from Bloody Sunday, our march is not yet finished. But we are getting closer. Two hundred and thirty-nine years after this nation's founding, our union is not yet perfect. But we are getting closer. Our job's easier because somebody already got us through that first mile. Somebody already got us over that bridge. When it feels the road's too hard, when the torch we've been passed feels too heavy, we will remember these early travelers, and draw strength from their example, and hold firmly the words of the prophet Isaiah:

> Those who hope in the Lord will renew their strength.
> They will soar on wings like eagles.
> They will run and not grow weary.
> They will walk and not be faint.

We honor those who walked so we could run. We must run so our children soar. And we will not grow weary. For we believe in the power of an awesome God, and we believe in this country's sacred promise.

May He bless those warriors of justice no longer with us, and bless the United States of America.

From *Trump: The Art of the Deal*

"You can't con people, at least not for long"

Before his television show, before his Twitter feed, Donald Trump became a national celebrity because of a book. Trump: The Art of the Deal, *which he wrote with journalist Tony Schwartz, became a huge bestseller in 1987 (and an excuse to appear on countless cable TV shows). It remains one of the best sources for understanding Trump's views on scandal, celebrity, and the media, three forces he relied on to reach the White House.*

You can have the most wonderful product in the world, but if people don't know about it, it's not going to be worth much. There are singers in the world with voices as good as Frank Sinatra's, but they're singing in their garages because no one has ever heard of them. You need to generate interest, and you need to create excitement. One way is to hire public relations people and pay them a lot of money to sell whatever you've got. But to me, that's like hiring outside consultants to study a market. It's never as good as doing it yourself.

One thing I've learned about the press is that they're always hungry for a good story, and the more sensational the better. It's in the nature of the job, and I understand that. The point is that if you are a little different, or a little outrageous, or if you do things that are bold or controversial, the press is going to write about you. I've always done things a little differently, I don't mind controversy, and my deals tend to be somewhat ambitious. Also, I achieved a lot when I was very young, and I chose to live in a certain style. The result is that the press has always wanted to write about me.

I'm not saying that they necessarily like me. Sometimes they write positively, and sometimes they write negatively. But from a pure business point of view, the benefits of being written about have far outweighed the drawbacks. It's really quite simple. If I take a full-page ad in the *New York Times* to publicize a project, it might cost $40,000, and in any case, people tend to be skeptical about advertising. But if the *New York Times* writes even a moderately positive one-column story about one of my deals, it doesn't cost me anything, and it's worth a lot more than $40,000.

The funny thing is that even a critical story, which may be hurtful personally, can be very valuable to your business. Television City is a perfect example. When I bought the land in 1985, many people, even those on the West Side, didn't realize that those one hundred acres existed. Then I announced I was going to build the world's tallest building on the site. Instantly, it became a media event: the *New York Times* put it on the front page, Dan Rather announced it on the evening news, and George Will wrote a column about it in *Newsweek.* Every architecture critic had an opinion, and so did a lot of editorial writers. Not all of them liked the idea of the world's tallest building. But the point is that we got a lot of attention, and that alone creates value.

The other thing I do when I talk with reporters is to be straight. I try not to deceive them or to be defensive, because those are precisely the ways most people get themselves into trouble with the press. Instead, when a reporter asks me a tough question, I try to frame a positive answer, even if that means shifting the ground. For example, if someone asks me what negative effects the world's tallest building might have on the West Side, I turn the tables and talk about how New Yorkers deserve the world's tallest building, and what a boost it will give the city to have that honor again. When a reporter asks why I build only for the rich, I note that the rich aren't the only ones who benefit from my buildings. I explain that I put thousands of people to work who might otherwise be collecting unemployment, and that I add to the city's tax base every time I build a new project. I also point out that buildings like Trump Tower have helped spark New York's renaissance.

The final key to the way I promote is bravado. I play to people's fantasies. People may not always think big themselves, but they can still get very excited by those who do. That's why a little hyperbole never hurts. People want to believe that something is the biggest and the greatest and the most spectacular.

I call it truthful hyperbole. It's an innocent form of exaggeration—and a very effective form of promotion. . . .

Much as it pays to emphasize the positive, there are times when the only choice is confrontation. In most cases I'm very easy to get along with. I'm very good to people who are good to me. But when people treat me badly or unfairly or try to take advantage of me, my general attitude, all my life, has been to fight back very hard. The risk is that you'll make a bad situation worse, and I certainly don't recommend this approach to everyone. But my experience is that if you're fighting for something you believe in—even if it means alienating some people along the way—things usually work out for the best in the end.

When the city unfairly denied me, on Trump Tower, the standard tax break every developer had been getting, I fought them in six different courts. It cost me a lot of money, I was considered highly likely to lose, and people told me it was a no-win situation politically. I would have considered it worth the effort regardless of the outcome. In this case, I won—which made it even better.

When Holiday Inns, once my partners at the Trump Plaza Hotel and Casino in Atlantic City, ran a casino that consistently performed among the bottom 50 percent of casinos in town, I fought them very hard and they finally sold out their share to me. Then I began to think about trying to take over the Holiday Inns company altogether.

Even if I never went on the offensive, there are a lot of people gunning for me now. One of the problems when you become successful is that jealousy and envy inevitably follow. There are people—I categorize them as life's losers—who get their sense of accomplishment and achievement from trying to stop others. As far as I'm concerned, if they had any real ability they wouldn't be fighting me, they'd be doing something constructive themselves. . . .

You can't con people, at least not for long. You can create excitement, you can do wonderful promotion and get all kinds of press, and you can throw in a little hyperbole. But if you don't deliver the goods, people will eventually catch on.

I think of Jimmy Carter. After he lost the election to Ronald Reagan, Carter came to see me in my office. He told me he was seeking contributions to the Jimmy Carter Library. I asked how much he had in mind. And he said, "Donald, I would be very appreciative if you contributed five million dollars."

I was dumbfounded. I didn't even answer him.

But that experience also taught me something. Until then, I'd never understood how Jimmy Carter became president. The answer is that as poorly qualified as he was for the job, Jimmy Carter had the nerve, the guts, the balls, to ask for something extraordinary. That ability above all helped him get elected president. But then, of course, the American people caught on pretty quickly that Carter couldn't do the job, and he lost in a landslide when he ran for reelection.

Ronald Reagan is another example. He is so smooth and so effective a performer that he completely won over the American people. Only now, nearly seven years later, are people beginning to question whether there's anything beneath that smile.

I see the same thing in my business, which is full of people who talk a good game but don't deliver. When Trump Tower became successful, a lot of developers got the idea of imitating our atrium, and they ordered their architects to come up with a design. The drawings would come back, and they would start costing out the job.

What they discovered is that the bronze escalators were going to cost a million dollars extra, and the waterfall was going to cost two million dollars, and the marble was going to cost many millions more. They saw that it all added up to many millions of dollars, and all of a sudden these people with these great ambitions would decide, well, let's forget about the atrium.

The dollar always talks in the end. I'm lucky, because I work in a very, very special niche, at the top of the market, and I can afford to spend top dollar to build the best. I promoted the hell out of Trump Tower, but I also had a great product to promote.

A Note on Texts, Sources, and Permissions

My main goal in selecting the texts for this anthology is right there in the title: I wanted the best presidential writing, with pieces qualifying because they were elegant or effective or historically important, even if some of them are troubling or ugly when read today. I was thwarted in some instances by modern copyright laws, but the texts here remain an unprecedented collection, with many of them appearing in print for the first time or the first time since their original publication.

My main goal in editing these texts has been to make them clear and readable for today's readers. I modernized the spelling, punctuation, and capitalization; added more paragraph breaks; expanded abbreviations; and changed the occasional *'tis* to *it is*, though I never added new words unless explicitly indicated with brackets. I excerpted aggressively, always indicating where with a "from" in the chapter titles and ellipses in the text. While most of my cuts focused on real-time policy debates that time has made tricky to follow, I also cut the occasion-driven throat-clearing that marks so many speeches—George Washington starting his first inaugural with "Fellow-citizens of the Senate and of the House of Representatives" and so on. I removed the footnotes and citations that appeared in the original texts with one exception: a footnote in Jefferson's *Notes*.

In a couple of cases, I made bigger changes. Consider James Madison's essay on Benjamin Franklin, for instance. Near the end of his draft, Madison wrote: "For the anicdote [*sic*] at the close of the Convention relating to the rising son [*sic*] painted on the wall behind the Presidts [*sic*] chair see note at the end of the Debates." I removed this sentence, following

Madison's clear wishes, and replaced it with the paragraph he mentioned. Readers who want to see the original texts and variants, along with superb editorial apparatuses, should turn to the definitive presidential editions like *The Papers of James Madison*, published across dozens of volumes by the University of Virginia Press.

In addition to those scholarly editions, I consulted a range of historical and bibliographical scholarship—too many to cite here, though my *Author in Chief: The Untold Story of Our Presidents and the Books They Wrote* (New York: Avid Reader Press, 2020) surveys many of these sources and adds additional context to some of the presidential documents themselves. There are two essential starting points to any study of presidential prose: Jeffrey Tulis's *The Rhetorical Presidency* (Princeton: Princeton University Press, 1987), though see more recent critiques like Mel Laracey's "The Rhetorical Presidency Today: How Does It Stand Up?," *Presidential Studies Quarterly* 39.4 (2009): 908–931; and Karlyn Kohrs Campbell and Kathleen Hall Jamieson's *Presidents Creating the Presidency: Deeds Done in Words*, 2nd ed. (Chicago: University of Chicago Press, 2008). As Campbell and Jamieson write, the president's "words are deeds; in their speaking, the presidency is constituted and reconstituted" (341). I found a few more focused works also invaluable: Robert Schlesinger's *White House Ghosts: Presidents and Their Speechwriters* (New York: Simon & Schuster, 2008); Kenneth Collier's *Speechwriting in the Institutionalized Presidency* (Lanham, MD: Lexington Books, 2018); Hendrik Booraem's *The Road to Respectability: James A. Garfield and His World, 1844–1852* (Lewisburg, PA: Bucknell University Press, 1988); Robert S. La Forte's "Theodore Roosevelt's Osawatomie Speech," *Kansas Historical Quarterly* 32.2 (1966): 187–200; and Anne Pluta's "Reassessing the Assumptions behind the Evolution of Popular Presidential Communication," *Presidential Studies Quarterly* 45.1 (2015): 70–90. For a skeptical view of presidents persuading the public, see George Edwards, *On Deaf Ears: The Limits of the Bully Pulpit* (New Haven, CT: Yale University Press, 2006); for a skeptical view of presidents persuading the legislature, see Frances E. Lee, *Beyond Ideology: Politics, Principles, and Partisanship in the U.S. Senate* (Chicago: University of Chicago Press, 2009). Douglas MacArthur shared the story about Theodore Roosevelt in his *Reminiscences* (New York: McGraw-Hill, 1964), 33.

Unless otherwise noted, all texts in this book come from The American Presidency Project, though I've compared the Project's texts to *The Public Papers of the Presidents* and *The Compilation of the Messages and Papers of the Presidents* series, along with specialized editions like the Madison one cited above.

Thanks to John Woolley and Gerhard Peters for their wonderful resource, which any history fan should explore further at www.presidency.ucsb.edu.

Washington's notes to his early biographer come from the Humphreys-Marvin-Olmstead Collection, Yale University Library, Manuscripts and Archives Division, Box 4. They are reprinted in full, with helpful editorial material, in *David Humphreys's Life of General Washington: With George Washington's Remarks*, ed. Rosemarie Zagarri (Athens, GA: University of Georgia Press, 1991).

Adams's autobiographical excerpt is reprinted with permission from *The Adams Papers: Diary and Autobiography of John Adams: Volume 3—Diary 1782–1804, Autobiography through 1776*, ed. L. H. Butterfield, Leonard C. Faber, and Wendell D. Garrett (Cambridge, MA: The Belknap Press of Harvard University Press) Copyright © 1961 by the Massachusetts Historical Society; his "Dissertation" comes from *Works of John Adams*, volume 3, ed. Charles Francis Adams (Boston: Little and Brown, 1850–1856).

Jefferson's autobiographical excerpt comes from *The Writings of Thomas Jefferson*, volume 1, ed. Paul Leicester Ford (New York: G. P. Putnam's Sons, 1892–1899); Jefferson's *Notes* comes from *Notes on the State of Virginia* (Philadelphia: Prichard and Hall, 1788).

Madison's notes come from *The Debates in the Federal Convention of 1787*, eds. Gaillard Hunt and James Brown Scott (New York: Oxford University Press, 1920). Madison's essay on Franklin is reprinted with permission: Madison, James. Edited by David B. Mattern, J. C. A. Stagg, Mary Parke Johnson, and Anne Mandeville Colony. *The Papers of James Madison: 1817–1820, Volume 1*. pp. 600–602. © 2009 by the Rector and Visitors of the University of Virginia. Reprinted by permission of the University of Virginia Press. Madison's *Federalist Papers* come from *The Federalist*, ed. Henry Cabot Lodge (New York: G. P. Putnam's Sons, 1888).

Monroe's autobiographical excerpt comes from *The Autobiography of James Monroe*, ed. Stuart Gerry Brown (Syracuse, NY: Syracuse University Press, 1959).

John Quincy Adams's diary entries come from *Memoirs of John Quincy Adams: Comprising Portions of His Diary . . .* , volumes 5, 8, and 9, ed. Charles Francis Adams (Philadelphia: Lippincott, 1874–1877); his poems come from *Poems of Religion and Society* (New York: William H. Graham, 1848).

Jackson's excerpt comes from John Henry Eaton, *The Life of Andrew Jackson* (Philadelphia: Samuel F. Bradford, 1824).

Van Buren's text comes from *Inquiry into the Origin and Course of Political Parties in the United States* (New York: Hurd and Houghton, 1867).

Polk's diary entries come from *The Diary of James K. Polk During His Presidency, 1845 to 1849*, volumes 2, 3, and 4, ed. Milo M. Quaife (Chicago: A. C. McClurg & Co., 1910).

Fillmore's autobiographical excerpt comes from the *Millard Fillmore Papers*, volume 1, ed. Frank H. Severance (Buffalo: Buffalo Historical Society, 1907).

Lincoln's selections are reprinted with permission from *The Collected Works of Abraham Lincoln*, volumes 3, 4, 5, 7, and 8, ed. Roy P. Basler (New Brunswick: Rutgers University Press, 1953–1955).

Grant's autobiographical excerpts come from *The Personal Memoirs of U. S. Grant* (New York: Charles L. Webster & Co., 1885–1886).

Garfield's notes come from James A. Garfield Papers, Library of Congress, series 17D.

Harrison's text comes from *This Country of Ours* (New York: C. Scribner's Sons, 1897).

Roosevelt's campaign remarks come from "Mr. Roosevelt's Speech at Milwaukee," *Outlook*, October 26, 1912; his autobiographical excerpt comes from *Theodore Roosevelt: An Autobiography* (New York: Macmillan, 1913).

Taft's text comes from *Our Chief Magistrate and His Powers* (New York: Columbia University Press, 1916).

Wilson's book excerpt comes from *Congressional Government* (Boston: Houghton Mifflin, 1885); his lecture comes from *Leaders of Men*, ed. T. H. Vail Motter (Princeton: Princeton University Press, 1952); his suffrage speech comes from "Wilson Pledges His Aid to Women in Fight for Vote," *New York Times*, September 9, 1916.

Harding's remarks come from *Speeches and Addresses of Warren G. Harding*, comp. James W. Murphy (Washington, DC: Government Printing Office, 1923).

Coolidge's Massachusetts Senate speech comes from *Have Faith in Massachusetts* (Boston: Houghton Mifflin, 1919); his autobiographical excerpt is reprinted from *The Autobiography of Calvin Coolidge* (New York: Cosmopolitan Book Service, 1929) with permission from the Coolidge family.

Hoover's text comes from *The Ordeal of Woodrow Wilson* (New York: McGraw-Hill, 1958).

Roosevelt's review comes from "Is There a Jefferson on the Horizon?" *New York World*, December 3, 1925.

Truman's autobiographical excerpts are reprinted from *Memoirs* (New York: Doubleday, 1955–1956) with permission from the Truman family.

Eisenhower's Pearl Harbor excerpt is reprinted with permission from *Crusade in Europe* by Dwight D. Eisenhower, copyright © 1948 by Penguin Random House LLC. Used by permission of Doubleday, an imprint of the Knopf Doubleday Publishing Group, a division of Penguin Random House LLC. All rights reserved. The excerpt from his essay on autobiography is reprinted with permission from a 1967 draft in the postpresidential files at the Dwight D. Eisenhower Presidential Library, Abilene, Kansas.

Kennedy's book excerpt comes from *Why England Slept* (New York: Wilfred Funk, 1940).

Johnson's dictations are filed as an 8/19/1969 oral history at (and reprinted with permission from) the Lyndon B. Johnson Presidential Library, Austin, Texas.

Nixon's Apollo draft comes from the National Archives and can be found at www.archives.gov/files/presidential-libraries/events/centennials /nixon/images/exhibit/rn100-6-1-2.pdf.

Carter's book excerpt from *An Hour Before Daylight: Memories of a Rural Boyhood* by Jimmy Carter. Copyright © 2001 by Jimmy Carter. Reprinted with the permission of Simon & Schuster, Inc. All rights reserved.

Reagan's book excerpt comes from *Where's the Rest of Me?* (New York: Duell, Sloan and Pearce, 1965).

Trump's book excerpt is reprinted from *Trump: The Art of the Deal* by Donald Trump, copyright © 1987 by Donald Trump. Used by permission of Random House, an imprint and division of Penguin Random House LLC. All rights reserved.

Once again, Jofie Ferrari-Adler, Carolyn Kelly, and everyone else at Avid Reader were the ideal collaborators. The production team, including Jessica Chin, Kyle Kabel, Linda Sawicki, Laura Ogar, Amanda Mulholland, Elizabeth Hubbard, and Brigid Black, deserve special praise—not just for producing a beautiful book, but for buying us extra time as we wrestled with copyright issues. Librarians like Tim Rives (at the Eisenhower Presidential Library) and Nicole Hartmann Hadad (at the LBJ Presidential Library) helped secure documents and clarify key points. I would also like to thank some scholars who discussed this project with me and answered questions: Richard Ellis, Jennifer Mercieca, David Greenberg, Scott Casper, and Andrew Seal. Any remaining errors are my own.

Index